VOLUME 27

Turkey

Revised Edition

Çiğdem Balım-Harding

Compiler

CLIO PRESS

OXFORD, ENGLAND · SANTA BARBARA, CALIFORNIA

DENVER, COLORADO

© Copyright 1999 by ABC-CLIO Ltd.

All rights reserved. No part of this publication may be reproduced, stored in any retrieval system, or transmitted in any form or by any means, electronic, mechanical, photocopying or otherwise, without the prior permission in writing of the publishers.

British Library Cataloguing in Publication Data

Balım-Harding, Çiğdem
Turkey – Rev. Ed. – (World bibliographical series; v. 27)
1. Turkey – Bibliography
I. Title
016.9'561

ISBN 1–85109–295–1

ABC-CLIO Ltd.,
Old Clarendon Ironworks,
35A Great Clarendon Street,
Oxford OX2 6AT, England.

———

ABC-CLIO Inc.,
130 Cremona Drive,
Santa Barbara,
CA 93117, USA.

Designed by Bernard Crossland.
Typeset by Columns Design Ltd., Reading, England.
Printed in Great Britain by print in black, Midsomer Norton.

Turkey

WORLD BIBLIOGRAPHICAL SERIES

General Editors:
Robert G. Neville (Executive Editor)
John J. Horton

Robert A. Myers   Hans H. Wellisch
Ian Wallace   Ralph Lee Woodward, Jr.

John J. Horton is Deputy Librarian of the University of Bradford and was formerly Chairman of its Academic Board of Studies in Social Sciences. He has maintained a longstanding interest in the discipline of area studies and its associated bibliographical problems, with special reference to European Studies. In particular he has published in the field of Icelandic and of Yugoslav studies, including the two relevant volumes in the World Bibliographical Series.

Robert A. Myers is Associate Professor of Anthropology in the Division of Social Sciences and Director of Study Abroad Programs at Alfred University, Alfred, New York. He has studied post-colonial island nations of the Caribbean and has spent two years in Nigeria on a Fulbright Lectureship. His interests include international public health, historical anthropology and developing societies. In addition to *Amerindians of the Lesser Antilles: a bibliography* (1981), *A Resource Guide to Dominica, 1493-198*6 (1987) and numerous articles, he has compiled the World Bibliographical Series volumes on *Dominica* (1987), *Nigeria* (1989) and *Ghana* (1991).

Ian Wallace is Professor of German at the University of Bath. A graduate of Oxford in French and German, he also studied in Tübingen, Heidelberg and Lausanne before taking teaching posts at universities in the USA, Scotland and England. He specializes in contemporary German affairs, especially literature and culture, on which he has published numerous articles and books. In 1979 he founded the journal *GDR Monitor*, which he continues to edit under its new title *German Monitor*.

Hans H. Wellisch is Professor emeritus at the College of Library and Information Services, University of Maryland. He was President of the American Society of Indexers and was a member of the International Federation for Documentation. He is the author of numerous articles and several books on indexing and abstracting, and has published *The Conversion of Scripts and Indexing and Abstracting: an International Bibliography*, and *Indexing from A to Z*. He also contributes frequently to *Journal of the American Society for Information Science*, *The Indexer* and other professional journals.

Ralph Lee Woodward, Jr. is Professor of History at Tulane University, New Orleans. He is the author of *Central America, a Nation Divided*, 2nd ed. (1985), as well as several monographs and more than seventy scholarly articles on modern Latin America. He has also compiled volumes in the World Bibliographical Series on *Belize* (1980), *El Salvador* (1988), *Guatemala* (Rev. Ed.) (1992) and *Nicaragua* (Rev. Ed.) (1994). Dr. Woodward edited the Central American section of the *Research Guide to Central America and the Caribbean* (1985) and is currently associate editor of Scribner's *Encyclopedia of Latin American History*.

THE WORLD BIBLIOGRAPHICAL SERIES

This series, which is principally designed for the English speaker, will eventually cover every country (and some of the world's principal regions and cities), each in a separate volume comprising annotated entries on works dealing with its history, geography, economy and politics; and with its people, their culture, customs, religion and social organization. Attention will also be paid to current living conditions – housing, education, newspapers, clothing, etc. – that are all too often ignored in standard bibliographies; and to those particular aspects relevant to individual countries. Each volume seeks to achieve, by use of careful selectivity and critical assessment of the literature, an expression of the country and an appreciation of its nature and national aspirations, to guide the reader towards an understanding of its importance. The keynote of the series is to provide, in a uniform format, an interpretation of each country that will express its culture, its place in the world, and the qualities and background that make it unique. The views expressed in individual volumes, however, are not necessarily those of the publisher.

VOLUMES IN THE SERIES

Contents

Contents

Contents

Contents

Contributors

Bahattin AKŞİT
Middle East Technical University
(Social Conditions)

Belma T. AKŞİT
Middle East Technical University
(Health and Welfare)

Elif E. AKŞİT
Middle East Technical University
(Social Conditions; Health and Welfare)

Neslihan AVCI
Hacettepe University
(Education)

Sedat AYBAR
School of Oriental and African Studies, University of London
(Economy, Finance and Banking)

Necate BAYKOÇ
Hacettepe University
(Education)

Brian BEELEY
Open University, England
(Geology and Geography; Population: General)

Vahit BIÇAK
Ankara University
(Constitution and Legal System)

Contributors

Pınar BİLGİN
Bilkent University
(Foreign Relations: General, the Middle East, the West)

Stuart CAMPBELL
University of Manchester, England
(Archaeology)

Dilek CİNDOĞLU
Bilkent University
(Women)

Bilge CRISS
Bilkent University
(Administration and Local Government: Ottoman administration)

Yorgo DEDES
School of Oriental and African Studies, University of London
(Literature)

Mevlüt ERDEM
University of Manchester, England
(Language)

Ömer Faruk GENÇKAYA
Bilkent University
(Administration and Local Government: Turkish Republic)

William HALE
School of Oriental and African Studies, University of London
(Politics)

Ahmet İÇDUYGU
Bilkent University
(Population: Ethnic minorities; Overseas Populations)

Haluk KASNAKOĞLU
Middle East Technical University
(Agriculture)

Zehra KASNAKOĞLU
Middle East Technical University
(Statistics)

Dilek KAYA
Bilkent University
(Film)

Selda ÖNDÜL
Ankara University
(Theatre)

Gamze ÖZ
Middle East Technical University
(Constitution and Legal System)

Tülin SAĞLAM
Ankara University
(Theatre)

Jennifer SCARCE
Edinburgh University
(Textiles and Costumes; Food)

Jeremy SEAL
Travel writer
(Travel and Tourism)

Erdal ŞEKEROĞLU
Çukurova University
(Flora and Fauna)

Mustafa ŞEN
Middle East Technical University
(Trade and Industry; Employment and Manpower)

Tansı ŞENYAPILI
Middle East Technical University
(Architecture; Environment)

David SHANKLAND
University of Wales
(Religion)

Gareth WINROW
Bilgi University
(Foreign Relations: the Balkans, Soviet Union, Russia and the former
Republics of the Soviet Union)

Contributors

Owen WRIGHT
School of Oriental and African Studies, University of London
(The Arts: Music)

Filiz YENİŞEHİRLİOĞLU
Hacettepe University
(The Arts: General, Ottoman decorative arts, Painting)

Introduction

Turkey is both a Balkan and a Middle Eastern country, not only because of its European and Asian territories, but also because of its strong historical, ethnic and religious ties with these two regions. Turkey is also a Black Sea country, due to its close proximity to the Caucasus, and a Mediterranean country, with much in common with other Mediterranean countries. Turkey's economy, security and stability are deeply affected by events in all of these regions. Moreover, it has ethnic and religious ties with the Turkic and Muslim communities of Central Asia and the Caucasus. Outside Turkey, Turkish nationals form one of Europe's major ethnic minorities, numbering almost three million. There are Turkish-speaking ethnic communities in the Balkans (including Bulgaria, Greece, Macedonia and former Yugoslavia), in Cyprus, and in the Middle East (including Iraq and Iran).

If its geographical location makes Turkey a gateway between the most volatile regions of the world, Turkey's own politics, social structure and economy match this volatility. It is a diverse country with a young and sizeable population of 64.6 million (1998 estimate), and 'dynamism' is probably its most important feature. Since the 1970s, Turkey has been deeply influenced by rapid social mobilization, ethnic strife and external conditions such as the end of the Cold War, and the European Union's refusal to admit Turkey as a full member.

Rapid social mobilization and change are the important aspects of life in Turkey. The migration of rural masses to urban centres has converted a country of peasants into one of urban dwellers (for example, sixty-one per cent of the inhabitants of İstanbul are of rural origin). As migration increasingly integrates rural and urban cultures, new forms of music, language and norms of behaviour are born. Rural ties, such as family and kinship, and traditional values are used by the immigrants to come to terms with a different environment.

As well as migration, other factors contribute to the volatile social scene. The boom in the media industry has rapidly introduced new values, expectations and life-styles to the masses. Since the 1970s, when more and more Turkish workers began to experience life in Europe, the life-styles and worldviews of the rural masses began to change, followed by the market-oriented economy of the 1980s which raised people's material expectations. The role of education and of the increase in the number of Turkish students educated outside Turkey should not be underestimated, nor should the effect of rising tourism which has led to more interaction with other nations than ever before. While Turkish citizens are ambitious to succeed materially and want their children to get a better education, the majority of them wish to achieve this within their traditional values. Nevertheless, rural communal interactions are changing, and traditional culture is undergoing a turbulent reorganization.

While the number of political parties is increasing (despite the tough electoral system), those parties which could join under one roof continue to divide because of personal power politics. In this chaotic climate, five decades of experience of multi-party democracy has created an electorate with a distinct dislike of oligarchic rule. The people support multi-party pluralism, and seem to correlate it with their own personal welfare. The most important indicator of the establishment of democracy in Turkey has been the growth of civil societies and the increase in the number of people who exercise their democratic rights through them. In the united reaction to militarism by groups on the moderate left and right, the importance of civil administration has surfaced. Turkey's young population and the growth in communications since the mid-1980s have had a large role to play in this development.

In the 1980s, the Turkish press began to employ the latest technology as a consequence of the transition to an information-based economy. This also marked the end of the monopoly of the state over television and radio broadcasting. Today there are 29 national and 800 local newspapers, and 36 national magazines. According to the General Directorate of Press and Information, 17 news agencies operate in Turkey. In addition to the channels of the Turkish Radio and Television Corporation (TRT), there are 19 national and 244 local television channels, and 36 national, 108 regional and 1,056 local radio stations. The monopoly of the state on radio and television broadcasts was abolished de facto in 1990, and then by law in 1993, and many of the broadcasts are now relayed by satellite. Although there are constant complaints about the quality of the programmes broadcast by the numerous channels, such a growth in the media industry has had a positive impact on Turkey. On the negative side, it is possible to talk about organizations and groups of companies controlling the Turkish media and exerting their power over the masses and over the government.

Turkey's relations with its largest minority, the Kurds, have been a major challenge over the past two decades. Economic deprivation of East and South-East Turkey was seen as the core of the problem, and it was hoped that big projects, such as the Southeast Anatolia Project (GAP), would help to remedy it. The GAP project, which is continuing, is based on the richest resource in the area: water. It is an integrated economic development project, which aims to create power, and also irrigate the area, by damming the rivers Euphrates and Tigris. However, since the 1980s, the armed activities of the separatist Kurdish PKK movement, in its campaign to establish an independent breakaway Kurdish state, has cost over 30,000 lives, and many more have been displaced. After the military coup of 1980, a state of emergency was declared in the Kurdish areas, reviewed and renewed by the parliament every four months. Ordinary Kurdish villagers have been squeezed between the PKK militants who demand their loyalty and need their ground support, and the Turkish military who want them to resist the PKK. As the PKK tried to enforce its rule in the south-east, for example by banning the distribution of national newspapers and the consumption of goods produced by the state, by taxing shop-keepers and private businesses in the area, and by assassinating teachers, doctors and civil servants sent to the area by the state and killing villagers who did not help them, a large portion of Turkey's military assets have been redeployed in southeastern Anatolia, and combatting the PKK has put an immense strain on Turkey's resources.

Turkey had to admit to the existence of a 'Kurdish problem' within its boundaries during the late 1980s, and as a part of accepting a separate Kurdish identity the government allowed the use of Kurdish, which had been banned indirectly. This brought to the agenda the use of Kurdish in education and broadcasting, which is still not resolved. Dispute over Kurdish minority rights in Turkey is a complex issue, which has not been helped by the demands of the PKK for an independent state, because anyone who threatens (by word or deed) the indivisibility of the Turkish state and nation can be prosecuted (according to the Turkish Constitution). An example is the case of some of the Kurdish members of parliament, who, following the 1991 elections, refused to swear to uphold 'the indivisible integrity of the country and the nation'; their immunity was lifted, and they were prosecuted. While there are Kurdish members of parliament in other political parties, the radical nationalists have their own smaller parties. However, their relationship with the PKK is always under close scrutiny by the courts.

Introduction

In 1987, Turkey applied for full membership to the EU. This membership is seen as most desirable by secular and republican Turkish citizens, because it would aid economic liberalization and the strengthening of democratic institutions. In an attempt to better its democracy, Turkey recognized the individual right of its citizens to apply to the European Human Rights Commission, signed the Council of Europe and the United Nations conventions on the 'prevention of torture and inhuman or degrading treatment or punishment', and set up a parliamentary human rights commission. In 1989, Turkey approved the European Social Charter. In 1990, European Community foreign ministers agreed to delay any negotiations with Turkey on its membership, but a Customs Union was realized in January 1996. Later, the Luxembourg Summit in 1997 outlined three areas which Turkey had to improve if it wanted better relations with the EU: the question of human rights and the Kurdish problem; the issue of Cyprus; and Turkey's macro-economic policy and status. It was made clear that there was no prospect of Turkey becoming a member in the near future, which caused concern in official circles given that the Republic of Cyprus' application to join had been accepted. The decision had two immediate effects, one on the domestic politics of Turkey, the other on negotiations over the future of Turkish Cypriots. The Turkish proponents of the union with Europe have had to face criticisms since the 1987 rejection, put forward by the Islamists and the nationalists, that European Union was principally a 'cultural club', and that the rejection of Turkey was more about its Muslim population and cultural differences than any other factors. The 1997 decision strengthened this belief, and gave the extremists a good hand to exploit. While the proponents of the Union do not deny that democracy in Turkey needs to improve, they also believe that Turkey is being punished and shut out, rather than encouraged and motivated to better its democracy, unlike for example, the eastern European democracies.

Following the inclusion of the Republic of Cyprus in the list of prospective members of the European Union, Greece and Cyprus agreed on a joint defence policy, and as a consequence Turkey declared closer economic ties with the Turkish Republic of Northern Cyprus (TRNC). When the Republic of Cyprus decided to purchase Russian-made S-300 surface-to-air missiles, Turkey threatened to destroy them if they were placed on the island. Since Greece also has plans to arm its Aegean islands, it is not obvious what the future will hold for the Greek and Turkish Cypriots.

For Turkey, the most important event in the international arena has been the collapse of the Soviet Union, which brought about independent Muslim states of Turkic origin, as well as making accessible other

Turkic communities, which are spread around the former Soviet bloc. To many living in Anatolia, it came as a surprise that they had kinship ties with peoples from Xinjiang (China) to Moldavia. Until then, only the adherents of pan-Turkist ideologies had occupied themselves with the study of peoples of Turkic origins, and who spoke Turkic languages. Pan-Turkism never enjoyed official support in Turkey after 1923, and state-sponsored nationalism was based on the borders of Turkey, relying on its own sovereignty. In any case official contacts between Turkey and these communities, which were mostly in the Soviet bloc, were almost non-existent. Most Turkish citizens learnt, with the rest of the world, that around 200 million people in the world spoke Turkic languages, and while some of them were quite distant from the Turkish spoken in Turkey, others were so close as to be dialects of one another. As a result, there was great euphoria in Turkey when the Turkic republics of Azerbaijan, Kazakhstan, Kirgizstan, Turkmenistan and Uzbekistan declared independence after 1991. Turkey recognized these states immediately, and saw itself as the route between them and the West. Leaders of the Turkic states, desperate for international recognition and support, were eager to cultivate close links with Turkey, and the West for a brief period saw Turkey as the ultimate model of development for these new states. During the same years, Turkey also agreed to play a role in the Gulf War, taking an active part in it. It also launched the Black Sea Economic Cooperation project (1992), and prepared to see itself as a major player in international affairs. As it turned out, Turkey had to lower its expectations for a variety of reasons, and the economic ties between Turkey and the new states in Central Asia never reached the levels they were expected to (the trade between Russia and Turkey is still higher), although educational and cultural relations continue at a much better rate. Turkey also enjoys a good relationship with the Caucasian Republics, its immediate neighbours, but it has been careful not to get directly involved in the disputes between the states and communities, although there have been pressures from the electorate on the Turkish governments to do so, for example during the war between Armenia and Azerbaijan. It is a delicate balance, and will be difficult to sustain.

The oil and gas reserves of the Caspian, and possible routes for new oil and gas pipelines across Central Asia and the Transcaucasus, have created tensions in the area, with the involvement of all major powers. Turkey, Russia and Iran have been competing for the passage of Azerbaijani and Kazakh oil and Turkmen gas over their territories. Turkey is trying to secure the building of a Tengiz (Kazakhstan)-Baku (Azerbaijan)-Ceyhan connection to transport Kazakh and Azerbaijani oil to the Turkish Mediterranean coast. The project would also bring in revenues for Turkey, and help to cover Turkey's energy deficit. Recently an agreement has been reached between Turkey and Turkmenistan for the transport of natural gas through an underwater trans-Caspian pipeline via Azerbaijan and Georgia, which is opposed by Russia and Iran. The project competes with the Blue Stream project to bring gas from Russia to Turkey via the Black Sea seabed, while Iran sees its territory as providing the shortest route between Turkmenistan and Turkey.

In October 1998, Turkey celebrated the seventy-fifth anniversary of its foundation as a Republic, with the realization that it had come a very long way indeed from the desolate country of the 1920s.

Geography

Turkey has an area of 780,580 sq km, bordering on Armenia, Azerbaijan, Bulgaria, Georgia, Greece, Iran, Iraq and Syria, between latitudes 36 to 42 degrees North and longitudes 26 to 45 degrees East. 24,378 square kilometres of its lands are in Europe, controlling the Straits (the Bosporus and the Dardanelles) that link the Black Sea and the Aegean.

The average altitude of Turkey is 1,132 metres, and one-fifth of the country lies below 500 metres. The Anatolian plain in the middle of the country is bordered by the Pontus mountain chain in the north (rising from 700 metres in the West and to 3,300 metres in the East), and the Taurus chain in the south. The two chains of mountains join in the north-east, and the peak is Mount Ararat at 5,165 metres. Along with the topography, the climate, flora and fauna vary across Turkey. The coastal areas enjoy milder climates, while inland Anatolia experiences extremes of hot summers and cold winters with limited rainfall.

The people

Turkey's population is 64.6 million (1998 estimate), with a life expectancy at birth of 72.8 years. 63 per cent of the population is between the ages of 15 to 64 years, and the population growth rate is 1.64 per cent per annum.

65 per cent of Turkey's population live in urban areas. The rate of migration to the urban centres is very high: between the years 1990 to 1997, the annual increase in the population of the urban areas was 28 per cent. Of the 80 provinces, 17 have populations of over a million, with İstanbul over 9 million, and Ankara and İzmir over 3 million each. These figures are dramatic when one remembers that in 1927 the

population of Turkey was 13.6 million, of which over 75 per cent was rural, and life expectancy at birth was 44 years.

The largest ethnic minority in Turkey are the Kurds, their number estimated between 10 to 20 million. The population is predominantly Muslim (98 per cent), the majority of which are Sunnites (orthodox Muslims). One fourth of the Muslim population are Alevis. Religion cuts across the boundaries of ethnicity, the majority of the Kurds being Sunnites.

The Turkish Republic is based on secularist principles and the constitution guarantees freedom of religion and belief. All religious affairs are carried out by the Directorate of Religious Affairs, connected to the Prime Ministry. Turkish citizenship and Turkishness are not based on ethnicity. The Turkish Constitution defines a Turk as 'Everyone bound to the Turkish state through the bond of citizenship' (Article 66).

Language

Turkish is the official language of Turkey, and has been written with a Latin-based alphabet since 1928. It belongs to the Turkic branch of the Altaic family of languages, and, within the Turkic languages, it is in the Southern Group (Oghuz), hence the Turkish spoken in Turkey is very similar to Azerbaijanian (spoken in the Republic of Azerbaijan and by 13 million Azeris in Iran), and to Turkmen (the majority of whose speakers live in the Republic of Turkmenistan and in northern Iraq), Gagauz (spoken mainly in Moldova, otherwise spread over the Balkans), and Crimean Tatar. When taken together, with all their branches and dialects, Turkic languages are spoken by almost 200 million people in a very wide geographical area from the Balkans to Siberia.

As well as in Turkey, Turkish is spoken in the Balkans (Western Thrace in Greece, Macedonia, Bulgaria, Kosova, Cyprus and the Middle East). Turkish of the period from the 13th century to 1923 is known as Ottoman (written in Arabic script).

Structure of the state

Turkey is a secular republic, and its constitution distributes the powers of the state as follows: legislative power is vested in the Grand National Assembly (Türkiye Büyük Millet Meclisi) which has 550 members, elected to serve for five years. Executive power and function are exercised by the President of the Republic, who is elected every seven years by the members of the Grand National Assembly, and by the Council of Ministers, who are appointed by the President on the nomination of the Prime Minister. The National Security Council serves as an advisory body to the Government. Judicial power is exercised by the independent secular Turkish courts. The Constitutional Court is composed of judges appointed by the President, and the Court of Appeal includes judges elected by the Supreme Council of Judges and Prosecutors.

The first three articles of the Turkish Constitution are irrevocable provisions: that the Turkish state is a secular Republic; that it is an indivisible unity with its territory and nation; and that its language is Turkish. The Preamble to the Constitution stresses the 'indivisible unity' of the nation and 'national interests', which are the core values of Turkish nationalism and expected of Turkish citizens: '. . . no protection shall be afforded to thoughts or opinions contrary to Turkish national interests, the principle of the indivisibility of the existence of Turkey with its State and territory', and that 'as required by the principle of secularism, there shall be no interference whatsoever by sacred religious feelings in State affairs and politics'.

Economy

According to the World Bank, Turkey is among the 'fast integrators'. According to 1997 figures, the Gross Domestic Product is 388.3 billion US dollars, the GDP real growth rate is 7.2 per cent per annum, and the GDP per capita is 6,100 US dollars. The inflation rate, which had reached astronomical figures in the early 1990s, came down to around 70-80 per cent in 1996.

As a result of government policies, the share of the agricultural sector in Gross National Product has rapidly decreased, and the share of agricultural exports has gone down to 10 per cent (from 80 per cent in the 1950s, and 40 per cent in the 1980s). Industrial Production is growing at 10.8 per cent. The composition of GDP by sector is: agriculture 15 per cent, industry 28.4 per cent, and services 56.6 per cent.

Of the total labour force of 21.6 million, 43.1 per cent work in agriculture, 30.1 per cent in services, and 14.4 per cent in industry. The official unemployment rate is 6 per cent, although another 6 per cent is considered to be underemployed (1996 figures).

Turkey's official exports total 26 billion US dollars, and unrecorded exports 6 billion US dollars. Of the 46.7 billion US dollars of imports, raw materials and fuels make up 24 per cent, and machinery 26 per cent. Major trading partners are Germany, the United States, Russia, France, the United Kingdom and Italy. Textiles, food processing, automotive industry products, mining and the construction industry have all expanded dramatically since the 1950s.

Economic recovery has been dependent on foreign capital inflows during the last two decades. Although the tax burden has gradually increased, consolidated budget deficits continue to grow. Successive governments have pursued a programme of privatization of the state controlled industries since 1985, but progress has been slow.

Education

Education is centrally administered by the Ministry of National Education. The literacy rate of the over-15 population is 82.3 per cent. (As late as 1935, only 20 per cent of the population was literate.) Compulsory basic education, previously for five years only, has been extended to eight years since 1997. Higher education is affiliated to the Higher Education Council, which is an autonomous public juridical body with the authority and responsibility to administer the activities of all institutions of higher learning. There are 53 state and 19 private universities, and non-university institutions of higher education (police and military academies and colleges).

A brief outline of history and political developments

Origins of the 'Turks'

Turkey is a young Republic which was born out of the Ottoman Empire (like many other states in the region), but the history of the people known as Turks goes back much further. The name 'Turk' originates from outer Mongolia, where, living as nomadic tribes, they formed confederations. One such confederation was the Hsiung-nu/Asian Hunnic union, who threatened China from the 3rd century BC, and the first written mention of the Turks is found in the Chinese annals (Chinese *T'u-chüe* = Türküt). The legends reported in the Chinese sources associate the Türks with the Hsiung-nu and point to migrations that brought them to southern Siberia/northern Mongolia in the mid-5th century AD. In the 6th and 7th centuries AD, the Türküt Kaghanate ruled from the Aral Sea to the borders of the Chinese Empire and into Mongolia. In the 8th and 9th centuries the Uyghur Turks covered the lands to the south of Lake Baikal, and they were superseded by other Turkic groups throughout Central Asia. Records written in Turkic date from the 8th century AD: the Yenisey-Orkhon inscriptions which were written in Runic script, and Manichean and Buddhist texts written in the Uyghur script. Turkic or Turkicized people came into contact with Islam through trade on the Silk Road, and through the Arabs and Persians who expanded into Central Asia. During the 10th century AD, the Karakhanid dynasty adopted Islam, became the first Muslim Turkic state, and actively promoted Islam in the Turkic world. Their territory extended from Western Turkistan to Eastern Turkistan, including Bukhara and Kashghar. As the Turks became Muslims in groups, they first proved very useful as troops for the Muslim rulers of the Middle East, but later when conditions were favourable they overthrew their rulers and set up their own states, only to be defeated by other Turkic groups. One example is the Ghaznavids, who ruled Afghanistan, part of eastern Iran and much of India; another is the Memluks of Egypt. However, in the early 11th century another group, known later as the Seljuks (of the Oghuz tribe), defeated them, and also took Baghdad and founded the empire known by the same name. The Seljuks extended their rule by becoming overlords of the regions overrun by the Turkish nomads, such as the Caucasus. Syria, most of Palestine, Mecca and Medina also came under their rule, as well as the Karakhanids in Transoxania.

In 1071, the Byzantine defeat by the Seljuks at Manzikert (eastern Anatolia) opened Anatolia to Turkish settlement. Oghuz tribesmen, independent of the dynasty, began to migrate into Anatolia. At the end of the 11th century the Great Seljuk Empire disintegrated into smaller states. The Khwarazmshah state (again of Oghuz origin) replaced the Seljuks during the 12th and 13th centuries in Western Turkistan and Iran. The Seljuks in Anatolia, who had established themselves as the Sultanate of Rum (= East Roman), founded an independent state. Waves of Turkish migration from Central Asia into Anatolia continued for a very long time in unknown numbers. The Seljuks fought with the Byzantines and the Crusaders, and other Turkish *beys* throughout the 12th century. However, following a defeat by the Mongols in 1243, they accepted Mongol suzerainty after which they disintegrated. During these centuries, other peoples of Anatolia (Greeks, Kurds, Armenians and others) lived with the Turks and shared the land; many adopted the Turkish language, converted to Islam, and came to be known as Turks themselves. The Mongol invasion changed the demography of the Middle East and even Central Asia. Turkic tribesmen migrated in large numbers into the Middle East, turkicizing Anatolia, northern Iran and central Eurasia.

The distinct character of the Seljuk administrative structure, institutions, art and architecture carried traces not only of Central Asia, but also of Persian and Arabic Muslim civilizations, and the influences of the ancient Anatolian civilizations. Among the people who migrated from western Asia to Anatolia in order to escape the invading Mongol armies were merchants, academics, artisans and religious scholars, who enriched the culture. The Seljuk rulers practised Sunni Islam and guarded and developed its social and scholarly institutions. However, they were also attracted by the more mystical interpretations brought to

Anatolia by the sufis of Central Asia and beyond. Out of these grew Anatolian interpretations of Shiism (the Alevi), and orders like the Bektashi. Religious folk poetry and hymns composed and sung in Anatolian Turkish by the many dervish poets of the time continue to stand as masterpieces of Turkish literature. Among them, Yunus Emre's messages of divine love and wisdom never lose their relevance: 'Come, let us all be friends for once/ Let us make life easy on us/ Let us be lovers and loved ones/ The earth shall be left to no one' (translated by Talat Halman).

The Ottomans

During the 13th century, when Seljuk power was dissolving, the Ottomans were one of the principalities (beylik) in Anatolia. They settled in the North-West, around Söğüt. Their success in turning their principality into a great empire was due not only to their warring ability, but also to their diplomacy and leadership. Contrary to tradition, the Ottomans preferred to gain land and power by exploiting the weaknesses of the settlements surrounding them, either by marrying into influential families, or by using persuasive negotiations, concilia- tion and promises of vassalage. While they gained land in the Balkans, they also united the other principalities in Anatolia under their rule. In 1453, Constantinople fell to the Ottomans under Sultan Mehmet II (Mehmet the Conqueror), an event which established the Ottomans as a major power. The golden age of the Empire lasted until the failure of the second siege of Vienna in 1683. The peak of the period was the rule of Sultan Suleiman (1520-66) ('Suleiman the Magnificent' or 'Suleiman the Lawgiver' as he is known by the Turks). During his time, the Empire had control over the Mediterranean and most of the Middle East, the Black Sea, and Europe up to Vienna. After the conquest of Egypt, as well as gaining control of the Muslim holy cities of Mecca, Medina and Jerusalem, the Ottoman Sultans were also Caliphs (leaders of the Muslims as successors of Prophet Mohammed).

Over the centuries, the Ottomans developed their own peculiar administrative and legal system. The Empire was made up of peoples of various ethnic origins and religious groups. Non-Muslims, in exchange for the payment of a special tax, were allowed to live within the Muslim state without forced conversion. They lived in their local communities with a certain degree of autonomy. The Empire did not have a centrally administered cultural or educational policy, and for centuries it was able to rule by tolerating cultural diversity.

One of the more interesting features of Ottoman administration was the creation of an army, from the 14th century, from male children gathered from the Christian lands which they occupied and ruled. These male children would be raised by the state as Muslims and trained as soldiers to form a section of the Ottoman army, the Janissaries. From their ranks, the more able and scholarly inclined would be further educated and made officers and officials of the Ottoman Empire. Along with the members of the Sunni Muslim religious institutions, they constituted the ruling group, who did not pay taxes. For several centuries this system ensured the existence of a group of soldiers and administrators who were loyal only to the Sultan and to the existence of the state.

The decline and fall of the Empire took nearly three centuries to be completed. In the mid-18th century the Empire consisted of the Balkans, Anatolia, most of the Arab world, and parts of Saudi Arabia, Egypt, Libya, Tunisia and Algeria. However, it was no longer a great power, and when it started losing land to the western powers, the Ottomans realized they had to reform and westernize their army and weapons. This also necessitated fundamental reforms in education and technology.

In the early 19th century (1826), the traditional Janissary corps was abolished, and a new, mostly Prussian-trained, conscript army was put in its place. The Reform Period, which started officially in 1839, introduced a more important reform: while the traditional Ottoman state offered its subjects protection from foreign powers, fostered religion, and kept order, it was now to concern itself with the education and social welfare of its subjects, to provide roads, bridges and railways, and to be involved in areas which had been the province of private charity. Hence, the centralization of the administration of the Empire began. Government offices and ministries were established, legislative bodies were appointed, and salaried bureaucrats replaced those officials who were paid by the people who used their services. Provincial armies were put under orders from İstanbul, and a new postal system was installed.

It was recognized that ignorance of European languages restrained government officials from understanding Europe, so government offices opened training schools in foreign languages, especially in French. Translations from European languages and the training of translators were initiated. Technical schools which taught mathematics and science as well as languages were opened, attached to government departments. The members of the armed forces were destined to be at the forefront of the educational reforms, and the first medical and engineering schools were military schools. Middle schools were opened for boys who had come out of traditional Muslim elementary schools, with the aim of training them in science and technology in preparation for further education.

The centralization of administration and the improvement of communication systems started a new era for the masses. One important example is the introduction of the printing press. The first printing press in the Ottoman Empire was set up half a century after its invention, by Jews who had fled to the Ottoman Empire from persecution in Spain. Although there were thirty-seven printing houses in the Ottoman Empire set up by minorities and foreign missions (between 1494 and 1729), permission to set up a Turkish printing house was first given in 1727, and the first newspaper in Turkish was not published until 1831.

From the 19th century, Ottoman Anatolia experienced waves of immigration from the surrounding areas of the Empire. It was swamped by thousands of refugees who fled persecution especially in the Crimea, the Balkans and the Caucasus. Because the Ottoman lands were composed of mixed groups of peoples, every time a new state was carved out of its lands, the victorious proceeded to cleanse the land of its Muslims and/or Turks. Some were forced to immigrate because they were potential Ottoman sympathizers. Most of the migration movements followed the ups and downs of the wars between Russia and the Ottoman Empire. For example, in 1828-29, in accordance with the treaties signed, Armenians moved to Yerevan, Nakhitchevan, Karabagh, Akhaltsike and Akhalkalali. While this established the Armenian presence in the southern Caucasus, the Turkish population were forced to leave. Following the Crimean War (1853-56), the Russians retained Crimea, and they either exterminated or expelled the Crimean Tatars. In 1864, the Circassians came in their hundreds of thousands into Anatolia. Lazes and Adjarians followed in 1878, fleeing the Russian occupation of Batumi.

Towards the end of the 1860s, unrest among the new bureaucrats of the Ottoman Empire was growing. Known as the 'Young Ottomans', they wanted a move towards a constitutional government. They based their arguments on the democratic tradition inherent in Islam and formulated the concept of 'Ottomanism' to hold the Empire together. In 1876, the first constitutional period started with the establishment of a parliament. As well as a two-chamber parliament and cabinet ministers, an independent judiciary and taxes assessed according to the income of the taxpayer were introduced. Voting and elections took place according to division of religions. However, the Sultan retained extensive powers, including the convening and dissolving of parliament.

One of the most important events in the history of the Ottoman Empire was the Russo-Turkish war, which the Ottomans lost in 1878. Russia occupied north-east Anatolia (Batumi, Kars, Ardahan, Doğu Beyazit), and a large section of Bessarabia. Russian domination of the Balkans and Anatolia alarmed the Western powers, and led to negotiations with the involvement of Austria and Britain, with the aim of solving the 'Eastern Question'. After the Treaty of Berlin which followed, Romania, Serbia and Montenegro gained their independence, and an autonomous Bulgaria was created. Austria occupied Bosnia-Herzegovina, and Britain occupied Cyprus. Macedonia and Albania remained in the Empire. Following this, the lands which were nominally in the Empire were lost one after the other: in 1881 the French occupied Tunisia, and in 1882 the British occupied Egypt.

Meanwhile Sultan Abdülhamit II autocratically dissolved parliament. However, he was challenged in this on two fronts: by the 'Young Turks' (composed of army officers, bureaucrats and some professionals); and by non-Turkish nationalist groups, including the Arabs. The Young Turks formed the Committee for Union and Progress (CUP), and intensified their opposition to Ottoman administration outside the country. Although the constitutional government was reinstalled in 1908, in 1909 a violent conservative reaction took place. Pro-CUP officers and two parliamentary deputies were killed by religious factions of students and soldiers, and the CUP-backed cabinet resigned. The Third Army stationed in Macedonia marched on İstanbul and took control. Although a new Sultan was installed, his powers were restricted and the cabinet was made responsible to parliament. Abdülhamit II was deposed, and power passed to the army and the CUP. In Turkish politics, this incident can be taken as the beginning of the intervention of the army as the progressive force.

During the period known as the Young Turk era (1909-18), three trends of thought competed in bringing unity and social solidarity to the Empire. One was Ottomanism, which was based on the equality of all Ottoman subjects regardless of language and religion and their loyalty to a common state; another was Islamism, which opposed rapid westernization and promoted the unity of Muslims under one state; and the third was Turkism, which emphasized the unity of peoples who spoke Turkish and had a common Turkish culture. Growing nationalism, separatist movements among the non-Muslim subjects of the Empire, and nationalist movements in the Arab provinces soon proved that Ottomanism and pan-Islamism were not workable solutions.

The nationalist feelings of the Ottoman élite were fed by the disastrous fate of the Turks and Muslims living in the Balkans. The first nationalist revolt in the Balkans was in Greece in 1821, and resulted in the killing or exile of the Muslim/Turkish population in the Morea. This was followed by the eviction of thousands of Muslims from Serbia. But perhaps the worst events took place during revolts after 1876 in Bulgaria, which was heavily populated by Turks and Muslims. Over half a million people tried to escape the massacres, which were aided by the Russians, and fled to enclaves protected by the Ottoman army, and ultimately into Anatolia. Only a minority survived. Of the estimated 1.5 million Muslim population in Bulgaria, only half remained after the dust settled. Although accurate numbers are not known, Jews were also subject to persecution, partly because they were considered to be loyal Ottoman subjects, and partly because of anti-Semitism.

In 1912, Greece, Bulgaria, Serbia and Montenegro declared war against the Ottoman Empire. This led to the immediate extinction of the remaining Muslim population in the area, and those who could reached İstanbul on foot. They settled in western Anatolia and in eastern Thrace. By 1913, the Ottomans had lost the Balkans as far as İstanbul. However, when the Balkan allies fell into disagreement among themselves, the Ottomans were able to attack and retake eastern Thrace, more or less to its present boundaries. Thus, when the First World War started, the Ottoman Empire was flooded with thousands of refugees who had lost their lands and possessions.

In 1914, the CUP government entered the First World War on the side of Germany. The Ottomans had to fight on all fronts: the East, Iraq and Syria, Gallipoli, Galicia and Arabia. The Gallipoli campaign was a success for the Ottoman army, led by Mustafa Kemal, but they lost on other fronts. In 1916, the Russian army took most of eastern Anatolia, and Iraq and Palestine fell to the British. As a result of these occupations more people fled into Anatolia from their homelands. Meanwhile, in the East, the Armenian conflict flared up. The Armenians had revolted in the 1890s, but, without help from outside the Empire, they were not successful. When the First World War started, Armenian bands began new attacks with Russian support. Following the Armenian massacre of the Muslim population in Van and the surrounding area, the Ottoman Council of Ministers organized the evacuation of the Armenian population to the north of present-day Syria during 1915-16, which resulted in the death of thousands of Armenians.

In 1918, the War ended with an unconditional surrender by the Ottomans at the Armistice of Mudros, and the occupation of Anatolia and Thrace by the Allies began. Resistance to invaders by the local Anatolian population first came in the form of guerrilla attacks, but the CUP members and local leaders soon formed Societies for the Defence of the Rights of Turks, and were joined by what was left of the Ottoman army. The leaders of the resistance movement, including the members of the last Ottoman parliament, signed a manifesto called the National Pact (Misak-i Millî), which was based on the earlier resolutions of the congresses organized by the nationalists in Erzurum and Sivas. The pact declared the borders of the Ottoman Empire (of that time) sacred and an indivisible unit. The terms of this pact are still held sacred and are reflected in the Constitution of the Turkish Republic.

The last Ottoman parliament was dissolved by the British, and its members joined the representatives of the resistance forces in Ankara. On 23 April 1920, the Grand National Assembly (GNA) was formed with Mustafa Kemal as its President.

In 1920, İstanbul accepted the Treaty of Sèvres, leaving the control of only a portion of inner Anatolia to the Turks. Eastern Thrace and the area around İzmir was given to Greece, the Straits were internationalized, an independent Armenia was to be created in eastern Anatolia, France was to establish mandates in Syria and Lebanon, and Britain in Palestine, southern Syria and Mesopotamia (Iraq), including Mosul. Italy received south-western Anatolia, and the Kurds in the north of Mosul were to receive autonomy. The Allied powers expected resistance, and accepted the Greek offer to enforce the Treaty by military occupation. The War of Independence (1920-22) was subsequently fought between the Greeks and the Turks.

The War ended on 9 September 1922 in İzmir, with Turkish victory, and in the same year the victorious Turkish GNA in Ankara abolished the Sultanate (because the West had continued to recognize the İstanbul administration). The Treaty of Lausanne was signed in 1923 by the Ankara Government where the borders of Turkey were drawn as decided by the National Pact.

On 29 October 1923, the Turkish Republic was declared by the Grand National Assembly, and Mustafa Kemal was elected as its first President.

The Turkish Republic

Nation-building

After fighting for a century, what remained of the population were poor beyond belief. In some areas widows and children were in the majority. If the men had survived the long wars, they were ill, unskilled and mostly illiterate. Moreover, the Wars had brought hundreds of thousands of refugees into Anatolia. Economically, the country was in ruins without any infrastructure. During the Wars, the people had joined under the common cause of saving their lands, local rights and influence, and protecting their religion, but a modern nation state had to be formed out of a mosaic of peoples, most of which were Muslim, and who had functioned according to Islamic communitarian values.

What followed was a series of daring reforms which were aimed both at nation- and state-building, and which were executed quickly. Mustafa Kemal excelled as the mastermind behind the reforms which would determine the future of the Republic. The centralization of power and authority was essential, and a new identity other than Muslim and Ottoman had to be created to unite the people. The members of the Grand National Assembly, who represented different interest groups, were not unified in their ideas about the future. Some were military heroes of the Wars like Mustafa Kemal, and leaders of their communities, and some of them were against the total control Mustafa Kemal began to exercise. However, Mustafa Kemal and his close group of colleagues succeeded in passing the reform laws in a planned and orderly fashion.

In March 1924, the GNA abolished the Caliphate and the religious courts. After this date, all religious affairs in Turkey would be regulated by the Presidency of Religious Affairs, a central government organization under the Prime Ministry. All instruction in religious culture and ethics would be conducted under state supervision, and all religious textbooks would have to be licensed. At the same time the Ministry of Education was formed, and all schools were attached to the ministry. By centralizing education, schools run by sects and brotherhoods were banned, and pious foundations and Islamic schools were closed. In 1925, all religious orders were suppressed, and the wearing of various types of head-dress (the fez, turban, skullcaps, etc.) which showed the religion and the rank of an individual were outlawed. Women were encouraged to take off their veils. In addition, the international calendar and time system were adopted.

In 1926, a new Civil Code based on Swiss law was adopted. It prohibited polygamy; civil marriage was made compulsory, and equal rights were given to women in inheritance and property ownership. Women became equal before the law, and they were given the same rights to education and employment as men. This was followed by the adoption of the new Criminal and Commercial Codes. However, the right to vote was not given to women until 1930, when they were permitted to vote in municipal elections; in 1934, they could vote in national elections and be elected to the National Assembly. Mustafa Kemal actively promoted the image of the new Turkish woman: equal with men in the eyes of the law, unveiled, visible in the public domain, well-educated and taking part in the state-building process with her male counterparts. The new republican identity was expected to complement the virtues already required of an ideal Turkish female: modest and asexual in image, and a good sister, wife and mother.

Introduction

In 1928 the use of Arabic script for Turkish was banned and the new Latin-based Turkish alphabet was adopted. In fact this marked the beginning of a period of language planning, and the cleansing of Persian and Arabic origin words which had infested Ottoman Turkish for centuries. In 1932, the Turkish Language Society was formed in order to carry out research into Turkish and language planning. The Turkish Historical Society was also established to undertake research into Turkish history.

Also in 1928, the new Turkish state was declared 'secular'. Contrary to common belief, this reform was an extension of what the Ottoman rulers used to practice: first make the decision, then have it endorsed religiously. In other words, Ottoman rulers had used religion as a legitimizing power, putting religion to the service of the state. Moreover, civil ordinances often replaced the holy law of Islam, the Shari'a. Hence, secularizing the state in effect only meant the removal of the legitimizing power of religion in state and personal affairs.

In 1932 People's Houses (Halk Evi) were opened. They formed a vital component of the war on illiteracy. They spread to all provinces of Turkey, serving as centres of culture with libraries and activities – lectures and classes on many subjects, including foreign languages, drama, concerts and exhibitions.

In 1934, a law requiring all citizens to adopt family names was passed, and during the process the National Assembly bestowed on Mustafa Kemal the surname 'Atatürk' (father of Turks or Father Turk), by which he would thenceforth be known.

The early days of the Republic were not devoid of internal or external conflict. The inhabitants of the new Republic had diverse ethnic origins, but they all found a niche in the new Republic and accepted the Turkish identity which it promoted. The common Turks in the Ottoman Empire, which formed the majority, were only aware of their identity as Muslims. It was first the outsiders and much later the pan-Turkic intellectuals who identified them as 'Turks'. In the process of rebuilding, the national identity envisaged by Mustafa Kemal and his colleagues had the features of a civic nation but was based on Turkish ethnicity in language and culture as its core. Being Turkish did not necessitate being an ethnic Turk, but did require belief in the protection of Turkey's geographical borders and in its independence, working towards its prosperity and continuance as a secular state, and using Turkish as the language of education and communication.

Resistance to the Turkish Republic came from the Kurds, who were not only the largest ethnic minority in the country, but who were also spread over different states in the areas surrounding Turkey. The Kurds had supported the national resistance movement after 1920, in spite of the efforts of the British agents to influence them and the autonomy promised to them under the Treaty of Sèvres. They served in the national resistance committees, and fought in the War. However, the insistence of the new state on the total centralization of power, secularism and Turkish national identity, their numbers, their history, the social structures of their communities, and the fact that they were spread outside the borders of Turkey were all contributing factors in their resistance. Kurdish discontent was expressed violently in the revolts of 1925 and 1927 to 1938. The revolts did not involve all of the Kurdish population, and divisions among them helped the government to suppress them.

When Atatürk died in 1938, a new nation had been formed, and it had gained outside recognition. Atatürk was an intelligent and charismatic leader. His success stemmed from his clear vision and his ability to synthesize, plan and execute. He was a man of the Enlightenment, with a firm belief in science and positivism. However, he was also aware of the importance of religion; by ensuring that religion and religious teaching were controlled by the state, he was able to use the power of religion in creating a civic national identity. His pragmatism was reflected in his economic and foreign policies. Atatürk saw civilization as a common pool of mankind, and believed that the Ottomans had declined because they fell out of the mainstream of development. Civilization was not under the monopoly of the West, and like all nations Turkey could be a member of it. It is true that Atatürk did not work in a vacuum: many reforms had already started in the 19th century and before, and the majority of his opponents, even in their opposition to him, agreed with him on the preservation of the national unity.

1940 and after

Turkey had a single-party régime for a long time. In 1923 the People's Party (Halk Fırkası) was formed by Mustafa Kemal, changing its name to the Republican People's Party (RPP) in 1924, but it was only in 1931 that the party defined its programme. The six arrows on its symbol reflected the principles of the new Republic: Republicanism, Populism, Nationalism, Étatism, Laicism and Reformism. Later, these principles were written into the 1937 Constitution, and came to be known as the principles of Kemalism or Atatürkism.

The one-party régime continued in Turkey during the Second World War, under the leadership of İnönü. Although Turkey managed to stay neutral during the War, it had economic difficulties, and there were different ideological movements in the Republic. Atatürk's cadre of intellectuals (civil servants and military) formed the new élite in an otherwise classless society. As early as 1929, communist propaganda was suppressed in Turkey, and pan-Turkist movements were not allowed. During the 1946 elections, Turkey progressed to multi-party politics, and the Democrat Party (DP), founded by Celal Bayar, a colleague of both Atatürk and İnönü, won seats in the Parliament. This was to be followed by the Democrats winning elections in 1950, 1954 and 1957. Perhaps the most important difference between the two parties and their voters was that whereas the RPP traditionally represented the élite bureaucrats, the military and staunch secularists, the Democrats were in general conservatives with their roots in rural Turkey.

During their first period of rule, the Democrats liberalized the economy, and with the help of US aid Turkey embarked on a rapid industrialization programme. Roads and dams were built, agriculture was mechanized, and Turkish farmers and villages prospered compared with earlier times. At the same time government control over religion was relaxed, and religious orders which had gone underground began to exert their influence. However, by law, political parties could not be based on ethnicity, religion or class. Hence the Nation Party, which was formed in 1950, was dissolved by court order in 1954 because it sought to use religion for political purposes. (Two weeks later, the Republican Nation Party was founded as its successor.) This strict law meant that the catchment areas of the Turkish parties were nationwide and gave interest groups bargaining power. Parties recruited Kurdish notables from the East and South-East, who, armed with the weight of the votes they brought, were able to bargain with the parties for privileges. The same was true of religious sects and brotherhoods.

During this period, Turkey was forced to make clear choices in foreign policy. It had signed the United Nations Charter in 1945, and had bilateral agreements with various nations. Following the end of the Second World War in 1945, the Soviets demanded the revision of the Montreux Agreement governing the status of the Turkish Straits, and the situation worsened when Stalin made territorial demands on two Turkish provinces bordering the USSR. By then Turkey's geo-strategic significance had become a valuable asset for US foreign policy, and Turkey became a beneficiary of the Truman Doctrine of 1947, and of the Marshall Plan which was launched the following year. In 1949, Turkey was admitted to the Council of Europe. Following its participation in the Korean War in 1950, Turkey became a member of NATO in 1952. During the Cold War years, Turkey was to provide critical military base facilities for the United States, who in turn, provided economic and military aid to Turkey.

The relations between the two NATO allies, Greece and Turkey, began to be strained over Cyprus after 1955. In 1955, Greek nationalists started a terrorist campaign to unite Cyprus with Greece. In 1959, Greek, Turkish and British representatives agreed to establish a bi-communal independent Republic of Cyprus.

In the mid-1950s, inflation and the problems associated with unplanned rapid growth hit Turkey; hardest hit were the civil servants. Opposition to the DP government grew, and under criticism it began to take tough action, such as restricting the freedom of press and parties, and limiting the holding of public meetings. Finally, on 27 May 1960, the military took over.

In 1961, a new constitution was prepared, which broadened the scope of personal rights and liberties. It also introduced a Constitutional Court, the National Security Council (chaired by the President, and composed of the Chief of the General Staff, the commanders of the armed forces and the gendarmerie, and the government ministers concerned) as an advisor to the government, and the State Planning Organization. Elections were held the same year, and until 1965 Turkey was ruled by coalition governments.

In 1963, Turkey became an associate member of the European Community. The same year, a new crisis developed over Cyprus. Greek Cypriots, under the leadership of Archbishop Makarios, proceeded to change the Constitution, removing the entrenchment rights of the Turkish Cypriots, Turkish Cypriots were removed by force from all state organs, Turkish villages were besieged and the inhabitants were forced to migrate and live in enclaves. This unfortunate event also meant that Turks and Greeks could no longer live in mixed communities. Turkish intervention was averted by America, but the contents of a letter sent to Prime Minister İnönü by President Johnson fuelled anti-American sentiment in Turkey. Turkish foreign policy makers then realized that Turkey had to look after itself, and proceeded to open up to the rest of the world.

In 1965, the Justice Party (JP), heir to the banned Democrat Party, won the elections with a landslide victory. The JP had a broad base of supporters, including industrialists, small merchants and peasants as well as large land owners. Its leader, Süleyman Demirel, was a newcomer to the political scene. An engineer by training, and of rural origins, he was enthusiastic about big industrial projects and economic development. He was a popular leader with the masses, but was intensely disliked and looked down upon by the intellectuals. The Justice Party governments, led by Demirel, ruled the country until 1971. Although in economic terms these were better days for Turkey than before, Demirel was finding it difficult to keep unity in his own party, which lacked ideological coherence at a time when ideology was becoming increasingly important.

In 1967 problems flared up again in Cyprus. Turkish villages were overrun by the Greeks, but the crisis was resolved when the mainland Greek troops were made to withdraw.

During the late 1960s and early 1970s, Turkish society was undergoing extreme fragmentation and polarization. Demirel, while flirting with the more conservative sections of society, began to crack down on the socialist movements among university students and lecturers. Student demonstrations began to spread outside the universities, and Marxist revolutionary groups, Islamist fundamentalist groups and pan-Turkic groups clashed on the streets; this was followed by kidnappings and murders, which were supported by the political parties. While the Justice Party was weakened by a definite internal split, the pro-Islamic National Order Party (NOP) was formed by Necmettin Erbakan in 1970, and Bülent Ecevit led the RPP's transformation to a left-of-centre party. On 12 March 1971, the army intervened with a memorandum demanding a strong government to fight anarchy, and Demirel resigned. Martial law was imposed, the constitution was amended, Islamic and Marxist parties were closed down, and there were widespread arrests and trials. Elections were held in 1973, and until 1980 Turkey was ruled by minority or coalition governments. The first coalition was between two unlikely partners: the pro-islamic National Salvation Party (which replaced the National Order Party) and the new left-of-centre RPP, under Bülent Ecevit.

In 1974, the Cyprus problem flared up once again. The president of Cyprus, Archbishop Makarios, was overthrown in a coup by the military junta of Greece, which aimed to unite Cyprus with Greece. Turkey asked for intervention from the other coguarantors (Greece and Britain), and when no response came, it intervened on its own. Turkish troops landed in northern Cyprus and occupied one-third of the island. This led to the subsequent proclamation of the Turkish Republic of Northern Cyprus (TRNC) in 1983, recognized only by Turkey.

During 1975-77, Turkey was ruled by the 'National Front' coalitions of the JP, the NSP and the pan-Turkist Nationalist Action Party of Türkeş. Following the 1977 elections, the RPP, under Ecevit, formed the government, followed by the minority government of the JP under Demirel. During this time, while national security deteriorated, the economy suffered badly. 1979 was marked by assassinations and sectarian killings.

The Kurdistan Workers' Party (PKK), whose objective was the formation of a separate Marxist Kurdish state, was founded in 1978, supported by sister Marxist parties and underground Marxist organizations in Turkey. Their activities gained momentum, and towards the end of the 1970s governments declared martial law on several occasions to restore order. The PKK was not ideologically sophisticated, and consciously aimed at town and village youth who were poor and uneducated, stressing armed action. Its leader, Abdullah Öcalan, settled in Damascus in 1980, and, with the help of the Syrian government, set up training camps in the Beqa'a valley, where his guerrillas were trained.

On 12 September 1980, the military intervened again. All political parties and trade unions which represented the extreme left or right or ethnic and religious factions were closed. Officials and militants of radical parties and radical underground organizations (both from the left and right) who were involved in the street violence and terrorism in the 1970s were arrested and tried.

In 1982 a new constitution was prepared. It increased the powers of the National Security Council, and brought all universities under the supervision of the newly created Higher Education Council. The Atatürk Higher Council of Culture, History and Language was formed to replace the former Language and History Societies. Strikes were banned, and the military backed the economic measures adopted before the intervention, which placed more emphasis on market forces. The military also encouraged the development of Islam in a Turkish context to counter other ideologies, and to stabilize and de-politicize the country.

Turkey returned to multi-party politics in 1983. Among the three parties allowed to enter the elections, the newly founded Motherland Party (MP), led by Turgut Özal, received the majority of votes. The party combined economic liberalism with cultural conservatism, and represented different interest groups and political views from the centre to the far right. The Özal government extended trade liberalization laws, and import-substitution was abandoned in favour of an export-oriented economy. The private sector was supported and encouraged, and a new group of Turkish entrepreneurs appeared on the scene, as did corruption. The first years led to a boom in the economy, but the problems of high inflation and insufficient investment remained. After 1987, the popularity of the Motherland Party began to fall. Several new parties appeared on the scene, some of which were continuations of the old parties which had been closed down in 1980. Both the left and the centre-right were split; however, the True Path Party (TPP), led by Demirel, appeared as the real contender. In 1989 Prime Minister Özal was elected President, thus having to give up the formal leadership of the Motherland Party. In the 1991 and 1995 elections the Motherland Party lost its majority in parliament, and Turkey has been governed by coalition and minority governments ever since. In 1993 Demirel was elected President (until 2000), following the death of President Özal. The leadership of the True Path Party passed on to Mrs Tansu Çiller, who later became Turkey's first female Prime Minister.

During the 1995 elections, the pro-Islamic Welfare Party (WP), led by Necmettin Erbakan, received 21 per cent of the votes. Although the party had taken part in the governments of the 1970s, albeit under a different name, this created anxiety about a political Islam in a secular country. The secular Republicans in Turkey believe that political Islam, with its authoritarian conception of democracy, is not only a threat to the secular Republic, but that it is actually incompatible with democracy. Meanwhile, after the elections, the coalition of the WP with the TPP under Erbakan as Prime Minister particularly upset the defence and national security establishments, who saw his policies and *rapprochement* with extremist organizations of political Islam outside Turkey as damaging to Turkish national interests. Inside the country, provocations by WP mayors, calling for Islamic revolution and urging the masses to rise up against the régime of the secular Republic, gave cause for concern. During its ordinary meeting on 28 February 1997, the National Security Council (NSC) met under the chairmanship of the President. The government was advised that the greatest threat to Turkey was from Islamic fundamentalists and from their foreign supporters. It proposed a series of steps to cope with the new threat. These suggested measures gained support from the media and from non-WP voters. Meanwhile, the military establishment, the parliamentary opposition, trade unions and much of the economic élite united to oppose the WP/TPP coalition, which was also tainted with allegations of corruption at all levels. The coalition was abandoned, to be replaced by another coalition, and finally, in January 1999, by the minority government of the Democratic Left Party, with its leader Bülent Ecevit as the Prime Minister. Meanwhile the Welfare Party was closed by the Constitutional Court, and the Fazilet Partisi (Virtue Party) was formed to take its place.

Local and national elections were held in Turkey in April 1999. Although the Turkish electoral system, which uses mitigated proportional representation with a barrier of ten per cent, makes it difficult for any of the parties to have a majority of the seats, twenty-one parties took part in the elections. The Democratic Left Party of Bülent Ecevit, which received 22.19 per cent of the votes and gained 136 seats in parliament, emerged as a contender, followed by the surprising rise of the Nationalist Action Party with 17.98 per cent of the votes and 129 seats. The Virtue Party, the successor to the Islamic Welfare Party, received 15.41 per cent of the votes and gained 111 seats; the Motherland Party received 13.22 per cent of the votes and gained 86 seats; and the True Path Party, of Mrs Çiller, received only 12.01 per cent of the votes and gained 85 seats.

Another major political party of the past, the Republican People's Party, gained no seats in parliament because it received 8.71 per cent of the votes and could not reach the ten per cent barrier.

The 57th Government of Turkey is a coalition between the Democratic Left Party, the Nationalist Action Party and the Motherland Party, under Bülent Ecevit as the Prime Minister.

About the present work

The present volume has been prepared under the general guidelines of the World Bibliographical Series. It is designed for the English speaker, and aims to reach an expression of the country and its people, and an appreciation of its national aspirations. It hopes to guide the reader towards an understanding of Turkey. Hopefully it will also inspire future researchers to become interested in Turkish studies. This is not a comprehensive bibliography, and only those works which will serve as a starting point and which are easily available and accessible have been included. Works in languages other than English have been included only if there are no alternatives in English.

The first edition of this volume was published in 1982, and since then research on every field of Turkish studies has increased, and the number of works published in English on Turkey has more than doubled. Hence, although the present volume is a 'Revised Edition', the reader will find that very few items have been incorporated from the earlier volume. The majority of the works cited in the present volume have been published since 1980.

In order that the choice of works to be included in the volume should not be arbitrary, for some sections I consulted colleagues who specialize in different subject areas. For those sections I have edited their contributions, some of them more than others, and I have added works which I find useful, and works which were published after they submitted their contributions. The other sections have been prepared solely by me, but I carry the responsibility for any errors in all sections.

The works cited in the volume follow an order: first come the books, followed by chapters in books, government publications, and some articles. I have also given Internet addresses for several of the entries, which I believe the reader may find beneficial, especially for data which changes rapidly. Theses and dissertations have not been included unless there were no alternative publications, for the simple reason that the vast number of research students working on Turkish studies, and writing in English, made it impossible to choose from their works.

The entries for some subject areas such as 'Language' and 'Science and Technology' are shorter than for other sections; this is because I have not included works which were theoretical and specialized. For some areas, such as 'Health and Welfare', 'Constitution and Legal System', 'Employment and Manpower', 'Education', 'Oral tradition', 'Theatre' and 'Film', there are only a few works available in English.

The works are ordered alphabetically by the surname of the author, or the name of the organization which prepared them. When a work is relevant to more than one subject, it is annotated in one section, and cross-referenced in the other sections. The subject, author and title indexes at the back of the book should be helpful in locating the works.

There are many sites on the Internet which the reader can refer to for information on Turkey. The homepage of the Turkish Embassy in Washington, DC at <http://www.turkey.org> is very useful since it contains introductory information about Turkey; SOTA Turkish World at <http://www.turkiye.net/sota/sota.html> is also recommended, especially because it carries information about all Turkic peoples and states. The Bilkent University site at <http://www.bilkent.edu.tr> carries an almost comprehensive list of all Internet services in Turkey, divided into interest areas. The homepage of the Institute of Turkish Studies at Washington, DC also gives useful links for Turkish studies and Turkey, as well as for various organizations; the address is <http://turkishstudies.org/>. The State Institute of Statistics site at <http://www.die.gov.tr> provides up-to-date statistics about Turkey. For Turkish-language sources and links, the reader is advised to look at the homepage of the Center for Turkish Language and Speech Processing at Bilkent University, at <http://www.nlp.cs.bilkent.edu.tr/>. For science and technology, the homepage of the Scientific and Technical Research Council of Turkey at <http://www.tubitak.gov.tr> is a good starting point. The homepage of the Turkish Council of Higher Education at <http://www.yok.gov.tr/> is highly recommended for up-to-date information on education, especially higher education. The English text of the Turkish Constitution can be viewed at the Turkish Ministry of Foreign Affairs site at <http://www.mfa.gov.tr>. This site also provides Turkish news in English, as well as other publications. The Textile Museum at Washington, DC is an excellent Internet source for the reader interested in textiles. Its 'Textile Arts of the Islamic World' page offers a list of books, many of which are not included in this volume. The address is <http://www.textilemuseum.org/>. Links to and information about various archival organizations in Turkey can be reached at <http://www.archimac. marun.edu.tr>.

Acknowledgements

I would like to thank all those who contributed to the volume, as well as those whose names are not mentioned in the list of contributors, for helping me during the preparation of this volume. Bülent Aras, Laurance M. Cook, Özkul Çobanoğlu and Nezih Erdoğan are among those. I also thank Diana Erdoğan, Zeki Okar, Yankı Pürsün, Firdevs Robinson and Sevinç Türker of the Scientific and Technical Research Council of Turkey (TÜBİTAK).

I would also like to thank my colleague Brian Beeley for his support during the preparation of this book, and for sending me reminders and entries for many publications. Even when they were of works I had already seen, it made me confident to know that they had been noticed by another colleague. I would also like to thank Ted Harding for preparing the indexes for the volume, and Julia Goddard of ABC-CLIO for her patience and competent editing. A part of this volume was prepared while I received a Leverhulme Trust Research Grant.

Çiğdem Balım-Harding
June 1999

The Country and Its People

Contemporary

1 **The making of modern Turkey.**
Feroz Ahmad. London; New York: Routledge, 1993. 272p. bibliog.
The book focuses on the period from 1900 to 1991, and concentrates on the military, political, economic and to a lesser degree on the ideological issues related to that period. The first three chapters deal with the final days of the Ottoman Empire, and the later chapters successively chart the progress through the single-party regime set up by Atatürk (1923-45), and the multi-party period (1945-89). In contrast to most current analyses of modern Turkey, the author emphasizes the socio-economic changes rather than continuities as the motor of politics. This is a useful introduction to Turkish studies.

2 **The Turkic peoples of the world.**
Edited by Margaret Bainbridge. London; New York: Kegan Paul International, 1993. 403p. bibliog.
This is a collection of essays on the Turkic peoples of the world, including the Turkish nationals living beyond Turkey. The essays look at the Turkic peoples in terms of their populations, economic and social structures, languages, beliefs and life styles. The introduction by Jean Paul Roux summarizes the history of Turkic migrations from Central Asia to various parts of the world over a broad period of time. Unfortunately the essays were out of date before they were published, and there are some factual mistakes. However, it is a useful book for a general view of the Turkic peoples of the world.

3 **Turkey from the air.**
Murat Belge, Stefanos Yerasimos. London: Thames & Hudson, 1993. 192p. maps.
This is a collection of aerial photographs of Turkey taken by the photographer G. A. Rossi. The images include İstanbul, and the ancient cities of Ephesus, Miletus and

1

Aphrodisias. Also featured are the plains of Thrace, the uplands of Central Anatolia and Mount Ararat. The images are complemented by knowledgeable commentary. There is also a list of works for further reading.

4 Turkey: a country study.
Edited by Helen Chapin Metz. Washington, DC: Library of Congress, Federal Research Division, 1996. 5th ed. 458p. maps. bibliog. (Area Handbook Series, DA Pam: 550-80).

Like its predecessor of 1988 (*Turkey: a country study*, edited by P. M. Pitman), this comprehensive survey treats in a compact but accessible manner the dominant aspects of contemporary Turkey. The five main chapters are: 'Historical setting' (Steven A. Glazer), 'Society' (Eric Hooglund), 'Economy' (Fareed Mohammedi), 'Government and politics' (Eric Hooglund), and 'National security' (Jean R. Tartter). The bibliography, which refers almost exclusively to titles in English, is especially useful, while the seventeen maps, diagrams, and tables are clear and informative.

5 Turkey: a short history.
Roderic H. Davison. Huntingdon, England: The Eothen Press, 1998. 235p.

This is an updated version of earlier editions with the same title. It is a useful introductory study, which concentrates on the Ottoman period from 1453 to 1923, followed by the evolution of the Republic up to 1967. The final chapter, by C. H. Dodd, carries the story forward to the mid-1980s.

6 Turkey's religious sites.
Anna G. Edmonds. İstanbul: Damko, 1997. 268p. map. bibliog.

An introduction to the religions and cultures of Anatolia within the context of famous sites. The introduction contains general information about Turkey and the history of Anatolia. The section on religion starts with Paganism, its myths and folklore, before moving onto Judaism, Christianity and Islam. The section on the religious sites describes the locations, history and characteristics of each site, which are classified by geographical region.

7 An introduction to the history of the Turkic peoples: ethnogenesis and state-formation in medieval and early modern Eurasia and the Middle East.
Peter B. Golden. Wiesbaden, Germany: Otto Harrassowitz, 1992. 483p. maps. (Turkologica, no. 9).

This comprehensive study concerns practically all Turkic entities over three millennia. It is structured around the rise and fall of major empires, notably that of the Mongols, and has a later section surveying the ethnogenesis of the various Turkic groups across a range of countries today. The Turks of contemporary Turkey itself are described, and there is a substantial bibliography.

8   **Türkei/Turkey.**
Edited by Klaus-Detlev Grothusen. Göttingen, Germany: Vandenhoeck
& Ruprecht, 1985. maps. 844p. (Südosteuropa-Handbuch, no. 4).
This comprehensive volume on Turkey contains essays in German and in English. The
essays in English include: 'Historical foundations', S. J. Shaw; 'Domestic politics', K.
Karpat; 'Kemalism', D. A. Rustow; 'Political institutions', J. Landau; 'Political
parties and elections', E. Özbudun; 'Economic policies', Z. Y. Herschlag; 'Industry,
handicraft and tourism', M. Hiç; 'Foreign trade', A. O. Krueger; 'Population
structure', R. Keleş; 'Social structure', M. Kıray and N. Abadan-Unat; 'Theatre', M.
And; 'Film', O. Onaran; 'Folklore', İ. Başgöz; and 'Fine arts', R. Arık. Unfortunately
the work is somewhat out of date, but it is nevertheless useful.

9   **Living in Turkey. Turkish style.**
Photographs by Ara Güler, Samih Rıfat, text by Stefan Yerasimos,
illustrations by Kaya Dinçer. London: Thames & Hudson, 1992. 240p.
The pictures in this album show how traditional houses are used in modern life, and
how the material culture from the Ottoman period (ceramics, metal works, woodcarving,
calligraphy, glass, panels, carpets, kilims, and miniatures) are integrated into the
interior decorations of modern houses. There are 300 colour illustrations which reveal
the interiors and exteriors of Turkish houses throughout the country's regions. The
book can be viewed at: http://www.arzu.com/turknet/turkishstyle/first.html.

10   **Historical dictionary of Turkey.**
Metin Heper. Metuchen, New Jersey; London: The Scarecrow Press,
1994. 593p. maps. (European Historical Dictionaries, no. 2).
The reader should not be misled by the title of this work, because although it does
give a chronology of Turkish history, it is more valuable for its glossary of important
concepts, terms and prominent Turkish people, and for the twenty pages of general
information about the country. It also contains a list of rulers of Turkey and the results
of general elections in the Republican period. It has a useful unannotated bibliography
of works on Turkey.

11   **Turkey: a timeless bridge.**
Peter Holmes. London: The Stork Press, 1988. 252p.
Magnificent photographs account for most of this volume. The pictures range widely
over time in Turkey's past and present, and cover towns, villages, and rural areas. A
substantial introductory essay is followed by eight regional chapters, each with a
location map and some text highlighting distinctive features of the places shown in the
photographs.

12   **The Turks of Central Asia.**
Charles Warren Hostler. London: Praeger, 1993. rev. ed. 237p. maps.
bibliog.
A revised and updated edition of the author's 1957 book *Turkism and the Soviets*. It is a
study of the Turkish-speaking peoples in Turkey, and the Turkic peoples of the former
Soviet Union, China, Afghanistan, Iran and other countries. The book also dwells on
the development of nationalism and pan-Turkism in the 19th and 20th centuries.

13   **Turkey: a portrait.**
Foreword by Jacques Lacarrier, text by Ferid Edgü, translated from the
Turkish by Talat Halman.   Singapore: Archipengo Press (in association
with Eczacıbaşı Group and the Turkish Ministry of Culture), 1993.
195p.

This beautiful, visual introduction to Turkey contains photographs of Turkey and its
everyday life by eighteen contemporary Turkish photographers. Ferid Edgü, a contemporary Turkish author, has written the text, which has been translated into English
masterfully by Talat Halman.

14   **Turkey: the challenge of a new role.**
Andrew Mango.   Westport, Connecticut; London: Praeger, with the
Centre for Strategic and International Studies, Washington, DC, 1994.
144p.

This book offers a short but lively introduction to contemporary Turkish politics and
foreign relations, society and economy, and it effectively supersedes the author's
earlier book, *Turkey: a delicately poised ally* (Beverley Hills, California; London:
Sage, 1975). Topics covered include the Kurdish problem, Islam, and Turkey's relations
with the European Union, the states of Central Asia, the Middle East, and Greece and
Cyprus.

15   **The Turkish labyrinth: Atatürk and the new Islam.**
James Pettifer.   London: Penguin, 1998. 245p. maps. bibliog.

A general introduction to Turkey. It examines the importance of Turkey during different
periods of history and today. The author looks at Turkey's diversity, its strategic role,
the Ottoman heritage, the culture of its peoples and the different ethnic groups who
live in Turkey.

16   **The transformation of Turkish culture.**
Edited by Günsel Renda, C. Max Kortepeter.   Princeton, New Jersey:
The Kingston Press, 1986. 293p.

This book presents an overview of the Turkish culture of the Republican era up to
1986. The reader will find good factual information about (in the order of chapters):
Turkish opera and ballet, language reform, cinema, sculpture, literature, theatre, radio
and television, music, the press, painting, drama, and architecture. The essays are by
well-known authorities in each field and, although it is somewhat out of date, the book
is a recommended source of information.

17   **The Turkish landscape.**
Republic of Turkey Ministry of Tourism.   İstanbul: Ministry of
Tourism, 1996. 208p.

This coffee-table book contains beautiful colour photographs of Turkey, structured
around the themes of geography, nature, history, people, culture, arts and crafts. Each
section is accompanied by a brief introductory text.

18   **A cultural atlas of the Turkish world.**
Türk Kültürü Hizmet Vakfı.   İstanbul: Türk Kültürü Hizmet Vakfı,
1997- . 6 vols.

Türk Kültürü Hizmet Vakfı (Turkish Cultural Service Foundation) has been working
since 1991 on this project, which will comprise six volumes when completed. Only
two volumes have been published so far: 'The pre-Islamic period'; and 'The Seljuk
period'. The volumes aim to cover history, living geography, political history,
language, religion, music, architecture, city planning, folklore, ethnography, economy,
scholarship and intellectual life, arts, the military and sports. The English and Turkish
texts run parallel in facing pages or columns.

19   **Discovering Turkey.**
Edited by Ernest Warburton.   London: BBC World Service, 1995.
128p.

Based on the 'BBC World Service Turkish season', broadcast during the autumn of
1994, this book includes chapters on Turkish society, science and technology, arts and
heritage, and history. This is an informative and easy to read volume on Turkey,
written with a journalistic approach. The book is not for sale, but can be obtained by
writing to the BBC World Service in London.

20   **Turkey: a modern history.**
Erik J. Zürcher.   New York; London: I.B. Tauris, 1998. 4th rev. ed.
405p. bibliog.

The book was written originally as a textbook for students of Turkish studies, and
probably owes its success to this fact. The coverage begins in the 19th century and the
work brings the reader up-to-date on fundamental Turkish history, society, and
economic and social structure.

Culture shock! Turkey.
See item no. 43.

Insight guide: Turkish coast.
See item no. 54.

Cornucopia. Turkey for Connoisseurs.
See item no. 1323.

Newspot.
See item no. 1353.

Historical

21 **Under the Turk in Constantinople. A record of Sir John Finch's Embassy, 1647-1681.**
G. F. Abbott. London: Macmillan, 1920. 418p.

The volume is based on the letters of Sir John Finch, who was British ambassador to İstanbul between 1674 and 1681. Extracts from the letters present a vivid picture of the Turkish administration, and the way in which the representatives of European countries dealt with it.

22 **From the rising of the sun: English images of the Ottoman Empire to 1715.**
Brandon H. Beck. New York: Peter Lang, 1987. 151p. bibliog.

The author surveys the books written by the English about the Ottomans, and tries to unravel the images that were created in the minds of the readers. The bibliography is extremely useful since it provides a comprehensive list of primary sources, and numerous secondary sources. The appendix includes chronological tables of the Ottoman Sultans, and of the English ambassadors in İstanbul up to the 18th century.

23 **The Turkish letters of Augier Ghislen de Busbecq, Imperial Ambassador at Constantinople, 1554-1562.**
Augier Ghislen de Busbecq. Oxford: Clarendon Press, 1968. 265p. (Oxford Reprints).

Busbecq became the Flemish ambassador to İstanbul in 1554, during the time of Sultan Suleiman the Magnificent. The four letters by him give a full account of his mission, which was to keep a check on any attacks by the Turks on Hungary. Busbecq is known to be the first European to penetrate many parts of Asia Minor. The author presents an interesting view of the 16th-century Ottoman Empire as well as a personal appreciation of the Turkish character. This volume is a translation of the Elzevier edition of 1633, and a reprint of the 1927 Clarendon Press edition.

24 **Diversions of a diplomat in Turkey.**
Samuel S. Cox. New York: Charles L. Webster, 1887. 685p.

Written by the American ambassador to İstanbul in 1885, the book is a first-hand observation of life in the Ottoman Empire during the late 19th century. It covers a variety of subjects, such as the army, religion, minorities, customs, social beliefs, children, women, ceremonies, and bazaars.

25 **An English woman in Angora.**
Grace M. Ellison. London: Hutchinson; New York: Dutton, 1923. 344p.

The author was the only Englishwoman in Ankara when the War of Independence in Turkey began. This book describes the impressions she gained throughout her travels in Turkey, and provides accounts of her meetings with several outstanding personalities of the time, including Mustafa Kemal (Atatürk). The illustrations are reproduced from the author's own sketches. The work also contains photographs.

26   **Turkish life in town and country.**
Lucy Mary Jane Garnett.   New York: G. P. Putnam's Sons, 1905.
336p.
The book covers the country and its people as they were at the beginning of the 20th
century, under such diverse topics as town and country life, religious thought and
practice, education and culture, the Albanian highlands, the Macedonian nationalities,
the Armenian communities, the Jews, nomads and brigand life.

27   **Modern Turkey; a politico-economic interpretation, 1908-1923
inclusive, with selected chapters by representative authorities.**
Edited by Eliot Grinnell Mears.   New York: Macmillan, 1924. 779p.
maps. bibliog.
The book was intended as a reliable and practical reference book, giving general
information about Turkey as it was in 1924. It aimed to serve the statesman, the
financier, the merchant, the missionary and the educator. The chapters are written by
the most qualified persons of the time, who cover a variety of subjects, such as racial
characteristics, religions, public health, transport, agriculture, press, international relations,
and government.

28   **Secrets of the Bosphorus, 1913-1916.**
Henry Morgenthau.   London: Hutchinson, 1921. 275p.
The memoirs of ambassador Morgenthau were written at a time when Germany's
influence on the Ottoman Empire was strong. The book covers the events of those
years, such as the sale of American warships to Greece, the smuggling of the ships
Goeben and *Breslau* through the Dardanelles by Wangenheim (the personal representative of the Kaiser), Germany's closure of the Dardanelles, Turkey's abrogation of
the capitulations, the Allied fleet's bombardment of the Dardanelles, Talat and Enver
Pashas, the Armenians, and the author's views on the Armenian question.

29   **Turkey and its people.**
Edwin Pears.   London: Methuen, 1911. 409p.
An account of the social structure of the Ottoman Empire in the early 20th century. It
gives an account of the various ethnicities and groups within the Empire. Among the
many topics it covers are, for example, Turks as distinguished from the Ottomans,
Turkish domestic life and habits, the Greeks and the Greek church, the Vlachs, the
Pomaks, the Jews, the Albanians, the Macedonians and the Armenians, as well as the
Islamic sects of Anatolia.

30   **The Turk in French history, thought, and literature (1520-1660).**
Clarence Dana Rouillard.   Paris: Ancienne Librairie Furne, 1973.
reprint. 700p.
This is a useful source for the reader who is looking for a comprehensive source on
the cultural interaction between France and the Ottoman Empire. The sections are: the
historical background to Franco-Turkish relations; French books of travel and description
dealing with the Turks before 1520; and the Turk in French literature. This is a reprint
of a former edition (Paris: Boivin & cie, 1938).

31 **A traveller's history of Turkey.**
Richard Stoneman. Moreton-in-Marsh, England: The Windrush Press, 1993. 256p. maps. (The Traveller's Histories).

This is at the same time a history, a travel book, and also an introduction to the country. It starts with Neolithic settlements in Konya, and ends in recent times. It succeeds in depicting the diversity and the richness of Anatolia for those who feel that they need more background information on Turkey.

32 **Letters on Turkey: an account of the religious, political, social and commercial condition of the Ottoman Empire.**
Jean Henri Ubicini, translated from the French by Lady Easthope.
New York: Arno Press, 1973. 2 vols. in 1.

The book is a reprint of the two-volume set published in 1856 by John Murray in London. Through letters, the author set out to answer several questions about the social and political makeup of the Empire. The first volume covers administrative organization, politics, education, agriculture, industry, commerce, and the Muslim population of the Empire; the second volume dwells on the Christian and Jewish populations.

33 **Turkish embassy letters.**
Lady Mary Wortley Montagu, edited and annotated by Malcolm Jack with an introduction by Anita Desai. London: Pickering & Chatto, 1993. 190p. (Pickering Women's Classics).

This work was first published in 1763, then in 1965-66 as *Letters from the Levant during the embassy to Constantinople, 1716-1718*, edited by Robert Halsband (Oxford: Clarendon Press, 1965-66. 2 vols.), and later in 1988 as *Embassy to Constantinople: the travels of Lady Mary Wortley Montagu*, edited and compiled by C. Pick (London: Century, 1988. 224p.). These imagined letters – they were never actually sent, and usually not addressed – deal with Lady Wortley Montagu (1689-1762)'s travels and, residence in the Ottoman Empire (1716-18) as the wife of the British ambassador to İstanbul. The book offers fascinating insights into the customs, religion and morality in Ottoman Turkey, as well as containing an excellent, lively account of Turkish women's costumes and social life.

Turkey romanticized: images of the Turks in early 19th century English travel literature (with an anthology of texts).
See item no. 90.

Turkish house in search of spatial identity.
See item no. 939,

Three centuries: family chronicles of Turkey and Egypt.
See item no. 1193.

Arabesque.
See item no. 1195.

Travel and Tourism

Travel maps

34 **Turkey travel atlas.**
   Tom Brosnahan.   Hawthorn, Victoria, Australia: Lonely Planet
   Publications, 1997. 118p. (Lonely Planet Travel Atlases).
The publication contains full colour maps and a comprehensive index.

35 **Turkey, East. With Cyprus. Large scale national map.**
   Brentford, England: Roger Lascelles, updated regularly.
This soft cover map, to a scale of 1:800,000, covers eastern Turkey from Ankara to
Van. It includes plans of important towns, and shows in detail the full network of
roads. The reverse side contains information on the area which will be useful for
tourists.

36 **Turkey, West. Large scale national map.**
   Brentford, England: Roger Lascelles, updated regularly.
This soft cover map, to a scale of 1:800,000, covers western Turkey from Edirne to
Kayseri. It includes plans of important towns, and shows in detail the full network of
roads. On the reverse side important telephone numbers and addresses in Turkey are
listed to help tourists.

37 **Globetrotter travel map of Turkey.**
   London: New Holland Publishers, 1998. 1000 × 750mm. (Globetrotter
   Travel Maps).
This map caters for tourists and visitors, and shows areas of special interest in greater
detail, including İstanbul, İzmir, Marmara and the Turquoise coast. Places to stay are
pinpointed and there are charts showing distance and climate. It is to a scale of
1:1,820,000.

9

38 **Turkey travel maps.**
   Berlin: Ryborsch, 1994-95.

There are seven maps in the series covering all of Turkey, to a scale of 1:500,000. The areas covered are as follows: Sheet 1 – Edirne, İstanbul, Marmara region; sheet 2 – West and Southwest coast, İzmir; sheet 3 – West coast of Black Sea, Ankara, Cappadocia; sheet 4 – South coast, Konya and Cyprus; sheet 5 – East coast of Black Sea, Central Anatolia; sheet 6 – Eastern Anatolia, Erzurum, Lake Van; and sheet 7 – Southern Anatolia up to the Syrian border.

39 **Mount Ararat region.**
   London: West Col Productions, 1988. 32p.

The booklet has a folding map to a scale of 1:200,000, showing the main routes up Mount Ararat. It shows contours, spot elevations of mountains, trekking trails, and villages. An accompanying booklet gives trekking information.

Travel guides

40 **Landscapes of Turkey (Bodrum and Marmaris).**
   Brian Anderson, Eileen Anderson.   London: A & C Black Publishers, 1991. 136p. maps.

A very useful, step-by-step guide to tours, walks and picnics along one of the most well loved and best visited stretches of the Turkish coast. It contains 136 illustrations, 33 photographs, 12 walking maps, a touring map, and drawings. The maps and precise information present this stretch of coast as an excellent area to explore.

41 **Rough guide to Turkey.**
   Rosie Ayliffe, Marc Dubin, John Gawthorp.   London: The Rough Guides, 1997. 831p. maps.

This title possesses all the usual strengths of this series of guidebooks: it is clear, objective, comprehensive and imaginative. It is also thoroughly practical and provides an excellent aid to the general visitor. The guide covers Turkey by district, and contains eighty maps and plans, sections on the history, literature, language, music, and cinema in Turkey, and a list of books to read about the country. There is also a glossary and an index. Updates on the information given in the book can be viewed at the Rough Guides website: http://www.roughguides.com.

42 **Baedeker's Turkey.**
   Basingstoke, England: Automobile Association (distributors for the United Kingdom and Ireland), 1994. 571p. map.

This comprehensive guide is arranged by itineraries. The main focus is on classical and other historic sites but there is also coverage of the modern country, including travel guidance and general introductory section. The text is accompanied by site plans, coloured illustrations and a folding map of Turkey.

43   **Culture shock! Turkey.**
      Arın Bayraktaroğlu.   Singapore: Times Books International, 1996.
      176p.

This lively book about Turkey and the Turks is not a travel guide, but is rather written in anticipation of the concerns and interests of the visitor. It contains short chapters on the country, the Turks, language and communication, social life, culture and leisure, finding a home in Turkey, and doing business there.

44   **Turkey's southern shore: an archaeological guide.**
      George E. Bean.   London: Ernest Benn, 1979. 2nd ed. 154p. maps.
      bibliog.

Although the ancient cities on the southern coast of Turkey are, in general, less well known than those on the west coast, this area contains an amazing variety of classical monuments. The book covers the ancient cities of Perge, Sillyon, Aspendos and Side. The historical background is discussed in detail and is complemented by descriptions of individual sites. Bean is a wonderful companion, accessible, enthusiastic and always successful in describing the many sites that he visited during a long life of pioneering archaeology.

45   **Turkey beyond the Meander: an archaeological guide.**
      George E. Bean.   London: Ernest Benn, 1980. 2nd ed. 236p. map.

Ancient Caria, in the modern province of Muğla in the south-west corner of Turkey, contains many important classical remains. Perhaps the most notable are the cities of Halicarnassus and Aphrodisias. Bean, in his typically accessible style, makes this book suitable for use by both archaeologists and visitors with a casual interest in Turkey's extensive ruins. The book provides detailed summaries of the monuments and history of this area with comprehensive plans and photographs.

46   **İstanbul city guide.**
      Tom Brosnahan.   Hawthorn, Victoria, Australia: Lonely Planet
      Publications, 1997. 279p. maps.

The guide contains practical information for visitors to İstanbul. It describes a variety of walking tours, detailing hard-to-find sights, and accommodation and restaurant recommendations for all budgets. A shopping guide is also included. There are 276 colour illustrations.

47   **Turkey: a travel survival kit.**
      Tom Brosnahan, Pat Yale.   Hawthorn, Victoria, Australia: Lonely
      Planet Publications, 1997. 752p.

This best known of the working guidebooks provides all the information the typical traveller in Turkey will need. It is full of practical information but also finds space to give due coverage to the country's wealth of history and culture.

48   **Guide to Eastern Turkey and the Black Sea coast.**
      Diana Darke.   London: Michael Haag, 1987. 384p.

This is an excellent, all-purpose guide which is unique in devoting the space to Turkey's less-visited parts that they thoroughly deserve.

49   **Trekking in Turkey.**
     Marc Dubin, Enver Lucas.   Hawthorn, Victoria, Australia: Lonely
     Planet Publications, 1995. 152p.

A specialist guide to the walking, hiking and climbing opportunities offered by
Turkey, which are becoming increasingly popular. The guide covers all the main
trekking areas, and gives useful general information about the country.

50   **Cadogan guide to Turkey.**
     Dana Facaros, Michael Pauls.   London: Globe Pequot Press, 1998.
     4th ed. 256p.

This is a highly authoritative, interesting and inquisitive guidebook. It conveys the
writers' evident delight in the country – there are explanatory mini-essays on every-
thing from Turkish football and tulips to whirling dervishes and aubergines – while
also offering a wealth of useful practical information. The series is regularly updated.

51   **Classical Turkey.**
     John Freely.   London: Penguin Books, 1991. 160p. (Traveller's
     Architecture Guides).

Provides a historical context for the buildings of Turkey, followed by a discussion of
the development and the characteristics of the architecture, and an account of the
architects involved. There are lists of important examples of the style, and of a selection
of less important buildings. It also contains photographs, prints and drawings.

52   **The companion guide to Turkey.**
     John Freely.   Woodbridge, England: Boydell & Brewer Ltd., 1996.
     520p. maps. (Companion Guides).

Freely's guide, first published in 1960 and updated several times since, concentrates
on Turkey's archaeology and history. Highly authoritative but entirely accessible to the
layman, the work provides excellent coverage of İstanbul but also of more far-flung
sites in the country's hinterland.

53   **Blue Guide: İstanbul.**
     John Freely.   London: A & C Black; New York: W. W. Norton, 1997.
     4th ed. 360p. maps. bibliog. (Blue Guide).

In a series of carefully planned walks, the historic sites and monuments of İstanbul are
covered from the Byzantine walls to Haghia Sophia, Topkapı Sarayı and other museums, the Covered Bazaar, the shores of the Bosphorus and the Princes' Isles. There are
twenty-five ground plans, and a sixteen-page coloured map which identifies principal
streets. Practical information includes hotel and restaurant recommendations, details
of local transport, museum opening times, and useful addresses. The book has been
updated and published several times.

54   **Insight guide: Turkish coast.**
     Edited by Hans Hoefer, Metin Demirsar.   Singapore: APA
     Publications, 1998. 377p. maps. (Insight Guides).

Good photography and writing are the traditional strengths of this series. There are
chapters on many aspects of Turkish life, including music and cuisine, textiles and the

role of Islam. The book is intended as a background source rather than a comprehensive practical guide although it has a practical 'travel tips' section.

55   The turquoise coast of Turkey.
Rod Heikel.   İstanbul: Net Publishing, 1996. 180p.

A much needed regional guidebook that covers coastal Turkey from Bodrum to Kekova in unique detail. The book contains a general cultural and practical introduction to visiting Turkey but is particularly well-suited to the boatman, be he on a gullet or a flotilla holiday.

56   Turkish waters and Cyprus pilot: a yachtsman's guide to the Mediterranean and Black Sea coasts of turkey with the island of Cyprus.
Rod Heikel.   St. Ives, England: Imray Laurienorie & Wilson, 1997. 5th ed. 290p.

This is another good guidebook from the master of books on sailing. The volume provides practical suggestions, and general cultural introductions.

57   Fodor's Turkey : the complete guide with ancient ruins, Ottoman sites and the best beach resorts.
Edited by Nancy van Itallie.   London: Fodor's Travel Publications, 1997. 3rd ed. 272p. maps. (Fodor's Gold Guides).

This publication, which has been produced annually since 1969, is a complete guide to Turkey for all travellers. It aims to cover all areas of interest for all budgets. Sections of the book include walking and driving tours (with visits to historical sites), unspoiled Black Sea and Mediterranean beaches, and Aegean cruises. There are tips on shopping and on places to stay and eat for every budget and taste. There is also an A-to-Z section of important contact addresses in Turkey, travel tips, list of festivals, and other useful information.

58   İstanbul: a traveller's companion.
Lawrence Kelly.   London: Constable, 1987. 390p.

A selection of travellers' accounts of İstanbul through the ages, from the founding of the city by the Byzantines to the fall of the Ottomans and the emergence of the Republic. The book covers life, customs and morals, and architecture as well as the city's great monuments in history.

59   İstanbul: the Halı rug guide.
London: Laurance King Publishing, 1997. 144p. bibliog.

A guide to the choice and purchase of rugs in İstanbul, which includes essays on carpets and textiles of the area, and lists recommended businesses. It also contains a fact file to assist buyers in finding hotels and eating places. It contains 200 colour illustrations and a glossary.

60   **Turkey: the Aegean and Mediterranean coasts.**
Bernard McDonagh.   London: W. W. Norton & Co., 1995. 2nd ed.
736p. maps. (Blue Guide).

This is the best and most authoritative guidebook to Turkey's art, history and architecture.
The text is supported by maps and plans (by John Flower), and there is an historical
overview, with advice on customs, food, and travel in Turkey.

61   **The best small hotels of Turkey.**
Sevan Nişanyan, Müjde Nişanyan.   İstanbul: Intermedia, 1998. 239p.
(Go See Series, no. 7).

This is an independent and very useful guide to small hotels (with twenty-five rooms
or fewer), including bed and breakfast establishments, chosen by the writers. The book
includes information about the cities and provinces where these hotels are located.

62   **Eat smart in Turkey: how to decipher the menu, know the market
foods and embark on a tasting adventure.**
Joan Peterson, David Peterson, illustrated by S.V. Medaris.   Madison,
Wisconsin: Gingko Press, 1996. 140p.

This is not simply a recipe book, nor a travel guide, but both as it guides the reader
through markets, delicatessens, supermarkets, and eateries in Turkey as well as
providing recipes. The book aims to help the foreigner to discover the joys of Turkish
cuisine by guiding them through the mysteries of menus in Turkish, ingredients, and
modes of preparation. It also gives basic Turkish phrases for ordering food in Turkey.
It contains glossaries of menu items, foods, spices, kitchen utensils, and cooking
terminology. It is a useful and entertaining book.

63   **Wining and dining in İstanbul.**
İstanbul: Intermedia, 1996. 182p.

The book contains information about the city of İstanbul and about Turkish cuisine in
general, followed by a list of places to eat in the city.

64   **Wining and dining in Ankara.**
İstanbul: Intermedia, 1996. 182p.

This book contain information about Ankara in general, and provides a list of places
to eat in the city.

65   **The mountains of Turkey.**
Karl Smith.   Milnthorpe, England: Cicerone Press, 1994. 176p. maps.
(A Cicerone Guide).

This is a pocket book aimed at trekkers and peak-baggers. It gives the descriptions of
the easiest means of ascent of most major Turkish mountains. It covers the Kaçkar
mountains, Mount Ararat, Lake Van area (Nemrut, Süphan, Çandır mountains),
Aladağlar range, Bolkar Toros, Western Toros, Erciyes, and others such as Uludağ,
the Munzur range, and the Cilo-Sat range. It contains brief background information on
Turkey in general, and useful information for trekkers including useful addresses.
There is also a bibliography for further reading on Turkish flora and fauna, and mountains. The book is illustrated with photographs.

66   **Turkey: a traveller's historical and architectural guide.**
James Steel.   Buckhurst Hill, England: Scorpion Publishing, 1990.
172p. map.

This guidebook takes the reader through the seven geographical regions of Turkey in order to make it comprehensible and to arrive at a descriptive outline of its great diversity. The journey starts in İstanbul, proceeds to the Aegean coast, from the ruins of ancient Troy to Bodrum, covering archaeological evidence remaining in cities like Assos, Pergamon, Sardis, Ephesus, Priene, Miletus, Didyma and others. The Mediterranean region is the third geographical zone followed by the adjoining land border with Syria and Iran that defines the lower edge of the south-eastern region. The first riverine civilizations that evolved along the banks of Tigris and Euphrates are covered. The Eastern region bordering on both Iran and Russia, Central Anatolia and the Black Sea are also visited. The main architectural works, monuments and buildings visited in these areas are discussed, each within its historical and cultural context. There are coloured photographs and plans.

Contemporary travellers' accounts

67   **A Byzantine journey.**
John Ash.   London; New York: I. B. Tauris, 1995. 330p. map. bibliog.

Ash is a British poet who travelled in modern Turkey in search of remnant echoes of Byzantium. The result is an account of journeys in İstanbul, Bursa, Eskişehir, Konya and Cappadocia that is, at times, almost visionary in its approach.

68   **A traveller on horseback in Eastern Turkey and Iran.**
Christina Dodwell.   London: Hodder & Stoughton, 1979. 191p.

Christina Dodwell discovers the mountains and high pastures between Mount Ararat and Lake Van, and the rock churches of Cappadocia on horseback. This is an adventurer's account of travels in Turkey's hinterland.

69   **İstanbul: the imperial city.**
John Freely.   London: Penguin Books, 1998. 432p. bibliog.

This is a more of an anecdotal history than a guidebook in the usual sense of the word, covering as it does the travellers and gossips of every period. It presents the history of the city from the time of its founding up to the present day, and contains notes on the monuments that have survived from the epochs of its past.

70   **Journey to Kars.**
Philip Glazebrook.   London: Viking, 1984. 246p.

Covering his travels from the Balkans to Kars, on the border with the former Soviet Union, Philip Glazebrook's travelogue recounts a modern journey through the old Ottoman Empire. The descriptions of his sojourns in Marmaris, Selçuk, Cappadocia, Erzurum and Kars, then back via Trabzon and İstanbul, make interesting reading.

71   **A fez of the heart: travels around Turkey in search of a hat.**
      Jeremy Seal.   London: Picador; New York: Harcourt Brace Harvest,
      1996. 295p.

The author combines a 1990s journey through the Turkish hinterland from İstanbul, along the Black Sea, to Cappadocia and to Eastern Turkey, with the extraordinary history of the banned fez, Turkey's one-time popular hat. The result is a unique portrait of a country at odds with itself.

72   **East of Trebizond.**
      Michael Pereira.   London: Geoffrey Bles, 1971. 256p.

Pereira's account of a walking tour in the Pontic Mountains along the Black Sea is as much about the area's Georgian origins as it is about customs and life in the 1970s in Turkey's remote north-eastern region. The book covers Erzurum, Trabzon, Rize, Artvin and Hopa, and much of the surrounding countryside.

73   **Beyond Ararat: a journey through eastern Turkey.**
      Bettina Selby.   London: Little, Brown & Co., 1994. 224p.

This is an account of the author's journey by bicycle, beginning along the Black Sea coast of Turkey. She cycled south to Mount Ararat, then to the supposed site of the Garden of Eden, and to the borders of Iran, Iraq and Syria.

74   **Turkish reflections: a biography of a place.**
      Mary Lee Settle.   London: Grafton Books, 1991. 233p.

The American novelist, Mary Lee Settle, has travelled widely in Turkey. This book is a distillation of the best of those travels, an impressive meander through the country's history and mythology, as well as an articulate account of Turkey's profound effect upon the author.

Past travellers' accounts

75   **On horseback through Asia Minor.**
      Frederick G. Burnaby.   Oxford: Oxford University Press, 1996. 384p.
      map.

A fascinating account of a journey taken through Turkey during the winter of 1876/77, and originally published in 1877. In order to see for himself the tense relationship between Russia and Turkey, the author set out to cross 2,000 miles of Asia Minor, armed with a rifle, a stock of medicines, and some warm clothing, and accompanied by his servant.

76 **Travels in Asia Minor, 1764-1765.**
Richard Chandler, edited and abridged by Edith Clay.   London:
Trustees of the British Museum, 1971. 253p. bibliog.
The author travelled in Anatolia and Greece from 1764 to 1766, accompanied by
William Pars whose watercolours are reprinted in the book. The descriptions of people
and places are vivid and detailed, and the observations powerful. The book is based on
the 1825 edition.

77 **Evliya Çelebi's *Book of travels*. Land and people of the Ottoman
Empire in the seventeenth century. A corpus of partial editions.**
Edited by Klaus Kreiser.   Leiden, the Netherlands: E. J. Brill, 1988-96.
3 vols.
Evliya Çelebi was born in İstanbul in 1611 during the reign of Sultan Ahmed II. He
travelled for forty-one years until 1670, when he was sixty-one years old, and spent
the remaining ten years of his life writing about his experiences. His travels extended
to all parts of the Ottoman Empire, Europe, Asia and Africa. The result is an extraordinary treasure of period description. Evliya Çelebi's *Book of travels* is a vast
panorama of the Ottoman world, and not simply a travel account. Although frequently
highly fantastical, it provides a chronicle of the author's life and time, and therefore
also partly an autobiographical memoir. English versions of this massive work are
fairly inadequate, and Klaus Kreiser's series of excerpted texts and annotated translations of Evliya Çelebi is extremely useful, because the texts are reliably established
on the basis of the original manuscripts. The series contains: *Evliya Çelebi in
Diyarbekir: the relevant section of the Seyāḥatnāme* by Evliya Çelebi, edited and
translated from the Turkish with commentary and introduction by Martin Van
Bruinessen, Hendrik Boeschoten (Leiden, the Netherlands: E. J. Brill, 1988. 270p.
map. bibliog.); *Evliya Çelebi in Bitlis: the relevant section of the Seyāḥatnāme* by
Evliya Çelebi, translated from the Turkish with a commentary and introduction by
Robert Dankoff (Leiden, the Netherlands: E. J. Brill, 1990. 435p. map. bibliog.); and
Evliya Çelebis Anatolienreise: aus dem dritten Band des Seyāḥatnāme (Evliya
Çelebi's travels in Anatolia: from the third volume of the *Seyāḥatnāme*), edited with
translation, commentary and introduction by Korkut M. Buğday (Leiden, the
Netherlands: E. J. Brill, 1996. 456p. map. bibliog.).

78 **Evliya Çelebi seyahatnamesi.** (Evliya Çelebi's travelogue.)
Evliya Çelebi, prepared for publication by Orhan Şaik Gökyay with Y.
Dağlı, İ. Gündağ.   İstanbul: Yapı Kredi Yayınları, 1996. 498p. bibliog.
This is an annotated transcription and index of 17th-century traveller Evliya Çelebi's
travelogue. The edition is based on the manuscript in the library of the Topkapı
Museum (ref. no. Baghdat 304), which is considered to be the original copy of the
work. The text is supplemented by the transcription schema, a bibliography, and an
index.

79 **Across Asia Minor on foot.**
W. J. Childs.   New York: Dodd, Mead; Edinburgh, London: William
Blackwood & Sons, 1917. 459p.
The author, accompanied by a Turk, travelled about 1,300 miles in Asia Minor in five
months. The book describes the land and the people of the Black Sea region, Central

and Eastern Anatolia. Samsun, Tokat, Sivas, Talas, Cappadocia, Cilicia, Adana, Maraş, and Aleppo are among the provinces he visited.

80 Travels and researches in Asia Minor, more particularly in the province of Lycia.

Charles Fellows. Hildesheim, Germany; New York: Georg Olms Verlag, 1975. 510p. maps.

The volume is a reprint of the 1852 edition published by John Murray of London. The author's travels covered inner and southern Anatolia, and by marking his route on a map, he drew a map of the area, as well as several sketches of places he visited. He describes the ancient cities and ruins, his discoveries and excavations, and gives an account of life and of the people in the region. His journal was made public at the request of the Royal Geographical Society.

81 Ben kendim: a record of Eastern travel.

Aubrey Herbert. London: Hutchinson, 1932. 2nd ed. 380p. maps.

The author worked in the British Embassy in İstanbul, travelled extensively, and later became an expert on the Middle East. He was elected to Parliament in 1911. The volume covers his diplomatic activities, and journeys into obscure parts of Europe of the time. He also gives an account of the events leading up to the establishment of the new Turkey. ('Ben kendim' means 'I, myself' in Turkish.)

82 The day of the crescent: glimpses of old Turkey.

Gilbert Ernest Hubbard. Cambridge, England: Cambridge University Press, 1920. 243p.

The volume covers the travels of the author as well as his summaries of the most interesting parts of old travel books written from the 16th to the early 17th centuries.

83 Eothen: traces of travel brought home from the East.

Alexander Kingslake. Oxford: Oxford University Press, 1991. 279p.

First published in 1844, Kingslake's accounts of his grand tour around the Near East created such an impression that the author was widely known as 'Eothen' thereafter. Praised for its vivid impression, *Eothen* covers much of the Levant. The opening sixty pages on Turkey – mainly Constantinople and Smyrna – are essential period reading.

84 The towers of Trebizond.

Rose Macaulay. London: Futura, 1986. 222p.

First published in 1956, this is the travel account that never was. Nevertheless, this eccentric account of an entirely fictional jaunt along the Black Sea coast to modern Trabzon is memorable, moving and a surprisingly convincing depiction of place.

85 **Journal of a tour of Asia Minor, with comparative remarks on the ancient and modern geography of that country.**
William Martin Leake.   Hildesheim, Germany: Georg Olms Verlag, 1976. 362p. maps.

The book was first published by John Murray of London in 1824. It is written as a guide to the explorer and traveller. Maps show the maritime and the interior parts of the country. The book is principally a geographical survey which describes the landscape and natural resources, but it also gives information on the history of the land, its inhabitants and antiquities.

86 **With the Turk in wartime.**
Marmaduke Pickthall.   London: J.M. Dent & Sons, 1914. 216p.

Pickthall, translator of the *Koran*, loves Turkey and the Turks. He is also a shrewd political commentator, writing with great insight and enlightenment about issues such as religious tolerance and the emancipation of women.

87 **Impressions of Turkey during twelve years' wanderings.**
W. M. Ramsay.   London: Hodder & Stoughton, 1897. 296p.

During his residency in Turkey, the author travelled extensively, and this book contains his travel notes and impressions. It covers many topics from archaeology to religion, from minorities in the Empire to American missionaries.

88 **The historical geography of Asia Minor.**
W. M. Ramsay.   Amsterdam: Adolph M. Hakkert, 1972. 495p. maps.

This book, which was first prepared in 1886 to be read before the Royal Geographical Society after an exploration to Asia Minor, is in two parts. Part I recalls the travels of the author, and covers such topics as Hellenism and orientalism, the royal road, the eastern trade route, and the Roman roads. Part II is about the historical geography of the cities of Byzantine Asia, Lydia, Phrygia, the roads of the Province Asia, Galatia and northern Phrygia, and Cappadocia.

89 **A relation of a journey beegun A. Dom. 1610. Foure bookes. Containing a description of the Turkish Empire of Aegypt, of the Holy Land, of the remote parts of Italy and Islands adjoyning.**
George Sandys.   London: Chetwin, 1670. 6th ed. 240p.

This is a rich source of information on people and places in the Ottoman Empire at an early date. The author left Venice for the Greek Islands and the Dardanelles, then spent some time in Constantinople. From there he travelled by boat to the Holy Land and Egypt, before returning to England via southern Italy. Lively accounts are given of these places and their occupants.

90 **Turkey romanticized: images of the Turks in early 19th century English travel literature (with an anthology of texts).**
Reinhold Schiffer. Bochum, Germany: Studienverlag N. Brockmeyer, 1982. 183p. bibliog. (Materialia Turcica, no. 5).

After a long and interesting introductory essay (p. 1-56), where the author analyses and summarizes the contents of the early 19th-century English travel literature on Turkey, part two contains extracts from selected travel literature under the thematic headings of 'The genius of a place', 'The natural Turk: cultural divergence and cultural bias', 'Turkish society', 'The Sultans', and 'The traveller's lot'. Extracts are from travellers such as J. Dallaway, T. Walsh, W. Hunter, T. Thornton, C. Macfarlane, and others. One of the common points between the texts presented here is that for their authors 'the Orient and the Oriental are different by nature, and not only this, but that Europe and Asia stood in contrast, or even antagonism' (p. 24). This is a useful and interesting collection both for the general reader and the researcher, who may proceed to read the complete texts of the mentioned books.

91 **Washed by four seas.**
H. C. Woods. London: Fisher Unwin, 1908. 316p.

An account of travels in Turkey by an ex-officer of the Grenadier Guards. Much of the book consists of general impressions of Turkish life, but with emphasis on the army, the military significance of buildings and fortifications, railway developments, etc. It deals mostly with Anatolia, but there are some chapters on the Balkans and the recently (at that time) created State of Bulgaria.

Turkish embassy letters.
See item no. 33.

Aegean Turkey.
See item no. 127.

Lycian Turkey: an archaeological guide.
See item no. 128.

Geology and Geography

Maps

Topographic maps

92   **Topographic quadrangle map set.**
      Moscow: Soviet Government, 1973-86. 162 sheets.
This is a set of high quality maps produced by the Russian government. Each sheet
has a descriptive text on the reverse written in Russian. The scale is 1:200,000.

93   **Türkiye fiziki haritası.** (Turkey: physical map.)
      Ankara: Harita Genel Komutanlığı, 1997.
This is a three-sheet set in colour, with detail and to a scale of 1:1,000,000. They have
hypsometric shading, and shaded relief. The maps show roads, towns, and pipelines.

94   **Türkiye – Balkanlar – Ortadoğu.** (Turkey – Balkans – the Middle
      East.)
      Ankara: Harita Genel Komutanlığı, 1982.
This is a one-sheet map in colour, to a scale of 1:1,300,000. It uses hypsometric tints
for elevation.

Geological and thematic maps

95   **Türkiye jeoloji haritası.** (Turkey: geological map.)
      Ankara: Maden Tetkik Arama Genel Müdürlüğü, 1989.
An official geological map of Turkey, to a scale of 1:200,000. It is bilingual in
Turkish and English.

96   **Türkiye'nin bilinen maden ve mineral kaynakları.** (The mines and minerals of Turkey.)
Ankara: Maden Tetkik Arama Genel Müdürlüğü, 1989. 108p.
This is a one-sheet map with an accompanying booklet listing individual mines, deposits, and ore reserves. It is bilingual in Turkish and English. The scale is 1:2,000,000.

97   **Türkiye enerji haritası.** (Turkey: energy map.)
Ankara: Harita Genel Komutanlığı, 1996.
This is a two-sheet map of Turkey, with information on energy resources overprinted. It shows pipelines, oil and gas fields, hydroelectric plants and resources, tanker terminals, and refineries. It is bilingual in Turkish and English, to a scale of 1:1,250,000.

98   **Balkanlar.** (The Balkans.)
Ankara: Harita Genel Komutanlığı, 1993.
This is a set of four sheets to a scale of 1:1,100,000. It is in colour and shows roads, pipelines, and towns. It is in Turkish.

99   **Kafkaslar.** (The Caucasus.)
Ankara: Harita Genel Komutanlığı, 1993.
This is a set of two sheets to a scale of 1:1,100,000. It is in colour, and shows roads, pipelines, towns, and international boundaries. It is in Turkish.

100   **Kıbrıs.** (Cyprus.)
Ankara: Harita Genel Komutanlığı, 1987.
This is a coloured, detailed map to a scale of 1:250,000. It is topographic, and bilingual in Turkish and English.

101   **Türk Cumhuriyetleri.** (Turkic republics.)
Ankara: Harita Genel Komutanlığı, 1997.
This one-sheet colour map covers Turkey and the Turkic peoples and republics of the world. It shows oil and gas pipelines, refineries, nuclear energy plants, and tanker terminals. It provides a summary of energy resources in the area (Eastern Europe, Middle East, Caucasus, and Central Asia).

Geology

102   **The seismicity of Turkey and adjacent areas. A historical review, 1500-1800.**
N. N. Ambraseys, C. F. Finkel.   İstanbul: Eren Yayıncılık, 1995.
240p. maps. bibliog.
A reference work for historians, civil engineers, earth scientists and others concerned with the seismic hazard within the area of present-day Turkey. All significant

earthquakes which occurred in the period covered are described, with full bibliographical references included for each entry. There is an introductory account of previous attempts to compile earthquake catalogues for the area and a discussion of primary source material.

103 **Geology of Turkey.**
R. Brinkmann. Amsterdam; New York; Oxford: Elsevier Scientific, 1976. 156p. maps. bibliog.
This is a brief introduction to the geology of Turkey, containing some references to the palaeontology and ore deposits; palaeogeographic and tectonic relations to the neighbouring areas are also shown. It includes an extensive bibliography, maps and tables giving detailed information.

Geography

104 **The Middle East: a geographical study.**
Peter Beaumont, Gerald H. Blake, J. Malcolm Wagstaff. London: David Fulton Publishers, 1988. 2nd ed. 623p. bibliog.
This up-dated edition offers a comprehensive account of the environmental setting and human geography of the region. The substantial treatment of Turkey can be identified with the help of the detailed list of contents, bibliography and index.

105 **Turkey: geographic and social perspectives.**
Edited by Peter Benedict, Erol Tümertekin, Fatma Mansur. Leiden, the Netherlands: E. J. Brill, 1974. 446p. map. bibliog. (Social, Economic and Political Studies of the Middle East, no. 9).
The essays in this volume deal with the human geography, rural and village settlements, land ownership and land tenure (part one); problems of socio-economic change in the villages, including the role of the state and the local government and leaders (part two); and problems of urban centres, migration to urban centres, modernization in 19th-century Turkey, and Turkish workers abroad (part three). Although dated, the volume is still important for the light it sheds on Turkish social history and social geography.

106 **La Turquie d'Asie: géographie administrative, statistique descriptive et raisonnée de chaque province de l'Asie Mineure.**
(Asiatic Turkey: administrative geography and descriptive statistics for each province in Asia Minor.)
Vital Cuinet. Paris: Ernest Leroux, 1890-95. 4 vols.
This detailed and descriptive geography of Anatolia (and other Ottoman territories in south-west Asia) provides a very valuable survey account of the reality prior to the collapse of the Ottoman Empire. The work systematically reviews resources, population and religious/ethnic groups, economic and political patterns, etc. by province and

sub-province divisions. The text, which is substantially supported by statistical tables and by maps of each province (vilayet), is in accessible French and each paragraph section is clearly headed for ease of identification (and translation). Volume four includes an index of places covering the whole four-volume work in forty-eight separately numbered pages.

107 **Turkey: an introductory geography.**
John C. Dewdney. London: Chatto & Windus; New York: Praeger, 1971. 214p. maps. bibliog. (Praeger Introductory Geographies).

This book is the first modern geography of Turkey written in English, and remains a valuable systematic coverage of the country in three main sections: physical, human and economic. A fourth section gives a region-by-region account of the country, each one supported by an effective map.

108 **The Middle East: a physical, social and regional geography.**
William Bayne Fisher. London: Methuen, 1978. 7th ed. 571p. maps. bibliog.

Fisher's highly respected regional geography includes an account of the physical and environmental basis of the country under the 'Physical geography of the Middle East' in part one of the book; in part three, 'Asia minor' is discussed on pages 323-62.

109 **Atlas of Islamic history.**
Harry W. Hazard. Princeton, New Jersey: Princeton University Press, 1954. 3rd ed. 49p.

The maps show the changes in the political boundaries in the area which occurred between the 7th and 20th centuries. There are also separate maps of the area showing geographical features, the Crusades, the Ottoman Empire, central and south Asia and the Far East.

110 **Middle East patterns. Places, peoples, and politics.**
Colbert C. Held. Boulder, Colorado: Westview Press, 1994. 2nd ed. 484p. maps. bibliog.

This leading American geographical study of the Middle East, offers a systematic account of physical and cultural patterns in the region (including Turkey) in part one. Part two treats countries separately and chapter twenty-one (p. 375-95) is devoted to a geographical survey of Turkey, with sections on the country's location, regional patterns, historical background, population, economic development, and foreign links. The volume includes an index.

111 **Türkei.** (Turkey.)
Wolf-Dieter Hütteroth. Darmstadt, Germany: Wissenschaftliche Buchgesellschaft, 1982. 584p. 116 maps. bibliog. (Wissenschaftliche Länderkunden, no. 21).

The most comprehensive geographical study of Turkey available. Readers with some knowledge of German may be helped by a very detailed 5-page contents list, 116 maps, plans and figures, and a 36-page bibliography which is a valuable aid to study in itself with titles in English as well as in German, French and Turkish. The book has strong sections on physical structure, climate, and bio-geography and a brief historical overview, followed by a close examination of population, settlement, agriculture, industry, resources and urbanization. The text ends with an interesting discussion of İstanbul and Ankara, and a look at the pattern of inter-regional disparities in Turkey.

112   **An historical geography of the Ottoman Empire from earliest times to the end of the sixteenth century, with detailed maps to illustrate the expansion of the Sultanate.**
      Donald Edgar Pitcher.   Leiden, the Netherlands: E. J. Brill, 1972. 171p. maps.

This book outlines the history of the Ottoman Empire and its changing political boundaries from the pre-Ottoman period to 1606. It has been described by critics as the standard and only work in political geography for the Ottoman state. The work includes sixty maps.

113   **Provincial and regional statistics, 1994.**
      State Institute of Statistics (SIS).   Ankara: State Institute of Statistics, 1997. 570p.

This annual publication breaks down information by the five regions of Turkey as well as its seventy-three provinces. It covers information on population, marriages, divorces, deaths, suicides, health care, school enrolment, prisons, net production, number of animals, animal products, mining, electricity and power, manufacturing, construction, transport, tourism, wholesale and retail prices, prices received by farmers, finance, and national accounts. It is also available on diskette.

Turkey: a country study.
See item no. 4.

SEAP provincial statistics, 1950-1996.
See item no. 765.

Flora and Fauna

114 **Flora of Turkey and the east Aegean islands.**
Edited by P. H. Davis, with J. Cullen, M. J. E. Coode. Edinburgh:
Edinburgh University Press, 1965-85. 9 vols.

This magisterial work was produced under the direction and general editorship of
P. H. Davis. It provides a systematic account of the flora of Turkey, and the Greek
islands of the eastern Aegean. The first volume contains an account of the topography
and climate, a description of the main phytogeographic regions and a consideration of
the extent of endemism. A list of general works on Turkish vegetation is given. The
volumes provide a comprehensive and detailed description of the flora.

115 **Food from the fields: edible wild plants of Aegean Turkey.**
Evelyn Lyle Kalças. Bornova, Turkey: Birlik Matbaası, 1980. 2nd ed.
146p. map.

The book describes approximately ninety edible wild plants originating in the Aegean
area. Each plant is illustrated with a sketch by the author. The three indexes provide
the scientific names, as well as the Turkish and English common names, for the plants.

116 **Türkiye kardelenleri.** (Turkish snowdrops.)
N. Zeybek, E. Saner. İzmir: Ege Üniversitesi Basımevi, 1995. 95p.
maps. (Süsbitkileri Tarım & Sanayi A.Ş., Karamürsel).

The text of this publication, which is a detailed study of the types of Galanthus found
in Turkey, is in German and Turkish. It contains maps, plates, and illustrations.

117 **Important bird areas in Turkey.**
Gernant Magnin, Murat Yarar. İstanbul: Doğal Hayatı Koruma
Derneği, 1997. 320p. maps. bibliog.

This publication by the Society for the Protection of Nature in Turkey (DHKD) lists
ninety-seven important bird areas (IBAs) in Turkey that are of outstanding importance

26

for birds and bird conservation. Each site description details geographical and hydro-logical features, the importance of the area for the birds, and a full list of relevant conservation issues. The site descriptions are accompanied by full-colour maps that show main habitats, access roads and important land features. Introductory chapters include a section on nature conservation legislation. Appendices contain recent information on bird populations, wetland loss in Turkey, and the first widely accepted English-Turkish bird name list. Vast number of references are provided in the biblio-graphy.

118 **Wetlands of Turkey.**
Environmental Problems Foundation of Turkey. Ankara:
Environmental Problems Foundation of Turkey, 1989. 178p. maps.

Information about the geographical position and area, general information, ornithological importance, and forms of use, and human activities are given for the wetlands of Turkey. A total of seventy wetlands are described in the Black Sea, the Marmara, the Aegean, the Mediterranean, Central Anatolia, and Eastern Anatolia regions. The threat to Turkey's wetlands are discussed and solutions to problems are suggested.

119 **Türkiye kuşları.** (Birds of Turkey.)
İlhami Kiziroğlu. Ankara: OGM Yayınevi, 1989. 314p. maps.

This publication is in Turkish, but its introduction is in English and in German. It not only provides general information about birds, but also, in the third section, a list of birds in Turkey, and in the fourth section it contains a map for Turkish birds, and a description of their general characteristics. Coloured photographs of 'passeres' (song-birds) are given.

120 **Türkiye omurgalılar tür listesi.** (Species list of vertebrate in Turkey.)
Edited by Aykuy Kence, Can Bilgin. Ankara: TÜBİTAK, 1996.
206p.

One of the publications of the Turkish Fauna Database project supported by the Scientific and Technical Research Council of Turkey (TÜBİTAK). It lists the vertebrate of Turkey (mammals, fish, birds, reptiles, and amphibians).

121 **Herb drugs and herbalists in Turkey.**
K. H. C. Baser, G. Honda, W. Miki. Tokyo: Institute for the Study of Languages and Cultures of Asia and Africa, 1986. 300p. (Studia Culturae Islamicae, no. 27).

The volume gives a list of herbs, discusses the principal forms in which medicines (compounds) are prepared (pills, powders, ointments, etc), and lists the names of various complaints with prescribed medicines for each one.

122 **Where to watch birds in Turkey, Greece and Cyprus.**
Hilary Welch. London: Mitchell Beazley, 1996. 216p. maps.

The guide, illustrated by M. Langman, describes 180 bird-watching sites in the Eastern Mediterranean. Information given includes expected species, general introduction to sites, and best times to watch.

123 **Songbirds of Turkey.**
Cees S. Roselaar.   Mountfield, England: Helm Information, 1995.
240p. maps. bibliog.

Provides information on the taxonomy, morphology and distribution of Turkish song-birds, and compares the data with similar data from other countries. Most of the data collected is the result of a twenty-year research programme entitled 'Birds of the western Palaearctic'. Characteristics and measurements of all the subspecies of passerine of the region are given.

124 **The bulbous plants of Turkey. An illustrated guide to the bulbous petaloid monocotyledons of Turkey: amaryllidaceae, iridaceae, liliaceae.**
Turhan Baytop, Brian Mathew.   London: B. T. Batsford with Alpine Garden Association, 1984. 132p. map. bibliog.

The book is based on the knowledge and the material gathered by the authors on their collecting trips in Turkey over a period of twenty years, and the herbarium specimens from Kew, Edinburgh, and İstanbul University (Faculty of Pharmacy). It is richly illustrated with photographs, and where possible vernacular names of the species are also given. There is a chapter containing short biographies of earlier collectors in Turkey.

Bilim ve Teknik. (Science and Technology.)
See item no. 1300.

Turkish Journal of Botany.
See item no. 1369.

Turkish Journal of Zoology.
See item no. 1377.

Archaeology and Prehistory

125 **Ancient civilisations and ruins of Turkey, from prehistoric times until the end of the Roman Empire.**
Ekrem Akurgal. İstanbul: NET Turistik Yayınları with University of Pennsylvania, 1993. 8th ed. 398p.

This well-known introduction to the antiquities of Turkey has seen many editions. It provides a useful illustrated overview of the major periods since prehistory, looking at many of the key sites, and more spectacular artefacts are discussed in detail. It contains 112 pages of plates.

126 **Town and country in south-eastern Anatolia II. The stratigraphic sequence at Kurban Höyük.**
Edited by Guillermo Algaze. Chicago: The Oriental Institute, University of Chicago Press, 1990. 438p.

Kurban Höyük is one of the most important recent excavations in south-eastern Turkey. The largest area exposed dated to the 3rd millennium but parts of a long sequence of settlements from prehistoric and historic periods were also excavated. Although the site is now submerged by one of the new dams on the Euphrates, this publication gives an up-to-date, detailed account of the artefacts from a wide range of periods typical of this region.

127 **Aegean Turkey.**
George E. Bean. London: Ernest Benn, 1974. 2nd ed. 250p. bibliog.

A survey of the classical sites of the Aegean coast of Turkey. The area includes some of the most famous and best preserved sites in Turkey, such as Ephesus, Pergamon, Miletus and Smyrna (modern-day İzmir).The volume is well illustrated, and discusses the historical context and the individual sites in a readable manner.

128 **Lycian Turkey: an archaeological guide.**
George E. Bean.   London: Ernest Benn, 1978. 197p. maps. bibliog.

Continuing Bean's classic survey of the archaeology of Turkey (see item no. 127), this books deals with the history and visible remains of Lydia, concentrating heavily on the classical period. The book strikes a balance between academic rigour and readability, combined with a good selection of illustrations.

129 **Hittite myths.**
Edited by Gary M. Beckman, translated from the Hittite by Harry A. Hoffner Jr.   Georgia, Atlanta: Scholars Press, 1990. 92p. (SBL Writings from the Ancient World, no. 2).

Hittite mythology is a rich mix from both Anatolia and from the regions bordering it. This book provides a useful general introduction to individual Hittite myths and very readable translations of both Hittite and other Anatolian myths.

130 **The Aegean, Anatolia and Europe: cultural interrelations in the second millennium B.C.**
Jan Bouzek.   Gothenburg, Sweden: Paul Åströms Forlag, 1985. 267p. (Studies in Mediterranean Archaeology, no. 29).

The archaeology of the western part of Turkey is strongly connected to that of Greece and south-east Europe. This is especially true of the second millennium BC, the end of which provides the historical setting for the Homeric epics. This book presents the evidence from the area as a whole, is well illustrated and is particularly strong on stylistic analysis.

131 **Ancient Anatolia: aspects of change and cultural development. Essays in honour of Machteld J. Mellink.**
Edited by Jeanny Vorys Canby, Edith Porada, Brunilde Ridgway, Tamara Stech.   Madison, Wisconsin: University of Wisconsin Press, 1986. 137p.

This edited volume provides a variety of essays on different areas of the archaeology of Turkey, from prehistory to the 1st millennium BC and ranging from the health of the people in the Bronze Age to the interpretation of ancient seals. It provides a good indication of several different approaches to the ancient evidence in a well-presented format.

132 **Anatolian Iron Ages: the proceedings of the second Anatolian Iron Ages colloquium held at Izmir, 4-8 May 1987.**
Edited by A. Çilingiroğlu, D. H. French.   Oxford: Oxbow Books, 1991. 164p. (British Institute of Archaeology at Ankara, Monograph no. 13; Oxbow, Monograph no. 13).

The articles in the volume provide a rich source of information on recent work on the 1st millennium in Turkey, a period during which vibrant indigenous states, such as the Urartu and Phrygia, came into contact with the surrounding powers, such as the Assyrians and classical Greece.

133 **Anatolian Iron Ages: the proceedings of the third Anatolian Iron Ages colloquium held at Van, 6-12 August 1990.**
Edited by A. Çilingiroğlu, D. H. French.   London: British Institute of Archaeology at Ankara, 1994. 352p. (British Institute of Archaeology at Ankara, Monograph no. 16).

The articles in the volume provide a rich source of information on recent work on the 1st millennium in Turkey, a period during which vibrant indigenous states, such as the Urartu and Phrygia, came into contact with the surrounding powers, such as the Assyrians and classical Greece.

134 **Chronologies in old world archaeology.**
Edited by Robert W. Ehrich.   Chicago: University of Chicago Press, 1992. 2 vols.

This edited book attempts to provide an authoritative chronology and general account of cultural developments in the ancient Near East. It is important to see Turkey in its wider geographical context and, as well as a number of sections which offer summarized information on prehistoric and historic periods in Turkey, this volume provides a valuable summary of the developments in the neighbouring regions.

135 **Studies in the history and topography of Lycia and Pisidia: in memoriam A.S. Hall.**
Edited by David French.   London: British Institute of Archaeology at Ankara, 1994. 122p. maps. (British Institute of Archaeology at Ankara, Monograph no. 19).

South-west Turkey is one of the less well known parts of the country, but is the location of a number of important classical sites. The articles in this volume provide a scholarly overview of the historical topography of the area, inscriptions found there and more detailed accounts of three of the ancient cities, Sinda, Isinda and Lagbe.

136 **Sardis: twenty-seven years of discovery.**
Edited by Eleanor Guralnick.   Chicago: Chicago Society of the Archaeological Institute of America, 1987. 87p.

The site of Sardis in the west of Turkey has been the subject of a long running excavation. This volume brings together a variety of data from many of the different periods of occupation on the site, from prehistoric to Roman, Byzantine and medieval. It presents both a good range of information and some indication of the detail that lies behind it.

137 **The Hittites.**
Oliver R. Gurney.   Harmondsworth, England; New York: Penguin, 1990. 214p.

The Hittites dominated central Anatolia in the 2nd millennium BC and their remains are among the most striking of any in Turkey. This book is the classic one-volume summary of the Hittites. It provides a very good overview of the evidence, both archaeological and historical.

138 **Sardis from prehistoric to Roman times: results of the
    archaeological exploration of Sardis 1958-1975.**
    George M. A. Hanfmann.   Cambridge, Massachusetts: Harvard
    University Press, 1983. 512p.

The most comprehensive account of the excavations at Sardis, illustrating what lies
behind the visible ruins. The excavated architecture is surveyed, and discussions cover
the pottery and other finds.

139 **Recent Turkish coin hoards and numismatic studies.**
    Edited by C. S. Lightfoot.   Oxford: Oxbow Books, 1991. 347p. maps.
    bibliog. (British Institute of Archaeology at Ankara, Monograph
    no. 12; Oxbow, Monograph no. 7).

The history of coins in Turkey is both long and rich. This volume presents a series of
papers covering a very wide range of topics, from the detailed to the general, concerned
with Turkish numismatics, their chronology and their social context.

140 **Architecture and society in Hecatomnid Caria: proceedings of the
    Uppsala symposium.**
    Edited by Tullia Linders, Pontus Hellström.   Uppsala, Sweden:
    University of Uppsala, 1989. 104p. (Uppsala Studies in Ancient
    Mediterranean and Near Eastern Civilization, no. 17).

The Swedish excavations at Labraunda were initiated in 1948. Although the aim was
to find a link between Minoan Knossos and Bronze Age Labraunda, Greek architecture
promoted by indigenous philhellenism in the 4th century was discovered. In later
years scholars from many countries focused their interest on Hecatomnid Caria and its
blending of Greek, Carian and Oriental cultures. When, in 1987, the Turkish authorities
consented to send to the Medelhavsmuseet (the Mediterranean Museum, Stockholm)
an exhibition of excavated finds from Labraunda belonging to the museums of İzmir
and Bodrum, as a temporary loan, an architectural symposium on Hecatomnid Caria
became relevant, and was held in October 1987. A number of scholars still working on
various aspects of this period were brought together in this symposium to discuss the
results. The proceedings include: some general trends in the architectural layout of
4th-century Caria; the Mausoleion; an interpretation of the freestanding sculptures
from the Mausoleum; the sculptures from the Mausoleum; the sculptors of the
Mausoleum friezes; metrology and planning in Hecatomnid Labraunda; formal ban-
queting at Labraunda; and rock tombs in Hecatomnid Caria and Greek architecture.
The book includes several photographs, elevations, sections and plans.

141 **Anatolia in the second millennium B.C.**
    Maurits N. van Loon.   Leiden, the Netherlands: E. J. Brill, 1985. 94p.
    (Iconography of Religions, no. 12).

The iconography of 2nd millennium BC Anatolia is rich, amongst the Hittites and also
among other ethno-linguistic groups and includes indigenous elements and elements
drawn from further afield, Mesopotamia and even Egypt. Interpretations are provided
for a wide range of iconography and an attempt is made to place them in the context of
local religious beliefs.

142 **Anatolia in the earlier first millennium B.C.**
Maurits N. van Loon.   Leiden, the Netherlands: E. J. Brill, 1991. 97p.
(Iconography of Religions, no. 15).
During the first half of the 1st millennium BC, Anatolia was home to a rich and fascinating mix of artistic styles and subjects. Culturally the Phrygians, the Neo-Hittites
and other pre-classical groupings had distinctive styles in some regards but they had
many common themes. This book describes a wide range of objects, detailing their
meaning, their links elsewhere and providing individual bibliographies.

143 **The Hittites and their contemporaries in Asia Minor.**
J. G. Macqueen.   London; New York: Thames & Hudson, 1986. 174p.
(Ancient Peoples and Places).
Another wide-ranging summary of what is known of the Hittites in Turkey. Although
it covers rather less detail than Gurney's book (see item no. 137), it is markedly better
illustrated. Sections deal with origins of the Hittites, their history and various aspects
of the organization of the Hittite state, as well as their eventual disappearance towards
the end of the 3rd millennium.

144 **Çatal Hüyük: a neolithic town in Anatolia.**
James Mellaart.   New York: McGraw Hill, 1967. 232p. bibliog.
(New Aspects of Archaeology).
Çatal Hüyük is, without doubt, of one of the most spectacular Neolithic sites in the
Middle East, dating from the end of the 6th millennium BC and being of exceptional
size for its time; much of the spectacular preservation is due to accidental fires in the
tightly packed settlement. The site is located in the Konya plain and is now the
renewed subject of excavations. This well illustrated volume provides a detailed and
accessible account of the main results of the original series of excavations undertaken
between 1961 and 1965.

145 **Urartu: a metalworking centre in the first millennium B.C.**
Edited by Rivka Merhav.   Jerusalem: The Israel Museum, 1991. 372p.
The Iron Age kingdom of Urartu in Eastern Turkey produced some of the most
impressive artefacts of the 1st millennium BC. This exhibition catalogue, with extensive
illustrations, many in colour, gives an impression of the riches that must once have
existed as well as providing a useful historical summary and set of commentaries.

146 **Anatolia: land, men, and gods in Asia Minor.**
Stephen Mitchell.   Oxford: Clarendon Press, 1993. 2 vols.
The incursions of the Galatians into Anatolia in the 3rd century BC marked a period of
profound change in Turkey, which led to the Roman and Byzantine periods and saw
the growth of Christianity as the major religion. This publication covers both the history and the archaeological remains, looking at the developments during this time in
rural and urban life, as well as the impact of new religious practices. Volume one is
entitled 'The Celts in Anatolia' and volume two 'The impact of Roman rule'.

147 **Cremna in Pisidia: an ancient city in peace and war.**
Stephen Mitchell. Swansea, Wales: Classical Press of Wales, 1996.
244p.

Provides a detailed reconstruction of the life and history of an important town in southern Roman Turkey, based on an extensive survey carried out during the 1980s. It explores many characteristics of civic life – the water supply, housing, and public buildings – as well of techniques of Roman siege warfare.

148 **Tille Höyük 1: the medieval period.**
John Moore. Oxford: Oxbow Books, 1993. 205p. (British Institute of
Archaeology at Ankara, Monograph no. 14).

The site of Tille Höyük was excavated between 1979 and 1990 by the British Institute of Archaeology at Ankara as a part of the Turkish Lower Euphrates Rescue Project. The site reveals important remains of the Late Bronze and Iron Ages, and of the Achaemenid and Hellenistic periods, as well as the medieval phase which is presented in this volume.

149 **The lost treasures of Troy.**
Caroline Moorehead. London: Weidenfield & Nicolson, 1994. 306p.

The recent rediscovery in Russia of many of the treasures from Troy has drawn new attention to the spectacular nature of these finds. This accessible work provides a compelling account of Heinrich Schliemann and the original discovery of the objects. It gives the background to their rediscovery, discusses the nature of the objects and also provides a considerable amount of information on the older excavations of the site of Troy.

150 **Reflections upon the great theatre at Ephesus.**
Peter W. Parsons. *Journal of the Faculty of Architecture, Middle East
Technical University*, vol. 9, no. 2 (1989), p. 109-16.

Of all the archaeological remains from antiquity, one of the most impressive is the Great Theatre at Ephesus. This paper discusses some of the most important buildings in Ephesus, and the reasons that the Theatre has endured so far, and gives general information about the ruins and the Theatre in particular.

151 **The Caucasian region in the early Bronze Age.**
Antonio Sagona. Oxford: British Archaeological Reports, 1985.
563p. (British Archaeological Reports, International Series, no. 214).

Eastern Turkey forms a distinct region and its archaeological links are as close to north-west Iran and Trans-Caucasia as to central Anatolia. This study looks in particular at this region in the 4th and 3rd millennia BC and, in addition to a general account of the period, includes a gazetteer of sites and a comprehensive pottery corpus.

152 **Ancient Turkey: a traveller's history of Anatolia.**
Lloyd Seton. Berkeley, California: University of California Press,
1989. 240p.

Provides an excellent overview of the archaeology and history of pre-Islamic Turkey. The detailed summaries of all periods are well written and accessible, giving excellent and reliable accounts of the main cultures, with more detail on some specific sites. It is accompanied by good photographs and a bibliography.

153   **The Late Bronze Age and the Iron Age transition.**
G. D. Summers.   Oxford: Oxbow Books, 1993. 205p. (British Institute of Archaeology at Ankara, Monograph no. 15).
The volume presents a full description of the finds from the period of the Hittite Empire, including a Mycenaean stirrup jar sherd. It also discusses the local hand-made pottery from the earlier part of the period, which is unlike anything previously known.

154   **Eastern Turkey: an architectural and archaeological survey. Volume I: Van, Kars and Ararat. Volume II: the Pontus, Erzurum, Sivas, the Ani-Taurus and the upper Euphrates. Volume III: The lower Euphrates and the Tigris. Volume IV: Edessa, the Hatay.**
T. A. Sinclair.   London: The Pindar Press, 1987. 4 vols. bibliog.
Eastern Turkey has an exceptionally rich range of material remains of the past. This series of books provides a very detailed survey of the monuments of various periods from the Neolithic to the Ottoman. As well as the site descriptions, the period and geographical summaries are excellent, as are the accompanying illustrations and bibliography.

155   **Schliemann of Troy: treasure and deceit.**
David A. Traill.   New York: St. Martin's Press, 1996. 365p.
The spectacular treasures of Troy were found by Schliemann in the 19th century but then passed by a tortuous route through many different hands, disappearing completely until their rediscovery in Russia. This book describes the original discovery and the subsequent events, as well as providing new information on the character of their original excavator.

156   **Çatal Hüyük in perspective.**
Ian A. Todd.   Menlo Park, California: Cummings, 1976. 167p.
bibliog. (Cummings Modular Program in Anthropology).
The large Neolithic settlement of Çatal Hüyük, located in the Konya plain, was excavated between 1961 and 1965 and has recently been the subject of further excavations. This book summarizes the spectacular results of the earlier series of excavations, including details of the buildings, their wall paintings, burial practices, the economy and the importance of trade.

157   **Town and country in south-eastern Anatolia I. Settlement and land use at Kurban Höyük and other sites in the lower Karababa basin.**
T. J. Wilkinson.   Chicago: The Oriental Institute, University of Chicago, 1990. 315p.
One of the more recent developments in archaeology in the Middle East is the use of intensive study of pottery and other artefacts lying on the surface of sites. From this it is possible to reconstruct not simply what happened at individual sites, but entire past landscapes and settlement systems. This study is one of the most sophisticated of its kind.

158 **The later prehistory of Anatolia: the late Chalcolithic and early Bronze Age.**
Jak Yakar. Oxford: British Archaeological Reports, 1985. 2 vols. bibliog. (British Archaeological Reports: International Series, no. 268).

This book covers the period between approximately 4,000 BC to 2,000 BC, a period from which there are perhaps fewer spectacular remains but in which key developments in society were taking place, such as the rise of states and cities. It reviews the general developments against the environmental background; however, the bulk of the publication consists of an invaluable summary of all the excavated sites of this period.

159 **Prehistoric Anatolia: the Neolithic transformation and the early Chalcolithic period.**
Jak Yakar. Tel Aviv: Tel Aviv University, Sonia & Marco Nadler Institute of Archaeology, 1991. 361p. bibliog. (Monograph Series of the Institute of Archaeology, Tel Aviv University, no. 9).

Yakar gives a summary of the exceptionally rich sequence of prehistoric cultures in Turkey, together with an overview of past environments.

160 **Prehistoric Anatolia. Supplement: the Neolithic transformation and the early Chalcolithic period.**
Jak Yakar. Tel Aviv: Tel Aviv University, Sonia & Marco Nadler Institute of Archaeology, 1994- . (Monograph Series of the Institute of Archaeology, Tel Aviv University, no. 9a).

The volume includes a comprehensive list of excavations throughout Anatolia, many of which are otherwise available in English, describing the major results and illustrating the architectural and material remains.

161 **The structure of the Urartian state.**
Paul Zimansky. Chicago: The Oriental Institute, University of Chicago, 1985. 141p. (Studies in Ancient Oriental Civilization, no. 41).

The Urartian kingdom in eastern Turkey was for a considerable period one of the great rivals to the Assyrian Empire in the 1st millennium BC. It has left a fascinating range of sites in a wide area. This book provides one of the best, recent surveys of the material remains, and is one of the most successful attempts at providing a coherent interpretation of the evidence.

Turkey's southern shore: an archaeological guide.
See item no. 44.

Turkey beyond the Meander: an archaeological guide.
See item no. 45.

Anatolian Archaeology: Reports on Research Conducted in Turkey.
See item no. 1311.

Anatolian Studies: Journal of the British Institute of Archaeology at Ankara.
See item no. 1312.

Anatolica: Annuaire International pour les Civilisations de l'Asie Antérieure.
See item no. 1313.

History

General

162 **The modern Middle East.**
Edited by Albert Hourani, Philip S. Khoury, Mary C. Wilson.
London: I. B. Tauris, 1993. 687p. bibliog. (Tauris Readers).
This is a useful reader for students of Middle Eastern studies, covering the period
from 1789 to the present. It contains twenty-seven essays, which have been published
before, arranged in four sections. The essays which concern the Ottoman Empire and
the Turkish Republic closely are: 'Reforming elites and changing relations with
Europe'; 'The Ottoman 'Ulemā and westernization in the time of Selīm III and
Maḥmūd II' by Uriel Heyd; 'Turkish attitudes concerning Christian-Muslim equality
in the nineteenth century' by Roderic H. Davison; 'Ottoman reform and the politics of
notables' by Albert Hourani; 'Egypt and Europe: from French expedition to British
occupation' by Roger Owen; 'War and society under the Young Turks, 1908-18' by
Feroz Ahmad; 'Ottoman women, households, and textile manufacturing, 1800-1914'
by Donald Quataert; 'Said Bey – the everyday life of an İstanbul townsman at the
beginning of the twentieth century' by Paul Dumont; 'Religion and secularism in
Turkey' by Şerif Mardin; 'From Ottomanism to Arabism: the origin of an ideology'
by C. Ernest Dawn; and 'The religious right' by Binnaz Toprak.

163 **Osmanlı devleti ve medeniyeti tarihi.** (History of the Ottoman state
and civilization.)
Edited with an introduction by Ekmeleddin İhsanoğlu. İstanbul:
Research Centre for Islamic History, Art and Culture (IRCICA), 1994- .
4 vols. bibliog.
The work will have four volumes when completed. Although the first two volumes
which have been published are in Turkish, translations into Arabic and English are
being prepared. The work is illustrated with photographs and paintings, and there is a
glossary, a bibliography and an index. The volumes will cover all aspects of the

Ottomans, including history, administration, legal system, economy, society, language, literature, art, music, and education.

164 Constantinople: city of the world's desire, 1453-1924.
Philip Mansel.   London: John Murray, 1995. 528p. maps. bibliog.

A comprehensive account of nearly five centuries of İstanbul. The book deals with the daily life and activities of the city on the rise and decline of Ottoman imperial power. There are chapters on the imperial family, on the international role of İstanbul, on viziers and dragomans, ambassadors and artists, janissaries, on the Young Turks, and on the loss of Greek Orthodox and other minorities. There is, throughout much of the book, some emphasis on the role of the Ottoman court and on the fortunes of the royal dynasty. The structure of this informative and reflective work is largely chronological and there is a substantial bibliography.

165 The Ottoman Turks: an introductory history to 1923.
Justin McCarthy.   London: Longman, 1997. 406p. maps. bibliog.

A general history of the Ottoman Empire from its beginnings (1288) to the end of the First World War. The book covers social history (family life, health), as well as diplomatic, military and political history.

166 History of the Ottoman Empire and modern Turkey.
Stanford Jay Shaw.   New York: Cambridge University Press, 1977.
2 vols. bibliog.

The first volume deals with the period from 1280 to 1803. As well as covering military, political, and economic topics, it also includes two chapters on the society, administration, arts and culture in the Empire. The second volume begins with the reforms in the Ottoman Empire, the Young Turk period, the War of Independence and the Turkish Republic. The final two chapters cover the period between 1923 and 1975. Each volume is accompanied by a bibliography, which lists major works in both Turkish and English.

167 The Ottomans.
Andrew Wheatcroft.   London: Viking Press, 1993. 322p. map.
bibliog.

A general history of the Ottoman Empire from its beginnings in 1288. It aims to explain who the Ottomans were, how they functioned, and why the West misunderstood them. It is aimed at the non-specialist reader, and its style is somewhere between academic and journalistic.

The making of modern Turkey.
See item no. 1.

Turkey: a short history.
See item no. 5.

An introduction to the history of the Turkic peoples: ethnogenesis and state-formation in medieval and early modern Eurasia and the Middle East.
See item no. 7.

Turkey: a modern history.
See item no. 20.

Atlas of Islamic history.
See item no. 109.

An historical geography of the Ottoman Empire from earliest times to the end of the sixteenth century, with detailed maps to illustrate the expansion of the Sultanate.
See item no. 112.

Belleten. Türk Tarih Kurumu. (Bulletin. Turkish Historical Society.)
See item no. 1316.

International Journal of Middle Eastern Studies.
See item no. 1333.

New Perspectives on Turkey.
See item no. 1352.

Osmanlı Araştırmaları. The Journal of Ottoman Studies.
See item no. 1355.

Tarih ve Toplum. (History and Society.)
See item no. 1360.

11th to 17th centuries

168   The Ottoman Empire: 1300-1481.
       Colin Imber.   İstanbul: ISIS Press, 1990. 288p. maps. bibliog.
This is a chronological history of the Ottoman Empire from its foundation until the death of Mehmed II in 1481. The narrative has been re-constructed from primary source materials, which the author discusses in detail in the introduction.

169   Süleymân the Second and his time.
       Edited by Halil İnalcık, Cemal Kafadar.   İstanbul: The ISIS Press, 1993. 394p.
This important volume is a collection of essays by well-known scholars who cover many aspects of Ottoman history in the age of Süleyman (Suleiman) the Magnificent (1520-66). They represent a variety of positions and scholarly traditions, ranging from political and social history to arts and architecture.

170   The Ottoman Empire: the classical age 1300-1600.
       Halil İnalcık.   London: Phoenix, 1995. 2nd impression. 258p. maps.
       bibliog.
A reprint edition of the earlier 1973, 1989 and 1994 editions by the same author. The
first part of the book gives an outline of Ottoman history from its beginnings to its
declining years in the 17th century. The second part describes the structure of the
Ottoman dynasty starting with the time of Osman (1281-1324?), the palace and its organization, and the central and provincial administrations. The third part covers economic
and social life, trade, cities, roads, population, guilds and merchants in the Empire. The
final section deals with religion and culture, including education and popular culture.

171   Between two worlds: the construction of the Ottoman State.
       Cemal Kafadar.   Berkeley, California; London: University of
       California Press, 1995. 221p. bibliog.
This volume looks at the rise of the Ottoman Empire and its transformation from a
small frontier group into a centralized imperial state.

172   The Seljuks of Anatolia: their history and culture according to
       local Muslim sources.
       Mehmed Fuad Köprülü, translated from the Turkish by Gary Leiser.
       Salt Lake City, Utah: University of Utah Press, 1992. 101p. bibliog.
The translation of an eighty-page article by a well-known Turkish scholar, first
published in Turkish in 1943. The article presents unique details on the most obscure
period of Anatolian history, and the translator's notes and comments on the text
provide a detailed update of the status of medieval Anatolian history since 1943. This
is a good source book for the libraries and researchers of Turkish, Byzantine and
medieval studies.

173   Suleyman the Magnificent and his age: the Ottoman Empire in the
       early modern world.
       Edited by Metin Kunt, Christine Woodhead.   London: Longman,
       1995. 218p. maps. bibliog.
The book comprises an introductory chapter by M. Kunt on the early development of
the Ottoman state up to the time of Süleyman (Suleiman), followed by eight essays in
two parts. Part one focuses on the problems and policies of the age of Süleyman, and
part two addresses the ideology of Ottoman rule. There is also a glossary of
Ottoman/Turkish terms.

174   Neshri's history of the Ottomans: the sources and developments of
       the text.
       V. L. Ménage.   New York; London: Oxford University Press, 1964.
       86p. bibliog. (London Oriental Studies, vol. 16).
Nearly all historians of the classical age in the Ottoman Empire used the work of
Neshri, who wrote during the reign of Sultan Bayezid II (1481-1512). This is a scholarly
study of Neshri and his work. The appendices give the concordance of texts and
sources, specimens of the text of the manuscript, Neshri's chronological list and
stemma of Neshri's manuscripts.

175 **Annals of the Turkish Empire from 1591 to 1659 of the Christian era.**
Naima, translated from the Turkish by Charles Fraser. London: Ayer Co. Publishers, 1932. 467p.

The book was first published under the same title in 1832 (London: Printed for the Oriental Translation Fund of Great Britain and Ireland by John Murray & Parbury, Allen & Co.). The Turkish annalist Naima narrated the most important and interesting events that took place within the Turkish dominions between the years 1591 to 1659, giving detailed account of the wars, foreign and domestic, in which Turks were engaged during that period, all negotiations, and treaties with foreign nations. Naima's work follows a chronological arrangement, listing the events under the years in which they took place.

176 **Theodore Spandounes: on the origins of the Ottoman emperors.**
Donald M. Nicol. Cambridge, England: Cambridge University Press, 1997. 191p.

Theodore Spandounes was a Greek refugee from Constantinople who settled in Venice. He was among many who published works about the origins, history and institutions of the Turks, after the Ottoman conquest of Constantinople. This particular work was published in 1538 in Italian, and the present volume is the first English translation of its complete text, with historical commentary and explanatory notes.

177 **The Seljuks in Asia Minor.**
Tamara Talbot Rice. London: Thames & Hudson; New York: Praeger, 1961. 280p. maps. bibliog. (Ancient Peoples and Places, no. 20).

The Seljuk Turks and their Empire, which lasted a little more than two centuries, formed the foundation of the Ottoman Empire. The book covers the Seljuks of Persia (1073-1157), the Seljuks of Syria (1095-1103), the Seljuks of Iraq (1131-34), and the Seljuks of Rum (1077 to about 1308). The book contains eighty photographs and fifty-six line drawings. It is one of the rare works in English on the Seljuks.

178 **The history of Mehmed the Conqueror.**
Tursun Beg, translated from the Turkish by Halil İnalcık, Rhoads Murphcy. Chicago: Bibliotheca Islamica, 1978. 263p. (American Research Institute in Turkey Monograph Series, no. 1).

'Tārīh-i Abu'l Fath' is the most important original source for the study of Mehmed the Conqueror's time. The author, Tursun Beg, belonged to the inner circle of the government throughout the Sultan's reign, and in his work gives a detailed account of the times. The present volume contains a section on the life and the work of Tursun Beg, followed by an English summary of the manuscript, facsimile text (Ayasofya library MS), and a glossary.

18th to 20th centuries

179 **After empire. Multiethnic societies and nation-building: the Soviet Union and the Russian, Ottoman and Habsburg Empires.**
Edited by Karen Barkey, Mark von Hagen. Boulder, Colorado: Westview Press, 1997. 208p.

A study of the causes and consequences of imperial decline and collapse. The contributors of the essays ask the following questions: is imperial decline inevitable; what is the balance of power between the centre and the peripheries; what coping mechanisms do empires tend to develop and what influence do these have; and is modernization the cause of imperial decline and collapse? Among the contributors are Charles Tilly, Çağlar Keyder, Şerif Mardin, and Roger Brubaker.

180 **Russia and the Armenians of Transcaucasia, 1789-1889. A documentary record.**
Annotated translation and commentary by George A. Bournoutian.
Costa Mesa, California: Mazda Publishers, 1998. 578p.

The author presents an annotated translation of documents written in Armenian, Russian, Persian, and Georgian, which primarily deal with the Armenians of Transcaucasia. However, the documents presented are also highly relevant to Ottoman history and migration studies. The documents have been selected from the twelve volumes of *Akty* (*Akty sobrannye Kavkazskoiu arkheograficheskoiu kommissieiu*), official publications, and published and unpublished documents from Russian, Georgian and Armenian archives. It also includes documents from the archives of the Turkish Prime Ministry.

181 **Italo-Turkish diplomacy and the war over Libya, 1911-1912.**
T. W. Childs. Leiden, the Netherlands: E. J. Brill, 1990. 271p. maps. bibliog. (Social, Economic and Political Studies of the Middle East and Asia, no. 42).

In 1911 Italy, an aspiring Great Power, attacked Ottoman Libya. Italy's military was ill-prepared for it, and the Ottoman Empire, distracted by internal dissension and unrest in the Balkans, was unready. This study examines how the belligerents dealt with the military and diplomatic stalemate into which the Libyan War degenerated, and which was ended only by the outbreak of the First Balkan War in 1912, when the Ottomans were obliged to make peace with Italy in order to face more dangerous enemies nearer home. The study is based on Ottoman archives, as well as on better-known Italian sources.

182 **Istanbul under Allied occupation (1918-1923).**
Nur Bilge Criss. Leiden, the Netherlands: E. J. Brill, 1999. 200p.
(The Ottoman Empire and its Heritage: Politics, Society and Economy, no. 17).

This study covers the socio-political, intellectual and institutional dynamics of underground resistance to the Allied occupation in İstanbul. The author asserts that the city was neither the seat of treason against the nationalist struggle for independence, nor was in collaboration with the occupiers. In that context, she claims that several factors helped the Turkish nationalists in their struggle for independence: inter-Allied rivalries in the Near East that carried over to İstanbul; the fact that the British, French and Italians, as major occupation forces, failed to establish a balance of strength among themselves in their haste to promote respective national interests; and the victors' underestimation of the defeated, engrossed as they were with bureaucracy and assailed by the influx of Russian refugees, Bolshevik propaganda, and the Turkish left.

183   **Reform in the Ottoman Empire, 1856-1876.**
        Roderic H. Davison.   Princeton, New Jersey: Princeton University
        Press, 1963; New York: Gordian Press, 1973. 483p. bibliog.

A primary source for the study of the Ottoman reform movement in the mid-19th century. Its focal points are the important political leaders of the period, the reform decree of 1856, the re-organization of the non-Muslim nationalities, and the influence of western and Russian diplomats in pressing for reforms.

184   **Essays in Ottoman and Turkish history, 1774-1923: the impact of
        the West.**
        Roderick H. Davison.   London: Saqi Books, 1990. 288p.

The book comprises a dozen essays (all but one previously published), in which the author surveys the influence of European ideas on the Ottoman Empire and the creation of the Turkish Republic.

185   **Churchill's secret war. Diplomatic decrypts: the Foreign Office
        and Turkey 1942-44.**
        Robert Denniston.   Stroud, England: Sutton Publishing, 1997. 208p.

The British Foreign Office had been reading Turkish diplomatic communications since 1922, as had the Germans. The information in this book comes from the release in 1994 of secret government archives. Churchill did his best to draw Turkey into the war on the side of the Allies, and even went to Turkey in 1943. The book contains much detail and many footnotes, and it is not an easy read. However, for the specialist it is a valuable source of information.

186   **The well-protected domains: ideology and the legitimation of
        power in the Ottoman Empire, 1876-1908.**
        Selim Deringil.   London: I. B. Tauris, 1997. 260p. map. bibliog.

The author asks the question 'how did the Ottoman Empire grapple with the challenge of modernity and survive?'. He rejects the explanations based on the concept of an Islamic empire, or the paradigm of the 'Eastern Question'. He argues that far richer insights can be gained by focusing on imperial ideology and drawing out the striking similarities between the Ottoman and other late legitimist empires like Russia, Austria and Japan. He traces the Ottoman state's pursuit of legitimation in public ceremonial, in the iconography of buildings, music, the honours system or the language of the chancery, in its proto-nationalist reformulation of the Islamic legal practices, in its efforts to inculcate, through an expanded educational system, and in the efforts of the Ottoman elite to present a 'civilized' image abroad.

187 **The slow rapprochement: Britain and Turkey in the age of Kemal Atatürk, 1919-38.**
Stephen F. Evans.   Huntingdon, England: The Eothen Press, 1982.
123p. bibliog.
This is a straightforward account of the relations between the two countries, based mainly on published British documentary sources.

188 **Clash of empires: Turkey between Russian Bolshevism and British Imperialism, 1918-1923.**
Bülent Gökay.   London: I. B. Tauris, 1997. 224p. bibliog.
The author deals with the aftermath of the 'Great Game', the struggle between Britain and Russia for influence in the Middle East and Central Asia in the 19th century. He shows how an alliance between Turkish nationalism and the Bolsheviks forced Britain to recognize that it did not have the resources to consolidate the spoils of its victory after the First World War.

189 **The Young Turks in opposition.**
Şükrü Hanioğlu.   New York; Oxford: Oxford University Press, 1996.
416p. bibliog. (Studies in Middle Eastern History).
A contribution to the history of the Committee of Union and Progress (or the Young Turks). The author writes about their activities in many cities inside and outside the Ottoman Empire. He provides insights into diplomatic relations between the Ottoman Empire and Europe in the early 20th century.

190 **Anglo-Ottoman encounters in the age of revolution. The collected essays of Allan Cunningham, volume I.**
Edited by Edward Ingram.   Ilford, England: Frank Cass, 1993. 360p.
Alan Cunningham traces the effects of involvement in the Revolutionary and Napoleonic Wars on the Ottoman Empire. This is the first volume of his collected essays on the 'Eastern Question', which was the most intractable problem of the 19th century.

191 **The revolution of 1908 in Turkey.**
Aykut Kansu.   Leiden, the Netherlands: E. J. Brill, 1997. 341p.
(Social, Economic and Political Studies of the Middle East and Asia, no. 58).
In Ottoman history, the year 1908 opened a new era of representative government and social and political developments. This is a detailed account and narrative history of the period between 1906-08, during which the prelude and aftermath of the revolution and elections of 1908 took place.

192 **The great powers and the end of the Ottoman Empire.**
Edited by Marian Kent.   London: Frank Cass Publications, 1996.
238p. bibliog.
The papers in this volume focus on the international rivalry among the European powers at the end of the 19th century (Russia, Italy, Germany, France, and Great

Britain), and the questions posed by the fall of the Ottoman Empire following the First World War. The authors include M. Kent, F. Ahmad, F. R. Bridge, R. J. B. Bosworth, A. Bodger, U. Trumpener, and L. B. Fulton.

193   **Death and exile: the ethnic cleansing of Ottoman Muslims, 1821-1922.**
Justin McCarthy.   Princeton, New Jersey: Darwin Press, 1995. 368p. bibliog.

One of the very few academic studies which document the nature and the degree of Muslim suffering in Anatolia and the Balkans during the 19th century. The author uses British consular reports sent from major Balkan and eastern Anatolian cities, the observations and findings of international commissions and foreign investigators, and information found in Turkish military documents. The book consists of seven chapters covering the period from the Greek revolt in 1821 to the Turkish War of Independence, which began in 1919. Specific emphasis is placed on the consequences of the Turco-Russian War (1877-78), the Balkan Wars (1912-13), the First World War, and the Greek invasion of western Anatolia in 1919.

194   **Gallipoli.**
Alan Moorehead.   Ware, England: Wordsworth Editions, 1997. 320p. (Wordsworth Military Library).

The Allied campaign against Gallipoli began in 1915, when the Ottoman Empire joined the First World War on Germany's side. The aim was to break the deadlock on the Western front by a naval operation, in which French and British warships would try to eliminate the Ottoman batteries and then sweep the minefields in the Dardanelles, finally capturing Constantinople. This would cut off the Ottoman Empire from German aid, and make it possible for the Allies to take supplies and arms to the Russians for their German front. Using official records and private papers, the author recounts what happened during the next nine months, namely a nightmare of confused planning, and military incompetence. This is the story of one of the most controversial campaigns of modern times.

195   **Imperial meanderings and Republican by-ways: essays on eighteenth century Ottoman and twentieth century history of Turkey.**
Robert Olson.   İstanbul: ISIS Press, 1996. 332p.

The essays in the first section of this collection deal with 18th-century Ottoman topics, particularly the Janissary revolt of 1730 and the Ottoman-Persian wars between 1730 and 1747. Most of the essays in the second section discuss various aspects of the Kurdish problem from 1920 onwards, and its strategic importance for the Middle East.

196   **Beginnings of modernization in the Middle East: the nineteenth century.**
Edited by William R. Polk, Richard L. Chambers.   Chicago: Chicago University Press, 1968. 427p. bibliog.

The collection includes the following papers on Turkey: 'Aspects of the aims and achievements of the nineteenth century Ottoman reformers', Stanford Shaw; 'Ottoman reform and the politics of notables', Albert Hourani; 'The land regime, social structure

and modernisation in the Ottoman Empire', Kemal H. Karpat; 'The advent of representation in the government of the Empire', Roderick H. Davison; 'The impact of
nationalism on the Turkish elite', Ercümend Kuran; 'Stratford Canning and the
Tanzimat', Allan Cunningham; and 'The *Mektebi-i Osmani* in Paris', Richard L.
Chambers.

197 Between old and new: the Ottoman Empire under Sultan Selim III, 1789-1807.
Stanford J. Shaw.   Cambridge, Massachusetts: Harvard University
Press, 1971. 535p. bibliog.

The book examines Selim III's reign as a force which gave rise to modern Turkish
reform. In five parts, the author gives an account of the events in different parts of the
Empire during the 19th century.

198 Atatürk and the modernization of Turkey. Political tutelage and democracy in Turkey: the Free Party and its aftermath.
Walter F. Weiker.   Leiden, the Netherlands: E. J. Brill, 1973. 317p.
bibliog.

The book provides valuable information on the first attempt at democratization in
republican Turkey, when Atatürk experimented with the idea of creating a 'loyal
opposition'. The reasons for the birth of the Free Party, its failures and dissolution,
and the effects of this on Turkey's subsequent political development are discussed in
detail. Important information is also given on the partial reform of the single-party
regime in the 1930s.

199 Ottoman diplomacy: Abdülhamid II and the Great Powers, 1878-1888.
Feroze A. K. Yasamee.   İstanbul: The ISIS Press, 1996. 293p. bibliog.
(Studies on Ottoman Diplomatic History, no. 7).

The author re-evaluates the conventional analyses of the 'Eastern Question'. He
demonstrates that the Ottoman Empire under Abdülhamid II possessed an independent
foreign policy, which encompassed deliberate choices, and that these choices affected
the interests and ambitions of the European Great Powers. The book is based on
archival sources.

200 Colmar Freiherr von der Goltz and the rebirth of the Ottoman Empire.
Feroze A. Yasamee.   *Diplomacy & Statecraft*, vol. 9, no. 2 (1998),
p. 91-128.

Colmar Freiherr von der Goltz, also known as the 'father of the Turkish army', played
a crucial role in the development of military relations between the German and
Ottoman Empires. In a semi-biographical essay, the author analyses the events during
three decades of German-Ottoman relations, until the end of 1916.

201 **Political opposition in the early Turkish Republic: the Progressive Republican Party 1924-1925.**
Erik Jan Zürcher. Leiden, the Netherlands: E. J. Brill, 1991. 177p. bibliog. (Social, Economic, and Political Studies of the Middle East, no. 44).
The author combines unused sources with a close reading of the known ones, in order to put together a history of opposition in the early Republic.

Étatism and diplomacy in Turkey: economic and foreign policy strategies in an uncertain world, 1929-1939.
See item no. 649.

Anadolu ve Rumeli'de gerçekleştirilen ulusal ve yerel kongreler ve kongre kentleri bibliyografyası. (Bibliography of national and regional congresses held in Anatolia and in Rumelia, and of provinces where they were held.)
See item no. 1421.

Bibliography on national sovereignty, democracy and human rights (1840-1990).
See item no. 1428.

Ottoman domains

202 **The Ottoman Gulf. The creation of Kuwait, Saudi Arabia, and Qatar, 1870-1914.**
Frederick F. Anscombe. New York: University Press of California, Columbia and Princeton, 1997. 288p. bibliog.
The author aims to dispel the notion that Britain was exclusively responsible for the formation of the Persian Gulf's modern states. He dwells on the roles played by the Ottoman Empire, and the Ottoman occupation of the Persian Gulf in 1871.

203 **Imperial legacy: the Ottoman imprint on the Balkans and the Middle East.**
Edited by L. Carol Brown. New York: Columbia University Press, 1996. 337p. maps.
Presents a re-evaluation of the Ottoman past not only of Turkey, but of the twenty-eight countries which are heirs to the Empire. The work includes seventeen articles in six sections, and each section has an introduction in which the editor summarizes the important points and implications of the articles, which demonstrate how the Ottoman legacy continues to shape patterns of behaviour and perception among the peoples of Western Asia, Northern Africa, and Southeastern Europe. The authors explore the way in which this complex history influenced nations and ethnic groups in the building of

ideologies and identities today through varying issues such as politics, diplomacy, education, language, and religion. The essays also address the different regional perspectives on the Ottoman legacy found in the Arab world, the Balkans, and Turkey.

204 **Modernization in the Middle East: the Ottoman Empire and its Afro-Asian successors.**
Edited by Cyril E. Black, L. Carl Brown. Princeton, New Jersey: Darwin Press, 1993. 418p. maps. bibliog. (Studies on Modernization of the Center of International Studies at Princeton University).
A comparative and historical study of how the region has responded to modernization, beginning two centuries ago and tracing development in the modern states of Egypt, Tunisia, Turkey, Iraq, Israel, Jordan, Lebanon, and Syria.

205 **Christians and Jews in the Ottoman Empire: the functioning of a plural society.**
Edited by Benjamin Braude, Bernard Lewis. London; New York: Holmes & Meier Publishers, 1982. 2 vols. bibliog.
The volumes present a collection of essays by experts on the non-Muslim communities in the Ottoman Empire. Volume one is subtitled 'The central lands', and contains twenty essays on the Islamic background, the early history of the non-Muslim communities under Ottoman rule, the structure of the non-Muslim communities in the 18th century and after, the role of Christians and Jews in Ottoman life during the 19th century and after, and sources which dwell on the Ottoman archival material. Volume two contains nine essays, and is subtitled 'The Arabic speaking lands'.

206 **Jewish life under Islam. Jerusalem in the sixteenth century.**
Amnon Cohen. Cambridge, Massachusetts: Harvard University Press, 1984. 267p.
This is a social history not only of the Jewish minority but of other inhabitants of Jerusalem as well. The author looks at the population characteristics of the Jewish community, leaders, laws, religious practice, social and judicial status, and economic activity.

207 **Economic life in Ottoman Jerusalem.**
Amnon Cohen. Cambridge, England: Cambridge University Press, 1989. 179p. bibliog. (Cambridge Studies in Islamic Civilization).
This study of Jerusalem and its local economy under Ottoman rule looks at butchers and meat consumption, soap production and olive oil, flour and bread production in detail, as well as at the trade relations of Jerusalem with its neighbours. Jerusalem conducted its economic and social life with little interference from the central authorities. According to the author, this was useful in the short term, but later contributed to further weakening of the Ottoman Empire.

208 **The politics of households in Ottoman Egypt: the rise of the Qazdağlis.**
Jane Hathaway. Cambridge, England: Cambridge University Press, 1996. 216p. maps.

The author studies the military society in Ottoman Egypt, and contends that the basic framework within which it operated was the household, a conglomerate of patron-client ties. The book focuses on the Qazdağlı household, a military group which came to dominate Egypt.

209 **Ottoman military administration in eighteenth-century Bosnia.**
Michael Robert Hickok. Leiden, the Netherlands: E. J. Brill, 1997. 190p. bibliog.

The book examines the administration of Bosnia during the 18th century from the perspective of the officials who were charged by the sultans with this task. The author uses the collection of letters, journals, reports, and occasionally poems to supplement the chronicles, left by the selected governors, to shed light on what they sought to do in Bosnia and, in some cases, their own thoughts concerning their service. The work shows how the people of the province – including the Christians – cooperated with the Ottoman state to realize societal needs, and that 'an explanation for the social disruptions in eighteenth-century Bosnia lies somewhere beyond one-dimensional claims of class warfare, emergent nationalisms, religious strife, or even Ottoman decline'.

210 **Endowments, rulers and community. Waaqf al-Haramayn in Ottoman Algiers.**
Miriam Hoexter. Leiden, the Netherlands: E. J. Brill, 1998. 192p. (Studies in Islamic Law and Society, no. 6).

This is a history of the *waqf* endowments (religious endowments regulated by Islamic law) in Algiers dedicated to the poor of Mecca and Medina over the last 170 years of the Ottoman Empire, based on their own registers. The history is discussed both within the context of the Islamic endowment institution and that of Algiers. The role of the foundation is seen as a major factor in the shaping of the Algerian public sphere.

211 **State and provincial society in the Ottoman Empire: Mosul, 1540-1834.**
Dina Rizk Khoury. Cambridge, England: Cambridge University Press, 1998. 328p. maps.

The book sets out to demonstrate that contrary to the accepted view, military, fiscal, and political links between the central Ottoman Empire and provincial Iraqi society were strengthened rather than weakened over the three centuries in question.

212   **National movements and national identity among the Crimean Tatars (1905-1916).**
       Hakan Kırımlı.   Leiden, the Netherlands: E. J. Brill, 1996. 242p. map.
       (The Ottoman Empire and its Heritage: Politics, Society and Economy, no. 7).

The volume dwells on the process of the formation of the modern national identity among the Crimean Tatars during the first decades of this century. Although the main focus of the study is the period 1905-16, a general portrayal of Crimean Tatar society during the first century of Russian rule over the Crimea is given as well as an account of the two formative decades of İsmail Bey Gaspirali's reforms prior to 1905. The author places the subject within the context of parallel processes of other Turkic and/or Muslim peoples.

213   **The Ottoman presence in Southeastern Europe, 16th-19th centuries: a view in maps.**
       Text by James P. Krokar for the Herman Dunlap Smith Center for the History of Cartography.   Chicago: The Newberry Library, 1997. (The Newberry Library Slide Set, no. 27).

The collection contains six slides of maps. There is an introductory text, and a short bibliography to accompany the maps, which gives information about their origins. The maps are: 'The Danubian Basin (1566)'; 'The Fortress at Szigetvar (1566)'; 'The Fortress of Klis and the city of Split (1605)'; 'Contemporary Illyria (1705)'; 'Hungary (1717)'; and an 'Ethnographic map of the Ottoman Balkans (1848)'.

214   **In the house of the law. Gender and Islamic law in Ottoman Syria and Palestine.**
       Judith E. Tucker.   Berkeley, California: University of California Press, 1998. 213p. map.

A study of Islamic law in 17th- and 18th-century Syria and Palestine under Ottoman rule. The author challenges the prevailing views on Islam and gender, revealing Islamic law to have been more fluid and flexible than previously thought.

215   **Egyptian society under Ottoman rule, 1517-1798.**
       Michael Winter.   London: Routledge, 1993. 336p.

The book presents a panoramic view of Ottoman Egypt from the overthrow of the Mamluk Sultanate in 1517 to Bonaparte's invasion of 1798, and the beginning of Egypt's modern period. It uses archive material, chronicles and travel accounts from Turkish, Arabic, Hebrew and European sources. It is intended to be a comprehensive social history which looks at the dynamics of the Egyptian-Ottoman relationship, and the ethnic and cultural clashes which characterized the period. The conflicts between Ottoman pashas and their Egyptian subjects and between Bedouin Arabs and the more sedentary population are presented, as is the role of women in this period and the importance of the doctrinal clash of Islam, Christianity and Judaism.

216   **Haifa in the late Ottoman period, 1864-1914. A Muslim town in transition.**
      Mahmoud Yazbak.   Leiden, the Netherlands: E. J. Brill, 1998. 264p. maps.

The author traces the beginnings of Haifa in the early 18th century, and reconstructs the vital elements of its society and administration from records. Haifa's demography, inter-communal relations, and the restructuring of the sources of elite power after 1864 are studied. The work also contains a study of the economic activities of Muslim women.

217   **An Ottoman century: the district of Jerusalem in the 1600s.**
      Dror Ze'evi.   New York: State University of New York, 1996. 258p. bibliog. (Suny Series in Medieval Middle East History).

The author integrates court records, petitions, chronicles, and local poetry to provide a detailed account of the Jerusalem area in the 1600s.

Muslims and minorities: the population of Ottoman Anatolia and the end of the Empire.
See item no. 295.

Ottoman social, cultural and economic history

218   **New approaches to the state and peasant in Ottoman history.**
      Edited by Halil Berktay, Suraiya Faroqhi.   London: Frank Cass, 1992. 282p.

A collection of studies which include: 'The Ottoman state and the question of state autonomy: comparative perspectives', J. Haldon; 'The search for the peasant in Western and Turkish history/historiography', H. Berktay; 'Ottoman history by inner Asian norms', I. Togan; 'In search of Ottoman history', S. Faroqhi; and 'Three empires and the societies they governed: Iran, India, and the Ottoman Empire', H. Berktay.

219   **Ottoman seapower and the Levantine diplomacy in the age of discovery.**
      Palmira Brummett.   Albany, New York: State University of New York Press, 1994. 285p. bibliog.

The book challenges the view that the 16th-century Ottoman Empire was a reactive economic entity, driven by the impulse to territorial conquest. The author sees the Ottoman state as an inheritor of Euro-Asian trading networks and participant in the contest for commercial hegemony stretching from Venice to the Indian Ocean, and in this context, studies the Ottoman navy, and the development of Ottoman sea-power.

220 **Revenue-raising and legitimacy: tax collection and finance administration in the Ottoman Empire, 1560-1660.**
Linda T. Darling.   Leiden, the Netherlands: E. J. Brill, 1996. 368p. bibliog. (The Ottoman Empire and its Heritage, Politics, Society and Economy, no. 6).

The book examines the finance procedures and documents of the post-classical Ottoman Empire. It provides an overview of institutional and monetary history and a detailed description of assessment and collection processes for different taxes. It constitutes a good source for the researchers of Ottoman economic and political history and the early modern Middle East, and historians of early modern Europe for imperial administration.

221 **Slavery in the Ottoman Empire and its demise, 1800-1909.**
Harkan Erdem.   New York: St. Martin's Press, 1997. 248p. bibliog.

This book attempts to understand how slavery persisted and then came to an end in the Ottoman Empire. It concentrates on the period 1800-1909, and examines the policies of the Ottoman state regarding slavery. It also looks at British involvement in the issue.

222 **Towns and townsmen of Ottoman Anatolia: trade, crafts, and food production in an urban setting, 1520-1650.**
Suraiya Faroqhi.   Cambridge, England: Cambridge University Press, 1984. 425p. maps. bibliog. (Cambridge Studies in Islamic Civilization).

This work is a contribution to the social and economic history of the Ottoman Empire. The author takes a period when there was an unusual period of growth and crisis in the Ottoman Empire, and aims to isolate some of the reasons behind both. She dwells on factors such as population growth (which increased the taxpaying population), and the establishment of a network of towns where previously urban centres had existed in isolation.

223 **Pilgrims and Sultans: the hajj under the Ottomans, 1517-1683.**
Suraiya Faroqhi.   London: I. B. Tauris, 1994. 244p. map. bibliog.

A comprehensive study of the pilgrimage to the holy cities of Islam during the first two centuries of Ottoman rule in the Hijaz. The author focuses mainly on the political, social and economic aspects of the topic, using Ottoman documents.

224 **Coping with the state: political conflict and crime in the Ottoman Empire, 1550-1720.**
Suraiya Faroqhi.   İstanbul: The ISIS Press, 1995. 205p.

A collection of eleven essays by the author, previously published elsewhere between 1985 and 1995. They focus on the relations between the Ottoman society and the state in the Ottoman provinces, where the peasantry and other 'marginals' and provincial officers were locked in a constant struggle to assert themselves. The author applies crime-solving methods to understand the workings of criminal behaviour in Ottoman provincial society.

225 **Making a living in the Ottoman lands, 1480-1820.**
Suraiya Faroqhi. İstanbul: The ISIS Press, 1995. 330p. (Analecta Isisiana, no. 19).

This collection of fourteen essays by the author, previously published elsewhere between 1985 and 1995, deals with Ottoman social and economic history. The articles focus on the ways in which Ottoman peasants, merchants, craftsmen, and what the author calls the 'marginals' dealt with the problems of survival in a harsh world. Several essays deal with the lives of artisans and craftsmen, where the author explores their mentalities, behaviour, and their reactions under certain conditions; others explore the impact of Ottoman administrators upon town development. There are ten essays on the 16th and 17th centuries, one on 15th-century Bursa, and two on the late 18th and early 19th centuries.

226 **Izmir and the Levantine world, 1550-1650.**
Daniel Goffman. Seattle, Washington: University of Washington Press, 1990. 254p. maps. bibliog.

The author focuses on one of the most important Ottoman commercial centres, İzmir, tracing its development into the dominant centre of Western Anatolia, and the focal point of Ottoman-European trade.

227 **The private world of Ottoman women.**
Godfrey Goodwin. London: Saqi Books, 1997. 260p. bibliog.

This illustrated book tells the story of Ottoman women during the six centuries of Ottoman rule. It also explores the issues of clothing and cooking, and family celebrations connected with birth, marriage and death. The final chapters of the book explore what it meant to be alive in the final years of the Ottoman Empire in the 19th century.

228 **The Janissaries.**
Godfrey Goodwin. London: Al-Saqi Books, 1997. 288p.

In this incredibly rich and readable book, the author explores the origins of the janissary corps of the Ottoman Empire, and follows their history through the centuries, until they were exterminated by Mahmud II in 1826. He brings to life one of the most extraordinary human institutions devised, the janissaries, who were both the greatest strength and greatest weakness of the Ottoman Empire.

229 **The rise of the bourgeoisie, demise of Empire: Ottoman westernization and social change.**
Fatma Müge Göçek. New York; Oxford: Oxford University Press, 1996. 200p. bibliog.

The author argues that the rise of a westernized Ottoman bourgeoisie in the 18th and 19th centuries caused the decline and the demise of the Empire.

230 **History of astronomy literature in the Ottoman period.**
Edited by Ekmeleddin İhsanoğlu. İstanbul: Research Centre for
Islamic History, Art and Culture (IRCICA), 1997. 2 vols. (History of
Ottoman Scientific Literature Series no. 1).

These volumes are in Turkish with a foreword in English. This is an in-depth study of
the scientific activities in the field of astronomy during the Ottoman period. The introduction reviews the scientific and cultural environment which prevailed under the
Seljuks of Anatolia and the Beyliks (emirates), and the Ottomans. The first volume
covers the works where the authors are known, by order of date of publication, including
biographies of 582 authors and citing 2,438 works. The second volume contains the
ten indexes and a bibliography.

231 **Studies in Ottoman history and law.**
Colin Imber. İstanbul: ISIS Press, 1996. 337p.

A collection, with introduction, of eighteen articles by the author published between
1972 and 1994, dealing with 16th-century naval history, the history of sects and heresies
in the Ottoman Empire, the history and historiography of the early Ottoman Empire,
Ottoman law and other subjects.

232 **Ebu's-su'ud: the Islamic legal tradition.**
Colin Imber. Edinburgh: Edinburgh University Press, 1997. 288p.
bibliog. (Jurists: Profiles in Legal Theory).

A study of the Ottoman Sheykh ul-Islam Ebu's-su'ud (d. 1574). The introductory
chapters place Ebu's-su'ud' s life and career within its legal and historical context,
and discuss the nature of the shari'a (Islamic law) and of Ottoman secular law. The
subsequent chapters discuss in detail his fatwas and other writings relating to specific
topics: the Sultan and legal sovereignty, the Caliphate, land and taxation, *waqfs*
(religious endowments regulated by Islamic law), family law, offences against the
property and offences against the person.

233 **The Middle East and the Balkans under the Ottoman Empire.**
Halil İnalcık. Bloomington, Indiana: Indiana University Turkish
Studies, 1993. 475p. bibliog. (Indiana University Turkish Studies,
no. 9).

A collection of the author's essays, some of them originally published in Turkish.
Topics covered include the economy, social conditions, and political history.

234 **An economic and social history of the Ottoman Empire.**
Edited by Halil İnalcık with Donald Quataert. Cambridge, England:
Cambridge University Press, 1997. 2 vols. maps. bibliog.

The first volume is by Halil İnalcık and covers the period between 1300 and 1600; the
second volume by Suraiya Faroqhi, Bruce McGowan, Donald Quataert and Şevket
Pamuk covers the period from 1600 to 1914. The volumes provide a detailed account
of the social and economic history of the Ottoman region, from the origins of the
Empire around 1300 to the eve of its destruction during the First World War. They
examine developments in population, trade, transport, manufacturing, land tenure, and
the economy.

235 **State and peasant in the Ottoman Empire: agrarian power relations and regional economic development in Ottoman Anatolia during the sixteenth century.**
Huri İslamoğlu-İnan. Leiden, the Netherlands; New York: E. J. Brill, 1994. 293p. bibliog.

Examines the conditions of peasantry and agriculture in Turkey in historical perspective, linking the conditions of Turkish agriculture to broader trends in the world. The topics addressed in the book include the political logic of the Ottoman peasantry, the conceptualization of state, peasant relations, Ottoman fiscal surveys as a source for social and economic history, appropriation and exchange of agrarian surpluses in north-central Anatolia, patterns of peasant economy in north-central Anatolia, and development of regional town markets.

236 **Self and others: the diary of a dervish in seventeenth century İstanbul and first-person narratives in Ottoman literature.**
Cemal Kafadar. *Studia Islamica*, vol. 69 (1989), p. 121-50.

The author takes issue with the dualistic framework of courtly versus popular opposition that dominates Ottoman literary theory. Within this framework, he then examines a diary entitled 'Şoḥbetnāme', kept by an Ottoman dervish Seyyid Ḥasan between the years 1661 to 1665, discussing the literary antecedents and parallels of the work. The diary records the dervish's social life as a member of his order, and and provides an intimate perspective on the social network of a dervish in 17th-century İstanbul.

237 **The Ottoman Empire and the world economy: the nineteenth century.**
Reşat Kasaba. Albany, New York: State University of New York Press, 1988. 203p. (SUNY Series in Middle Eastern Studies).

The book emphasizes the importance of the mid-19th century for Western Anatolia. Using Ottoman and British archival material, it analyses the rise of İzmir as the leading port of export between 1840 and 1876 for the Ottoman Empire.

238 **İstanbul: mekânlar ve zamanlar.** (İstanbul: places and times.)
Cahit Kayra. İstanbul: Ak Yayınları, 1990. 207p. maps. bibliog. (Ak Yayınları Kültür ve Sanat Kitapları, no. 52).

The author aims to show the reader the changes that İstanbul, as a place, has undergone through time. It is a valuable book even for those who do not know Turkish because it contains 162 maps and plans of the city from the 5th century onwards. There are also ten folded maps accompanying the book, including 'Ancien Plan de Constantinople' dated 1566-74.

239 **Landholding and commercial agriculture in the Middle East.**
Edited by Çağlar Keyder, Faruk Tabak. Albany, New York: State University of New York Press, 1991. 260p. bibliog.

A collection of eleven papers presented at the Second Biennial Conference on the Ottoman Empire and the world economy, held in 1986 at the State University of New York. The papers by various authors study different aspects of the emergence and implications of commercial agriculture in the Ottoman Empire, with particular emphasis on peasants, landlords, labour and property rights and the state.

240 **The Ottoman steam navy: 1828-1923.**
Bernd Langensiepen, Ahmet Güleryüz, translated from the Turkish by
James Cooper. London: Conway Maritime Press, 1994. 192p.

The book contains a full list of all ships with their technical details, and ship plans of
the principal classes, along with a chronology of naval developments before the
Republic. It sheds new light on the First World War Dardanelles campaign.
Appendices list all the ships of the period along with their basic specifications, accompanied by line drawings. The book has 300 photographs and line drawings.

241 **Studies in *Defterology*. Ottoman society in the fifteenth and
sixteenth centuries.**
Heath W. Lowry Jr. İstanbul: The ISIS Press, 1992. 275p. (Analecta
Isisiana, no. 4).

The term 'Defterology' has been coined by historian Lowry to describe research based
on Ottoman tax registers, a field which he himself has pioneered. The present volume
is a collection of thirteen of Lowry's formerly published articles based on Ottoman tax
registers ('tahrir defterleri'). The first section is entitled 'General studies', and as well
as presenting the author's introduction to the study of tax registers as a source for
social and economic history, it contains an article on the Ottoman provincial law-codes
(*kanunnames*). The second section, 'Urban history', contains articles on Ottoman
regions, such as Trabzon in Anatolia, the island of Limnos in the Aegean, and Selanik
(Thessaloniki) in Macedonia, Greece. The third section, 'Monastic history', contains
two articles on the monasteries of Mount Athos.

242 **A history of Middle East economies in the 20th century.**
Roger Owen, Şevket Pamuk. London: I. B. Tauris, 1998. 300p.
bibliog.

This is a very useful and informative book on the economic histories of principal Arab
countries, Israel and Turkey from 1918 to the present. Important trends, including the
patterns of colonial economic management, import substitution, the impact of the
1970s' oil boom, and the current process of liberalization and structural adjustment
are explored. The authors chart the growth of national income and issues of welfare
and distribution over two periods, 1918-45, and 1945-90. It includes tables of
economic indicators for each country for different periods, statistical data, and a very
useful bibliography.

243 **Ottoman nautical charts.**
Kemal Özdemir, translated from the Turkish by P. Mary Işın.
İstanbul: Creative Yayıncılık ve Tanıtım, 1992. 159p. maps. (The
Marmara Bank Publications).

The book contains over seventy colour reproduction maps, fifty of which are Ottoman
maps, all from the 16th century or earlier.

244   **Ottoman Empire and European capitalism, 1820-1913: trade, investment, and production.**
Şevket Pamuk.   Cambridge, England; New York: Cambridge University Press, 1987. 278p. map. bibliog.

Pamuk claims that European economic and financial penetration of the Ottoman Empire after the mid-19th century led to the full integration of the country into the European economic system. Trade was the mechanism of this penetration and in time the Ottoman Empire became subservient to the European capitalist system.

245   **Kitab-ı Bahriye.**
Pîrî Reis, edited by Ertuğrul Zekâi Ökte, transcription by Vahit Çubuk, Turkish text by Vahit Çubuk, Tülây Duran, English text by Robert Bragner. İstanbul: The Historical Research Foundation, 1989. 4 vols. maps. bibliog.

Kitab-ı Bahriye was written in 1520, and is among the most famous works of naval and maritime history. This is a facsimile reproduction of the work, including a transcription of the Ottoman text, its translation into modern Turkish, and an English translation.

246   **Social disintegration and popular resistance in the Ottoman Empire, 1881-1908: reactions to European economic penetration.**
Donald Quataert.   New York: New York University Press, 1983. 205p. (New York University Studies in Near Eastern Civilization, no. 9).

The author focuses on the resistance of some people in the Ottoman Empire to the process of Europeanization, the accommodation of other groups, and the benefits they derived from Western presence. The book contains case-studies focusing on European companies that were formed to exploit Ottoman agriculture, mining, transport, and commerce, and their relations with the Ottomans.

247   **Manufacturing and technology transfer in the Ottoman Empire, 1800-1914.**
Donald Quataert.   İstanbul, Strasbourg: ISIS Press and Université des Sciences Humaines de Strasbourg, 1992. 61p. (Études Turques-USHS, no. 2).

A volume of lectures given in Paris in 1989. The author questions some generally held notions about the performance and structure of late Ottoman manufacturing. He shows the vitality and degree of versatility of Ottoman manufacture in importing Western technology as well as its ability to react to market demands, although not always successfully. He claims that the Ottoman Empire was not a passive recipient of Western technology, and sees the transfer of technology as a part of the vitality of the Ottoman economy.

248 **Workers, peasants and economic change in the Ottoman Empire, 1730-1914.**
Donald Quataert. İstanbul: The ISIS Press, 1993. 203p. bibliog.

A valuable collection of fifteen essays by the author on Ottoman economic history, which have been previously published elsewhere. In the introduction, the author details the problems of researching Ottoman history.

249 **Ottoman manufacturing in the age of Industrial Revolution.**
Donald Quataert.   New York: Cambridge University Press, 1993.
244p. maps. bibliog. (Cambridge Middle East Library, no. 30).

A study of Ottoman manufacturing and manufacturers between 1800 and 1914. Using Ottoman, European and American archival sources, the author explains Ottoman technological methods of producing cotton cloth, wool cloth, yarn and silk, and the way in which they changed in the 19th century, as well as the organization of home and workshop production and trends in the domestic and international markets. The book shows that manufacturers of the Ottoman lands adopted a variety of strategies to confront European competitors and retain domestic and international customers.

250 **Manufacturing in the Ottoman Empire and Turkey, 1500-1950.**
Edited by Donald Quataert.   Albany, New York: State University of New York Press, 1994. 175p.

A collection of articles by leading social historians who provide case-studies of manufacturing activities in their social and political contexts. The work is important for historians, economists, and other interested parties. Contributions to the book include: 'Labor recruitment and control in the Ottoman Empire, sixteenth and seventeenth centuries', S. Faroqhi; 'Ottoman industry in the eighteenth century: general framework, characteristics and main trends', M. Genç; 'Ottoman manufacturing in the nineteenth century', D. Quataert; and 'Manufacturing in the Ottoman Empire and in republican Turkey, ca. 1900-50', Ç. Keyder.

251 **Piri Reis and Turkish map making after Columbus: the Khalili Portolan atlas.**
Svatopluk Soucek.   London; New York: Nour Foundation with Azimuth Editions and Oxford University Press, 1996. 2nd ed. 176p.
maps. bibliog. (Studies in the Khalili Collection of Islamic Art, no. 2).
(Nasser D. Khalili Collection of Islamic Art. Manuscript. MSS.718).

The Ottoman naval commander and cartographer Piri Reis (1475-1554) played a leading role in transmitting the discoveries of Columbus's voyage to the New World to the Ottomans. His work is known from two fragments of two world maps, and from his *Kitab-i Bahriye* (Book of Seamanship), which he illustrated with charts derived from medieval portolans. The Khalili Portolan Atlas is a hand-drawn example of the cartographic tradition established by Piri Reis. The book shows how Piri Reis's works fused the Islamic world view with European map making traditions, and were modified by his own experience as a navigator, and by the recent discoveries of Columbus.

252 **Ottoman foreign trade in the 19th century.**
State Institute of Statistics (SIS). Ankara: State Institute of Statistics, 1995. 106p. (Historical Statistics Series, no. 1).

This publication covers the content, coverage, problems and limitations of Ottoman foreign trade statistics, re-construction and general trends in Ottoman foreign trade. It also discusses Ottoman foreign trade by sub-period, commodity, composition and country.

253 **Agricultural statistics of Turkey during the Ottoman period.**
State Institute of Statistics (SIS). Ankara: State Institute of Statistics, 1995. 260p. (Historical Statistical Series, no. 3).

Presents information on Turkish agriculture in the early 20th century, agricultural censuses during the Ottoman period, the agricultural censuses of 1909, 1913 and 1914, and the area covered by the censuses.

254 **Ottoman industry: industrial census of 1913, 1915.**
State Institute of Statistics (SIS). Ankara: State Institute of Statistics, 1994. 228p. (Historical Statistics Series, no. 4).

This publication contains a discussion and explanation of the methodology used in these censuses, a summary of the censuses and data on food products, crops, leather, wood, textiles, paper products, and chemical and metal goods.

255 **The first statistical yearbook of the Ottoman Empire.**
State Institute of Statistics (SIS). Ankara: State Institute of Statistics, 1998. 370p. (Historical Statistics Series, no. 5).

This volume contains information on the population, health, education, libraries and antiques, state revenues and expenditures, public finance and debts, money and medals, silk and silk production, public debt administration, industry, sea and land transport, communication and selected pages from the original volume of the 1897 *Statistical Yearbook*. The text has been adapted to modern Turkish.

256 **The public works program and the development of technology in the Ottoman Empire in the second half of the 19th century.**
İlhan Tekeli, Selim İlkin. *Turcica*, vol. 28 (1996), p. 195-234.

During the 19th century, technology was introduced in the Ottoman Empire in five different sectors. The authors claim that although a significant amount of technology was transferred, it was not enough to reverse the peripheralization of the Empire.

257 **The Ottoman slave trade and its suppression 1840-1890.**
Ehud R. Toledano. Princeton, New Jersey: Princeton University Press, 1982. 307p. maps. bibliog.

Many members of the ruling elite of the Ottoman Empire were legally slaves (*kul*) of the sultan as he could theoretically surrender their labour and lives at any time. However, slavery provided a means of social mobility, political power within the military, the state or the household, forming an essential part of patronage networks. There was also a lucrative market in the slave trade, and the author explores its history and suppression in the 19th century.

258 **Slavery and abolition in the Ottoman Middle East.**
Ehud R. Toledano.   Seattle, Washington: University of Washington
Press, 1997. 204p. bibliog.
The author examines the major categories of slaves in the Ottoman Empire: the female
harem slaves, the sultan's military and civilian *kuls* (see item no. 257), court and elite
eunuchs, domestic slaves, Circassian agricultural slaves, slave dealers, and slave
owners. The author uses British and Ottoman sources, and offers an insight into the
life and thought of the Ottomans.

259 **Socialism and nationalism in the Ottoman Empire.**
Edited by Mete Tunçay, Erik Jan Zürcher.   London; New York:
British Academic Press in association with the International Institute of
Social History, Amsterdam, 1994. 222p.
A summary of the research on the interrelation between socialist and nationalist movements in the last decades of the Ottoman Empire. It includes six major contributions
by authors who have used resources in a multitude of languages. The introduction, by
Feroz Ahmad, is entitled 'Some thoughts on the role of ethnic and religious minorities
in the genesis and development of the socialist movement in Turkey', and the book
has chapters on the Greeks, Bulgarians and Armenians and Jews during the period
between 1878 and 1923. There are two sections on territorially-defined entities:
Macedonia and Thessaloniki.

260 **The politics of piety: the Ottoman ulema in the postclassical age
(1600-1800).**
Madeline C. Zilfi.   Chicago: Bibliotheca Islamica, 1988. 288p.
bibliog. (Studies in Middle Eastern History, no. 8).
The author traces the role of the official men of learning (the *ulema*) in their relations
with the state, from the 16th to 18th centuries. She claims that a decline in learning
among the ulema and their movement away from meritocracy and toward aristocracy
derived from the tensions of political instability, and the new reality helped preserve
the Empire into the 20th century. That is, a fusion between the 16th-century Ottoman
golden age and its 17th-century antithesis brought about an 18th-century synthesis
among the religious elite. The book contains a glossary, illustrations, and an index.

261 **Between death and desertion. The experiences of the Ottoman
soldier in WWI.**
Erik Jan Zürcher.   *Turcica,* vol. 28 (1996), p. 235-58.
The author depicts the state of the Ottoman soldier during the First World War. He
was badly clothed and undernourished, and there was a lack of medical care and of
transport. There was corruption, widespread hunger, diseases, and an adventurous war
strategy. The author examines the mentality of the Ottoman soldier, who kept on fighting among such horrors.

The population of the Ottoman Empire and Turkey (1500-1927).
See item no. 291.

The first population census during the Ottoman Empire, 1831.
See item no. 292.

The Arab World, Turkey and the Balkans (1878-1914): a handbook of historical statistics.
See item no. 294.

Ottoman and Turkish Jewry: community and leadership.
See item no. 325.

Religion and social change in modern Turkey: the case of Bediüzzaman Said Nursi.
See item no. 446.

The Ottoman lady.
See item no. 485.

Women in the Ottoman Empire. Middle Eastern women in the early modern era.
See item no. 507.

The origins of communism in Turkey.
See item no. 546.

Atatürk: founder of a modern state.
See item no. 560.

Atatürk and the modernization of Turkey.
See item no. 565.

Workers and the working class in the Ottoman Empire and the Turkish Republic, 1839-1950.
See item no. 850.

Biographies and memoirs

262 **An Ottoman statesman in war and peace. Ahmed Resmi Efendi, 1700-1783.**
Virginia H. Aksan. Leiden, the Netherlands: E. J. Brill, 1995. 253p. map. bibliog.

A well researched study of Ahmet Resmi Efendi, a civil servant and critic of the state. The book offers insights into 18th-century Ottoman society, politics and foreign relations. Of particular interest is section three, where Ahmet Resmi's career during the crucial years of the Russo-Turkish War (1768-74) is examined. Ahmet Resmi was the first of a new generation of statesmen, who saw virtue in the rationalization of war, and the need for peace within prescribed borders, and therefore in developing a polity which did not depend on the results of the battlefield.

263   **An English Consul in Turkey. Paul Rycaut at Smyrna, 1667-1678.**
      Sonia P. Anderson.   Oxford: Clarendon Press, 1989. 323p.
Sir Paul Rycaut (1629-1700) was a diplomat, historian of Turkey, and consul in
Smyrna (now İzmir) from 1667 to 1678. Anderson's book concentrates on Rycaut's
career in Turkey, and the English community at Smyrna.

264   **Early voyages and travels in the Levant. I. The diary of Master**
      Thomas Dallam, 1599-1600, II. Extracts from the diaries of Dr.
      John Covel, 1670-1679, with some account of the Levant Company
      of Turkey merchants.
      Edited by J. Theodore Bent.   New York: Burt Franklin, 1964. 305p.
      (Works issued by the Hakluyt Society, no. 87).
These are the manuscript diaries of two men who resided in İstanbul during the early
days of the Levant Company, which was established in 1581 with the help of William
Harborne (the first English ambassador to Constantinople) after the Ottomans granted
Capitulations to England. The Company set up factories in Smyrna (now İzmir), and
by 1640 there were twenty-five English firms in Constantinople dealing mainly in
cloth. Until the 19th century, the Levant Company, rather than the British government,
paid the salaries of the British ambassadors. The diaries contain information about the
Ottoman Empire and provide an account of the Levant Company which survived for
244 years.

265   **The Sultan's seraglio. An intimate portrait of life at the Ottoman**
      court.
      Ottaviano Bon, edited by G. Goodwin.   London: Al Saqi Books, 1997.
      160p.
Bon was a 17th-century Venetian representative at the court of Sultan Ahmed I. This
book gives a lively account of life and politics at the Topkapı Palace, and his description
of the social and religious mores of the period is fascinating.

266   **Turkey in revolution.**
      Charles Roden Buxton.   London: T. Fisher Unwin, 1909. 285p. map.
A first-hand account of the author's visits to Turkey and his observations immediately
before and after the revolution of 1908. Buxton was invited to be present at the
opening of the new parliament, as he was an ardent admirer of the Young Turks. The
book deals with the origins of the revolution, the author's personal observations of the
era, and his assessment of the personalities of the leaders of the Young Turks.

267   **Suleiman the Magnificent: the man, his life, his epoch.**
      Andre Clot.   London: Saqi Books, 1992. 399p. maps.
The author presents a vivid study of the famous Sultan and his era, and life in the
Ottoman Empire. The book concludes with a glossary.

268 **The intimate life of an Ottoman statesman Melek Ahmed Pasha (1588-1662) as portrayed in Evliya Çelebi's** *Book of travels* *(Seyāḥatnāme).*
Evliya Çelebi, translated from the Turkish with a commentary by Robert Dankoff. Albany, New York: State University of New York Press, 1991. 304p. (SUNY Series in Medieval Middle East History).

This volume contains the passages from the *Seyāḥatnāme* of Evliya Çelebi, which deal directly with the life and times of Evliya's most important patron and hero, Melek Ahmed Pasha, who was an outstanding military and administrative leader. The passages paint an unusually intimate portrait of the Pasha.

269 **A Turkish tapestry: the Shakirs of İstanbul.**
Şirin Devrim. London: Quartet, 1994. 243p.

Recounts the story of the Shakir Pasha family in the years before the Republic, and in Republican Turkey, written by one of its members. Through the story of the family members (prominent scholars, soldiers, loyal servants, artists, and writers), the reader traces the social history of Ottoman Turkey. The material comes from the author's conversations with her mother (Fahrelnissa, a painter) and her diaries.

270 **Memories of a Turkish statesman, 1913-1919.**
Djemal Pasha. New York: Arno Press, 1973. 302p. (Middle East Collection).

Djemal Pasha (Cemal Paşa) was the governor of Constantinople, the imperial Ottoman navy minister, and the commander of the fourth army in Sinai, Palestine, and Syria. The book begins with his direct participation in politics during the coup of 23 January 1913, and ends with the battles of Gaza, the Arab rebellion, and the Armenian question. The book was first published in 1922 (New York: George H. Doran).

271 **Britons in the Ottoman Empire, 1642-1660.**
Daniel Goffman. Seattle, Washington: University of Washington Press, 1998. 310p. bibliog.

Using Ottoman and British sources, the author recreates the lives of some of the Englishmen (Henry Hyde, Sir Sacville Crow, and Thomas Bendysh), and their experiences in the commerce and politics of the Ottoman Empire during the turmoil of the civil war at home.

272 **Memoirs of Halidé Edib: with illustrations.**
Halide Edib. London: John Murray, 1926. 472p.

Halide Edib Adıvar (1884-1964) was the most prominent female spokesperson for the War of Independence (1920-23) and new Turkey. Through her fiery speeches, novels and short stories, she supported the birth of the Republic. Some of her writings contain her descriptions of Anatolia during the War while she travelled with the army. This volume of her memoirs (translated into Turkish as *Mor salkımlı ev* in 1963) covers the period from her birth until 30 October 1918. It deals with her childhood years, her education and marriage, her life as a teacher in Syria, and the historical events which led to the foundation of the Republic.

273 **The Turkish ordeal: being the further memoirs of Halide Edib with a frontispiece in color by Alexandre Pankoff and many illustrations from photographs.**
Halide Edib. Westport, Connecticut: Hyperion Press, 1981. reprint.
407p. (First published, London: John Murray; New York: Century, 1928. 407p.).

The further memoirs of Halide Edib Adıvar (translated into Turkish under the title *Türkün ateşle imtihanı* in 1962) continues with events until the end of 1922 (see item no. 272). Halide Edib is at her best in these memoirs which are written in a fluent and natural style. They span the last days of the Ottoman Empire and the beginning of the modern Turkish Republic and give a personal insight into many political and literary figures of the day.

274 **Fatma Aliye Hanım.**
Ahmet Mithat Efendi, transliterated by Lynda Goodsell Blake, edited with an introduction by Müge Galin. İstanbul: The ISIS Press, 1998.
96p.

Fatma Aliye was one of the earliest leading female Ottoman novelists and activists. She was not only a pioneer in the publishing world, but also a historian, a public education reformer, and a proponent of equality between the sexes. She became involved in political mobilization, gave public speeches, and worked for charitable organizations. She wrote novels about liberated Ottoman women from the point of view of the female protagonists, with the aim of empowering her female readers. Her novels deal with the limitations placed on Ottoman women and show how the protagonist coped with partriarchal family life. This biography of Fatma Aliye Hanım (1862-1936) by Ahmet Mithat Efendi (1844-1913), which covers her childhood and the early years of her life as a writer, has been transliterated by Lynda Goodsell Blake (1906-89). The glossary from Ottoman Turkish to contemporary Turkish has been prepared by Şehnaz Aliş.

275 **İsmet İnönü: the making of a Turkish statesman.**
Metin Heper. Leiden, the Netherlands: E. J. Brill, 1998. 270p.
bibliog. (Social, Economic, and Political Studies of the Middle East, no. 62).

İsmet İnönü, who played a critical role in the founding of the Turkish Republic, is presented here as a highly motivated, self-critical and self-conscious political leader. The author suggests that İnönü complemented Atatürk, contrary to the popular claims that he played a secondary role to Atatürk and that he was a power hungry politician with an authoritarian frame of mind. The author suggests that while he remained a staunch guardian of the premises upon which the Republic was founded, over time he adopted liberal political views.

276 **Atatürk: the rebirth of a nation.**
Patrick Kinross. London: Orion Books, 1998. 3rd impression reprint.
542p. maps. bibliog.

Mustafa Kemal Atatürk (1881-1938) is one of the most outstanding statesmen of the 20th century, and the founder of the Turkish Republic. Born in Salonica, he became an officer in the Ottoman army, and served in Damascus, Macedonia, and Tripoli during his early career. His defence of the Dardanelles against the Allied forces during the First World War brought him fame as a commander. After the war, he led the Turkish resistance movement against the Allied forces, and was the commander of the Turkish army during the War of Independence. When the Turkish Republic was declared in 1923, he was elected the first president of the country. Until his death in 1938, he implemented the social, cultural and economic reforms which were to make Turkey a modern nation state. This work is the most well known of the biographies of Atatürk and is told within the context of the historical events of the time. The first section dwells on the decline and fall of the Ottoman Empire; the second section covers the War of Independence; and the third part deals with the rise of the Turkish Republic. The book contains photographs of Atatürk, and a chronology of events from 1876 to 1938. It was first published in 1964 (New York: William Morrow).

277 **Just a diplomat.**
Zeki Kuneralp, translated from the Turkish by Geoffrey Lewis.
İstanbul: The ISIS Press, 1992. 151p.

This is the English translation of the book *Sadece diplomat*, written by the well-known diplomat and statesman, Zeki Kuneralp, about his life and times.

278 **Ottoman and Persian odysseys. James Morier, creator of Hajji Baba of Ispahan, and his brothers.**
Henry McKenzie Johnston. London: I. B. Tauris, 1997. 264p.

The book is based on the family papers of the 19th-century author James Morier, and his brothers Jack and David Morier. It reveals how during the Napoleonic Wars, the brothers became involved in countering French activities, and gained influence in the Ottoman Empire and Persia.

279 **Atatürk.**
A. L. Macfie. London; New York: Longman, 1994. 217p. maps.

This is a simplified and 'gossipy' biography of Atatürk and account of Ottoman/Turkish history before and after the First World War. It does not use Turkish sources and documents, and has little to say about Atatürk's career after 1926.

280 **The life of Midhat Pasha: a record of his services, political reforms, banishment and judicial murder.**
Ali Haydar Midhat. New York: Arno Press, 1973. 292p.

This book by Midhat Pasha's son aims to show that the reforms associated with his father in the constitution of 1876 were not introduced hastily and prematurely as had been claimed. He discusses the early history of the Ottoman Empire, the treatment of the Christian subjects, the palace, Janissaries, and Mehmed Ali's revolt. The rest of the book revolves round Midhat Pasha's life, his first appointment as grand vizier by Sultan Abdül Aziz, his second grand vizierate under Sultan Abdül Hamid II, the constitution and its promulgation, and his arrest, trial, exile in Taif and assassination.

281 İstanbul boy: böyle gelmiş, böyle gitmez (that's how it was but not
   how it's going to be). The autobiography of Aziz Nesin, part I.
   Aziz Nesin, translated from the Turkish by J. S. Jacobson.   Austin,
   Texas: University of Texas Press, 1977. 227p.
Aziz Nesin (1915-95) is one of the most popular and widely read authors in Turkey.
Part one of his autobiography, *İstanbul boy*, is a translation of the first of the third and
revised printings (1972) of the first volume of his autobiography written in Turkish
(see also item nos. 282 and 283). The Turkish title of the first part is a telling negation
of a fatalistic proverb, 'That's how it was and will always be'. It starts with his
recollections of the 1920s in Turkey, a period of transition from the Ottoman Empire
to the Republic.

282 İstanbul boy: yol (path). The autobiography of Aziz Nesin, part II.
   Aziz Nesin, translated from the Turkish by J. S. Jacobson.   Austin,
   Texas: University of Texas Press, 1979. 181p.
This is a translation of the second part of the third and revised printing (1972) of the
first volume of Aziz Nesin's autobiography written in Turkish (see also item no. 281
and 283).

283 İstanbul boy: yokuşun başı (the climb). The autobiography of Aziz
   Nesin, part III.
   Aziz Nesin, translated from the Turkish by J. S. Jacobson.   Austin,
   Texas: University of Texas Press, 1990. 220p.
In part three of Nesin's autobiography, he continues the story of his youth in 1930s
Turkey. Amongst the biographical anecdotes, the reader finds frank impressions of a
young teenager, of the army, Atatürk, the dervishes, minorities, epilepsy, truancy, sex
education and war with the Greeks. Nesin frequently blends his biography with a
consideration of current problems or opinions. See also item nos. 281 and 282.

284 Envoy extraordinary: a most unlikely ambassador.
   Horace Phillips.   New York; London: Radcliffe Press, 1995. 256p.
The memoirs of Horace Philips, retired ambassador to Turkey. It covers the author's
remarkable and colourful life in the British civil service, his army years and diplo-
matic service, as well as his years as a businessman, and finally as a lecturer at Bilkent
University in Ankara.

285 İhsan Doğramacı: a remarkable Turk.
   Horace Phillips.   Bishop Wilton, England: Wilton, 1997. 106p.
A biographical study of Professor Doğramacı, founder of Hacettepe Children's
Hospital, Hacettepe Faculty of Medicine and Health Sciences, Hacettepe and Bilkent
Universities among many of his other achievements. The author has known İhsan
Doğramacı for over twenty years, and as well as using his personal interviews, he
draws on the books written about Doğramacı previously.

286 **This is my life.**
Sakıp Sabancı. Saffron Walden, England: World of Information, 1988. 360p.

The author of this autobiography is one of the leading businessmen of Turkey, and the owner of one of the biggest holding companies active in many sectors of the Turkish economy. The autobiography not only gives information about the business life of Sabancı, and the development of the private sector in Turkey, but it also reflects the world view of Sabancı, and the social activities of the Sabancı Group.

287 **Five years in Turkey.**
Liman von Sanders. Annapolis, Maryland: Williams & Wilkins for the United States Naval Institute, 1928. 326p. maps.

After 1914, in an attempt to reorganize the Ottoman army, a large part of the older officer corps was purged, and a German military mission of seventy officers, led by General Liman von Sanders, was given the task of reforming the army. The members of this mission became very influencial especially after their numbers reach over 700 officers in time. This book gives day-to-day information about the First World War, and about the condition of the Turkish lines of communication, and the character of the Turkish officers, and while it points out their defects, it emphasizes their endurance and heroism. It also analyses the errors of officers in high places in İstanbul and discloses the mistakes of the author himself.

288 **Sport and travel: East and West.**
Frederick Courteney Selous. London; New York: Longmans, Green & co., 1900. 311p.

F. C. Selous was a hunter, scout, explorer, writer, and adventurer. He spent most of his life in Africa, hunting and studying game animals. He first visited Turkey in 1894 for two months to learn more about the red deer (Cervus maral) and wild goats (Capra aegagrus), returning in 1895 and 1897. During the First World War, he was killed in Africa (1917). His memoirs carry vivid and memorable descriptions of the countryside, villages and towns of 19th-century Anatolia, as well as commentary on the flora and fauna. The book has been translated into Turkish by Derin Türkömer with the title *Av ve gezi* (İstanbul: Yapı Kredi Yayınları, 1998). A review of the book, which also includes Selous's photographs, appears in *Cornucopia*, vol. 3, no. 17 (1999), p. 108-11.

289 **The life of Hacı Ömer Sabancı.**
Sadun Tanju, translated from the Turkish by Geoffrey Lewis. Saffron Walden, England: World of Information, 1988. 186p.

Hacı Ömer Sabancı is the father of the Sabancı brothers, the famous Turkish industrialists. The book not only details the events in the life of Sabancı, but also presents a sixty-year social history of Turkey, beginning with the collapse of the Ottoman Empire which coincided with the birth of Sabancı (approximately 1903) to his death in 1966. The author rightly claims 'In this book I have tried to draw the picture of a man of Anatolia who started life as a poor peasant, but whose name came to be among the best-known in commercial and industrial circles in Turkey' (p. vii). Geoffrey Lewis's excellent English translation gives new life to the book, and makes it a very readable story. A useful glossary explains Turkish names and terms which may be unfamiliar to the reader, and the book is illustrated with photographs.

290 **Storm centers of the Near East: personal memoirs, 1879-1929.**
Robert Windham Graves.   New York: AMS Press, 1976. 375p.

The author spent fifty years in the Near East and Eastern Europe, and was a witness to the events that led to the First World War. He was in İstanbul during the Russo-Turkish War of 1877-78, and in Sophia during 1881-88, and witnessed the Bulgarian struggles against Russia, the eastern Rumelian Revolution, and the Serbo-Bulgarian War. He spent the years between 1892 and 1898 in eastern Turkey and Armenia. He also lived in Crete, Macedonia and Albania. The book was first published in 1933 in London by Hutchinson, and provides an account of the author's life and the events he witnessed during the most turbulent period for the area. The volume is a good source for Balkan and Turkish history.

Foundations of Turkish nationalism: the life and teachings of Ziya Gökalp.
See item no. 555.

Post peripheral flux: a decade of contemporary art in İstanbul.
See item no. 1120.

Population

General

Ottoman (13th century to 1923)

291 **The population of the Ottoman Empire and Turkey (1500-1927).**
Prepared by Cem Behar for the State Institute of Statistics (SIS).
Ankara: State Institute of Statistics, 1995. 138p. (Historical Statistics
Series, no. 2).

The volume contains information on some population estimates for the pre-Ottoman
period, populations of Ottoman provinces, the religious distribution of the population
in Ottoman cities, population estimates for some Anatolian cities, estimates for the
total and Muslim population of some Ottoman cities, and population growth according
to official statistics. The volume is in Turkish with an English summary.

292 **The first population census during the Ottoman Empire, 1831.**
Enver Ziya Karal.   Ankara: State Institute of Statistics (SIS), 1998.
2nd ed. 226p.

This volume, which was first published in 1950 by the SIS, gives the results of the
1831 population census as well as information about land registers and censuses in the
Ottoman Empire.

293 **Ottoman population, 1830-1914: demographic and social characteristics.**
Kemal Karpat. Madison, Wisconsin: University of Wisconsin Press, 1985. 242p. maps.
The first part of this book contains sections on the evaluation of Ottoman censuses, population movements, and the socio-economic transformation of İstanbul. The second and main part of the work includes more than seventy statistical tables based on the original Ottoman and other sources. The author presents data critically, noting problems of omission (e.g the under-estimation of females), and category defects (e.g. Muslims are not differentiated by ethnicity or sect).

294 **The Arab world, Turkey and the Balkans (1878-1914): a handbook of historical statistics.**
Justin McCarthy. Boston, Massachusetts: G. K. Hall, 1982. 309p.
Following a discussion of administrative subdivisions of the Ottoman Empire at the time of the 1884 census, the book contains chapters of data on climate, population, health, medicine, education, justice, money and finance, industry and transport. The chapter on population, which is mainly based on the survey of 1914, provides figures by province and district, including details of religious affiliation, age and economic group. The writer notes that the under-numeration of women and children (by twenty per cent or more) affected non-Muslims as well as Muslims.

295 **Muslims and minorities: the population of Ottoman Anatolia and the end of the Empire.**
Justin McCarthy. New York: New York University Press, 1983. 248p. bibliog.
An analysis of population gain and loss in the Ottoman lands during the early part of the 20th century. The text includes sections on Ottoman Anatolia; the Muslim, Armenian, Greek and other population groups; and a general picture of Anatolia in 1912. There are five appendices, which include: an analysis of the 1927 census; an evaluation of the sources used by the author; tables of figures showing migration from Turkey between 1921 and 1927; an explanation of the methodology used in the collection and evaluation of population data; and a comparative list of the provinces of the Republic (1927) and of the Ottoman provinces.

296 **La population de l'Empire Ottoman. Cinquante ans (1941-1990) de publications et de recherches.** (The population of the Ottoman Empire. Fifty years (1941-90) of publications and research.)
Daniel Panzac. Aix-en-Provence, France: Universités d'Aix Marseille I-II & III, Institut de Recherches et d'Études sur le Monde Arabe et Musulman, 1993. 97p. (Travaux et Documents de l'I.R.E.M.A.M., no. 15).
Of the 464 titles listed in the work, over 120 are in English, and a similar number are in French. The book includes an introductory review of the literature, and indices by time, topic, author, and periodicals involved.

Population. General. Turkish Republic (1923-)

The first statistical yearbook of the Ottoman Empire, 1831.
See item no. 255.

Turkish Republic (1923-)

297 **Who lives with whom in İstanbul.**
Gülbin Gökçay, Frederic Shorter. *New Perspectives on Turkey,* no. 9
(1993), p. 47-73.
The article presents tables derived from a three per cent sample of the 1985 population census data. Classifications are based on age, sex, sequence location, and relation to head within the household, which was the critical social group. There is a discussion of changes since 1907, and some detail on the regional origins and types of households.

298 **Earthquake vulnerable populations in modern Turkey.**
John Kolars. *Geographical Review,* vol. 72, no. 1 (1982), p. 20-35.
maps.
Reviews the distribution and intensity of earthquakes between 1933 and 1976, and combines the patterns of population potential, seismicity, and accessibility in order to identify critical areas. The writer suggests a strategy for disaster anticipation based on levels of development, and information infrastructure for those areas – both urban and rural.

299 **Population policy formation and implementation in Turkey.**
Ned Levine, Sunday Üner. Ankara: Hacettepe University
Publications, 1978. 264p. map. bibliog.
With sections on structure and policy makers, and possible future projections, this book tries to bring a holistic approach to the making and application of population studies. It reflects the ideological and historical dimensions of state interference.

300 **Population of Turkey by ethnic groups and provinces.**
Servet Mutlu. *New Perspectives on Turkey,* no. 12 (1995), p. 33-60.
The paper analyses the number and spatial distribution of the Kurds in Turkey as far as the available data permits.

301 **Trends in fertility and mortality in Turkey, 1935-1975.**
Frederic Shorter, Miroslav Macura. Washington, DC: National
Academy Press, 1982. 150p. (US National Academy of Sciences,
Commission on Population and Demography, Report, no. 8).
This account was written late in the transitional phase of Turkey's demographic transformation (1955-85), which was characterized by rapid population growth despite falling fertility rates. The writers foresaw the advanced stage of demographic transition (after 1985), when population growth slackened with low birth and death rates.

302 **The population of Turkey after the War of Independence.**
Frederic C. Shorter. *International Journal of Middle East Studies,*
vol. 17, no. 4 (1985), p. 417-41.

The article reconstructs an estimated census for 1923 by reverse population projection from 1935, and assesses the value of the 1927 census and of other data sources for the early years of the Republic. The author also considers the demographic impact of Turkey's wars, and of population exchanges (with Greece) and discusses the impact of the country's special demographic conditions on agricultural production and employment (especially of women).

303 **The crisis of population knowledge in Turkey.**
Frederic C. Shorter. *New Perspectives on Turkey,* no. 12 (1995), p. 1-31.

Discusses approaches to population issues and considers aspects of Turkey's macro-demography, urbanization, and patterns of health. The article draws on the larger work, to which the writer contributed substantially, produced by the State Institute of Statistics in Ankara (see item no. 308).

304 **Genel nüfus sayımı. İdari bölünüş. 21.10.1990. (Census of population: administrative division).**
State Institute of Statistics (SIS). Ankara: State Institute of Statistics, 1991. (Publication no. 1457).

The data is presented by province, district, sub-district, and village (with separate pagination for each province). An introductory section offers a summary of tables by province showing trends since recent census years. Previous comparable censuses were held at five-year intervals from 1935. The first census in the Republic was taken in 1927, though this was preceded by nearly a century when the first comprehensive count was conducted in 1831. The book is in Turkish and in English.

305 **Genel nüfus sayımı. İdari bölünüş (özet tablolar). 21.10.1990. (Census of population: administrative division – summary tables).**
State Institute of Statistics. Ankara: State Institute of Statistics (SIS), 1991. 36p. (Publication no. 1458).

Contains the summary of the census of population by province, which also appears in the full edition of this census. It is in Turkish and in English.

306 **1989 Turkish demographic survey.**
State Institute of Statistics (SIS). Ankara: State Institute of Statistics, 1993. 304p.

This publication reports the findings of the demographic survey conducted by the State Institute of Statistics in 1989. The next demographic survey is planned for the year 2000. The survey was administered to a sample of 17,675 households in 238 settlements. The first part of the report contains the social and economic characteristics of the population, such as household size, age and sex structure, education, marital status, and economic activity. The second part contains statistics on fertility such as births, number of children born alive, and number of children wanted. The third part contains statistics on death rates, and infant and child mortality. The survey questionnaire is also provided in an appendix.

307 **Census of population. Social and economic characteristics of population, 1990.**
State Institute of Statistics (SIS). Ankara: State Institute of Statistics, 1994. 216p.

The volume contains statistics which break down the population according to age, citizenship, place of birth, marital status, literacy, formal educational attainment, fertility of female population, last week's occupation, last week's economic activity, usual occupation, number of households and heads of households, province, district, sub-district, age group, household size, number of working people per household, and home ownership status.

308 **The population of Turkey, 1923-1994. Demographic structure and development, with projections to the mid-21st century.**
State Institute of Statistics (SIS). Ankara: State Institute of Statistics, 1995. 159p. bibliog. (Publication no. 1716).

Based on research carried out by Frederic C. Shorter and others at the Institute's Centre for Population and Demographic Analysis, this important study offers information on population trends since 1923, on the current status, and an assessment of prospects for the future. Topics considered include age and sex structure, fertility, mortality, migration, and regional and urban-rural differences. The study dates the first stage of demographic transition in Turkey from 1923 to about 1950. The second stage accounts for the next three decades and was characterized by declining fertility and death rates and by rapid urbanization. The third stage is expected to end in the mid-21st century with a population more or less constant at around 100 million.

309 **Death statistics from provincial and district centers, 1995.**
State Institute of Statistics (SIS). Ankara: State Institute of Statistics, 1996. 128p.

This annual publication contains information on deaths by year, month, province, district, sex, marital status, permanent residence, cause of death, and occupational group of deceased. It also provides a breakdown of infant deaths in the first year of life by province and sex.

310 **Suicide statistics, 1996.**
State Institute of Statistics (SIS). Ankara: State Institute of Statistics, 1998. 64p.

The publication gives data about suicides, including the demographic region, cause, method, and the sex, marital status, and education of the deceased.

311 **Marriage statistics, 1996.**
State Institute of Statistics (SIS). Ankara: State Institute of Statistics, 1998. 72p.

This annual publication gives number of marriages and crude marriage rate by year, province, district, age, educational attainment, and occupation. It also gives a break-down of non-crude marriages by province, age of partners, occupation, citizenship, and other related criteria.

312 **Divorce statistics, 1996.**
State Institute of Statistics (SIS). Ankara: State Institute of Statistics, 1998. 48p.
Provides information on divorces and divorce rates by year, age group, reasons for divorce, duration of divorce proceedings, duration of marriage, and other relevant criteria.

313 **Population issues in Turkey: policy priorities.**
Edited by Aykut Toros. Ankara: Hacettepe University, Institute of Population Studies, 1993. 518p.
This work is based on a project initiated by the Turkish State Planning Organization (SPO) in order to identify demographic and socio-economic factors influencing population growth during the past twenty years, as well as to evaluate the efficiency of education programmes for birth-control. This publication was prepared by specialists from different backgrounds working in different sectors related to the study of population. It is a contribution to the identification of the needs and the realization of policies and programmes in the fields of population and sustained development.

İstanbul households: marriage, family and fertility, 1880-1940.
See item no. 455.

Turkey. Demographic and health survey, 1993.
See item no. 519.

Turkey: political, social and economic challenges in the 1990s.
See item no. 530.

Ethnic minorities

314 **The Greek minority of İstanbul and Greek-Turkish relations: 1918-1974.**
Alexis Alexandris. Athens: Centre for Asia Minor Studies, 1992. 2nd ed. 380p.
This chronological study focuses on how the presence of the Orthodox patriarchate and Greek community in İstanbul figured in relations between Greece and Turkey. Alexandris contends that the minority community generally suffered from the hostility between the two states because it could easily become a bargaining point in Turkey's favour. He presents a well-documented study of the judicial and political context of the community's existence as a result of its special exemption from population exchanges in the 1920s.

315 **Ethnic groups in the Republic of Turkey.**
Compiled and edited by Peter Alford Andrews with Rüdiger
Benninghaus. Wiesbaden, Germany: Dr Ludwig Reichert Verlag,
1989. 659p. maps. bibliog. (Beihefte zum Tübinger Atlas des Vorderen
Orients, Reihe B [Geisteswissenschaften], no. 60).

This important volume contains an introduction, a catalogue of forty-seven different
ethnic groups, seven surveys, villages listed by ethnic group, a section of ethnographic
essays, bibliography, and two folding maps. The work discusses a map separately
published in two sheets – 'Tübinger Atlas des Vorderen Orients (TAVO) Map A VIII
14, Republic Türkei: Ethnische Minderheiten im ländlichen Raum' (Tübinger atlas of
the Near East [TAVO] Map A VIII 14, Republic of Turkey: ethnic minorities in the
countryside), scale 1:2,000,000, 1987. Groups are identified primarily by language and
secondarily by religion, though distinctions are in consequence sometimes arbitrary.
The data of the main study relates to the period 1960-70 but there is also a detailed
treatment of the south-east of the country based on the discontinued 'Köy Envanteri'
(Village Inventory) (1952-60). The two main maps, and the text discussions and
analysis omit data for towns. The picture of rural Turkey which is represented does
not reflect all the population movements of recent decades – notably in the south-east
where conflict has led to a substantial re-location of Kurds since the mid-1980s, much
of it to urban and western parts of Turkey. Topics discussed in this volume include:
ethnicity in eastern Turkey; kinship, tribalism and ethnicity in eastern Turkey; the
Kurdish language; and Christians and Jews in Turkey.

316 **Turkey's Kurdish dilemma.**
Henri J. Barkey. *Survival*, vol. 35, no. 4 (1993), p. 51-70.

This article examines the challenge posed by the Kurdish insurrection, led by the
Kurdistan Workers' Party (PKK), as well as the Turkish reactions to this insurrection.
It also deals with the domestic costs of the Kurdish rebellion in both political and
economic terms. It goes on to analyse the implications of this conflict for Turkey's
relations with the United States, Europe and regional actors, such as Syria, Iran, Iraq
and the Iraqi Kurds. The article concludes with an assessment of Turkey's options,
and a discussion of steps the West could take to help contain the conflict in Turkey.

317 **The Kurds in Turkey : a political dilemma.**
Michael M. Gunter. Boulder, Colorado: Westview Press, 1990. 151p.
(Westview Special Studies on the Middle East).

Analyses the current Kurdish problem in Turkey from the point of view of the Turkish
authorities and their supporters, as well as from the perspective of disaffected Kurds
living in Turkey and abroad. Some of the issues discussed include: the historical background; the political instability and terrorism rampant in Turkey during the late 1970s;
the legal suppression of the Kurds; the emergence of numerous Kurdish political parties in the 1970s (of which the PKK has been the most noteworthy); the current
activities of the PKK; and the transnational influences on the situation.

318 **The compulsory exchange of populations between Greece and
Turkey: the settlement of the minority questions at the Conference
of Lausanne, 1923, and its impact on Greek-Turkish relations.**
Kalliopi K. Kaufa, Constantinos Svolopoulos.   In: *Ethnic groups in
international relations.*   Edited by Paul Smith.   Aldershot, England:
Dartmouth Publishing Company, 1991, p. 275-308. (Comparative
Studies on Governments and Non-dominant Ethnic Groups in Europe,
1850-1940).

This work examines the bases for the decision to accept compulsory reciprocal migration,
based primarily on religious affiliation, in the Lausanne Exchange Convention of 1923
following the defeat of Greece in 1922 – though the first such exchange agreement
had been annexed to the 1913 Treaty of Constantinople between Bulgaria and Turkey.
A mixed commission, set up after 1922 to oversee property rights, etc., worked with
difficulty and there were exemptions on both sides (Greek Orthodox in İstanbul and
Muslims in Western Thrace).

319 **The Sephardim in the Ottoman Empire.**
Avigdor Levy.   Princeton, New Jersey: Darwin Press, 1992. 124p.
bibliog.

In 1492 (during the time of Sultan Bayezid II) the Jews were expelled from Castille,
with Aragon and Portugal following suit. The Ottoman Empire opened its frontiers to
Spanish Jews, and invited them to its lands. The quincentennial of Spanish Jews'
immigration to the Ottoman Empire was celebrated in 1987 by Brandeis University
with a conference on the Ottoman Jewry. Avigdor Levy edited the papers of the
conference in a volume (see item no. 320), and expanded his introduction to the
volume into this book-length overview of the conclusions reached during the conference.
Drawing from a range of traditional Hebrew sources, and based on Ottoman and
European archives, this work summarizes the conclusions of current and recent
scholarship following a 1987 conference on the subject.

320 **The Jews of the Ottoman Empire.**
Edited by Avigdor Levy.   Princeton, New Jersey: Darwin Press, 1994.
799p. bibliog.

This major study brings together most of the papers presented at a 1987 conference at
Brandeis University, and starts with a reprint of the editor's *The Sephardim in the
Ottoman Empire* (see item no. 319). The wide-ranging coverage, in both time and
space, reflects recent advances in Ottoman Jewish historiography, using Ottoman
archives, rabbinical responsa, and sources on the Alliance Israélite Universelle (for
more details on the latter, see item no. 324).

321 **Turks and Kurds.**
Andrew Mango.   *Middle Eastern Studies*, vol. 30, no. 4 (1994), p. 975-97.

The author seeks the reasons behind the Kurdish problem in Turkey by asking whether
it is only a problem of terrorism or whether a separate Kurdish ethnic community
exists in Turkey, and whether the historical argument, that a single community was
constituted under the Ottoman Empire and that there have been no ethnic barriers, has
ever been valid. The article uses the memoirs of Musa Anter, and works by authors
such as K. Burkay, P. Kinross, and R. Olson.

322 **The Kurds: a nation denied.**
David McDowell. London: Minority Rights Publications, 1992. 150p.

The book explores the identity of the Kurds, their bonds of loyalty and their historical and recent experience since the break-up of the Ottoman Empire. It looks at their position in the different countries in which they find themselves, and tries to pinpoint some of the internal and external factors and contradictions which exist today that both motivate and impede Kurdish nationalism.

323 **Ethnic Kurds in Turkey: a demographic study.**
Servet Mutlu. *International Journal of Middle East Studies*, vol. 28, no. 4 (1996), p. 517-41.

The author assesses the available data on the Kurdish population in Turkey, and explains the methodological basis of his estimates of numbers and population trends. Adjusted estimates by province provide a detailed breakdown, and indicate a total of just over 7 million (12.6 per cent of the Turkish national total) in 1990, compared to 3.1 million in 1965 (ten per cent). The massive movements of Kurds from east and south-east Anatolia towards western Turkey and into urban centres seems to rule out any ethnic based federal solution to Turkey's continuing Kurdish question.

324 **French Jews, Turkish Jews: the Alliance Israélite Universelle and the politics of Jewish schooling in Turkey, 1860-1925.**
Aron Rodrigue. Bloomington, Indiana: Indiana University Press, 1990. 248p.

A French-Jewish organization founded in 1860 to help 'Jews of the East' by education and other means, the Alliance Israélite Universelle established schools where there were significant Jewish communities in the Ottoman Empire, many of which operated into the 20th century. The Alliance taught French and Turkish, the first tending to distance Jews from Turkey and the second tending to integrate them. The schools were secular but this did not keep Jews in Turkey from being drawn into the dispute between the Zionists and Turkish nationalists. The work draws on archives in Paris, as well as Turkish and Hebrew sources.

325 **Ottoman and Turkish Jewry: community and leadership.**
Edited by Aron Rodrigue. Bloomington, Indiana: Indiana University Turkish Studies, 1992. 277p. bibliog. (Indiana University Turkish Studies, no. 12).

The volume contains nine essays with an introduction by Aron Rodrigue. The topics include: 'The Jewish society in the Ottoman Empire during the fifteenth to seventeenth centuries', Joseph Hacker; 'Rabbanite-Karaite relations in Constantinople', Jean-Christophe Attias; 'Jewish lay leadership in the Ottoman Empire', Leah Bornstein-Makovetsky; 'The extraterritorial status of Jews in Italy and the Ottoman Empire', Minna Rozen; 'The Sabbatean movement and the leadership of the Jewish communities in the Ottoman Empire', Jacob Barnai; 'The Sephardi community', Avner Levi; 'Pre-zionist Ashkenazi community in nineteenth century Palestine', Israel Bartal; 'Ottoman Jewish communities in the early twentieth century', Esther Benbassa; and 'The Jews of İstanbul', Riva Kastoryano.

326 Jews of the Ottoman Empire and the Turkish Republic.
Stanford J. Shaw. New York: New York University Press, 1991.
271p. bibliog.

A history of the Jews in the Ottoman Empire, which also covers little-known features such as the evolution of Ladino (a Sephardic Jewish language used especially in the Balkans and Asia Minor, which combines Spanish, Hebrew, and other elements), and the Sephardic musical heritage.

327 Turkey and the holocaust: Turkey's role in rescuing Turkish and European Jewry from Nazi persecution, 1933-1945.
Standford J. Shaw. New York: New York University Press, 1993.
330p. bibliog.

An account of the Turkish protection of the Jews before and during the Second World War. The author uses the documents in the archives of the Turkish embassy in Paris, and his interviews with people who were actively involved in protecting the Jews. He also unearths other relevant material and sources, which shed light on the subject. The study is rich in detail.

328 Ottomans, Turks, and the Jewish polity: a history of the Jews of Turkey.
Walter F. Weiker. Lanham, Maryland: University Press of America, 1992. 369p. bibliog. (The Milken Library of Jewish Public Affairs).

The book provides detailed historical coverage of Jews in the Ottoman Empire and Turkey up to the 1980s, beginning with the period before the 15th century. It reflects the archival and other source material in English, French, Turkish and modern Hebrew. Weiker, a political scientist, also draws directly on his own acquaintance with Turkey over several decades. He indicates that the Jewish experience in the Ottoman Empire was generally better than that of Jews in Europe. The book contains nineteen statistical tables.

329 The Jewish community of Turkey.
Adina Weiss-Liberles. In: *The Balkan Jewish communities: Yugoslavia, Bulgaria, Greece and Turkey.* Edited by Daniel J. Elazar, Harriet Pass Friedenreich, Baruch Hazzan, Adina Weiss-Liberles. Boston, Massachusetts: University Press of America, 1984, p. 127-70.

The attempt at extinction of Jewish communities in the world motivated an effort to map the structures and functions of the organized Jewish communities in different countries, and this chapter deals with the Jewish community in Turkey.

Christians and Jews in the Ottoman Empire: the functioning of a plural society.
See item no. 205.

Socialism and nationalism in the Ottoman Empire.
See item no. 259.

Muslims and minorities: the population of Ottoman Anatolia and the end of the Empire.
See item no. 295.

Population of Turkey by ethnic groups and provinces.
See item no. 300.

The Kurdish question and Turkey: an example of trans-state ethnic conflict.
See item no. 563.

Atatürk's children: Turkey and the Kurds.
See item no. 578.

Migration

330 **Population movements in southeastern Anatolia: some findings of an empirical research in 1993.**
Bahattin Akşit, Kayhan Mutlu, H. Ünal Nalbantoğlu, A. Adnan Akçay, Mustafa Şen. *New Perspectives on Turkey*, no. 14 (1996), p. 53-74.

In this article the economic and sociocultural structure of forty-seven villages and ten urban centres in south-east Anatolia are discussed in relationship to rural-urban migration, and on the basis of survey data sets gathered by the authors. Factors contributing to migration are assessed, and unemployment, underdevelopment and violence are singled out as the principal reasons.

331 **What mass migration has meant for Turkey.**
Gündüz Atalık, Brian Beeley. In: *Mass migrations in Europe. The legacy and the future.* Edited by Russell King. London: Belhaven Press, 1993, p. 156-73.

Since the 1960s substantial groups of Turks have been established in Germany and other countries of western Europe from where money has been sent back to Turkey. Within Turkey, the relocation of people has left more in urban than rural areas for the first time. Neither academics nor planners anticipated the scale of migration. The former have disagreed as to its causes, whereas the latter have been unable to propose measures to control movement, or use it in the national interest. Indeed, the increasing concentration of people in more developed parts of Turkey reduces prospects for any marked reduction in disparities between regions.

332 **Migration and reintegration in rural Turkey: the role of women behind.**
Adviye Azmaz. Göttingen, Germany: Edition Heradot, 1984. 253p. bibliog.

An empirical work which aims to understand the movement of labour from Turkish villages to Europe and development in Turkey. It is based on intensive interviews of men who worked in the Federal Republic of Germany and who returned to Turkey by 1973, and of their wives. The study is divided into four sections and covers the three provinces in the eastern half of Turkey. The first section describes the theoretical and methodological framework, the second deals exclusively with men and the third, and most voluminous, covers women.

333 **Migration and urbanization in rural Turkey.**
Brian Beeley. In: *The Middle Eastern village.* Edited by Richard Lawless. London: Croom Helm, 1987, p. 51-75.

Reviews the changing status of villages and villagers within the economic integration of the Turkish national space during the late 1980s. The author discusses competing analytical approaches to the study of village change, and comments on the impact of coordinated national planning after 1961. Rural modernization, reflecting changes in communication, division of labour, village functions, and migration, has been progressing against the background of questions about the country's future.

334 **Migration networks: Turkish migration to Western Europe.**
Anita Böcker. In: *Causes of international migration.* Compiled by the Netherlands Interdisciplinary Demographic Institute. Luxembourg: Office for Official Publications of the European Community, 1995, p. 151-67.

This chapter deals with the case of Turkish migration to Western Europe, and focuses on the roles of families in migration decision-making. Migration flows from other countries, and historical trends are discussed comparatively. The findings show that those Turkish immigrants who have settled in the Netherlands are pressurized by their relatives and friends in Turkey to help them immigrate as well.

335 **Migration movements from Turkey to the European Community.**
Centre for Turkish Studies (Bonn). Brussels: Forum des Migrants, 1993. 195p.

A review of the effects of three decades of Turkish migration on selected countries of the European Union, and on Turkey itself. The work is written as a report and is supported with sixty-three tables of data.

336 **Population policy in Turkey. Family planning and migration between 1960 and 1992.**
Erhard Franz. Hamburg, Germany: Deutches Orient-Institut, 1994. 358p. bibliog.

This well-documented study includes main sections on demographic data, family planning, population dispersal, and policy regarding migration. The list of these sections offers a valuable critical review of the censuses and other publications on population and demography of the State Institute of Statistics in Ankara, together with a comprehensive checklist. The study is part of a 1990-93 research project entitled 'Demographic Policies in the Middle East: Syria, Egypt and Turkey', including all measures or omissions which effect alternation in the demographic development of a country as a whole or of a region. It discusses immigration from the Balkans and Central Asia, political refugees, who are mainly from the Middle East, and the gradual exodus of non-Muslim minorities.

337 **Post Second World War immigration from Balkan countries to Turkey.**
Kemal Kirişçi. *New Perspectives on Turkey*, no. 12 (1995), p. 61-77.
The author analyses the size and causes of immigration since the Second World War. The data obtained from the General Directorate of Village Works in Ankara reveals that the Turkish Republic can be considered as an immigration country for Turks and Muslims from Bulgaria, Yugoslavia, Bosnia, and Romania.

338 **Refugees of Turkish origin: 'coerced immigrants' to Turkey since 1945.**
Kemal Kirişçi. *International Migration*, vol. 34, no. 3 (1996), p. 385-412.
The author describes the situation of and national policy towards the 800,000 refugees of Turkish origin/descent who have been officially admitted to Turkey since 1945. This is one of the few sources outlining the laws and policies of the Turkish state for obtaining citizenship.

339 **Symposium on international migration and Turkey.**
Edited by Kemal Kirişçi. *Boğaziçi Journal. Review of Social, Economic and Administrative Studies*, vol. 10, no. 1-2 (1996).
Seven articles in this volume examine how contemporary forms of international immigration have affected Turkey, as well as raising theoretical and conceptual questions about international migration and its consequences. Following an editorial introduction by K. Kirişçi, the articles are: 'The global refugee regime: continuity and change', Emek M. Uçarer; 'The European Union's third pillar justice home affairs (history-institutions-perspectives)', Cengiz Aktar; 'Refugee and asylum-seeking migration from Turkey to Western Europe', Anita Böcker; 'Unplanned resistance: Turkish immigrants in a postmodern Germany', Peter O'Brien; 'The current refugee situation in Bosnia-Hercegovina in the context of movements of peoples in the Balkans', Hugh Poulton; 'Forced migrations in the north and south Caucasus', Alexandre Toumarkine; and 'Transit migrants and Turkey', Ahmet İçduygu.

340 **The unfinished story: Turkish labour migration to Western Europe, with special reference to the Federal Republic of Germany.**
Philip L. Martin. Geneva: International Labour Organization, 1991. 123p. bibliog.
The author brings together a large number of previous studies and provides a useful summary of works on the impact of migration on communities in Turkey and in Germany. The post-war migratory flows are analysed in terms of the world economy,

and around the following questions: who benefited from these migrations; what the impact was on migrants' lives and on their regions of origin; and what the future holds for them, particularly with the development of the Single Market project.

341 **Between Western Europe and the Middle East: changing patterns of Turkish labour migration.**
Ian J. Seccombe, Richard Lawless. *Revue Européenne des Migrations Internationales*, vol. 2, no. 1 (1986), p. 37-56.
After the closure of the west European labour markets to new inflows from 1973 onwards, Turkey pursued a policy of migrant worker re-direction, based on the successful penetration of the Middle East construction market by Turkish contractors. The growth, organization and characteristics of these two phases in the country's migration history are compared and contrasted in this article.

342 **Migration movements from Turkey to the European Community.**
Edited by Faruk Şen, Sedef Koray. Brussels: Centre for Turkish Studies, 1993. 195p.
Assesses the effects of more than thirty years of Turkish migration on Turkey and on selected countries of the European Community, namely the Netherlands, France, Belgium and Denmark. The study concentrates predominantly on the Turkish migrants living in Germany, where approximately 1.8 million of the 2.4 million Turks in the EC (EU) countries live.

The socio-economic aspects of return migration in Turkey.
See item no. 452.

Peasant struggles and social change: migration, households and gender in a rural Turkish society.
See item no. 458.

Gecekondu: rural migration and urbanization.
See item no. 462.

Turkish families in transition.
See item no. 471.

Rural-urban migration and formation of squatters in Turkey.
See item no. 893.

Involuntary displacement and the problem of resettlement in Turkey from the Ottoman Empire to the present.
See item no. 894.

Boğaziçi Journal. Review of Social, Economic and Administrative Studies.
See item no. 1319.

Eurasian Studies.
See item no. 1330.

Nüfusbilim dergisi. The Turkish Journal of Population Studies.
See item no. 1354.

Türk dış göçü, 1960-1984: yorumlu bibliyografya. (Turkish out-migration, 1960-84: annotated bibliography.)
See item no. 1401.

Türkiye dışındaki Türk vatandaşları bibliografyası. A bibliography of Turkish citizens out of Turkey.
See item no. 1405.

Overseas Populations

343 Turkish community in Australia.
Edited by Rahmi Akçelik, Joy Ellen.   Melbourne: Australian-Turkish
Friendship Society Publications, 1988. 248p.

This publication brings together the papers presented at a one-day conference entitled
'Turkish community in Australia – migration, family, women, youth, education,
employment and health issues', held in Coburg, on 20 August 1988. The papers
demonstrate clearly that an understanding of the experiences of migrants is distorted
or incomplete if they are treated as people without a past. The pre-migration experience inevitably and powerfully influences the ways in which people react to and
interpret life in a new and often puzzling setting.

344 Turkish youth in Australia.
Edited by Rahmi Akçelik.   Melbourne: Melbourne Institute of
Technology, 1993. 140p.

The volume contains eight essays, which directly dwell on the issues and problems
concerning the Turkish youth in Australia. The authors put forward opposing views
regarding solutions to these problems. The reader also learns much about Australia
and its domestic policies regarding minorities.

345 The Turks in Australia: celebrating twenty-five years down under.
Hatice Hürmüz Başarın, Vecihi Başarın.   Hampton, Australia:
Turquoise Publications, 1995. 135p. bibliog.

This is an oral history project which aims at reflecting the settlement process of Turks
in Australia through the stories of those who migrated to Australia. It is an account of
twenty-five years, taking 1968 as the departure point for this migration. In the words
of the authors: 'Twenty-five years after the arrival of those first flights, it is timely to
ask: what happened to those Turks in Australia? What happened to their dreams, their
expectations and fears? How did their children fare?'.

346 **The experience of Turkish and Turkish Cypriot life in the United Kingdom.**
Peter Coggins. *Les Annales de l'Autre Islam*, no. 3 (1995), p. 125-45.
The author aims to provide an overview of the experiences of the Turkish Cypriot and Turkish mainland immigrants, who have arrived either as refugees or as non-refugees to Great Britain during the post-war period. By analysing the differences between the Turkish speakers who came from Cyprus and those who originated in mainland Turkey, Coggins tries to illustrate the influence that colonialism had upon migration, and the notion that shapes the collective and individual personalities and psychologies of ethnic minorities.

347 **State politics and Islamic institutions: Turks in Netherlands and Germany.**
J. Doomernik. In: *The Centre for Middle Eastern and Islamic Studies: Muslim Communities Project, volume 2: Muslim communities in the Netherlands and Germany*. Edited by Suha Taji-Farouki.
Durham, England: Centre for Middle Eastern and Islamic Studies, 1995, p. 7-19.
The author explains and illustrates the opportunities that the Dutch state offers for Islamic institutionalization, and compares this with the situation in Germany. He believes that the restriction of a mosque's function to religious activities may serve to emphasize the gulf between Muslim immigrant communities and the host country.

348 **Turkish and other Muslim minorities of Bulgaria.**
Ali Eminov. London: Hurst & Co., 1997. 219p. bibliog.
Bulgaria's Muslim population consists of three groups of people: Turks, Pomaks, and Gypsies. The author reviews the political, economic and social experience of Bulgaria's Muslims in the Ottoman and post-Ottoman periods, especially under Communism when they were subjected to forced assimilation, and since 1989. A chapter is devoted to the Turkish language as it is spoken in Bulgaria, the linguistic effects of the nationality policy of Todor Zhivkov (Bulgarian prime minister and titular head of state), and the efforts to reverse these effects since 1989.

349 **States, markets and immigrant minorities: second-generation Turks in Germany and Mexican Americans in the United States in the 1980s.**
Thomas Faist. *Comparative Politics*, vol. 26, no. 4 (1994), p. 439-60.
The article discusses public policies, their effects on processes of insertion of the children of labour migrants into labour markets, and the response of immigrants to the opportunities and constraints they have encountered in entering labour markets.

350 **Turkish culture in German society today.**
Edited by David Horrocks, Eva Kolinsky. Providence, Rhode Island;
Oxford: Berghahn Books, 1996. 207p. bibliog. (Culture and Society in
Germany, no. 1).

A collaborative work by scholars of migrant literature, specialists on German society,
and sociologists with a special interest in migration and immigration. The titles of the
essays in the volume are: 'Migrants or citizens? Turks in Germany between exclusion
and acceptance', D. Horrocks and E. Kolinsky; 'From "Pappkoffer" to pluralism: on
the development of migrant writing in the Federal Republic of Germany', S. Fischer
and M. McGowan; 'In search of a lost past', D. Horrocks; 'Living and writing in
Germany', D. Horrocks and E. Kolinsky; '"Black Eye and his donkey": a multi-cultural
experience', E. S. Özdamar; 'Non-German minorities in contemporary German
society', E. Kolinsky; 'The Turkish minority in German society', E. Kürşat-Ahlers;
'Turkish everyday culture in Germany and its prospects', D. Tan and Hans-Peter
Waldhoff; and 'Turkish cultural orientations in Germany and the role of Islam',
Yasemin Karakaşoğlu.

351 **Changing settlement intention of the Turkish immigrants in**
Australia and Sweden: some recent parallels.
Ahmet İçduygu. *Migration: A European Journal of International*
Migration and Ethnic Relations, vol. 26, no. 6 (1994), p. 49-73.

The article aims to give the reader some insight into the question of whether contemporary
Turkish settlements in Australia and Sweden are still temporary, or have gradually
become more long-term, or even permanent, in recent years. The analysis of settlement
intentions twenty to twenty-five years after the arrival of the immigrants suggests that
the subjective side of the settlement process is not yet complete. The results of studies
demonstrate the complexities involved in understanding the mechanisms, and the
changing intentions of the immigrants as regards permanent settlement.

352 **Facing changes and making choices: unintended Turkish**
immigrant settlement in Australia.
Ahmet İçduygu. *International Migration,* vol. 32, no. 1 (1994),
p. 71-95.

The case of migrants from Turkey to Australia between the late 1960s and mid-1970s
is analysed through three questions: why these migrants came to Australia with the
intention of staying only temporarily, despite the fact that at no time was the notion of
'guest-worker' a part of Australia's immigration policy; how they became more or
less permanent settlers in Australia; and the extent to which the original intention of
temporary migration and subsequent changes in this intention affected the incorporation
of individual migrants and their families into Australia's social structure.

353 **Turks in Nordic countries: an overview.**
Ahmet İçduygu, Orhan Tekelioğlu. *Les Annales de l'Autre Islam,*
no. 3 (1995), p. 205-14.

This work deals with the Turkish immigrant populations in the Nordic countries.
Turkish communities are significant for important reasons, namely, they are composed
of young families and children, and the age and sex structures of the immigrant
populations reflect their patterns of migration.

354 **Making something of myself.**
Christine Inglis, Joy Ellen, Lenore Manderson. Canberra:
Commonwealth Australian Government Publishing Service, 1992.
160p.

The purpose of this study is to explore the range of experiences of second-generation Turks reared in Australia, especially as to how they relate to education and to work. The earlier difficulties encountered by the Turkish migrants in settling in Australia have been extensively documented, and whether these difficulties continue for the younger generation is the major focus of this research. The conclusions drawn from this study indicate that the situation is far more complex, and that the stereotypes not only misrepresent much of the social reality but, more significantly, constitute a major barrier to Turkish young people striving to improve their situation.

355 **Muslims in Germany, with special reference to the Turkish-Islamic community.**
Yasemin Karakaşoğlu, Gerd Nonneman. In: *Muslim communities in the new Europe.* Edited by Gerd Nonneman, Tim Niblock, Bogdan Szajkowski. Reading, England: Ithaca Press, 1997, p. 241-67.

The authors provide a comprehensive analytical summary of the development of Islamic movements and organizations among the Turkish community in Germany.

356 **The Ottoman emigrates to America, 1860-1914.**
Kemal H. Karpat. *International Journal of Middle Eastern Studies,* vol. 17, no. 2 (1985), p. 175-209.

Using Ottoman and other sources, Karpat discusses the movement from Syria and neighbouring parts of the Ottoman Empire to America. He states that this emigration included substantial numbers of Muslims as well as Christians, and that it has to be studied in the context of the overall Ottoman policy on migration. He credits in- and out-migration with contributing substantially to the weakening of the imperial edifice and its replacement by national states.

357 **The Turks of Bulgaria: the history, culture and political fate of a minority.**
Edited by Kemal H. Karpat. İstanbul: The Isis Press, 1990. 257p.

This collection of articles explores the history, culture and condition of the Muslim Turks in Bulgaria. On the cover, the book is described by the publisher as follows: 'Written by European and Turkish scholars and based on information gleaned from objective factual research, these articles show that, contrary to the assertions by the Bulgarian government, the modern Turks of Bulgaria are the descents of people of genuine Turkish stock'.

358 **The Turks in America.**
Kemal H. Karpat. *Les Annales de l'Autre Islam,* no. 3 (1995), p. 229-52.

The survey outlines some of the major aspects of Turkish life in the United States and in Canada, and indicates that Turks in America have failed to create a truly living, authentic American Turkish community. This lack of a true community of American

Turks is suggested to be behind the cultural and linguistic discontinuity between parents and children, and the dearth of a truly Turkish socio-cultural core.

359   **From ethnic minority niche to assimilation: Turkish restaurants in Brussels.**
Christian Kesteloot, Pascale Mistiaen.   *Area*, vol. 29, no. 4 (1997), p. 325-34. map.
A twenty-five year observation of Turkish restaurants in the Turkish neighbourhood of Brussels shows many changes in their characteristics and distribution. The two dimensions of change are interrelated, and are explained by strategies of ethnic minority entrepreneurship and by the Hotelling effect (i.e. the phenomenon of spatial concentrations of similar businesses).

360   **A matter of honour: experiences of Turkish women immigrants.**
Tahire Koçtürk.   London: Zed Books, 1992. 145p. bibliog.
This book examines the social and cultural impact of western industrial society on Muslim Turkish immigrants, especially in terms of gender and family relations. The author provides a historical overview of the life styles of Turkish women, and in examining the status of women in Islamic thought, she argues that both religious ideology and the 'honour ethic' have been instrumental within the oppression of Turkish women. She discusses the circumstances that led to large-scale immigration out of the villages of Turkey into the alien industrialized West. Through interviews of Turkish immigrants, especially women, and their daughters, the author explores how these families lived according to a rural Islamic tradition as a reaction to living in modern Europe.

361   **Shifting centres and emergent identities: Turkey and Germany in the lives of Turkish *Gastarbeiter*.**
Ruth Mandel.   In: *Muslim travellers. Pilgrimage, migration, and the religious imagination.*   Edited by Dale F. Eickelman, James Piscatori. London: Routledge, 1990, p. 153-71.
The author shows how the experience of migration affects Alevi and Sunni Turks in Germany, who confront the foreign context in very different ways. However, their relations to each other are undergoing a transformation through their interactions with German society, and their different patterns of socialization influence the overall future orientations of Sunni and Alevi youth towards Turkey and Germany.

362   **Ethnic leadership, ethnic communities' political powerlessness and the state in Belgium.**
Marco Martiniello.   *Ethnic and Racial Studies,* vol. 16, no. 2 (1993), p. 236-55.
Examines the relations between the Belgian state and the political system on the one hand and the immigrant ethnic communities living in the country on the other. The political exclusion of immigrant groups is analysed as the survival strategy of a state which feels subjectively threatened by the potential emergence of a new ethnicity related to immigrant population in the political life, and this is compared with the position of the Italian community in relation to the Moroccan and Turkish communities.

363 **The political participation of Turkish immigrants in Europe and Denmark.**
Eva Ostergaard-Nielsen. *Les Annales de l'Autre Islam*, no. 3 (1995), p. 375-405.

Suggests that the analyses of the participation of immigrants in Turkish politics fall mainly outside the scope and interest of the society and politics of their country of residence, but that the factual political integration of the Turks in the politics of their country of residence is the object of increasing attention and debate. The author discusses the varying patterns of the issue.

364 **Muslim identity and the Balkan state.**
Edited by Hugh Poulton, Suha Taji-Farouki. London: Hurst & Co., 1997. 320p.

Apart from in Albania, where they form the majority, the Balkan Muslim communities which were left behind after the retreat of the Ottoman Empire from the area became minorities within the successor states. This work focuses on the current situation of Balkan Muslims. Among the papers in this volume are: 'From religious identity to ethnic mobilisation: the Turks of Bulgaria before, during and after Communism', Wolfgang Höpken; 'National identity among Muslims in Thrace and Macedonia: Turks, Pomaks and Roma', Hugh Poulton; 'Turkey as kin state: Turkish foreign policy towards Turkish and Muslim communities in the Balkans', Hugh Poulton; and 'Sustaining Turkish-Islamic loyalties: the *Diyanet* in Western Europe', Nico Landman.

365 **Turkish migrants in Austria.**
Gabriele Rasuly-Paleczek. *Les Annales de l'Autre Islam,* no. 3 (1995), p. 177-203.

The author provides a brief survey of the Turkish migrant community in Austria, which consists of migrant workers, students and asylum seekers.

366 **Turkish Islamic organizations and the Dutch state: new opportunities?**
Thijl Sunier. In: *The Centre for Middle Eastern and Islamic Studies: Muslim Communities Project, volume 2: Muslim communities in the Netherlands and Germany.* Edited by Suha Taji-Farouki. Durham, England: Centre for Middle Eastern and Islamic Studies, 1995, p. 20-32.

Discusses the nature of Turkish Islamic organizations, and their relationships with the Dutch society, and promotes the idea that if Islamic organizations cannot respond to the changing characteristics of their membership, they will eventually lose ground.

367 **Turkish immigrants in Sweden.**
Ingvar Svanberg. *Les Annales de l'Autre Islam*, no. 3 (1995), p. 215-27.

The varying ways of being a Turk in Sweden are discussed in terms of the immigrants' background, employment status, and ethnic and religious identity.

368 **Racism in Germany and its impact on the Turkish minority.**
Faruk Şen. *The Turkish Yearbook of International Relations*, vol. 24 (1994), p. 1-10.
Summarizing the situation of the Turks in Europe and especially in Germany, the author suggests ways of counteracting racism.

369 **The Turkish presence in Bulgaria: communications, 7 June 1985.**
Turkish Historical Society. Ankara: Publications of the Turkish Historical Society, 1986. 90p. maps. bibliog. (Serial VII, no. 87a).
This is a compilation of reports which discuss the Turkish presence in Bulgaria through detailed historical information supported by relevant tables and maps. The volume includes the following chapters: 'Bulgarians and the Turkish language', Hasan Eren; 'Turkish settlement in the Balkans and its consequences', Yaşar Yücel; 'The Turks of Bulgaria and the immigration question', Bilal N. Şimşir; and 'The question of Turkish minority in Bulgaria from the perspective of international law', Hamza Eroğlu.

370 **Bulgarian Turkish emigration and return.**
Darina Vasileva. *International Migration Review*, vol. 26, no. 2 (1992), p. 342-52.
Although the history of the emigration of Bulgarian Muslim Turks to Turkey is over a century old, the violation of the human rights of ethnic Turks by the totalitarian regime during the 1980s resulted in an even larger and unpredictable migration. This article emphasizes the complexity of the factors and motivations behind this emigration, with the aim of providing a better understanding of the character of ethnic conflicts in post-totalitarian Eastern Europe.

371 **Imaging 'us' as migrant diaspora: sentiments, history and identity among Turkish migrants in Germany and France.**
Lale Yalçın-Heckmann. *Les Annales de l'Autre Islam*, no. 3 (1995), p. 333-48.
The author discusses the collective identity of migrant Turks with an emphasis on the collectivization of sentiments and affect, and how sentiments are produced as belonging and depicting collectivity, and how these collective sentiments shape the collective identities of migrant Turks in Bamberg (Germany)and Colmar (France).

The Turkic peoples of the world.
See item no. 2.

An introduction to the history of the Turkic peoples: ethnogenesis and state-formation in medieval and early modern Eurasia and the Middle East.
See item no. 7.

Death and exile: the ethnic cleansing of Ottoman Muslims, 1821-1922.
See item no. 193.

Media, migrants and marginalization. The situation in the Federal Republic of Germany.
See item no. 1272.

Bitig: Journal of the Turkic World.
See item no. 1318.

Central Asian Survey.
See item no. 1322.

Eurasian Studies.
See item no. 1330.

Türkiye dışındaki Türkler bibliyografyası. A bibliography of Turks out of Turkey.
See item no. 1404.

Türkiye dışındaki Türk vatandaşları bibliyografyası. A bibliography of Turkish citizens out of Turkey.
See item no. 1405.

Irak Türkleri bibliyografyası. A bibliography of Iraqi Turks.
See item no. 1429.

Language

Reference works

372 The languages of the Soviet Union.
Bernard Comrie.   Cambridge, England: Cambridge University Press,
1981. 317p. bibliog.

The book introduces the languages and language families of the former Soviet Union,
as well as giving a brief synopsis of how they interacted with Russian. Chapter two
(p. 39-91) is devoted to Altaic languages (Turkic, Mongolian, and Tungusic). As well
as the general characteristics of the group, the phonological, morphological and
syntactic structures of individual languages are given. There is also a classification of
modern Turkic languages.

373 Turkic languages.
Bernard Comrie.   In: *International encyclopedia of linguistics.*
Edited by William Bright.   New York; Oxford: Oxford University
Press, 1994, vol. 4, p. 187-90.

Provides general information about Turkic languages, both historical and contemporary.
The article contains a bibliography, and a summary list of important facts, such as the
names of languages and the number of speakers.

374 Philologiae Turcicae fundamenta.
Edited by Jean Deny, Kaare Grønbech, Helmuth Scheel, Zeki Velidi
Togan.   Wiesbaden, Germany: Franz Steiner Verlag, 1959. 2nd ed.
vol. 1. 810p. map.

Although dated, this remains a valuable and important work on Turkic languages.
Essays in the volume are in Turkish, English, French or German, and they describe all
Turkic languages. After a general introduction on Turkic languages and peoples, each
language is presented in terms of its phonetics, morphology, syntax, followed by

specimen texts. Turkic languages are classified, Old Turkic, Middle Turkic, Eastern Middle Turkic, and Modern Turkic, including Ottoman, and dialects of Turkish are described. Although the volume may at times fail to reflect the contemporary structures of the languages, it is still the most complete and useful work on Turkic languages. The volume contains a folded map of 'Turkic linguistic regions'.

375 **Handbuch der Turkischen Sprachwissenschaft. Teil I.** (Handbook of Turkish linguistics. Volume I.)
Edited by Gyorgy Hazai. Wiesbaden, Germany: Otto Harrassowitz, 1990. 493p.

The articles in this work are in German and English. As well as summarizing the state of affairs in research into Ottoman and modern Turkish, the articles are accompanied by very useful bibliographies. The chapters in English cover phonetics and phonology, quantitative studies, Anatolian dialects, Balkan dialects, and the Turkish language reform and language policy in Turkey.

376 **The Turkic languages.**
Edited by Lars Johanson, Eva Csato. New York; London: Routledge, 1998. 504p. (Routledge Language Family Descriptions).

A survey of major Turkic languages. Each chapter combines modern linguistic analysis with traditional historical linguistics. The chapters are as follows: 'The speakers of Turkish languages'; 'The Turkic peoples: a historical sketch'; 'The structure of Turkic'; 'The reconstruction of proto-Turkic and the genetic question'; 'The history of Turkic'; 'Turkic writing systems'; 'Old Turkic'; 'Middle Kipchak'; 'Chagatay'; 'Ottoman Turkish'; 'Turkish'; 'Turkish dialects'; 'The Turkish language reform'; 'Azerbaijanian'; 'Turkmen'; 'Turkic languages of Iran'; 'Tatar'; 'Bashkir'; 'West Kipchak languages'; 'Kazakh and Karakalpak'; 'Nogay'; 'Kirghiz'; 'Uzbek'; 'Uyghur'; 'Yellow Uyghur and Salar'; 'South Siberian Turkic'; 'Yakut'; and 'Chuvash'. Each language is outlined in terms of its phonology, morphology, lexis and dialects, and a reading list is provided.

377 **Compendium of the Turkic dialects. (Diwan lugat at-Turk).**
Maḥmūd al-Kāşgarī, edited and translated with an introduction and indices by Robert Dankoff in collaboration with James Kelly.
Duxbury, Massachusetts: Harvard University Printing Office, 1982-85. 3 vols. map.

Dīvānü Lügāt-it-Türk, as it is commonly known, is the 11th-century masterpiece of Maḥmūd al-Kāşgarī. The aim of the author was to teach Turkic to Arabic speakers, therefore his work is a dictionary and grammar, as well as a collection of proverbs, poems and other samples taken from the living dialects of Turkic in the 11th century. It has 7,500 entries, and the meanings of the words are given in Arabic. It sheds light on where Turkic dialects were spoken, how the Turkic people lived, their history, folklore, beliefs and daily activities. The latest facsimile edition of the work, reproduced from the manuscript (MS AR. 4189, National Library in Fatih, İstanbul), is by the Ministry of Culture in 1990: *Dîvânü lûgat-it Türk: tıpkı basım*, by Mahmud Kashgari (Ankara: Kültür Bakanlığı, 1990. 320p. [Kültür Bakanlığı Yayınları, no. 1205]).

378   **Turkish and Turkic languages.**
      Jaklin Kornfilt.   In: *The world's major languages.*   Edited by
      Bernard Comrie.   London: Croom Helm, 1987, p. 619-44.
This is a useful and informative introduction to Turkic languages, Turkish, their
history and structure. After a brief introduction to Turkic languages, the author
concentrates on modern Turkish, outlining its phonology, morphology and syntax.

379   **Turkish.**
      Jaklin Kornfilt.   In: *International encyclopedia of linguistics.*   Edited
      by William Bright.   New York; Oxford: Oxford University Press,
      1992, vol. 4, p. 190-96.
The section on Turkish provides a summary of Turkish phonetics, phonology,
morphology, and syntax.

380   **The Turkic languages and peoples: an introduction to Turkic
      studies.**
      Karl Menges.   Wiesbaden, Germany: Otto Harrassowitz, 1995.
      2nd rev. ed. 248p. maps. bibliog.
Originally published in 1963, this is a general introduction to Turkic philology. The
contemporary reader will find the work cumbersome to follow, but it is full of
information about the Turkic languages, in terms of their comparative syntactic
properties, lexicology, sound systems, morphology, alphabets, and the languages they
have been in contact with. There are five folded leaves of plates and maps.

381   **Turkic languages.**
      Talat Tekin.   In: *The encyclopedia of language and linguistics.*
      Edited by R. E. Asher.   Oxford: Oxford University Press, 1994,
      vol. 9, p. 4780-85.
This article gives an overview of the historical development of Turkic languages and
their classification. It outlines the characteristics of their phonology, morphology, and
syntactic properties.

382   **Altaic languages.**
      Talat Tekin.   In: *The encyclopedia of language and linguistics.*
      Edited by R. E. Asher.   Oxford: Oxford University Press, 1994,
      vol. 1, p. 82-85.
Summarizes the structure of Altaic languages (Turkic, Mongolian, Manchu-Tungus,
and Korean). It gives the common characteristics of the group, together with a general
account of their phonological, morphological, syntactic and lexical properties.

383 **Turkish.**
Talat Tekin. In: *The encyclopedia of language and linguistics.*
Edited by R. E. Asher. Oxford: Oxford University Press, 1994,
vol. 9, p. 4785-87.
Turkish is presented as a descendant of Ottoman Turkish. The article gives an outline
of its history, followed by its phonological, morphological, syntactic and lexical
properties with examples.

Dictionaries

General

384 **Langenscheidt's English-Turkish, Turkish-English standard
dictionary.**
Resuhi Akdikmen. New York: Langenscheidt; London: GeoCenter
International UK Ltd, 1986. 438p.
The dictionary contains 80,000 items, and is accompanied by a brief explanation of
grammar, and a pronunciation guide.

385 **Langenscheidt's English-Turkish, Turkish-English pocket
dictionary.**
Resuhi Akdikmen. New York: Langenscheidt; London: GeoCenter
International UK Ltd, 1995. 776p. (Langenscheidt Pocket
Dictionaries).
The dictionary contains 50,000 items, and is accompanied by a brief explanation of
grammar, and a pronunciation guide.

386 **The Redhouse Turkish-English dictionary.**
V. Bahadır Alkım, Nazime Antel, Robert Avery. İstanbul: Sev
Matbaacılık ve Yayıncılık A.Ş., 1997. 1,292p.
This dictionary is based largely on the Turkish-English lexicon of Sir James Redhouse,
published in 1890. It has over 94,000 Turkish words and phrases defined by over
115,000 separate English definitions and equivalents. It gives full coverage of words
used both in Ottoman and modern Turkish. Each main entry is shown in Latin characters
and also in Arabic (handwritten *rika* print). The dictionary is also rich in proverbs,
folk sayings, and technical terms.

387   **The Redhouse contemporary Turkish-English dictionary.**
Robert Avery, Serap Bezmez, C. H. Brown, Mehlika Yaylalı.
İstanbul: Sev Matbaacılık ve Yayıncılık A.Ş., 1997. 545p.
Includes over 75,000 Turkish words, phrases and proverbs defined by over 125,000
English definitions, translations and idiomatic equivalents. It also includes slang
expressions, colloquial words, and technical terms pertaining to arts and sciences.

388   **The Redhouse English-Turkish dictionary.**
Robert Avery, Serap Bezmez, Anna G. Edmonds, Mehlika Yaylalı.
İstanbul: Sev Matbaacılık ve Yayıncılık A.Ş., 1997. 1,152p.
This dictionary includes over 70,000 English words and phrases with over 182,000
Turkish definitions. It also gives a pronunciation guide.

389   **The Redhouse portable dictionary.**
Robert Avery, Serap Bezmez, Anna G. Edmonds, Mehlika Yaylalı.
İstanbul: Sev Matbaacılık ve Yayıncılık A.Ş., 1997. 503p.
Contains 17,250 English words and phrases and 13,250 Turkish entries. The publishers
recommend this dictionary especially for language students.

390   **Redhouse English-Turkish, Turkish-English CD-ROM dictionary.**
Serap Bezmez, Richard Blakney, C. H. Brown.   İstanbul: Sev
Matbaacılık ve Yayıncılık A.Ş., 1997.
This CD runs on Windows 3.1 or a higher version. It contains approximately 75,000
entries (words, idioms, terms and proverbs), 20 hours of recorded speech, and over
5,000 example sentences.

391   **An etymological dictionary of pre-thirteenth century Turkish.**
Gerard L. M. Clauson.   Oxford: Clarendon Press, 1972. 989p.
This valuable reference work provides a list of words in the Turkish lexicon prior to
the 13th century with their etymologies. As well as being cross-referenced to other
etymologically related words, and similar words, each entry is also illustrated with a
quotation.

392   **The Oxford Turkish dictionary. (Türkçe-İngilizce, İngilizce-Türkçe).**
H. C. Hony, Fahir İz, A. D. Alderson.   Oxford; New York: Oxford
University Press, 1993. 619p.
This is a combined edition of *The Oxford Turkish-English dictionary* (3rd ed., 1984),
and *The Oxford English-Turkish dictionary* (2nd ed., 1978). Although dependable, it is
largely out-of-date.

393 **Dictionary of the Turkic languages: English: Azerbaijani, Kazakh, Kyrgyz, Tatar, Turkish, Turkmen, Uighur, Uzbek.**
Kurtuluş Öztopçu, Abuov Zhoumagaly, Nasir Kambarov, Youssef Azemoun. London; New York: Routledge, 1996. 384p.
The dictionary covers 2,000 English words in eight Turkic languages. Words are organized topically and alphabetically. Original spelling in Cyrillic and Latin transliteration are provided.

Specialized dictionaries

394 **English-Turkish Longman Metro dictionary of business English.**
J. H. Adam, translated into Turkish by İ. Önder, E. Ergin, M. Kaytaz, G. Evcimen. İstanbul: Longman & Metro, 1990. 300p.
This is an excellent and easy-to-use dictionary, which gives the different meanings of the words, where they are used, and explanations of their different meanings. It also contains a section on useful information on international measurements (length, weight, volume, etc.), chemical elements and symbols, and on the countries of the world. This dictionary doubles as a handbook for business studies.

395 **Türkçe-İngilizce, İngilizce-Türkçe hukuk, ticaret, işletme terimleri ve kısaltmalar sözlüğü.** (English-Turkish, Turkish-English dictionary of legal, commercial, managerial terms and abbreviations.)
Erhan Adal. İstanbul: Erk Yayıncılık, 1993. 256p. bibliog.
This is a standard and useful dictionary of commerce, management and law. It also provides the abbreviations commonly used.

396 **Pashas, begs, and efendis. A historical dictionary of titles and terms in the Ottoman empire.**
Gustav Bayerle. İstanbul: The ISIS Press, 1997. 169p. bibliog.
This handy volume is not only about titles but also contains translations and explanations of many important terms which a student of Ottoman studies will come across. Where possible, the author also gives a brief history of the word in question, citing sources. The volume is full of fascinating facts and makes for interesting reading.

397 **İngilizce-Türkçe, Türkçe-İngilizce teknik terimler sözlüğü.**
English-Turkish, Turkish-English dictionary of technical terms.
Fono Yayınları. İstanbul: Fono Yayınları, 1998. 736p.
This easy-to-use dictionary is also available in separate volumes, one for English to Turkish and the other from Turkish to English. It contains scientific and technical vocabulary.

398 **Turkish-English law dictionary.**
Mustafa Ovacık.   Ankara: Türkiye İş Bankası, Banka ve Ticaret
Hukuku Araştırma Enstitüsü, 1986. 2nd ed. 292p.

A learned dictionary of law oriented for the professional, although it explains the uses
and meanings of specialized terminology. It is comprehensive and easy-to-use.

399 **English-Turkish law dictionary.**
Mustafa Ovacık.   Ankara: Türkiye İş Bankası, Banka ve Ticaret
Hukuku Araştırma Enstitüsü, 1986. 2nd ed. 330p.

A learned dictionary of law for the professional, although it explains the uses and
meanings of specialized terminology. It is comprehensive and easy-to-use.

400 **Tıp sözlüğü.** (English-Turkish medical dictionary.)
Pars Tuğlacı.   İstanbul: ABC, 1997. 8th ed. 924p.

This dictionary was first published in 1964, and has been continuously revised since
then. It covers the larger field of medical sciences, and the entry for each word
includes details of the context in which the word is used, and what part of speech the
word belongs to. It provides the Turkish terms used for the English words in question,
and explains the meaning (in Turkish). Different meanings and uses of the same word
are also given.

401 **Türkçe-İngilizce iktisadi ticari hukuki terimler sözlüğü.** (Turkish-
English dictionary of economic, commercial, legal terms.)
Pars Tuğlacı.   İstanbul: ABC, 1997. 640p.

This is a practical dictionary covering many areas of law as well as economy and
commerce. Different uses of the same word are given, and brief explanations of the
specialized terminology are provided.

402 **Türkçe-İngilizce ansiklopedik askeri sözlük.** (Turkish-English
dictionary of military terms.)
İrfan Uğurlu.   Ankara: Meteksan Yayınları, 1991. 475p.

This is a mini-encyclopaedia and a dictionary of military terms. It also reads like a
handbook and is full of useful information for the specialist.

403 **A dictionary of Turkish proverbs.**
Metin Yurtbaşı.   Ankara: Turkish Daily News, 1993. 654p. map.
bibliog.

This volume contains 5,000 proverbs used currently or in the past, collected from
Turkic-speaking peoples. The proverbs are given in 172 topical categories. The author
first gives a literal translation of their meaning, then presents (with references) the
matching proverb (especially in English), if such exists.

Grammars

404 Chagatay manual.
János Eckmann. Richmond, England: Curzon Press, 1997. 340p.
bibliog. (Uralic & Altaic Series, no. 60).

Chagatay was the classical literary language of Central Asian Turkic languages between the 15th and 20th centuries. It is the continuation of the Karakhanid (Khakanian) of the 11th to 13th centuries, and Khorazmian Turkic of the 14th century, all literary languages. Chagatay was also used by the Muslim Turks of Europe until the 19th century, but was replaced by the Uzbek literary language in 1921. The book gives a concise grammar of Chagatay, and includes a reader and a glossary.

405 The Turkish grammar of Thomas Vaughan: Ottoman Turkish at the end of the XVIIth century according to an English 'transkriptiontext'.
Erika Hitzigrath Gilson. Wiesbaden, Germany: Otto Harrassowitz, 1987. 235p. (Near and Middle East Monographs, New Series, no. 2).

A linguistic study of the *Grammar of the Turkish language of 1709* by Thomas Vaughan (a merchant of the Levant Company). It is based on a facsimile of the original reprinted in 1968, which has a preface, a grammar, five dialogues with English translations, a fable, fifty-three proverbs and an extensive vocabulary.

406 Turkish.
Jaklin Kornfilt. New York; London: Routledge, 1997. 575p.

This is an up-to-date, comprehensive, descriptive grammar of modern Turkish. It covers all components of Turkish grammar, such as syntax, phonology, morphology, as well as some parts of the lexicon. Different levels of vocabulary (recent versus old; official versus colloquial or informal; polite versus impolite) are designated as such. Intended as a reference grammar, it is designated for structural typologists and theoretical linguists, students and teachers of linguistics and students and teachers of Turkish.

407 Turkish grammar.
Geoffrey Lewis. Oxford: Oxford University Press, 1986. 303p.
bibliog.

First published in 1967, this book has since been the most comprehensive, accessible, and therefore popular reference grammar for modern Turkish. It is written in a traditional framework, and benefits greatly from the author's vast knowledge of Ottoman and modern Turkish language and literature. It contains many colloquialisms, and the author's sense of humour shines through the book.

408 A grammar of Orkhon Turkic.
Talat Tekin. Richmond, England: Curzon Press, 1997. 419p. bibliog.

Originally published by Indiana University Press in 1968 as part of the Uralic and Altaic Series. Orkhon Turkic is the oldest form of Turkic for which there are written records. It was spoken by the Turks primarily in Mongolia in the first half of the 8th century AD. It is known through the inscriptions found in present-day outer Mongolia, mainly in the basin of the Orkhon River, which are the Kül Tigin, Bilgae Kagan, Tonyukuk, İşbara Tarkan (Ongin), and Küli Çor (Ikhe-Khushotu) inscriptions. The book consists of four parts. Part one provides a grammar of Orkhon Turkish, the second and third parts contain the texts and their translations, and the fourth part is a comprehensive glossary which includes the lexical items in all the inscriptions.

409 **Turkish grammar.**
Robert Underhill. Cambridge, Massachusetts: The MIT Press, 1993. 7th ed. 474p.

First published in 1976, this book is written within the conceptual framework of early generative grammar. It is a useful volume for grammar practice as well as a reference grammar. The chapters contain information on phraseology and idiomatic usage, and there are glossaries of suffixes and lexical items.

Textbooks

410 **Colloquial Turkish.**
Sinan Bayraktaroğlu, Arın Bayraktaroğlu. London; New York: Routledge, 1992. 245p. audio cassette.

The authors take a communicative approach to teaching Turkish. The book provides a useful source for the functions of the grammatical structures of Turkish in fifteen lessons, and it presents written and spoken Turkish as used in everyday situations. Although beginners may find it rather challenging, the book is useful for remedial teaching, or for intermediate learners of Turkish.

411 **Teach yourself Turkish.**
Asuman Çelen, David Pollard. London: Hodder & Stoughton Ltd, 1996. 300p. audio cassette.

The book, aimed at beginners, takes a communicative approach to teaching Turkish. By the end of the book, the learner should be able to master basic Turkish sentence structures, and a vocabulary of over 1,000 words. Although it is designed for self-study, it is best used with the help of a teacher and a grammar book for reference.

412 **Turkish sampler.**
Müge Galin. Bloomington, Indiana: Indiana Turkish Studies, 1989. 356p. bibliog.

This is a graded reader of modern Turkish. The volume contains samples of written Turkish from a variety of sources, with introductory notes in English and questions on the texts, followed by written assignments. There is also a brief summary of grammatical points and a Turkish-English glossary at the end of the volume. It is mainly designed for classroom use, although it can be used for self-study.

413   **Türkçe öğreniyoruz.** (We are learning Turkish.)
       Mehmet Hengirmen.   Ankara: Engin Yayınevi, 1990- . 6 vols. audio
       cassettes.

These are the textbooks of the Ankara University's Turkish Language Teaching
Centre: Türkçe Öğretim Merkezi (TÖMER). They aim to take the learner from a
beginner's level to advanced. The lessons are structured around situations presented at
the start of the lesson, followed by grammar and exercises. Since the books do not use
a cyclical approach, and are not based on functions, all the functions of a syntactic
structure may be given in the same lesson. The exercises tend to be repetitive. The
books are designed for classroom use.

414   **Turkish in three months.**
       Bengisu Rona.   London: Hugo Publishers, 1998. 206p. audio cassette.

A good summary reference grammar for all learners of Turkish. It is learner-friendly,
easy to follow, and highly recommended.

Linguistic studies

415   **The acquisition of aspect and modality: the case of past reference
       in Turkish.**
       Ayhan Aksu-Koç.   Cambridge, England: Cambridge University Press,
       1988. 245p. bibliog. (Cambridge Studies in Linguistics).

The book dwells on the acquisition of tense-aspect-modality in Turkish, and the
development of the semantic structures underlying the use of the appropriate verb
forms for talking about past events.

416   **Patterns of language mixing: a study in Turkish-Dutch
       bilingualism.**
       Ad Backus.   Wiesbaden, Germany: Otto Harrassowitz, 1992. 119p.
       bibliog.

The book deals with patterns of language mixing, and Turkish-Dutch language contact,
initiated through the Turkish-speaking immigrants and their children growing up in
the Netherlands.

417   **Symbolae Turcologicae. Studies in honour of Lars Johanson on his
       sixtieth birthday 8 March 1996.**
       Edited by Árpád Berta, Bernt Brendemoen, Claus Schönig.
       Stockholm: Svenska Forskningsinstitutet Istanbul, 1996. 246p.
       (Swedish Research Institute in Istanbul Transactions, no. 6).

The volume contains twenty-five articles (twelve of them in English), written by
Johanson's colleagues. They cover a diversity of turcological disciplines, such as
philological and linguistics studies of extinct literary Turkic languages (Orkhun

Turkic, Bolgar, Kipchak, Chagatay, and Ottoman), medieval Kipchak history, living Turkic languages and peoples, Anatolian dialectology, modern Turkish, historical syntax, and language contact.

418   **Studies on modern Turkish: proceedings of the Third Conference on Turkish Linguistics.**
Edited by Hendrik Boeschoten, Ludo T. Verhoeven.   Tilburg, the Netherlands: Tilburg University Press, 1987. 270p. bibliog.
Contains the papers presented at the Third International Conference on Turkish Linguistics. The topics of the papers include phonetics, phonology, syntax, computational linguistics, pragmatics, first and second language acquisition, and sociolinguistics.

419   **Acquisition of Turkish by immigrant children: a multiple case study of Turkish children in the Netherlands aged 4 to 6.**
Hendrik E. Boeschoten.   Wiesbaden, Germany: Otto Harrassowitz, 1990. 181p. bibliog.
This study describes the developmental patterns in the speech of the Turkish children born in the Netherlands during the two years they attend kindergarten classes.

420   **Turkish linguistics today.**
Edited by Hendrik Boeschoten, Ludo Verhoeven.   Leiden, the Netherlands: E. J. Brill, 1991. 193p.
Deals with the structural aspects of Turkish, and each chapter gives a view of the field as it stood in the early 1990s, namely phonology, syntax, semantics, language acquisition, and language variation. The book offers an introduction to current research in the field of synchronic Turkish linguistics.

421   **Old Turkic word formation: a functional approach to the lexicon.**
Marcel Erdal.   Wiesbaden, Germany: Otto Harrassowitz, 1991. 2 vols. bibliog.
A handbook of Old Turkic for linguists, produced meticulously. Volume one contains the formation of denominal and deadjectival nominals, deverbal nominals and adverbs. Volume two covers the formation of denominal verbs, types of action and inaction, diathesis and voice. All the formation types are given with examples and sources, followed by a lexicon of Old Turkic. The volumes also include an index of verb stems, an index of linguistic phenomena and morphemes, and an index of corrected or reinterpreted passages.

422   **The function of word order in Turkish grammar.**
Emine Eser Erguvanlı.   Berkeley, California: University of California Press, 1984. 179p. bibliog. (University of California Publications in Linguistics, no. 106).
The volume deals with the pragmatic functions of word order variation in Turkish.

423　**Immigrant languages in Europe.**
Edited by Guus Extra, Ludo Verhoeven.　Clevedon, England:
Multilingual Matters, 1993. 208p.

Contains, among other essays, the following titles which discuss Turkish as spoken in
northwest Europe: 'A bilingual perspective on Turkish and Moroccan children and
adults in the Netherlands', Guus Extra and Ludo Verhoeven; 'Turkish language
development in Germany', Carol Pfaff; 'Turkish language development in the
Netherlands', Anneli Schaufeli; 'Summative assessment of ethnic group language
proficiency', Jeroen Aarssen, Jan Jaap de Ruiter and Ludo Verhoeven; 'Parental
attitudes towards child bilingualism in the Nordic countries', Sirkku Latomaa; 'Code-
copying in immigrant Turkish', Lars Johanson; and 'Turkish-Dutch code-switching
and the frame-process model', Ad Backus.

424　**Relative clause constructions in Turkish.**
Geoffrey Haig.　Wiesbaden, Germany: Otto Harrassowitz, 1998.
254p. bibliog. (Turcologica, no. 33).

The author deals with the technical details of relative construction in Turkish in the
first and second chapters. The third and forth chapters introduce nominalization and
attribution. Later chapters deal in detail with case recovery and the problem of participle
choice. The language samples used in the book have been collected from different
texts which are cited in the appendix.

425　**VIII. Uluslararası Türk Dilbilimi Konferansı bildirileri, 7-9**
Ağustos 1996. Proceedings of the VIIIth International Conference
on Turkish Linguistics, August 7-9, 1996.
Edited by Kamile İmer.　Ankara: Ankara Üniversitesi, 1997. 377p.
maps. bibliog.

This is a collection of conference papers on different areas of Turkish linguistics.

426　**The Mainz meeting: proceedings of the Seventh International**
Conference on Turkish Linguistics (August 3-6 1994).
Edited by Lars Johanson, with Eva Agnes Csato, Vanessa Locke,
Astrid Menz, Dorothea Winterling.　Wiesbaden, Germany: Otto
Harrassowitz, 1998. 482p.

This volume contains the papers presented at a conference in 1994 in Mainz. The
papers address various issues in all branches of linguistics as they relate to Turkish
and Turkic languages. They cover phonology, morphology, communicative functions
and referentiality, converbs, voice, relative clauses, general syntax and semantics,
stylistics, language acquisition, dialect studies, historical and comparative Turkish
studies, contact linguistics, and applied linguistics.

427 **Studies on Turkish linguistics: proceedings of the Fourth
International Conference on Turkish Linguistics, 17-19 August
1988.**
Edited by Sabri Koç. Ankara: Middle East Technical University,
1988. 596p.
The volume contains thirty-one papers presented at the conference, covering different
areas of synchronic Turkish linguistics.

428 **The phonology of modern standard Turkish.**
Robert Lees. Richmond, England: Curzon Press, 1997. 76p. (Uralic
and Altaic Series, no. 6).
Originally published in 1961 by Indiana University Press, this is the first generative
phonology of Turkish.

429 **English writers on the Turkish language, 1670-1832.**
Geoffrey Lewis. *Osmanlı Araştırmaları* (The Journal of Ottoman
Studies), vol. 7-8 (1988), p. 83-96.
Lewis presents works in English on Turkish (Ottoman) up to 1846, when James
Redhouse published his first Turkish grammar. He also provides concise reviews for
the works. This is an important source, written with a good sense of humour, and
elegance.

430 **Central Asian monuments.**
Edited by Hüseyin B. Paksoy. İstanbul: The ISIS Press, 1992. 173p.
The volume contains essays by H. B. Paksoy, P. B. Golden, R. Frye, R. Dankoff,
U. Schamiloglu, K. Krisciunas, A. Altstadt, E. J. Lazzerini, and D. S. Thomas, on
different aspects of the literatures and languages of Central Asia. P. B. Golden's
'Codex Cumanicus' is of special importance, as it contains information on the
Kipchak-Cuman Turkic language and the Khazars, within the context of the 13th-
century manuscript known as 'Codex Cumanicus', which is housed in the library of
St Mark, in Venice. It is a collection of texts, a practical handbook of Cuman, with
glossaries in Italo-Latin, and Persian, religious texts, and folkloric material.

431 **The stories of the prophets. Qisas al-Anbiya. An eastern Turkish
version.**
Al-Rabghuzi, critically edited by H. E. Boeschoten, M. Vandamme,
S. Tezcan with the assistance of H. Braam, B. Radtke, translated into
English by H. E. Boeschoten, J. O'Kane, M. Vandamme. Leiden, the
Netherlands: E. J. Brill, 1995. 2 vols.
The first critical edition of Rabghuzi's *The stories of the prophets*, written in 1310 in
Khwarezmian Turkish, and one of the most important Islamic Turkish texts. The work
contains a mixture of theological discourse, popular stories and poems which together
form an important source both for historical linguistics and literary criticism, and for
Islamic studies. The first volume contains a critical text edition based on the British
Library manuscript (the oldest manuscript extant), but with additions from, and some
collation with, two manuscripts from libraries in St. Petersburg. The text edition is
accompanied by a selective glossary. The translation offered in the second volume is

directly based on the text as established in the first volume. Extensive indices are included.

432 **Current issues in Turkish linguistics: proceedings of the Fifth International Conference on Turkish linguistics, 15-17 August 1990.**
Edited by Bengisu Rona. Ankara: Hitit Yayınevi, 1996. 2 vols.
The volumes contain papers on different topics of Turkish linguistics.

433 **Studies in Turkish grammar.**
Gerjan van Schaaik. Wiesbaden, Germany: Otto Harrassowitz, 1996. 277p. bibliog.
This book applies Functional Grammar to Turkish. After an introduction of the terms of Functional Grammar, two chapters are devoted to the morphology and syntax of noun phrases. The chapter entitled 'Lexical representation' is concerned with nominal predicates, and the chapter 'On generation' describes possible applications of the principles derived. Another chapter investigates how nominal compounds of Turkish can be treated within the framework of Functional Grammar, and the last chapter addresses the similarity construction in Turkish. This study is ideally suited to researchers who are interested in the application of Functional Grammar to Turkish.

434 **Studies in Turkish linguistics.**
Edited by Isaac Slobin, Karl Zimmer. Amsterdam: J. Benjamins, 1986. 300p. (Typological Studies in Language, no. 8).
The book contains most of the papers presented at the Conference on the Turkish Language and Linguistics in Atatürk's Turkey (Berkeley, California on 15-16 May 1982). It includes: 'Turkish' by Robert Underhill (p. 7-21), which outlines the structure of modern Turkish grammar and gives a list of reference works; and 'Bibliography of modern linguistics works on Turkish', also by Robert Underhill (p. 23-51), which provides a list of academic works written in English from the 1960s to 1986.

435 **Language and identity in the Middle East and North Africa.**
Edited by Yasir Suleiman. Richmond, England: Curzon Press, 1996. 192p.
This collection of essays dwells on the importance of the relationship between language and identity. Three essays are relevant for Turkish studies: 'Turkish as a symbol of survival and identity in Bulgaria and Turkey', Çiğdem Balım; 'Turkish as a marker of ethnic identity and religious affiliation', Farida Abu-Haidar; and 'Language and ethnopolitics in the ex-Soviet Muslim republics', Jacob M. Landau.

436 **Language and society in the Middle East and North Africa: studies in variation and identity.**
Edited by Yasir Suleiman. Richmond, England: Curzon Press, 1999. 288p.
Covers the issues of collective identity and variation as they relate to language in different fields of social studies. The essays which are related to Turkish in this

volume are: 'The story of a failed attempt: 1997 draft bill on the correct use of Turkish language', Çiğdem Balım; 'Gender in a genderless language: the case of Turkish', Friederike Braun; and 'Language and diaspora: Arabs, Turks and Greeks', Jacob M. Landau.

437   *Irk bitig*: the book of omens.
Talat Tekin. Wiesbaden, Germany: Otto Harrassowitz, 1993. 133p.
Irk bitig is the only Old Turkic text written in the runic script and in the form of a book. It was written in the 'Manichean dialect', and although it cannot be precisely dated, it was probably written in the 9th century AD. After an introduction to the origins of the text and previous studies on it, Tekin provides an English translation, a study of the lexicon, and a glossary followed by the facsimiles of the book's pages.

Turkish and other Muslim minorities of Bulgaria.
See item no. 348.

Wisdom of royal glory (Ḳutaḍġu bilig): a Turko-Islamic mirror for princes.
See item no. 1066.

American Association of Teachers of Turkic Languages (AATT) Bulletin.
See item no. 1310.

Çağdaş Türk Dili. (Contemporary Turkish language.)
See item no. 1324.

Dil Dergisi. Language Journal.
See item no. 1327.

Dilbilim Araştırmaları Dergisi. (Journal of Linguistic Research.)
See item no. 1328.

Journal of Turkish Studies. Türklük Bilgisi Araştırmaları.
See item no. 1339.

Turkic Linguistics Post (TULIP).
See item no. 1365.

Turkic Languages.
See item no. 1366.

Türk Dili. (Turkish Language.)
See item no. 1385.

Türk Dilleri Araştırmaları. Researches on Turkic Languages.
See item no. 1386.

Türkiye, Türkler ve Türk dili bibliyografyası. (Bibliography of Turkey, Turks and the Turkish language.)
See item no. 1410.

Religion

438 **The rise of Islamic fundamentalism and its institutional framework.**
Sencer Ayata. In: *Political and socioeconomic transformation of Turkey*. Edited by A. Eralp, M. Tünay, B. Yeşilada. New York: Praeger Press, 1993, p. 51-69.

The author analyses the rise of Islamic fundamentalism in the context of relationships between the institutional spheres of religion, economy, education, and politics. The militancy of the Islamic media may signal further developments in the politicization of Islam in Turkey.

439 **The development of secularism in Turkey.**
Niyazi Berkes. London: Hurst & Co., 1997. 537p. bibliog.

This is a reprint of the 1964 edition, but it is still the only major work which concentrates purely on the secularization of Islam from the 18th century until the founding of the Republic. The work is important not just because of the quality of its writing, but also because it proclaims the continuity of the secularist tradition through the late (but still theocratic) Ottoman Empire into the Republic.

440 **Agha, sheik, and state.**
M. van Bruinessen. London: Zed Books, 1992. 373p. bibliog.

This work is not ostensibly about religion, but is rather a social study of eastern Anatolia, which gives the most detailed, comprehensive and credible analysis of the role played by the *tarikats* in tribal areas. It puts forward the important argument that the influence played by the religious sheik increases as the power of the centre declines. A chapter describes more specifically the role of the Nakshibendi tarikat in the area. The author is deeply influenced by E. Gellner, though this is scarcely acknowledged.

441 **The seed and the soil: gender cosmology in Turkish village society.**
Carol Delaney. Berkeley, California: University of California Press,
1991. 360p. bibliog.

An interesting work based on fieldwork carried out in a Turkish village outside
Ankara in 1980. The author's argument is that there is a deep cultural and religious
patterning whereby men regard women as 'fields' to be fertilized by their sperm.
According to Delaney, the implication of this is that the creative spark in procreation
is regarded as being provided by males, whilst the women are relegated to the role of
nurturing the growing foetus.

442 **Islam as a factor of change and revival in modern Turkey.**
Paul Dumont. In: *Turkic culture: continuity and change.* Edited by
Sabri M. Akural. Bloomington, Indiana: Indiana University Turkish
Studies, 1987, p. 126-58.

The author discusses how 'official' Islam in Turkey (as opposed to 'freelance' Islam)
has been transformed into a tool for spreading Republican ideals.

443 **Christianity and Islam under the sultans.**
F. W. Hasluck, edited by Margaret M. Hasluck. New York: Octagon
Books, 1973. 2 vols. bibliog.

Hasluck worked as a librarian at the British School at Athens, served in Greece in
intelligence during the First World War, and died in a Swiss sanatorium. His wife
edited his assorted papers which were based on numerous visits to Anatolia. His
Greek experience, combined with a sound background in classical scholarship (he was
a fellow of King's College, Cambridge), led him to a fascination with the Christian
past of Anatolia. He was also the product of an intellectual climate which was interested in the diffusion and inheritance of cultural characteristics. This research resulted
in a mass of material concerned with shrines common to both Islam and Christianity,
the longevity of folk beliefs and unorthodox religious practices. Anglo-Saxon
academia declared this approach out of court until very recently but Hasluck's un-
polished mixture of folklore, rumour, scholarship, legend and ethnography is now a
fascinating treasure trove for those who are trying to understand better the neglected
topic of Anatolia's second and most thorough transition from Christianity to Islam.

444 **Islamic World Report.**
London: Islamic World Report, 1996. vol. 1, no. 3, 133p.

The third issue of this new periodical is largely devoted to religion in Turkey and is
entitled 'Turkey: the pendulum swings back'. The diverse articles by Ş. Mardin,
C. Mansel, A. Algar and D. Shankland (among others) are all well informed by the
recent rise in Islam in Turkey. No answers are offered, but the authors do attempt to
sketch out the way that this Islamic resurgence will begin to influence Turkish society
in areas as diverse as economics, politics, nationalism, and international relations.

Religion

445 **Alevism in Turkey and comparable syncretistic religious communities in the Near East in the past and present.**
Edited by K. Kehl-Bodrogi, B. Kellner-Heinkele, A. Otter-Beaujean. Leiden, the Netherlands: E. J. Brill, 1997. 255p. bibliog. (Studies in the History of Religions, no. 76).
This volume brings together the collected papers of the international symposium of the same name, held in Berlin (14-17 April 1995). The text is in English, German and French.

446 **Religion and social change in modern Turkey: the case of Bediüzzaman Said Nursi.**
Şerif Mardin.   Albany, New York: State University of New York Press, 1989. 267p. bibliog.
The masterpiece of one of the most distinguished writers on religion in modern Turkey. In it, the author attempts to place the life of Said Nursi (Islamic scholar, 1876-1960) within its social context, interweaving analysis of Nursi's religious philosophy with succinct, illuminating comments on the final period of the Ottoman Empire and the subsequent development of the Republic. There is a slight lack of ethnographic (as distinct from textual or documentary) material, but in spite of this, this is a valuable book, which will influence much future research on the development of religion in modern Turkey.

447 **Bektashis in Turkey.**
J. D. Norton.   In: *Islam in the modern world.*   Edited by Denis MacEoin, Ahmed Al-Shahi.   London: Croom Helm, 1983, p. 73-87.
This chapter outlines the development of this Sufi order, especially since the founding of the Republic of Turkey, and assesses the nature of Bektashi activity and allegiance in the 1980s. Attendance at the mid-August festivals in Hacıbektaş and visits to the *tekke* (dervish lodge) show that the order has survived the ban which made it illegal after 1925.

448 **Alevi identity. Cultural, religious and social perspectives.**
Edited by Tord Olsson, Elisabeth Özdalga, Catharina Raudvere. Richmond, England: Curzon Press, 1998. 188p. (Swedish Research Institute in Istanbul).
The articles in the book address social and political issues related to Alevi religious and cultural identity in Turkey.

449 **Official secularism, popular Islam and the veiling issue in Modern Turkey.**
Elisabeth Özdalga.   Richmond, England: Curzon Press, 1997. 128p. (NIAS Reports, no. 33).
While focusing on the issue of veiling in Turkey, the author considers a wider picture of tension between official secularism and popular Islam in present-day Turkey. She argues that the fact that the Islamic movements are on the rise does not mean that they threaten the foundations of modern Turkish society.

450   **Diverse paths of change: Alevi and Sunni in rural Anatolia.**
David Shankland.   In: *Culture and the economy: changes in Turkish
villages*.   Edited by Paul Stirling.   Huntingdon, England: The Eothen
Press, 1994, p. 46-64.

This article is concerned with the contemporary place of religion in society. The
author attempts to show that the Sunni belief and practices in rural Anatolia are able to
modernize more easily than the Alevis, leading to quite different ethics of modernization.
The article also contains a description of an Alevi collective ritual, central to their
religious philosophy, in which peoples' conflicts are resolved through a prescription
on conflict.

451   **Islam in modern Turkey: religion, politics and literature in a
secular state.**
Edited by Richard Tapper.   London: I. B. Tauris, 1991. 307p. bibliog.

The book brings a multi-dimensional perspective to contemporary issues in Turkey in
the context of Islam. Part one discusses the treatment of both Islam and nationalism as
political ideologies in recent Turkish history; part two deals with the different aspects
of the production of Islamic knowledge in Turkey; and part three dwells on Islamic
revivalism.

The forbidden modern: civilization and veiling.
See item no. 491.

**Becoming the 'other' as a muslim in Turkey: Turkish women vs islamist
women.**
See item no. 499.

Living Islam: women, politics and religion in Turkey.
See item no. 500.

Women in modern Turkish society. A reader.
See item no. 504.

Women and fundamentalism.
See item no. 505.

Islam and political development in Turkey.
See item no. 588.

Political Islam and the Welfare (Refah) Party in Turkey.
See item no. 589.

**The political economy of Islamic resurgence in Turkey: the rise of the
Welfare Party in perspective.**
See item no. 756.

Social Conditions

452 The socio-economic aspects of return migration in Turkey.
Nermin Abadan-Unat. *Migration*, no. 3 (1988), p. 29-59.
This paper examines return migration from Europe to Turkey between 1973 and 1985, including returns caused by both official pressure and individual choice.

453 Rethinking modernity and national identity in Turkey.
Edited by Sibel Bozdoğan, Reşat Kasaba.   Seattle, Washington:
University of Washington Press, 1997. 270p.
The aim of the contributions to this volume is to examine the extent to which Turkey can incorporate both its commitment to modernity and its traditionalism. According to the editors, in order to understand the complexity of modernity in Turkey, a multi-disciplinary approach is necessary. The contributions include: 'Kemalist certainties and modern ambiguities', Reşat Kasaba; 'Whither the project of modernity? Turkey in the 1990s', Çağlar Keyder; 'Modernization policies and Islamist politics in Turkey', Haldun Gülalp; 'Project as methodology: some thoughts on Modern Turkish social science', Şerif Mardin; 'The quest for the Islamic self within the context of modernity', Nilüfer Göle; 'The project of modernity and women in Turkey', Yeşim Arat; 'Gendering the modern: on missing dimensions in the study of Turkish modernity', Deniz Kandiyoti; 'The predicament of modernism in Turkish architectural culture: an overview', Sibel Bozdoğan; 'Once there was, once there wasn't: national monuments and interpersonal exchange', Michael Meeker; 'Silent interruptions: urban encounters with rural Turkey', Gülsüm Baydar Nalbantoğlu; 'Arabesk culture: a case of modernization and popular identity', Meral Özbek; 'The Turkish option in comparative perspective', Ernest Gellner; 'Modernizing projects in Middle Eastern perspective', Roger Owen; and 'Finding the meeting ground of fact and fiction: some reflections on Turkish modernization', Joel S. Migdal.

454 **Crowds and public order policing: an analysis of crowds and interpretations of their behaviour based on observational studies in England, Wales and Turkey.**
İbrahim Cerrah.   Aldershot, England: Ashgate Publishing Group, 1998. 268p.

Analyses crowds and their behaviour based on observational studies of thirty-three crowd events in England, Wales and Turkey between 1992 and 1995. All the events involved large police deployment. There are also interviews with key figures who are involved in police public order training.

455 **İstanbul households: marriage, family and fertility, 1880-1940.**
Alan Duben, Cem Behar.   Cambridge, England: Cambridge University Press, 1991. 276p. bibliog. (Cambridge Studies in Population, Economy and Society in Past Times, no. 15).

A systematic historical study of the family and population in Turkey. Combining the methods and approaches of social anthropology, historical demography and social history, the authors construct a social history of marriage, family and population in İstanbul during the transition period from empire to republic. Using census records, marriage registers, archives, private papers, contemporary periodicals, travel accounts, novels, biographies and retrospective interviews, they reconstruct İstanbul's social and economic conditions. The authors show how İstanbul set the tone for many social and cultural changes in Turkey and the Muslim world.

456 **Turkish state, Turkish society.**
Edited by Andrew Finkel, Nükhet Sirman.   London; New York: Routledge, for SOAS Centre of Near and Middle Eastern Studies, 1990. 312p.

This collection of papers bridges the gap between political and sociological studies. The contributions cover issues of state and gender in village society, the Turkish army in politics during the 1960s and early 1970s, the 'Grey Wolves' (an ultra-nationalist youth organization), the 1987 elections and constitutional issues, class and clientalism, municipal politics, the politics of economic development strategies, women's associations, and tribal organization and politics in a Kurdish rural community.

457 **Tea and the domestication of the Turkish state.**
Chris M. Hann.   Huntingdon, England: The Eothen Press, 1990. 106p. bibliog.

A study of tea-growing in north-east Turkey, which traces the social, economic and political effects of the development of this industry.

458 **Peasant struggles and social change: migration, households and gender in a rural Turkish society.**
Suzan M. Ilcan.   *International Migration Review*, vol. 28, no. 3 (1994), p. 554-79.

The author has chosen the Saklı community in north-east Turkey to illustrate the inter-relationship between seasonal migration, subsistence production and peasant relations.

This case-study shows that migration can be experienced as a transgressor of hierarchies but at the same time as an expander of tradition.

459 **Blood feud in Turkey. A sociological analysis.**
Tülin Günşen İçli. *The British Journal of Criminology*, vol. 34, no. 1 (1994), p. 69-74.

This article focuses on blood feud in the eastern and south-eastern regions of Turkey. The study indicates that most of the murders were committed with a gun, and the majority of the subjects have low educational status and large families, with farming being the main occupation. The main causes of murders are disputes over land and water supplies, and matters of honour, or abduction.

460 **The paradox of Turkish nationalism and the construction of official identity.**
Ayşe Kadıoğlu. *Middle Eastern Studies*, vol. 32, no. 2 (1996), p. 177-93.

The author discusses the 'paradox' of Turkish nationalism and the role of the state elites during the single-party regime, in manufacturing an official republican ideology.

461 **Sex roles, family and community in Turkey.**
Edited by Çiğdem Kağıtçıbaşı. Bloomington, Indiana: Indiana University Press, 1982. 414p. bibliog. (Turkish Studies, no. 3).

An important collection of essays which use a micro-analytical approach to understand the nature of complex interrelations between the sexes in Turkey. Some of the topics covered are: the construction of the myth of extended family; women's place in Turkey until the 1980s; double standards concerning the education of women; the value given to children relating to attitudes about fertility; the 'working woman' and the delicate power relations between men and women in the Turkish family; migration and its effects on women's roles in Turkey; the evolution of the economic function of the family in three consecutive decades; the changing structures of a village (Taşköprü) in the western Marmara region; the psychopathological aspects of the inward dynamics of the Turkish family; and crime and patterns of homicide according to gender.

462 **Gecekondu: rural migration and urbanization.**
Kemal H. Karpat. London; New York; Melbourne: Cambridge University Press, 1976. 291p. bibliog.

The study investigates the migration and urbanization of the people in the settlements outside urban centres (*gecekondu*) in the 1970s. It is based on fieldwork carried out in the northern hills of İstanbul along the Bosphorus. It covers the *gecekondu* in comparative perspective, the historical roots of migration in Turkey, the establishment and the growth of the *gecekondu*, its social and economic structure, the urbanization of the *gecekondu*, village relations and rural change, politics and party affiliation. It is a useful study for social historians.

463 Social and economic aspects of decision making related to labor
     utilization and choice of technology: a case study of a Turkish
     village.
     H. Kasnakoğlu, H. Akder, A. A. Gürkan, N. Sirman, N. Ekinci,
     M. Ecevit. In: *Labor, employment and agricultural development in
     west Asia and north Africa.* Edited by Dennis Tully. Boston,
     Massachusetts: Kluwer Academic Publishers, 1990, p. 55-78.

The coexistence and competition of irrigated and rain-fed farming pose problems for
the agricultural policy, which stem from the image of economic development that is
associated with irrigation and modern technology. Rain-fed farming is usually
neglected by researchers as a symbol of traditional farming. Kınık, the village studied
in this article, symbolizes the rain-fed farming aspects of Anatolia, and team work. As
such, it represents a beginning for the modern study of traditional means of agriculture.

464 Paths of rural transformation in Turkey.
     Çağlar Keyder. In: *The Middle East.* Edited by Talat Asad, Roger
     Owen. London: Macmillan Press, 1983, p. 163-77. (Sociology of
     Developing Societies Series).

This chapter describes the multiplicity of development paths which can be observed in
the transformation of agriculture in the context of five villages, which represent
various parts of Turkey, and different dynamics of agricultural change.

465 Outline of a practical theory of football violence.
     Anthony King. *Sociology*, vol. 29, no. 4 (1995), p. 635-51.

An analysis of an incident of football violence that occurred at the Hotel Tamsa in
İstanbul in 1993, the night before a European Cup game between Manchester United
and Galatasaray. The author concludes that structural and objective factors are insufficient in explaining the occurrence of football violence. The national and
masculine consciousness of certain Manchester United fans, and the political context
and ideological condition of the Turkish state are seen as preconditions for the
violence.

466 Anatolia's loom: studies in Turkish culture, society, politics and
     law.
     Paul J. Magnarella. İstanbul: The ISIS Press, 1998. 279p. map.
     bibliog. (Analecta Isisiana, no. 28).

A collection of the author's twenty-one previously published essays, brought together
with an introduction in five headings: 'Anthropology in Turkey and the Mediterranean'; 'Family, kinship and society'; 'Customs, peoples, and lives in change'; 'Politics
and society'; and 'Law and society'.

467 **Culture, change and the intellectual: a study of the effects of secularization in Modern Turkey.**
Şerif Mardin. In: *Cultural transitions in the Middle East.* Edited by Şerif Mardin. Leiden, the Netherlands: Brill, 1993, p. 189-214.

The links between the media, changing social and cultural structures and practices, and Islam are masterfully analysed through the 'poet' figure, exemplified by Necip Fazıl Kısakürek, and Nazım Hikmet Ran.

468 **Agrarian change: 1923-70.**
Ronnie Margulies, Ergin Yıldızoğlu. In: *Turkey in transition: new perspectives.* Edited by Irvin C. Schick, Ertuğrul Ahmet Tonak. Oxford: Oxford University Press, 1987, p. 269-92.

The article elaborates on the development of agriculture throughout the Republican period. The point of taking agriculture as a field for the observation of transition becomes clear, when the duality in the seemingly unchanging pattern and the rapid changing mechanisms is considered.

469 **Turkey: insolvent ideologies, fractured state.**
Middle East Report, vol. 26, no. 199 (1996), 48p.

Articles by distinguished theorists concerning Turkish Islam and the Kurdish question can be found in this issue.

470 **Symposium on İstanbul: past and present.**
Edited by Ferhunde Özbay. *Boğaziçi Journal. Review of Social, Economic and Administrative Studies,* vol. 11, no. 1-2 (1997).

The city of İstanbul is the theme of this important issue of *Boğaziçi Journal.* After an editorial introduction by F. Özbay, the essays include: Cem Behar's 'Fruit vendors and civil servants: a social and demographic portrait of a neighbourhood community in intra-mural İstanbul (The Kasap İlyas Mahalle) in 1885'; Lonas Tanatar-Baruh's 'At the turn of the century textile dealers in an international port city: İstanbul'; Edhem Eldem's 'İstanbul 1903-1918: a quantitative analysis of a bourgeoisie'; Ayşe Buğra's 'Tale of two cities: the evolution of İstanbul businessmen and their relations with the Ankara government'; and Ferhunde Özbay's 'Migration and intra-provincial movements in İstanbul between 1985-1990'.

471 **Turkish families in transition.**
Edited by Gabriele Rasuly-Palaczek. Frankfurt am Main, Germany: Peter Lang Europaischer Verlag der Wissenschaften, 1996. 215p.

The collected papers in this book provide an overview of the structure of Turkish families, and the changes which come about during a process of transition in that structure. The papers trace these changes in rural and urban families as well as migrant Turkish workers' families in Western Europe. The papers by G. Rasuly-Palaczek, M. Meeker, P. Stirling, E. O. İncirlioğlu, and D. Shankland dwell on issues which relate to families in Turkey. A. Güneş-Ayata provides information about domestic migration in Turkey, and compares features of solidarity in different ethnic groups. I. Beller-Hann looks at the Laz community in the Black Sea region. The last three papers by S. Pflegerl, L. Yalçın-Heckmann, and B. Wolbert relate to migrant workers, their families, and their reintegration in Turkey.

472 **Sports structures in Europe. Situation in the countries of the Committee for the Development of Sport of the Council of Europe.**
A. Remans, M. Delforge.   Brussels: The Clearing House, 1997.
4th rev. ed. 586p.

After an introductory chapter, the volume contains an inventory of sports structures in European countries, including Turkey. There are six appendices, which reproduce the Convention on Violence (1985); the Anti-Doping Convention (1992); the European Sports Charter (1992); and the Code of Sports Ethics (1992).

473 **From economic integration to cultural strategies of power: the study of rural change in Turkey.**
Nükhet Sirman.   *New Perspectives on Turkey*, no. 14 (1996),
p. 115-25.

This article reviews most of the studies on rural change in Turkey, revealing a shift from studies oriented towards socioeconomic development and integration to a culture and power oriented approach.

474 **Dispute and settlement in modern Turkey: an ethnography of law.**
June Starr.   Leiden, the Netherlands: E. J. Brill, 1978. 304p. bibliog.

The local settling of disputes in Turkey is studied through an empirical study of one Turkish village, Mandalinci, on the Bodrum peninsula. The book is an example of the study of village social life through conflicting claims, and an ethnography of law.

475 **Turkish village.**
Paul Stirling.   London: Weidenfield & Nicholson, 1965; New York:
John Wiley, 1966. 316p. maps. bibliog.

The two villages of Kayseri – Sakaltutan and Elbaşı – are the subjects of this anthropological, social, political, and economic analysis. It reflects life in Anatolia during the 1960s and is one of the classics of Turkish anthropology.

476 **Culture and the economy: changes in Turkish villages.**
Edited by Paul Stirling.   Huntingdon, England: The Eothen Press,
1993. 231p.

A collection of articles by well known social scientists, who focus on change, and the interpenetrations of the relationship between economy and culture in Turkish villages. After an introduction by Stirling, entitled 'Growth and changes', which outlines the unbelievable performance of growth and development in Turkish villages during a seventy-year period, from the foundation of the Republic to the beginning of the 1990's, the contributors look at the various aspects of this change. The essays in the book are: 'Sheep and money' by Lale Yalçın-Heckmann, about the organization of small-scale illegal animal trade in Hakkari, where an interesting socio-cultural analogy between sheep raising and money is constructed; 'Hazelnuts and lutes' by Martin Stokes, a musical and sociological comparison of two villages in the Black Sea region; 'Alevi and Sunni in rural Anatolia' by David Shankland; 'Peasants without pride' by Werner Schiffauer, on migration patterns, and their social and psychological aspects; 'Gender and household resource management in agriculture' by Behrooz Morvaridi; 'Labour migration among Bursa muhacirs' by Gabriele Palaczek;

Social Conditions

'Marriage gender relations and rural transformation in Central Anatolia' by Emine Onaran İncirlioğlu; 'The sexual division of labour in Lazistan' by Chris Hann; 'Traditional modes of authority and co-operation' by Carol Delaney; 'Rural health-seeking' by Belma T. Akşit; 'The genesis of petty commodity production in agriculture' by Çağlar Keyder; 'Studies in rural transformation in Turkey, 1950-1990' by Bahattin Akşit; and 'Impact of external migration on rural Turkey' by Nermin Abadan-Unat.

477 **'Strong as a Turk': power, performance and representation in Turkish wrestling.**
Martin Stokes. In: *Sport, identity and ethnicity.* Edited by Jeremy MacClancy. Oxford: Berg, 1996, p. 21-41.

The author discusses the influence of wrestling in the politics of Turkey, with reference to the use of the tough-man figure in popular cartoon satirical magazines. He also draws more general conclusions for sports, for example: Turkish wrestling seems to indicate that sport brings people together, and coordinates them in culturally specific ways; the ritualistic aspects of sport focus individuals on collective assumptions; and sport is one means by which a culture addresses the contradictions of everyday life.

478 **Peasants without ploughs: some Anatolians in İstanbul.**
Peter T. Suzuki. *Rural Sociology,* vol. 31, no. 4 (1966), p. 428-38.

Focuses on the villagers of Kırıntı in Anatolia, who migrated to İstanbul. Their transition from rural to urban life, their achievements, and their retention of rural patterns of life in the city are discussed. The features of village life such as mutual aid, endogamy and ritual kinship are considered to be important mechanisms in the villagers' transition to urbanism.

Who lives with whom in İstanbul.
See item no. 297.

Population movements in southeastern Anatolia: some findings of an empirical research in 1993.
See item no. 330.

Migration and urbanization in rural Turkey.
See item no. 333.

The unfinished story: Turkish labour migration to Western Europe, with special reference to the Federal Republic of Germany.
See item no. 340.

The seed and the soil: gender and cosmology in Turkish village society.
See item no. 441.

Money makes us relatives: women's labour in urban Turkey.
See item no. 506.

Turkey: political, social and economic challenges in the 1990s.
See item no. 530.

Turkey and the West: changing political and cultural variables.
See item no. 553.

Small employers in Turkey: the OSTİM estate at Ankara.
See item no. 791.

Structural change in Turkish society.
See item no. 890.

Tradition and change in a Turkish town.
See item no. 892.

The Arabesque debate: music and musicians in modern Turkey.
See item no. 1138.

Boğaziçi Journal. Review of Social, Economic and Administrative Studies.
See item no. 1319.

CEMOTI: Cashiers d'Études sur la Méditerranée Orientale et le Monde Turco-Iranien.
See item no. 1321.

International Journal of Middle Eastern Studies.
See item no. 1333.

The Middle East Journal.
See item no. 1344.

Middle East Review of International Affairs (MERIA).
See item no. 1345.

Middle East Studies Association Bulletin.
See item no. 1346.

New Perspectives on Turkey.
See item no. 1352.

Toplum ve Bilim. (Society and Science.)
See item no. 1363.

Toplumbilim. (Sociology.)
See item no. 1364.

Turkish Review of Middle East Studies.
See item no. 1381.

Turkish Studies Association Bulletin.
See item no. 1382.

Women

479 **Women in the ideology of Islamic revivalism in Turkey: three Islamic women's journals.**
Feride Acar. In: *Islam in modern Turkey: religion, politics and literature in a secular state.* Edited by Richard Tapper. London; New York: I. B. Tauris, 1991, p. 280-301.

This study looks at the revivalism of Islam in Turkey, and considers the issue of women as a major battleground in the struggle between secularists and Islamists. It reports the findings of an analysis of three Islamic monthly journals for women in Turkey, and identifies the similarities and differences on the basis of contents, themes, approaches, and messages.

480 **The patriarchal paradox: women politicians in Turkey.**
Yeşim Arat. Rutherford, New Jersey: Fairleigh Dickinson University Press, 1989. 162p. bibliog.

In a patriarchal society such as Turkey, it is assumed that the unequal power relationship between men and women would work against women, and keep them away from public life. However, the reforms introduced by the male Kemalist intelligentsia allowed a status for women which did not exist even in many western countries at the time. Arat calls this situation the 'patriarchal paradox', and shows that the reforms were a part of a broader project to westernize and secularize social life. Within this context, she then proceeds to analyse female politicians after the foundation of the Republic in 1923.

481 **Toward a democratic society: the women's movements in Turkey in the 1980s.**
Yeşim Arat. *Women's Studies International Forum*, vol. 17, no. 2/3 (1994), p. 241-48.

The author explains how the women's movements played a unique role in the process of redemocratization in Turkey throughout the 1980s. The movements did not merely grant more women the opportunity to participate in politics through grassroots organizations, but also helped them by extending the political space allotted to civil society. Within the context of a statist polity, feminist women upheld individualism. Organized independent of, and in opposition to the state, these women generated power through civil society.

482 Deconstructing images of 'the Turkish woman'.
Edited by Zehra F. Arat.   New York: St. Martin's Press, 1998. 292p.

This collection of essays seeks to combat the efforts to push Turkish women into a particular prototype. The multi-disciplinary study includes papers on political science, economics, business, ethnography, history, and literature, the common theme of which is the changes and continuities in the images of Turkish women from the late 19th century to the present.

483 State policy in the 1990s and the future of women's rights in Turkey.
Günseli Berik.   *New Perspectives on Turkey*, no. 4 (1990), p. 81-96.

The 1980s witnessed the rise of feminist and Islamic movements in Turkey. In diametrically opposed ways, both movements pushed the debate on women's status in society into the spotlight of public discussion. In response to the heightened debate concerning women's status, in the latter half of the 1980s the government put legal measures into effect, creating legal obligations at international level and institutional structures to address issues concerning women. Berik's article scrutinizes these measures, and explains how these measures in effect signal a threat to the future of women's rights in Turkey.

484 Symposium on gender and society.
Boğaziçi University.   *Boğaziçi Journal, Review of Social, Economic and Administrative Sciences*, special issue, vol. 8, no. 1-2 (1994).

A collection of essays on gender and society in Turkey, which examine various aspects of womanhood and femininity. The contributions include: 'Women's labor in rural urban settings', Ferhunde Özbay; 'Some observations on the position of women in the labor market in the development process of Turkey', Şemsa Özar; 'Organizational characteristics as correlates of women in the middle and top management', Hayat Kabasakal, Nakiye Boyacıgiller, Deniz Erden; 'Female participation in the Turkish university administration: econometric and survey findings, 1992', Gülay Günlük Şenesen; 'Liberalization or introdoctrination: women's education in Turkey', Zehra F. Arat; 'Women in the legislature', Ayşe Güneş Ayata; 'Purple Roof Women's Labor Foundation: democratic aspirations in institution building', Yeşim Arat; 'The image of women in Turkish television commercials (1991-93)', Perran Akan; and 'A model of gender relations in the Turkish family', E. Olcay İmamoğlu.

485 The Ottoman lady.
Fanny Davis.   New York: Greenwood Press, 1986. 321p. bibliog.

The study of upper-class Ottoman women is a much neglected subject, probably due to lack of sources. The Ottomans did not write about their women, therefore it has been necessary to use western sources. This book makes use of two sources: western women observers; and the surviving members of Ottoman families, their memories of the last decades of the Ottoman Empire, and family archives. The book shows that especially after the 15th century, the public role of women in the Ottoman Empire was increasingly coming to an end. However, this should not lead one to think that the Ottoman woman was a prisoner. Within limitations, she was the centre of considerable activity, and she was influential, although this influence was not openly wielded.

486 **Supporting women owned business in Turkey.**
Development Alternatives, Inc. and The Strategic Research Foundation.   Bethesda, Maryland: Development Alternatives Inc. & The Strategic Research Foundation, 1995. 200p. bibliog. (A report prepared for the Republic of Turkey, Ministry for Women's Affairs and Social Services, Directorate General on the Status and Problems of Women).

The study was carried out by a team of international and Turkish experts. The report provides a conceptual and analytic framework to guide the Government of Turkey in developing a project that would increase the number of female-headed small businesses.

487 **The report prepared in accordance with article eighteen of the Convention on the Elimination of All forms of Discrimination against Women.**
Directorate General on the Status and Problems of Women.   Ankara: Prime Ministry, 1993. 65p.

A second report on the legislative, administrative, judicial and other measures provided by Turkey towards the effectiveness of the Convention's clauses and also the establishment of its progress.

488 **The status of women in Turkey.**
Directorate General on the Status and Problems of Women.   Ankara: Prime Ministry, 1994. 69p.

This is the text of the Turkish national report to the fourth world conference on women. It contains twelve tables of figures, and useful factual information.

489 **Women in statistics.**
Directorate General on the Status and Problems of Women.   Ankara: UNICEF, 1995. 15p. (Republic of Turkey Ministry of State, Directorate General on the Status and Problems of Women & Prime Ministry, State Institute of Statistics).

A colourful little booklet, which provides facts and figures concerning women in Turkey. The text is short and to the point, and the statistics simplified. This constitutes a very good basic information source.

490 **The women of Turkey and their folklore, with an ethnographical map and introductory chapters on the ethnography of Turkey.**
Lucy Mary Jane Garnett. London: David Nutt, 1890. 2 vols. map.
The book deals with women of varying religious and ethnic backgrounds of the Ottoman Empire: Christians, including Vlach, Greek, Armenian, Bulgarian and Frank women; Jewish women; and Muslims, including Kurdish, Circassian, Yürük, Albanian, Tatar and Gypsy women. Each section provides information on their social status and activities, family ceremonies, beliefs and superstitions, occupations, culture and amusements.

491 **The forbidden modern: civilization and veiling.**
Nilüfer Göle. Ann Arbor, Michigan: University of Michigan Press, 1996. 173p. bibliog.
The major concern of this book is the East/West opposition which has been shaped to a great extent by the orientalist discourse. The 'woman' question, that is the debate over women's position and their status in society, has always been at the centre of the opposition between the eastern and western civilizations. The modernizing elites of the Ottoman Empire and the Turkish Republic tried to improve women's position in order to overcome that opposition, and nowadays the discourse of political Islam focuses on the status of women in order to emphasize the difference and incompatibility between them. The author claims that the veiling of women is a politicized practice that conceptually forces people to choose between the 'modern' and the 'backward', and that it also provides an insightful way of looking at contemporary Islam-West conflict, and sheds light on what is a more complex phenomenon than is commonly portrayed.

492 **Disseminating health information to women in Turkey.**
Hacettepe Institute of Population Studies. Ankara: Hacettepe University Institute of Population Studies, 1994. 66p.
This report details the results of a field survey conducted in 1991 by Hacettepe Institute of Population Studies. It scrutinizes the effectiveness of the media (radio, television, the press, and other forms of communication, including sermons delivered at mosques, teachers serving in rural parts of the country) with respect to their approach to maternal child-health issues such as consanguineous marriages, prenatal care and child birth, swaddling, breast feeding, supplementary food and health controls, immunization, diarrhoea, and information and practice on family planning.

493 **Turkey: women in development.**
Prepared by Sandra Hadler. Washington, DC: World Bank, 1993. 205p. bibliog. (A World Bank Country Study).
The report gives factual information about the situation of women in Turkey, including legal and health issues, and examines government strategy to increase the involvement of women in national policies and programmes. The main focus is on developing women's participation in the labour force by improving relevant education and training. More than half of the report consists of tables and charts, and there is a substantial bibliography.

494 **Women's subordination in Turkey: is Islam really the villain?**
Ayşe Kadıoğlu. *Middle East Journal*, vol. 48, no. 4 (1994),
p. 445-60.

The author explains how the ever-deepening rift between political Islamists and the westernized, native secularists has crystallized over the issue of veiling. She claims that the categories that constitute the clash between them do not emerge from the native home context nor are they exclusively Islamic, rather they reflect the struggle over the identity of women.

495 **End of empire: Islam, nationalism and women in Turkey.**
Deniz Kandiyoti. In: *Women, Islam and the state.* Edited by Deniz
Kandiyoti. London: McMillan, 1991, p. 22-47.

Examines the relationship between Islam, the nature of state projects, and the position of women in the modern nation states of the Middle East and South Asia. The chapter on Turkey traces the transformation that the country went through in the transition from a multi-ethnic empire to a secular nation state. The author shows how the appearance of women as objects of political discourse and as political actors and citizens was intimately bound up with the changing nature of the Ottoman/Turkish polity.

496 **Gendering the Middle East.**
Edited by Deniz Kandiyoti. London: I. B. Tauris, 1996. 177p.
bibliog.

Gender-aware scholarship has made remarkable inroads into the social sciences and humanities, and has prompted a critique and re-evaluation of the central analytic categories of most disciplines. Studies on women in the Middle East contribute to the advancement of women's studies in Turkey, and therefore it is useful to read this volume, which is an attempt to evaluate the extent to which gender analysis has succeeded in both informing and challenging established views of culture, society, and literacy in the Middle East.

497 **A world of difference: Islam and gender hierarchy in Turkey.**
Julie Marcus. London: Zed Books, 1992. 201p.

Offers a new theoretical analysis of the relationship between religious beliefs and the structuring of gender hierarchies. Central to the book is an exploration of the politics of knowledge. The author maintains that history and the difference between cultures must take account of feminist critiques of knowledge, which demonstrate that gender is the hidden factor essential to constructing a racialized east, and sexualized, eroticized Orient. An analysis of popular and scholarly travel writing illustrates how women and sexuality play a crucial role in the subordination of the East to West.

498 **The imperial harem: women and sovereignty in the Ottoman
Empire.**
Leslie P. Peirce. New York; Oxford: Oxford University Press, 1993.
374p. bibliog. (Studies in Middle Eastern History).

The main argument of the book is that changes in the nature of Ottoman state and society in the 16th and 17th centuries have increased royal women's participation in various demonstrations of sovereignty. In the first part of the book, the author challenges the general belief that in traditional Islamic society, gender segregation made women play only a subordinate role within the household. She argues that the segregation of sexes has led to a hierarchy of status and authority among women, which paralleled the one that existed among men. In the second part, she looks at the nature of Ottoman sovereignty.

499 Becoming the 'other' as a muslim in Turkey: Turkish women vs islamist women.

Ayşe Saktanber. *New Perspectives on Turkey,* no. 11 (1994), p. 99-134.

One of the consequences of the re-Islamification of modern Turkey is that the traditionally private role played by women in the creation of the religious tradition is becoming more public. In urban Turkey today, women identify themselves publicly as Islamic through their dress, demeanour, and often through political activity. In this article, the author brings out the complexities of such 'coming out', in that it can be interpreted at once as being in the sway of religion and emancipation. She stresses the partial success of the orthodox feminist movement.

500 Living Islam: women, politics and religion in Turkey.

Ayşe Saktanber. London: I. B. Tauris, 1998. 256p.

The author attempts to answer the following questions: how and why women have come to play a central role in the political project of Islamic revivalism, and in the power struggles between Islamic and secular forces in Turkey; and what Islam means for the position of women. She deals with families who have come together 'to live Islam' as 'conscious Muslims' in a suburb of Ankara.

501 Forced prostitution in Turkey: women in the 'genelev's (whorehouse).

Anne-Marie Sharman. London: Anti-Slavery International, 1993. 43p. (ASI Human Right Series, no. 6).

A report by Anti-Slavery International. ASI accepts that Turkey is one of the countries that has formally legalized the practice of prostitution, but is concerned for the coercive aspects of the system currently in operation in Turkey. The report is based on the results derived from interviews with twelve prostitutes who work in two major brothels, and with nineteen external sources, whose occupations give them some familiarity with the various conditions which affect the lives of prostitutes in Turkey.

502 Feminism in Turkey: a short history.

Nükhet Sirman. *New Perspectives on Turkey,* vol. 3 (1989), p. 1-34.

The author gives a concise and insightful account of the debates over the position of women in Turkish society from the middle of the 19th century to the present. The last part of the article dwells exclusively on women's movement in the 1980s, and the political demands articulated by these women, and she tries to define those parameters that may constitute feminism in contemporary Turkey.

503 **Women in statistics, 1927-1992.**
State Institute of Statistics (SIS). Ankara: State Institute of Statistics, 1992. 260p.
Provides a historical perspective on the status of women in Turkey relative to men. The statistics given include the age and gender structure of the population, education, marital status, economic activity, fertility, marriage and divorce characteristics, mortality, schooling rates, teachers, labour force participation rates, unemployment, convictions and political participation.

504 **Women in modern Turkish society. A reader.**
Edited by Şirin Tekeli. London: Zed Books, 1995. 324p.
The volume contains eighteen essays by prominent Turkish social scientists, following an introductory section by the editor. The authors and topics include: Nora Şeni on women's clothing and satire at the end of the 19th century; Feride Acar and Yeşim Arat on Islam and women, especially in the context of women's magazines; F. Yıldız Ecevit, Ferhunde Özbay and Günseli Berik on the female labour force; Fatma Gök on education; Yakın Ertürk on rural women and modernization; Ayşe Saktanber on the representation of women in the media; Hale Cihan Bolak on working-class married women as breadwinners; Nükhet Sirman on a case-study of a village and women's networks; Lale Yalçın-Heckmann on gender roles among the Kurdish tribes of Turkey; Ayşe Güneş-Ayata on women's participation in politics; Fatmagül Berktay on the Turkish Left and women; Nilüfer Çağatay and Yasemin Nuhoğlu-Soysal on feminism and nation-building process; Şahika Yüksel on domestic violence; Arşalus Kayır on sexual problems in Turkey; and Deniz Kandiyoti on patriarchy patterns in Turkey.

505 **Women and fundamentalism.**
Binnaz Toprak. In: *Identity politics and women: cultural reservations and feminism in international perspective.* Edited by Valentine Moghadam. London: Westview Press, 1994, p. 292-304.
The author claims that Islamic fundamentalist politics reflect a struggle to redefine women's status in Turkish society. The general characteristics of the Islamic movement in Turkey, which have been transmitted into identity politics, are especially visible in relation to the gender question. What differentiates the goals of Islamic fundamentalist movement from secular political alternatives is its demand to shape social organization and economic structure on Islamic principles. Central to its vision is its view of the family and of women, which is intimately connected with Islamic definitions of morality and community life. The movement sees the Muslim society's conception of women as its defining characteristic.

506 **Money makes us relatives: women's labour in urban Turkey.**
Jenny B. White. Austin, Texas: University of Texas Press, 1994. 162p. bibliog.
The aim of the book is to make visible certain interconnections within the lives of urban dwellers who share characteristics of gender and class and who participate in some form of small-scale commodity production. The book is based on two years of anthropological fieldwork carried out in İstanbul, among peasant families who have migrated to the city and live in *gecekondu* (squatter) districts and in poor working-class neighbourhoods.

507 **Women in the Ottoman Empire. Middle Eastern women in the
early modern era.**
Edited by Madeline C. Zilfi.   Leiden, the Netherlands: E. J. Brill,
1997. 312p. bibliog. (Ottoman Empire and its Heritage, no. 10).
A collection of essays by fourteen historians, who attempt to reconstruct the history of
Muslim women's experience in the Ottoman Empire between the 17th and 19th
centuries prior to the westernization movements in the Empire.

The private world of Ottoman women.
See item no. 227.

Migration and reintegration in rural Turkey: the role of women behind.
See item no. 332.

The seed and the soil: gender cosmology in Turkish village society.
See item no. 441.

Sex roles, family and community in Turkey.
See item no. 461.

**Women and household production: the impact of rural transformation
in Turkey.**
See item no. 844.

**Kadın süreli yayınları bibliyografyası: 1928-1996. Hanımlar Âlemi'nden
Roza'ya.** (A bibliography of women's periodicals: 1928-96. From 'The World
of Women' to 'Roza'.)
See item no. 1409.

Health and Welfare

508 Contraception, abortion and maternal health services in Turkey.
Edited by Ayşe Akın, Münevver Bertan. Calverton, Maryland:
Demographic and Health Surveys Macro International Inc., 1996.
136p. bibliog. (Ministry of Health, Hacettepe University Institute of
Population Studies, and Demographic and Health Surveys Macro
International Inc.).

The book is based on the 1993 Turkish demographic and health survey data, and
analyses contraceptive prevalence, contraceptive dynamics, induced abortion, and the
utilization of maternal health services in Turkey.

**509 Socio-cultural determinants of infant and child mortality in
Turkey.**
Belma T. Akşit, Bahattin Akşit. *Social Sciences and Medicine*,
vol. 28, no. 6 (1989), p. 571-76.

Attempts to review and integrate international and Turkish research on infant and
child mortality. According to the authors, existing studies in Turkey seem to suggest
that mother's and father's education link socio-economic, psychocultural, and biomedical
variables with each other at the community, household, and individual level, providing
clues for the formulation of future research designs and policy decisions.

**510 Community participation in primary health care: an
anthropological action research in a squatter-housing district of
Antalya.**
Belma T. Akşit, Bahattin Akşit. Ankara: UNICEF, 1994. 23p.
bibliog.

This report is based on a study of the Turkish predicament of community participation
in primary health care, and in family planning in the poor urban districts of Third
World countries. The advantages of community participation lie in its consolidation of

the democratic rights of citizens, and its enhancement of the status of women as well as its role in reducing infant/child mortality levels. The paper reports the findings of an anthropological action research which led to the expansion of women's health education and other organizational networks in a squatter housing district of a city in Turkey.

511 **Mother's education, differential child valuation and infant/child mortality: a review of literature and conceptual framework.**
Bahattin Akşit, Belma T. Akşit. In: *Mother's education and child survival.* Edited by John Simons, Leela Visaria, Peter Berman. Delhi: Vikas Publishing House, 1997, p. 128-36. bibliog.
The authors review Turkish and international literature on the effect of mother's education on family planning, valuation of children and gender differentials for their survival. They also discuss transformations in family structures and infant/child survival in the contexts of Islamic beliefs and secularization.

512 **The nature and extent of drug abuse in İstanbul: rapid assessment study, 1996.**
AMATEM Team (Y. Akdavar, J. Aral. S. Aytaçlar, D. Çakmak, A. Karalı, A. Türkcan) and Hacettepe Halk Sağlığı Vakfı (Belma T. Akşit, Selen Onaran). Vienna: United Nations Drug Contol Programme (UNDCP), 1996. 5 vols. bibliog.
These five volumes of reports give the results of 'The Nature and Extent of Drug Abuse in İstanbul' project, which was conducted jointly by Hacettepe University and a team from the Alcohol and Drug Addiction Research and Treatment Centre (AMATEM). The project involved qualitative studies, and comprised four phases as reflected in the titles of the reports; the assessment of the second-hand data about drug abuse in Turkey; methodology development studies; the qualitative study; and quantitative research. The final report summarizes the findings of all the phases of the project.

513 **Prenatal, neonatal, and under-five mortality in İstanbul based on representative samples on burial records.**
Ayşen Bulut, Gülbin Gökçay, Olcay Neyzi, Frederic Shorter. In: *Measurement of maternal and child mortality, morbidity and health care: interdisciplinary approaches.* Edited by J. Ties Boerma. Liege, Belgium: Editions Derouaux-Ordina, 1992, p. 153-73.
The Institute of Child Health at İstanbul University assessed the extent to which current data can be obtained from the city's burial records for the period 1987-88. The aim, which was to a large extent achieved, was to categorize deaths below the age of five by age, sex, place and cause in order to identify 'soft spots' in İstanbul, to enable targeted improvement in health care.

514 **Health and social inequalities in Turkey.**
Necati Dedoğlu. In: *Social Science and Medicine*, vol. 31, no. 3
(1990), p. 387-92.
This paper sets out to demonstrate the negative effects of recent governmental policies
on the health of the Turkish population.

515 **Abortion in Turkey: a matter of state, family or individual
decision.**
Akile Gürsoy. *Social Science and Medicine*, vol. 42 (1996),
p. 531-42.
Discusses the relationship between the legal structures concerning reproduction and
Islamic and secular traditions. The author claims that gender relations are directly
related to decision making processes regarding reproduction. She discusses the Islamic
and secular attitudes to non-fertility and to abortion as well as the formation of the
legal discourse throughout Turkish history.

516 **Beyond the orthodox: heresy in medicine and the social sciences
from a cross-cultural perspective.**
Akile Gürsoy-Tezcan. *Social Science and Medicine*, vol. 43, no. 5
(1996), p. 577-99.
The article claims that the frame of mind resulting from the Christian conceptualization
of medicine and the marginalization of Islamic medical scholars, such as Avicenna
and Avennesar, have shaped modern approaches to medicine, and have marginalized
alternative medicine. In the Turkish context, she discusses the effects of the foundation of
the modern school of medicine by Mahmud II in the 19th century, and the processes of
non-traditionalism, westernization, nationalism and secularism.

517 **Fertility trends, women's status, and reproductive expectations in
Turkey: results of further analysis of the Turkish demographic
and health survey.**
A. Hancıoğlu, Banu A. Ergöçmen, Turgay Ünalan. Calverton,
Maryland: Demographic and Health Surveys Macro International Inc.,
1997. 127p. (Hacettepe University Institute of Population Studies &
Demographic and Health Surveys Macro International Inc.).
In the first section of the book, Hancıoğlu analyses fertility in Turkey between 1978
and 1993. In the second part, Ergöçmen points out to the relationship between
women's status and fertility. Reproductive expectations and fertility trends in Turkey
are analysed by Ünalan in the final section.

518 **Proceedings of International Congress on Health and Recreation
Management. Antalya 17-20 September, 1989.**
Edited by B. Kocaoğlu, M. Korzay. İstanbul: Boğaziçi University
Publications, 1992. 339p.
The publication contains thirty-six contributions, mostly by Turkish authors, on
tourism, recreation, and the management of tourism in Turkey.

519 **Turkey. Demographic and health survey, 1993.**
Ministry of Health, Hacettepe University Institute of Population
Studies, Demographic & Health Surveys Macro International Inc.
Ankara: State Institute of Statistics, 1994. 247p.
Summarizes the findings of the 1993 survey in ten individually edited chapters and
appendices, detailing the design and implementation of the survey. There are 111
summary tables of data, and 27 graphs and diagrams. This nationwide sample survey,
conducted by the Institute of Population Studies at Hacettepe University in Ankara
among women of reproductive age, aims to provide, among other things, information
on fertility, family planning, child survival and children's health, based on interviews
conducted with 6,519 women. The results of the survey can be compared with earlier
surveys conducted by the Institute, particularly the '1988 Turkish population and
health survey', the '1983 Turkish fertility and health survey', and the '1978 Turkish
fertility survey'.

520 **Results of an educational intervention study on promotion of
breastfeeding.**
Olcay Neyzi.   In: *Maternal and child care in developing countries:
assessment, promotion, implementation.*   Edited by E. Kessel, A. K.
Awan.   Thun, Switzerland: Ott Publishers, 1989, p. 188-99.
The author stresses the importance of the education of health carers, who have been
known to give wrong information or feedback to mothers.

521 **The situation analysis of mothers and children in Turkey.**
Republic of Turkey and UNICEF Programme of Cooperation.
Ankara: UNICEF, 1995. 332p.
Deals primarily with the factors in education, administrative structure, social infrastructure, and economy that effect the health of mothers and children. The connection
between the state of children and development, and cooperation between the government
of Turkey, UNICEF and the Non-Governmental Organizations are discussed.

522 **Negotiating reproduction gender and love during the fertility
decline in Turkey.**
Frederic Shorter, Zeynep Angın.   New York: The Population Council,
1996. 48p. bibliog. (The Population Council, Regional Papers, West
Asia and North Africa Series, no. 42).
The paper discusses the reasons behind the decline of fertility in Turkey to near-
replacement levels, which was based primarily on male methods of contraception.

523 **1996 statistical yearbook.**
Social Insurance Institution.   Ankara: İlkiz Ofset, 1996. 135p. (Sosyal
Sigortalar Kurumu Genel Müdürlüğü, no. 593).
This yearbook, which has been published annually since 1946, gives detailed numerical
information on the insurance and health services offered by the Social Insurance
Institution (SSK). The Institution is responsible for 28 million people: 4,624,000
insured and 2,539,696 retired persons, widows, orphans, and family members. The
text is in English and Turkish.

Health and Welfare

524 **Pharmacy in Turkey.**
M. Tanker, D. Nebioğlu. *International Pharmacy Journal*, vol. 4, no. 3 (1990), p. 120-24.
A survey of the organization, management and education of pharmacy in Turkey.

525 **Cigarette demand, health scares and education in Turkey.**
Aysıt Tansel. *Applied Economics*, vol. 25 (1993), p. 521-29.
Tansel elaborates on the outcome of the introduction of cigarette health warnings in 1982, which resulted in an eight per cent decrease in cigarette demand despite the introduction of foreign cigarettes and associated advertising in 1984. Health warnings seemed to be more effective than the pro-smoking advertisements.

526 **Infant mortality in Turkey: basic factors.**
Edited by Ergül Tunçbilek. Ankara: Hacettepe University Institute of Population Studies, 1988. 69p. bibliog.
An overview of the causes and consequences of infant mortality in Turkey, which emphasizes the importance of education.

527 **Health statistics year book of Turkey. 1987-1994.**
M. Yalçın, M. Bardak. Ankara: Ministry of Health, 1997. 298p. (Ministry of Health, Department of Research, Planning & Coordination).
The 1997 edition of a yearbook which has been published since 1964. It contains information gathered from all health care institutions in Turkey, excluding military hospitals. It contains statistics on health establishments and budgets, health man-power, hospitals, infectious diseases, death, and preventive medicine.

Trends in fertility and mortality in Turkey, 1935-1975.
See item no. 301.

Population policy in Turkey. Family planning and migration between 1960 and 1992.
See item no. 336.

Sex roles, family and community in Turkey.
See item no. 461.

Culture and the economy: changes in Turkish villages.
See item no. 476.

Disseminating health information to women in Turkey.
See item no. 492.

Sağlık ve Sosyal Yardım Vakfı Dergisi. (Journal of Health and Social Welfare.)
See item no. 1358.

Politics

528 **The Turkish experiment in democracy, 1950-1975.**
Feroz Ahmad.   London: Hurst & Co., 1977. 474p. bibliog.
After describing the transition to multi-party politics during the period 1945-50, this
well informed study offers a detailed account of political developments up to the
mid-1970s. It contains a great deal of detailed information which is not available in
other sources.

529 **Political participation in Turkey: historical background and
present problems.**
Edited by Engin D. Akarlı, Gabriel Ben Dor.   İstanbul: Boğaziçi
University Publications, 1975. 192p. bibliog.
This valuable pioneering study is now somewhat out-of-date, but unfortunately there
has been little subsequent academic research in this field, except for that of Özbudun
(see item no. 573). It contains important contributions by Şerif Mardin, Ergun
Özbudun, Ayşe Kudat, Kemal H. Karpat, Sabri Sayarı and the editors, who deal with
the historical background, political participation in rural Turkey and squatter settlements,
patron-client relations and the role of the state.

530 **Turkey: political, social and economic challenges in the 1990s.**
Edited by Ç. Balım, E. Kalaycıoğlu, C. Karataş, G. Winrow, F.
Yasamee.   Leiden, the Netherlands: E. J. Brill, 1995. 302p. bibliog.
This is a valuable collection with informative and interesting essays on contemporary
Turkey. The essays include: 'New patterns of Turkish foreign policy behaviour',
Kemal Kirişçi; 'Regional security and national identity: the role of Turkey in former
Soviet Central Asia', Gareth Winrow; 'The Turkish Grand National Assembly: a brief
inquiry into the politics of representation in Turkey', Ersin Kalaycıoğlu; 'The Turkish
party system and the future of Turkish democracy', Üstün Ergüder; 'Parties and the
electorate: a comparative analysis of voter profiles of Turkish political parties',
Yılmaz Esmer; 'Islam and the secular state in Turkey', Binnaz Toprak; 'Recent trends
in Turkey's population', Cem Behar; 'The political economy of export-oriented

industrialization in Turkey', Ziya Öniş; 'Fiscal policy in Turkey: public debt and the changing structure of taxation and government expenditure, 1980-1993', Cevat Karataş; 'Pricing and distribution in an economy with an import public sector', Süleyman Özmucur; 'Inflation tax in a post-liberalization environment: evidence from Turkey, 1980-1990', Cevdet Akçay; 'The development and nature of small and medium-scale manufacturing enterprises in Turkey', Mehmet Kaytaz; 'Support for Turkish agriculture relative to developing and OECD countries', Haluk Kasnakoğlu; and 'Social order of the accounting profession in Turkey: the state, the market, and the community', İstemi Demirağ.

531 **Interest groups and political developments in Turkey.**
Robert Bianchi. Princeton, New Jersey: Princeton University Press, 1984. 426p. bibliog.
A thorough, methodological and sophisticated study of the subject, though now slightly out-of-date. Part one deals with the basis of interest group politics and their relationship to political culture. Part two describes and analyses the network of interest group politics, and the emergence and diffusion of interest groups. The final chapter discusses the theme in a comparative international perspective.

532 **The Generals' coup in Turkey: an inside story of 12 September 1980.**
Mehmet Ali Birand, translated from the Turkish by M. A. Dikerdem. London: Brassey's Defence Publishers, 1987. 220p.
This blow-by-blow account of the events leading up to the coup of 1980, by one of Turkey's best known journalists, is packed with important first-hand information. The final chapter deals with developments just after the coup, but there is unfortunately no information on the military regime's actions between then and its end in 1983. The work was originally published in Turkish as *12 Eylül, saat 0400* (İstanbul: Karacan, 1984).

533 **Shirts of steel: an anatomy of the Turkish armed forces.**
Mehmet Ali Birand, translated from the Turkish by Saliha Paker, Ruth Christie. London: I. B. Tauris, 1991. 485p.
This is a shortened translation of the author's Turkish original, *Emret Komutanım* (İstanbul: Milliyet, 1986). It is an intriguing study, based primarily on interviews with both senior and junior officers, which gives fascinating information on the training and political culture of the Turkish officer corps. As such, it offers invaluable background and an explanation of the armed forces' political role.

534 **Politics and government in Turkey.**
Clement H. Dodd. Manchester, England: Manchester University Press; Berkeley, California; Los Angeles: University of California Press, 1969. 335p. bibliog.
After an introductory chapter on the Ottoman background and the Republican period up to 1960, the second section of this important study covers political developments between 1960 and 1965. The third and fourth sections discuss the constitution of 1961, political parties, pressure groups, trade unions, the parliament, cabinet and the presidency, and public administration. It remains an excellent source for politics in the early 1960s.

535 **Democracy and development in Turkey.**
Clement H. Dodd. Huntingdon, England: The Eothen Press, 1979.
231p.

A systematic analysis of the Turkish political system, as it was in the late 1970s; this
has since been superseded by the same author's *Crisis of Turkish democracy* (see item
no. 536) and other studies. The opening chapter provides an outline of Turkish history,
society and government. Subsequent chapters discuss political elites, political culture
and ideas, the constitution of 1961, political parties and voting, the military and
bureaucracy, and pressure groups.

536 **The crisis of Turkish democracy.**
Clement H. Dodd. Huntingdon, England: The Eothen Press, 1990.
2nd ed. 236p. bibliog.

The second edition of a book first published in 1983. This valuable and scholarly
survey gives a useful account of events leading to the *coup d'état* of 1980 and
developments between 1983 and 1990, and considers the prospects for Turkish
democracy. The text of the 1982 constitution, with its amendments of 1987, is
reprinted in an appendix.

537 **The Turkish political élite.**
Frederick W. Frey. Cambridge, Massachusetts: The MIT Press, 1965.
483p. bibliog.

This book had great significance when it was published in 1965, as it added an
important social and cultural dimension to our understanding of political conflicts in
the pre- and post-war eras; unfortunately, there have been no further editions to bring
this work up-to-date. In an introductory chapter, the political significance of Turkey
and the Grand National Assembly are discussed. The second part of the book
examines the developments of the education system, its political significance,
occupations, and their importance in Turkish society. The third and most important
section analyses the social backgrounds of all members of the first ten Grand National
Assemblies.

538 **Political parties in Turkey: the role of Islam.**
Mehmet Yaşar Geyikdağı. New York: Praeger, 1984. 176p. bibliog.

A historical account of Turkish political parties, which takes the story from the Young
Turk era to the early 1980s. This is a useful study, but it must be remembered that
developments since its publication now make it rather out-of-date.

539 **Fifty years of Turkish political development, 1919-1969.**
İsmet Giritli. İstanbul: İstanbul University, 1969. 228p.

The author gives a straightforward, though somewhat uncritical, account of political
developments up to the 1960s. The text of the 1961 constitution is reprinted in an
appendix.

540   **Political cartoons: cultural representation in the Middle East.**
       Edited by Fatma M. Göçek.   Princeton, New Jersey: Markus Wiener
       Publishers, 1998. 155p.

The papers in the volume focus 'on the multiple cultural spaces that political cartoons
in the Middle East create across societies'. Ayhan Akman discusses modernity in
Turkey in 'From cultural schizophrenia to modern binarism: cartoons and identities in
Turkey (1930-1975)', and Palmira Brummett analyses the images of women in the
Ottoman cartoons. The reference notes which follow each article are useful for readers
who are interested in Turkish political cartoons.

541   **Turkish nationalism and western civilization.**
       Ziya Gökalp, translated from the Turkish and edited with an
       introduction by Niyazi Berkes.   London: Allen & Unwin; New York:
       Columbia University Press, 1959. 336p.

Contains an important selection of the works of Ziya Gökalp (1876-1924), covering
his views on culture, civilization, nationalism, the evolution of society, social values
and institutions, religion, education and family, the programme of Turkism, language,
literature, music, law, politics and economy.

542   **The principles of Turkism.**
       Ziya Gökalp, translated from the Turkish and annotated by Robert
       Devereux.   Leiden, the Netherlands: E. J. Brill, 1968. 141p.

This is a seminal text by Ziya Gökalp (1876-1924), one of the most influential Turkish
writers of the 20th century, and Turkey's pioneer sociologist, which was an important
intellectual inspiration for the Kemalist revolution.

543   **Roots and trends of clientelism in Turkey.**
       Ayşe Güneş-Ayata.   In: *Democracy, clientelism and civil society.*
       Edited by Luis Roniger, Ayşe Güneş-Ayata.   Boulder, Colorado:
       Lynne Rienner Publishers, 1994, p. 49-64.

The author discusses the process of the gradual integration of wider sections of civil
society into the political system in Turkey, by focusing on the patron-client relations,
from earlier dyadic forms of patronage to clientelistic brokerage typical of contemporary
Turkey. The chapter covers: the centre and periphery in Republican history; multi-
party politics and patronage; democracy and machine politics; structural reasons for
clientelism; and contradictions of contemporary patronage.

544   **Aspects of modern Turkey.**
       Edited by William Hale.   New York; Epping, England: Bowker, 1976.
       129p. maps. bibliog. (Centre for Middle Eastern and Islamic Studies
       of the University of Durham).

This collection of papers, mainly on political themes, is unfortunately now rather
out-of-date in parts. The volume includes; 'Political change between 1960 and 1974',
Geoffrey Lewis; 'The intellectual background to radical protests in the 1960s', David
Barchard; 'Particularism and universalism as modes of political participation, and the
trades union movement', William Hale; 'Cause, knowledge and change in a Turkish
village', Paul Stirling; 'Agricultural problems and rural development', John C.

Dewdney; and 'Political and social aspects of planning', John Bridge, Özer Baykay, Kutlu Ataç.

545 Turkish politics and the military.

William Hale. London; New York: Routledge, 1994. 369p. bibliog.

After three introductory chapters covering the late Ottoman and Kemalist periods, the author concentrates on a historical survey of Turkish politics and the military between 1960 and 1993. The final chapter analyses the Turkish army's political role in an international comparative perspective.

546 The origins of communism in Turkey.

George S. Harris. Stanford, California: Hoover Institution, 1967. 215p. bibliog.

Describes the radical currents which began towards the end of the Ottoman Empire. The book discusses communist activities, the leaders of the movement in Turkey, the Soviet Union and the Turks, the establishment of the Republic, the end of the legal communist movement in Turkey in 1925, and the 1926 penal code which was remodelled after the Italian code.

547 Turkey: coping with crisis.

George S. Harris. Boulder, Colorado: Westview Press, 1985. 240p. maps. bibliog.

This is a useful introduction to the Turkish politics of the mid-1980s, by a skilled writer experienced in the subject. After chapters on the geographical, historical, and economic background, the author examines the constitution, political dynamics, the role of the military, and foreign policy.

548 The plot to kill the Pope.

Paul B. Henze. London: Croom Helm, 1984. 216p.

This book is a gripping read, even though the author's argument that the Soviet and Bulgarian secret services were behind the attempt by Mehmet Ali Ağca to murder Pope John Paul II in 1981 may be disputed by many readers. Apart from this, the book supplies much information on political terrorism in Turkey during the 1970s.

549 The state tradition in Turkey.

Metin Heper. Huntingdon, England: The Eothen Press, 1985. 218p. bibliog.

This is not a book for newcomers to the subject, or those unfamiliar with the current academic discourse on the state and society. Nevertheless, it offers an important and original perspective on modern Turkish history and politics. It analyses the relationship between the Turkish state and society in terms of 'transcentalism', that is (among other things) 'the belief that man primarily belongs to a moral community'. This proposal is discussed in relation to the Ottoman, Kemalist, and post-Kemalist states; the author concludes that developments after 1980 led to the 'resurrection of a partially transcendental state'.

550 **State, democracy and the military: Turkey in the 1980s.**
Edited by Metin Heper, Ahmet Evin. Berlin; New York: Walter de
Gruyter, 1988. 265p.

This title is slightly misleading since the book does not cover the period after 1985:
nonetheless, it remains a very useful source for Turkish politics during the first half of
the 1980s. The first section deals with general theoretical approaches to state and society,
political modernization, and freedom from the Ottoman perspective, with papers by
Metin Heper, C. H. Dodd and Şerif Mardin. The remainder of the book focuses on the
early 1980s, with papers on political structures (Ergun Özbudun, Ersin Kalaycıoğlu),
political processes and actors (İlter Turan, Üstün Ergüder, Richard I. Hofferbert,
Frank Tachau, Binnaz Toprak), the military and the state (Kemal H. Karpat, William
Hale, George Harris) and the state and democracy (Ahmet Evin, Christian Rumpf,
Dankwart A. Rustow).

551 **Political parties and democracy in Turkey.**
Edited by Metin Heper, Jacob M. Landau. London; New York: I. B.
Tauris, 1991. 225p. bibliog.

This is the only thorough study of the development of political parties in Turkey, from
the beginning of the Republic up to 1990. After an introduction by Metin Heper and a
broad overview of the topic by Dankwart A. Rustow, there are important papers on the
period up to 1945, dealing with the general theme of Atatürk and political parties
(C. H. Dodd), and accounts of the development of the Republican People's Party from
1923 to 1945 (Kemal H. Karpat), the Progressive Republican Party of 1924-25 (Feroz
Ahmad) and the Free Party of 1930 (Walter F. Weiker). The following chapters deal
with the period since 1945, starting with the Republican People's Party (Frank
Tachau), the Democrat Party (Ali Yaşar Sarıbay) and the Justice Party (Avner Levy),
and their successors, the Motherland Party (Üstün Ergüder), the Social Democrat
Populist Party (Andrew Mango) and the True Path Party (Feride Acar). A revised and
updated edition, with information on the pro-Islamic Welfare Party, would be a very
valuable addition to the literature on this topic.

552 **Strong state and economic interest groups: the post-1980 Turkish
experience.**
Edited by Metin Heper. Berlin; New York: Walter de Gruyter, 1991.
198p. bibliog.

A valuable collection of specialist papers, which takes off from where the earlier study
by Bianchi (q. v.) left off. After an introductory chapter by the editor, the papers deal
with economic and legal factors affecting interest groups during the 1980s (Ziya Öniş,
Ergun Özbudun), the state and different interest groups, including labour (Ümit Cizre
Sakallıoğlu), agriculture (Üstün Ergüder), commercial groups (Ersin Kalaycıoğlu),
banking (Ayşe Öncü and Deniz Gökçe), manufacturing industries (Yılmaz Esmer) and
big business (Yeşim Arat). Concluding chapters are by Ayşe Buğra and the editor.

553 **Turkey and the West: changing political and cultural variables.**
Edited by Metin Heper, Ayşe Öncü, Heinz Kramer. London; New
York: I. B. Tauris, 1993. 289p. bibliog.

This is not a book on Turkey's international relations, as the title might suggest, but
instead it concentrates on attitudes towards the west on the part of different groups in

Turkish society. These groups and their attitudes are scrutinized by the following: army officers (Ali L. Karaosmanoğlu), bureaucrats (Metin Heper), journalists (Şahin Alpay), novelists (Ahmet Evin), politicians (İlter Turan), academics (Ayşe Öncü), businessmen (Selim İlkin), engineers (Nilüfer Göle), workers in Europe (Yasemin Soysal), and Islamist intellectuals (Binnaz Toprak).

554 **Politics in the third Turkish republic: the transition to democracy.**
Edited by Metin Heper, Ahmet Evin. Boulder, Colorado: Westview, 1994. 288p. bibliog.

The papers in this collection concentrate on Turkish politics between 1980 and the early 1990s, and are written by a large number of distinguished contributors. Successive sections deal with the 1980 *coup d'état* and the aftermath of the military regime of 1980-83, the transition towards a liberal-democratic state, economic transformation and governmental change, international dynamics and domestic politics, economic growth, eduction and Islam, the role of elites, and the state, civil society and democracy.

555 **Foundations of Turkish nationalism: the life and teachings of Ziya Gökalp.**
Uriel Heyd. London: Luzc & Harvill Press, 1950. 174p. bibliog.

Although the academic literature on Ziya Gökalp is now more extensive than it was when this book was written, this remains a very valuable analytical account of his ideas. After a biographical introduction, successive chapters deal with the sociological concepts which underlay his proposals (examining, in particular, his debts to sociologists Durkheim and Tonnies), westernization, Islam, Turkism, and the combination of these principles. The third part of the text presents an appreciation of his work as a scholar and poet, and his ideas on nationalism.

556 **Turkey's politics: the transition to a multi-party system.**
Kemal H. Karpat. Princeton, New Jersey: Princeton University Press, 1959. 522p. bibliog.

An invaluable scholarly study of political developments between 1945 and 1950, which is still the only detailed work in English on this topic.

557 **Political and social thought in the contemporary Middle East.**
Edited by Kemal H. Karpat. New York; Washington, DC, London: Praeger, 1968. 397p.

A collection of translated articles and extracts, with useful introductory notes by the editor, which helps to fill a gap in the scholarly literature on political thought and ideology in Turkey. The section on Turkey includes articles on Kemalism, socialism and statism, by a variety of prominent authors.

558 **Social change and politics in Turkey: a structural-historical analysis.**
Edited by Kemal H. Karpat. Leiden, the Netherlands: E. J. Brill, 1973. 373p. bibliog.

When it originally appeared, this was a very valuable collection of papers on a subject on which there was little literature. Unfortunately, it is now beginning to show its age, but there is still no more recent comparable study available. The historical introduction contains papers by the editor and Dankwart A. Rustow. These are followed by chapters on the middle classes, the integration of the villager into national life, and the effects of the system of free boarding schools (Nezih Neyzi, John F. Kolars, İlhan Başgöz). The final section, on politics and the ideologies of social groups, contains papers by Frank Tachau and the editor. The chapter on 'Labor in Turkey as a new social and political force' by Bülent Ecevit (later Prime Minister) is perhaps more important for what it tells us about the author, than for its subject matter.

559 **Populism and democracy in Turkey.**
Reşat Kasaba. In: *Rules and rights in the Middle East: democracy, law, and society.* Edited by Ellis Goldberg, Reşat Kasaba, Joel S. Migdal. Seattle, Washington: University of Washington Press, 1994, p. 43-68.

The author discusses the 'pressures that ensure the repeated restoration of multiparty democracy in Turkey', with special reference to the 1946-61 period. He believes that the key to understanding the resilience of Turkish democracy lies in understanding and explaining the enduring strength of a conservative appeal even as the country and the people are affected by wide-ranging economic and political changes.

560 **Atatürk: founder of a modern state.**
Edited by Ali Kazancıgil, Ergun Özbudun. London: Hurst & Co., 1997. reprint. 256p.

This introduction to the ideas and achievements of Kemalism, written by distinguished contributors, was first published in 1981 with the same name. The reprint contains a new introduction by the editors which evaluates the development of the Kemalist ideal since 1981. The contents are as follows: 'The principles of Kemalism', E. Z. Karal; 'The Ottoman-Turkish state and Kemalism', Ali Kazancıgil; 'Atatürk as an institution-builder', D. A. Rustow; 'The nature of the Kemalist regime', E. Özbudun; 'Kemalism and world peace', V. I. Danilov; 'The Kemalist revolution in comparative perspective', S. N. Eisenstadt; 'The political economy of Kemalism', F. Ahmad; 'Kemalist economic policies and étatism', K. Boratav; and 'Religion and secularism in Turkey', Ş. Mardin.

561 **Turkey: identity, democracy, politics.**
Edited by Sylvia Kedourie. *Middle Eastern Studies*, special issue, vol. 32, no. 2 (1996), 272p.

There are several original and informative papers in this special issue, but unfortunately it lacks a clear central focus, and probably assumes too much prior knowledge to be of value to newcomers to the subject. The first four papers deal with the late Ottoman palace establishment (S. Tanvir Wasti), and aspects of Turkey's foreign policy and foreign relations between 1906 and 1948 (Hasan Ünal, Bülent Gökay, Ekavi Athanassopoulou). These are followed by five papers on aspects of contemporary politics, specifically: the press (Metin Heper and Taner Demirel); democratic transition in the period 1980-83 (İhsan Dağı); the True Path Party (Ümit Cizre-Sakallıoğlu); urbanization and voting trends (Aryeh Shmuelevitz); and Turkish nationalism and the construction of official identity (Ayşe Kadıoğlu). The last three papers deal with the historical background of Turkish popular music (Orhan Tekelioğlu), the Turkish state discourse and the exclusion of Kurdish identity (Mesut Yeğen), and small employers in Ankara (Theo Nichols and Nadir Sugur).

562 **State and class in Turkey: a study in capitalist development.**
Çağlar Keyder.   London; New York: Vereso, 1987. 252p.

In his interpretative history of Turkey's social, economic and political history since late Ottoman times, the author adopts the framework of the Marxian discourse on peripheral development to argue that the lack of a dominant landlord class and the continued existence of an independent peasantry had a formative influence on the country's political and economic development. This is certainly not a book for beginners, but those with experience of the subject will be in a position to judge whether Keyder's original approaches and intellectual framework seem realistic.

563 **The Kurdish question and Turkey: an example of trans-state ethnic conflict.**
Kemal Kirişçi, Gareth M. Winrow.   London; Portland, Oregon: Frank Cass, 1997. 256p. bibliog.

This book is easily the most valuable source for those interested in the position of the Kurds in Turkey, and the impact of the Kurdish question on contemporary Turkish politics. It is remarkably dispassionate and objective, and is based on thorough research on both Turkish and non-Turkish sources. It begins with an informative general discussion of questions related to minority rights and the issue of self determination. This is followed by a historical summary of the evolution of the Kurdish question in Turkey from the 1920s to the 1980s. The most important and original part of the book details developments during the 1990s, and considers international aspects of the problem, as well as possible solutions.

564 **Radical politics in Turkey.**
Jacob M. Landau.   Leiden, the Netherlands: E. J. Brill, 1974. 315p. bibliog.

An extremely thorough and scholarly study of intellectual and ideological trends among radicals of both left and right during the 1960s. The description of Islamist ideas at the time is also important.

565 **Atatürk and the modernization of Turkey.**
Edited by Jacob M. Landau.   Leiden, the Netherlands: E. J. Brill; Boulder, Colorado: Westview, 1984. 268p.

This collection of papers covers a much wider disciplinary field than most purely historical and biographical studies. The first section, on Kemalist ideology, has an important general comparative paper by S. N. Eisenstadt, followed by more specific contributions by Rachel Simon, Paul Dumont and Osman Okyar. The second section deals with political culture and bureaucracy (Frank Tachau, Udo Steinbach, Metin Heper, İlter Turan), while the third takes up social and economic issues (Sabri Akural,

William Hale, Z. Y. Herschlag). Westernism and culture is dealt with in the fourth section, with papers by Michael Winter, Geoffrey Lewis, Metin And and David Kushner. The last two chapters examine the Kemalist reform of Turkish law (Vakur Versan), and Kemalism as an ideology of modernization (İsmet Giritli).

566 Pan-Turkism: from irredentism to cooperation.
Jacob M. Landau. London: Hurst & Co., 1995. 275p. bibliog.

An enlarged edition of the author's earlier book, *Pan-Turkism in Turkey: a study in irredentism* (London: Hurst & Co., 1981), revised to take account of the effects of the dissolution of the Soviet Union on pan-Turkist ideology in Turkey. With his customary thoroughness and scholarship, Landau provides a mine of information on the generation and flowering of this school of thought in the late Ottoman period, its 'latent' stage during the early republic, and its gradual return as part of the political mainstream in later years. The penultimate chapter examines pan-Turkism as an irredentist phenomenon from an international comparative perspective, while the last chapter describes and analyses the most recent developments.

567 The political philosophy of Mustapha Kemal Atatürk as evidenced in his published speeches and interviews.
Frederick P. Latimer. Ann Arbor, Michigan: University of Michigan Press, 1963. 229p.

A useful source, for which the material is otherwise only available in Turkish.

568 Catalysts of change: Marxist versus Muslim in a Turkish community.
Arnold Leder. Austin, Texas: University of Texas at Austin, Centre for Middle Eastern Studies, 1976. 56p. bibliog.

A fascinating and original study of politics in the 1970s in the town of Saruhanlı, where political conflicts mirrored those at the national level. The relationship between social groups and political alignments is well analysed. Though short, this is an important book, in a field on which there has been relatively little academic literature.

569 Modern Turkey.
Geoffrey L. Lewis. London: Benn, 1974. 235p.

The third and final edition of a book, previously entitled *Turkey*, and issued by the same publishers in 1955 and 1965. It gives a lively introductory summary of political developments from the 1920s to 1974.

570 The socialist movements in Turkey, 1960-1980.
Igor P. Lipovsky. Leiden, the Netherlands: E. J. Brill, 1992. 194p. bibliog.

This book, which was apparently originally written in Russian in the former Soviet Union, gives an extremely detailed account of Marxist movements and parties in Turkey during the 1960s and 1970s, explaining their evolution and complex internecine disputes. Unfortunately, it tells us relatively little about social democrat movements (such as that within the Republican People's Party at the time) and does not draw on any of the literature in English on the subject.

571 **A modern history of the Kurds.**
David McDowall. London; New York: I. B. Tauris, 1996. 427p.
This is the most thorough and up-to-date account of the overall history of the Kurds. It covers the position of the Kurds in Iraq and Iran as well as Turkey, and makes extensive use of British state archives as well as other primary sources. Chapters three and four deal with the Kurds within the Ottoman empire, chapter nine focuses on the Kurds in Turkey during the Atatürk era, and the last two chapters cover the evolution of Turkey's Kurdish problem since 1946. However, the coverage on Turkey is less full than in the book by Kirişçi and Winrow, *The Kurdish question and Turkey: an example of trans-state ethnic conflict* (see item no. 563).

572 **The role of the military in recent Turkish politics.**
Ergun Özbudun. Cambridge, Massachusetts: Harvard University Press, Centre for International Affairs, 1966. 54p. bibliog.
This short analytical study examines the political system in relation to the military's role, military intervention and social change, and contests between military radicals and moderates. Unfortunately, events since it was written have now rendered it rather out-of-date, but it still has value as an analysis of the military regime of the period 1960-61.

573 **Social change and political participation in Turkey.**
Ergun Özbudun. Princeton, New Jersey: Princeton University Press, 1976. 254p.
This important and original study examines the effects of socio-economic change on forms of political participation, the relationship between social cleavages and the party system, urban and rural differences in political participation, and related topics in the 1970s.

574 **The social and political thought of Ziya Gökalp, 1916-1924.**
Taha Parla. Leiden, the Netherlands: E. J. Brill, 1985. 157p. bibliog.
An important critical account of Gökalp's ideas, which adds to the earlier studies by Heyd and Berkes by relating the main themes to subsequent developments in Turkish politics. It starts with a biographical introduction, which is followed by chapters on Gökalp's social and political philosophy, the social basis of his political ides, his theory of politics and political organization, and problems in his theory. An important final chapter discusses the contemporary relevance of Gökalp.

575 **Turkey unveiled: Atatürk and after.**
Nicole Pope, Hugh Pope. London: John Murray, 1997. 373p. bibliog.
Potential readers should not be put off by the rather over-dramatic title of this book, which is actually a very accessible introduction to Turkey's modern political development up to the mid-1990s, and which contains a great deal of original information on the most recent period. The authors are two of the foremost foreign journalists currently working in Turkey, and make extensive use of Turkish sources as well as personal experience and interviews, although their exploration of social and economic issues seems rather weak.

576 **Top hat, grey wolf and crescent: Turkish nationalism and the Turkish Republic.**
Hugh Poulton. London: Hurst & Co.; New York: New York University Press, 1997. 350p. bibliog.

A valuable and topical study of the ideology of Turkish nationalism and its variants. After examining the question of group identities in the Ottoman empire and the early rise of Turkish nationalism, it discusses the secular nationalism of Kemalism and of the radical right, pan-Turkism and Islam in relation to Turkish nationalism, the position of ethnic and religious minorities, and the attitudes of Turkish minorities in other countries who have regarded Turkey as a 'kin state'.

577 **The first Turkish Republic: a case study in national development.**
Richard D. Robinson. Cambridge, Massachusetts: Harvard University Press, 1963. 367p.

A very informative study of the evolution of Turkish politics from the time of the foundation of the Republic up to 1961. The author lived and worked in Turkey for the American Universities Field Staff during the late 1950s and early 1960s. Besides having a through knowledge of the published literature, he adds valuable first-hand insights, although readers may feel that he is too critical of the Menderes government of 1950-60, and too uncritical of the military regime of 1960-61. At the end of the book, there is a very useful chronology of the main events in Turkey's political history during the period covered.

578 **Atatürk's children: Turkey and the Kurds.**
Jonathan Rugman, photographs by Roger Hutchings. London: Cassell, 1996. 128p.

A short and lively first-hand account of Turkey's current Kurdish problem, by the former correspondent of the BBC and *The Guardian* in Turkey. It is reasonably fair to both sides, and critical of both where necessary, though readers will probably wish to turn to the books by McDowell, Kirişçi and Winrow, and Gunter (q. v.) for more thorough and scholarly treatments of the same topic. The book also contains some striking illustrations by the photographer Roger Hutchings.

579 **Political patronage in Turkey.**
Sabri Sayarı. In: *Patrons and clients in Mediterranean societies.* Edited by Ernest Gellner, John Waterbury. London: Duckworth, with the Centre for Mediterranean Studies of the American Universities Field Staff, 1977, p. 103-13.

The author explores the role of patronage in Turkish electoral politics in terms of clientelistic behaviour, formal organizations such as the bureaucracy, trade unions, civil associations, and informal social groups.

580 **Turkey in transition: new perspectives.**
Edited by Irvin C. Schick, Ertuğrul Ahmet Tonak, with translations
from Turkish by Rezan Benatar, Irvin C. Schick, Ronnie Margulies.
New York; Oxford: Oxford University Press, 1987. 405p.

An informative collection of papers, covering politics and the economy, mostly during
the 'Özal era' of the 1980s. The first section deals with the historical political background up to 1945 (Taner Timur, Çağlar Keyder, and Stephane Yerasimos), and the
establishment of multi-party rule between 1945 and 1971 (Cem Ertuğrul). The second
section examines the political forces of the 1980s, with chapters on the left (Ahmet
Samim), the ultra-nationalist right (Mehmet Ali Ağaoğulları), the religious right
(Binnaz Toprak) and the army (Semih Vaner). The final section focuses on economic
developments (agriculture, labour, trade unions), which are explored in contributions
by Ronnie Margulies and Ergin Yıldızoğlu, Çağlar Keyder, Alpaslan Işıklı, and the
editors.

581 **The results of elections of local administration, 23.3.1994.**
State Institute of Statistics (SIS). Ankara: State Institute of Statistics,
1996. 686p.

The publication contains a breakdown of the results of elections for general provincial
assemblies, members of municipal assemblies, and mayors of major cities.

582 **General election of representatives: results by provinces,
24.12.1995.**
State Institute of Statistics (SIS). Ankara: State Institute of Statistics,
1996. 28p.

The publication gives the detailed results of the 1995 general elections in Turkey by
provinces.

583 **General election of representatives: results by districts, 24.12.1995.**
State Institute of Statistics (SIS). Ankara: State Institute of Statistics,
1996. 142p.

The publication gives the detailed results of the 1995 general elections in Turkey by
districts.

584 **Results of general election of representatives: summary tables,
24.12.1995.**
State Institute of Statistics (SIS). Ankara: State Institute of Statistics,
1996. 554p.

Contains a summary of the results of the 1995 general elections in Turkey.

585 **Results of general election of representatives, 24.12.1995.**
State Institute of Statistics (SIS). Ankara: State Institute of Statistics,
1996. 2 vols.

These volumes contain data on the results of the general elections of 1983, 1987, 1991
and 1995 in Turkey.

586   **A political analysis of student activism: the Turkish case.**
       Joseph S. Szyliowicz.   Beverley Hills, California; London: Sage,
       1972. 77p. bibliog.
This short study traces the history of student activism and political involvement from
the mid-16th century to the time of the 1960 *coup d'état*.

587   **Turkey: the politics of authority, democracy and developments.**
       Frank Tachau.   New York: Praeger, 1984. 224p. bibliog.
A useful account of the Turkish political system, as it was in the 1980s, which places
emphasis on the social and economic dimensions, and draws extensively on the work of
other researchers. Successive chapters concentrate on tradition and national identity,
political institutions and structures, parties and changing sociopolitical structures,
economic development, relations between villages and towns and the effects of rural-
urban migration. The last chapter, on foreign relations, is out-of-date since the end of
the Cold War, but the rest of this book remains valuable as an exploration of socio-
economic themes.

588   **Islam and political development in Turkey.**
       Binnaz Toprak.   Leiden, the Netherlands: E. J. Brill, 1981. 164p.
This is a thorough and well-balanced study of an important theme, namely the role of
Islam in Turkish politics up to the 1970s. After initial chapters which examine general
theoretical perspectives on religion and political development and Islam as a political
religion, the author relates Islam to the project of nation-building in Turkey, the
political mobilization of the Turkish peasantry, and Islam and political behaviour.
There is much valuable information, supported by statistical surveys, on the relationship between Islam and social and political attitudes.

589   **Political Islam and the Welfare (Refah) Party in Turkey.**
       M. Hakan Yavuz.   *Comparative Politics*, vol. 30, no. 1 (1997),
       p. 63-82.
The author describes Turkey's policy towards Islamist groups as a dual track policy of
cooptation and containment. He also illustrates that through the externalization of
Islamic identity in the public domain, the Welfare Party has helped to promote the
inner secularization of Islam, and a new synthesis has been created in which Islam is
radically reimagined within modern concepts and institutions.

The making of modern Turkey.
See item no. 1.

Turkey: the challenge of a new role.
See item no. 14.

The development of secularism in Turkey.
See item no. 439.

**Islam in modern Turkey: religion, politics and literature in a secular
state.**
See item no. 451.

Turkish state, Turkish society.
See item no. 456.

Boğaziçi Journal. Review of Social, Economic and Administrative Studies.
See item no. 1319.

International Journal of Middle Eastern Studies.
See item no. 1333.

The Middle East Journal.
See item no. 1344.

Middle East Review of International Affairs (MERIA).
See item no. 1345.

Middle East Studies Association Bulletin.
See item no. 1346.

Middle Eastern Studies.
See item no. 1347.

New Perspectives on Turkey.
See item no. 1352.

Turkish Review of Middle East Studies.
See item no. 1381.

Turkish Studies Association Bulletin.
See item no. 1382.

Constitution and Legal System

590 Introduction to Turkish law.
Edited by Tuğrul Ansay, Don Wallace Jr.   The Hague; Boston,
Massachusetts; London: Kluwer Law International, 1996. 224p.
bibliog.

This textbook also serves as a preliminary reference and key to the basic institutions,
principles and rules of Turkish law for foreign lawyers and scholars. Detailed explanatory
footnotes and bibliographies are provided at the end of each chapter. It comprises of
chapters on public law (such as Turkish constitutional, administrative and criminal
law), private law (civil law including property law), Turkish law of obligations, and
the procedural laws.

**591 Improperly obtained evidence: a comparison of Turkish and
English laws.**
Vahit Bıçak.   Ankara: Karmap Publishing, 1996. 232p. bibliog.

Provides a comparative analysis of the rules governing the admissibility of improperly
obtained evidence in Turkish and English law. The main objective is to consider how
the issues in question can most appropriately be solved under the different legal
circumstances of both countries.

592 The constitution of the Republic of Turkey.
In: *Constitutions of the countries of the world: a series of updated
texts, constitutional chronologies and annotated bibliographies.*
Edited by Albert Blaustein, Gisbert H. Flanz.   Dobbs Ferry, New
York: Oceana Publications Inc., vol. 19, 183p. (loose-leaf).

The section of the book on Turkey provides a translation of the 1982 Constitution of
Turkey, with amendments of 1987 and 1995. Flanz introduces the important constitutional
and political events in Turkey between 1983 and 1994, and the supplement by Ö. F.
Gençkaya covers the period 1994-95. There is also a two-page bibliography on
Turkish law.

593 **Foreigners in Turkey: their judicial status.**
Philip Marshall Brown. Princeton, New Jersey: Princeton University
Press; London: Humphrey Milford, Oxford University Press, 1914.
157p. bibliog.

The rights and privileges of foreigners was a complex issue in the Ottoman Empire.
The author clarifies the regime of capitulations (commercial treaties going back to
1536, by which Western states could trade freely in Ottoman ports, having freedom of
religion and redemption from taxes), and provides a clearer understanding of the exact
rights of foreigners as distinguished from their privileges. The author was an official
in the American Embassy in Constantinople for several years.

594 **Turkey and Article 25 of the European Convention on Human
Rights.**
Ian Cameron. *International and Comparative Law Quarterly*, vol. 37
(1988), p. 887-925.

On 29 January 1987 Turkey became the nineteenth member of the Council of Europe
to declare, under Article 25 of the European Convention on Human Rights, its recognition of the competence of the Commission to receive applications from individuals
alleging violations of their rights and freedoms guaranteed by the Convention. The
article argues that the unprecedented and highly controversial provisos attached to the
declaration raise important questions regarding the nature, purpose and legal effect of
the optional declarations in the Convention.

595 **The first Ottoman constitutional period: a study of the Midhat
constitution and parliament.**
Robert Devereux. Baltimore, Maryland: Johns Hopkins Press, 1963.
310p. bibliog. (Johns Hopkins University. Studies in Historical and
Political Science, Series 81, no. 1).

The book covers the period between 1876 and 1878 which coincides with the first
Ottoman constitutional period. It discusses Midhat's constitution and the structure of
the Ottoman constitutionalism, and the period of one month and seventeen days when
he was the Grand Vizier. This is a valuable book for the specialist.

596 **Environment law of Turkey.**
Environmental Problems Foundation of Turkey. Ankara: Önder
Matbaası, 1983. 24p.

This booklet is an unofficial English translation of the Turkish Environment Law
no. 2872 enacted in 1983.

597 **Environment law and its application in Turkey.**
Environmental Problems Foundation of Turkey. Ankara: Önder
Matbaası, 1987. 59p.

Contains the papers presented at a meeting on the implementation of the Environment
Law. They discuss the Environment Law from the standpoints of Civil Law,
Administrative Law and Penal Law, and the environmental treaties which Turkey has
signed. In the 'Appendix' section the Environmental Law of Turkey is given.

598 **Environmental legislation in EC and Turkey.**
Environmental Problems Foundation of Turkey.   Ankara: Önder
Matbaası, 1989. 115p.

Following Turkey's application for full membership of the European Community in
1987, the necessity of bringing the country's policies and legal arrangements into
harmony with those of the EC gained importance. This book is the result of such an
attempt, and aims to identify the similarities and differences between environmental
regulations in the EC and in Turkey. Turkish and EC legislation are compared.

599 **Turkish environment law and some other related legal provisions.**
Environmental Problems Foundation of Turkey.   Ankara: Önder
Matbaası, 1988. 78p.

In the Turkish legal system, apart from the Environment Law itself, there are a large
number of legal sources containing provisions either directly or indirectly related to
the environment. In this book, the complete text of the Environment Law is given, and
some articles of important laws directly concerning the environment, and of particular
interest to foreigners, have also been included. For technical reasons the book does not
contain those legal sources which have become effective since 1 November 1988. The
volume does not give an exhaustive account of Turkish environmental legislation, but
rather aims to provide an overall picture of the main regulations pertaining to the
environment in Turkey.

600 **Non-governmental Organizations guide (main establishments).**
Economic and Social History Foundation of Turkey NGO Centre.
İstanbul: Economic & Social History Foundation of Turkey, 1996.
520p.

The guide is a catalogue comprising information on national, regional and local
organizations. It provides systematic information on the NGOs in Turkey (title,
purpose, scope of activities, board of directors, activities at present and in the past,
contact person and details).

601 **Studies in old Ottoman criminal law.**
Ureyl Heyd, edited by V. L. Ménage.   Oxford: Clarendon Press, 1973.
3340p. bibliog.

Deals with the fundamental problems of the criminal law, the reasons for its decline
and the criminal procedure. The chapters in the first section cover the development of
the Ottoman criminal code, criminal law in the provincial *kanunname*s (secular laws
issued by the Ottoman ruler), and the Ottoman criminal code in practice. The second
section discuss the legal character of *kanun* legislation and its relation to the *shari'a*, the
courts, the authorities administering criminal justice, the trial procedure (particularly
with reference to the *kadı* court) and punishment.

602 **The domestic application of international human rights norms.**
The International Centre for the Legal Protection of Human Rights,
and the Ankara University Human Rights Centre. Ankara: Ankara
University Press, 1992. 86p. (Faculty of Political Sciences Publication,
no. 576; Human Rights Center Publication, no. 7).
This is a collection of papers presented at a colloquium in Ankara (13-14 September
1990) on the application of human rights in Turkey.

603 **Turkish constitutional developments and assembly debates on the
constitutions of 1924 and 1961.**
Suna Kili. İstanbul: Robert College Research Center, 1971. 209p.
bibliog.
The book covers Turkish constitutional developments, discusses the *senedi ittifak*
(document of alliance), the *Gülhane Hatt-ı Hümayun* (the Imperial Decree of
Gülhane), and the constitutions of 1876, 1921, 1924 and 1961. The texts of the four
constitutions are given in the appendix.

604 **The reception of Swiss family law in Turkey.**
Paul J. Magnarella. *Anthropological Quarterly,* vol. 46, no. 2 (1973),
p. 100-16.
The adoption of Western legal codes by the Turkish Republic is discussed with special
reference to Swiss Family Law. The author examines traditional Islamic law and
traditional and modern marriage ceremonies. Polygamous marriages and family
inheritance traditions are also outlined.

605 **The Cyprus question and the Turkish position in international law.**
Zaim M. Necatigil. Oxford: Oxford University Press, 1993. 2nd ed.
482p. maps. bibliog.
Provides a recent history of Cyprus and examines the legal issues that have been
raised in connection with various developments. It is argued that the events in Cyprus
since December 1963 raise a number of interesting issues for international law.
Special consideration is given to the Treaty of Guarantee and principles of international law relating to statehood and recognition, as well as the principles of
self-determination and its application to the situation in Cyprus.

606 **The Ottoman land code.**
F. Ongley. London: William Clowes & Sons, 1892. 396p.
A translation of the land laws of the Ottoman Empire, which also includes notes on
Ottoman legislation.

607 **An introduction to law and the Turkish legal system.**
Arif Payaslıoğlu. Ankara: Higher Education Council Publications,
1993. 175p.
A textbook prepared for introductory law courses at Turkish universities, where the
medium of teaching is English.

608 **The Turkish straits.**
C. L. Rozakis, Petros N. Stagos.   Dordrecht, the Netherlands: Kluwer
Academic Publishers Group, 1987. 220p. (International Straits of the
World, no. 9).
This book discusses the legal and political issues affecting Turkey's straits, covering
the history, and the provisions of the international law regarding their status.

609 **The protection of human rights in Turkey and the significance of
international human rights instruments.**
Christian Rumpf. *Human Rights Law Journal*, vol. 14, no. 11-12
(1993), p. 394-433.
The article focuses on legal practice under the most important human rights instruments,
and the implementation of human rights within the Turkish legal system.

610 **Turkish Labor Law.**
Michael N. Schmitt, Mehmet Nur Tanışık.   New York: Transnational
Publishers, 1997. 275p.
After an overview of the general principles, the relevant provisions of the Turkish
Constitution and extracts from the Turkish Labour Law are given. The legislation,
such as the relevant parts or articles from Labour Code no. 1475, Collective Labour
Agreement, Strike and Lock-out Law no. 2822, Unions Law no. 2821, and Law
no. 2007 on the trading and services reserved for Turkish citizens, is explained.

611 **Judicial statistics, 1996.**
State Institute of Statistics (SIS).   Ankara: State Institute of Statistics,
1998. 262p.
An annual publication which contains data on the activities of judicial agencies and
courts in Turkey, including the military justice organization, the Department of
Forensic Medicine, notaries, the Constitutional Court, the Supreme Court, the Council
of State, the High Board of Arbitration, and Public Prosecutors' Offices, as well as
criminal, civil, and administrative courts, and law enforcement offices.

612 **Human rights in Turkey.**
Hikmet Sami Türk.   *Perceptions: Journal of International Affairs*,
vol. 3, no. 4 (December 1998-February 1999), p. 5-24.
The author gives a history and summary of present human rights legislation in Turkey,
the draft laws, and the activities of the Ministry in charge of human rights as well as
those of other offical bodies.

613 **Privatization in Turkey: the law and the implementation.**
Sponsored by Türk Ekonomi Bankası (TEB).   İstanbul: Intermedya,
1995. 140p.
This booklet gives an overview of privatization implementation in Turkey since 1990.
It provides information about relevant legislation, and those authorities and organs
established under the legislation. Although the date of publication is quite recent, parts
of the legislation have been subject to amendments, or have been repealed by the

Constitutional Court at certain times. Therefore, the book must be read with some caution.

614 **Handbook of Turkish law.**
Engin Ural. Ankara, İstanbul: Önder Matbaası, 1997. 3rd ed. 200p.
Provides basic information for foreigners about the Turkish legal system on a wide range of topics such as banking, marriage and divorce, passports, certain misdemeanours and felonies, estate rentals and sales.

615 **Fortunes made, fortunes lost. The saga of the İstanbul Stock Exchange.**
Abdurrahman Yıldırım, translated from the Turkish by Lucy Wood. İstanbul: Intermedya, 1996. 261p.
The book provides introductory information on the Turkish capital markets, and details experiences which may be helpful for the investors. It also gives a ten-year review of investments in Turkey and discusses the evolution of the Capital Market Board, investors, and the evolution of the İstanbul Stock Exchange.

616 **Türk Anayasa Mahkemesi.** (Turkish Constitutional Court.)
The Turkish Constitutional Court (Anayasa Mahkemesi). Ankara: Anayasa Mahkemesi, 1995. 52p. bibliog.
This booklet is in Turkish but contains an English translation (p. 13-24), where introductory information is given on the establishment, composition, tasks, and duties of the Constitutional Court, and procedures to challenge the unconstitutionality of laws before the Court. The bibliography contains reference material in English, French and German.

In the house of the law. Gender and Islamic law in Ottoman Syria and Palestine.
See item no. 214.

Studies in Ottoman history and law.
See item no. 231.

Ebu's-su'ud: the Islamic legal tradition.
See item no. 232.

The development of Turkish trade unionism: a study of legislative and socio-political dimensions.
See item no. 838.

Ten years with seventeen-ten: a decade in the conservation of traditional vernacular houses 1973-1983.
See item no. 958.

Ankara Üniversitesi Hukuk Fakültesi Dergisi. (Journal of Ankara University Faculty of Law.)
See item no. 1314.

Constitution and Legal System

Banka ve Ticaret Hukuku Dergisi. (Journal of Banking and Commercial Law.)
See item no. 1315.

İstanbul Üniversitesi Hukuk Fakültesi Dergisi. (Journal of İstanbul University Faculty of Law.)
See item no. 1335.

Administration and Local Government

Ottoman administration

617 **Problems in the Ottoman administration in Syria during the 16th and 17th centuries: the case of Sanjak of Sidon-Beirut.**
Abdul-Rahim Abu-Husayn. *International Journal of Middle East Studies,* vol. 24, no. 4 (1992), p. 665-75.
By using the Ottoman chancery documents and the local chronicles, the article elaborates on the formation and problems of Ottoman administration in the Druze country, namely the sanjak of Sidon-Beirut. The author explains why Druzes, who were not regarded as true Muslims in the Ottoman system, resisted the Ottoman government, and underlines the social, religious and administrative-fiscal factors as important elements.

618 **Bandits and bureaucrats: the Ottoman route to state centralization.**
Karen Barkey. Ithaca, New York: Cornell University Press, 1997. reprint. 304p.
First published in 1994, this study presents a structuralist model of state formation by analysing the nature of change in the Ottoman Empire during the 17th century. The author examines three groups: regional elites, rural populations of peasants and nomads, and bandits.

619 **Town officials, tımar-holders, and taxation: the late 16th century crisis as seen from Çorum.**
Suraiya Faroqhi. *Varia Turcica,* no. 18 (1986), p. 53-82.
The author investigates the relationship among local officials, their relations with the central administration and the way in which taxes were levied at the local level. The author uses a record book by the *kadı* (judge and governor) of Çorum during the

period 1595-97. When the state officials decided to levy *avarız* (supplementary payments above and beyond the regular taxes), the community financed the town *kethüda*'s (steward) trip to İstanbul to petition against such injustice. Urban cohesion was intact in Çorum, and it seems that many townships exercised a freedom of manoeuvre within the larger frame of the Ottoman administration.

620 **Bureaucratic reform in the Ottoman Empire: the Sublime Porte, 1789-1922.**
Carter V. Findley. Princeton, New Jersey: Princeton University Press, 1980. 455p. bibliog. (Princeton Studies on the Near East).

This monograph reviews the evolution of the civil bureaucracy in the central administration of the Ottoman Empire from the accession of Selim II in 1789 to the end of the Empire in 1922. The first three chapters of the book deal with the origin and the expansion of the traditional scribal service in the Empire. The foundation and development of the civil bureaucracy at the centre of the State are analysed in chapters four to seven.

621 **Ottoman civil officialdom.**
Carter V. Findley. Princeton, New Jersey: Princeton University Press, 1989. 342p. bibliog.

This book is a sequel to the author's *Bureaucratic reform in the Ottoman Empire: the Sublime Porte, 1789-1922* (see item no. 620). While the former examined the administrative system and reforms, this book is a social history of the administrators and discusses the transformation of the scribal service (*kalemiye*) to the civil service (*mülkiye*). Accordingly, governmental assertiveness, chronic economic crisis, egalitarianism, and cultural dualism (i. e. religious as opposed to secular nationalist identity) were the forces which transformed Ottoman civil officialdom. Individual portraits of civil servants, mostly associated with the Foreign Ministry, as drawn by the author, familiarize the reader with the system, and with their aspirations, humour, successes and failures. This humanization of the bureaucracy makes the book most readable as well as insightful.

622 **Ottoman civil administration.**
Carter V. Findley. Princeton, New Jersey: Princeton University Press, 1989. 399p.

The book begins with the Ottoman service in the days when Sultans' administrators were still technically slaves. After reviewing the Tanzimat reforms of 1830, the author deals with issues such as the social origin, recruitment, education, promotion, intellectual orientations, and career patterns of Ottoman civil servants until the dissolution of the Empire. The main focus of the work is on the Foreign Office.

623 **Bureaucrat and intellectual in the Ottoman Empire: the historian Mustafa Ali.**
Cornell H. Fleischer. Princeton, New Jersey: Princeton University Press, 1986. 348p. bibliog.

Mustafa Ali was a poet, translator of treatises (on sex as well as on government) from Persian, historian, and socio-political critic. As a bureaucrat he served four sultans, from Suleiman the Magnificent to his great-grandson Mehmed III. The author presents a portrait of 16th-century Ottoman political and intellectual thought through the person of Mustafa Ali.

624 Preliminaries to the study of the Ottoman bureaucracy.

Cornell Fleischer. *Journal of Turkish Studies*, vol. 10 (1986), p. 135-41.

The article examines the human formation and structure of Ottoman bureaucracy, the *kalemiye,* in the early 16th century. The author concludes that Kanuni Sultan Süleyman (Suleiman the Magnificent) formulated a deliberate policy to increase the scope and number of the bureaucratic body in order 'to build a professional, self-sustaining bureaucracy as a distinctive part of the Ottoman administration'. The professionalization and expansion of the bureaucracy also paved the way for social mobility, and thus might have been caused by pressure from below, to find distinguished jobs for graduates of a *medrese* (Muslim high-school for the teaching of the Sunni law) and sons of dignitaries. As a result, a new professional path was established between men of the sword and those of learning with the 'new men' being learned in protocol and finance.

625 The Ottoman State and the question of state autonomy: comparative perspectives.

John Haldon. In: *New approaches to state and peasant in Ottoman history.* Edited by Halil Berktay, Suraiya Faroqhi. London: Frank Cass, 1992, p. 18-108.

Haldon's article attests that socio-economic factors cannot be divorced from administration: the fact that 'some political leaderships are able for a while to pursue policies and promote strategies which are in fact fundamentally in contradiction to the interests of major sections of society does not, of course, mean that absolute political autonomy is a real possibility' (p. 87). The ruling elite in the Ottoman Empire was neither class-based nor hereditary and hence was seemingly autonomous. Struggles among the ruling class were to a large degree based on the distribution of surpluses appropriated from the countryside. Moreover, patronage networks which tied the central government to the provinces reduced the Sultan's absolutism. Socio-economic dynamics defy categorizations such as 'absolutism' or 'oriental despotism'.

626 The Sultan's servants: the transformation of Ottoman provincial government, 1550-1650.

Metin I. Kunt. New York: Columbia University Press, 1983. 181p. bibliog.

An account of the transformation of the Ottoman Empire into a highly centralized and consolidated state. At the provincial level, the 'households' were a reflection of the central palatial establishment and this is a key-word for the author. While regionalism, localism, nepotism and patronage are prevalent in contemporary democracies, the roots of patronage systems in the medieval Ottoman Empire give fascinating insights into the history of such networks. The author bases his research on Appointments and Registers, i. e. on the personnel records for the Ottoman provinces in the 16th century. In sum, this is the history of how central government officials were promoted to take over provincial administration and, perhaps more importantly, how patronage, which stemmed from household affiliations, became a dominant factor in the polity.

627 **Palestinian peasants and Ottoman officials: rural administration around sixteenth-century Jerusalem.**
Amy Singer. Boston, Massachusetts: Cambridge University Press, 1994. 207p. bibliog. (Cambridge Studies in Islamic Civilization).

A case-study of the relationship between the Palestinian peasants and the state in the 16th century. The peasant, as producer and taxpayer, was an important economic component of the Empire. Taxes were pre-calculated based on the expected amount of production. However, when less tax was paid, conflict became inevitable. An agricultural economy, therefore, was precariously balanced between state bankruptcy and the pauperization of the producers. The book reveals the relationship between the administrators, and the Palestinian *reaya* (non-Muslim subjects), through a consultation of both the cadastral and court registries.

628 **The Seljuk vezirate: a study of civil administration, 1055-1194.**
Carla L. Klausner. Cambridge, Massachusetts: Harvard University Press, 1973. 143p. bibliog. (Harvard Middle Eastern Monographs, no. 22).

The study analyses the government organization of the Seljuks in general, and the institution of the *vezirate* in particular, the functions of which included financial, military, judicial, religious and ceremonial matters and the exercise of patronage.

629 **From the Ottoman experiment in local government to the first constitutional parliament of 1876-77.**
İlber Ortaylı. *The Turkish Yearbook of International Relations*, no. 21 (1982-91), p. 17-24.

Local government was quite a recent phenomenon in the Ottoman Empire for Muslims and non-Muslims alike; indeed, some scholars assert that certain craft guilds or religious orders constituted the local government. The author argues that this was not the case because any local government must be based on economic and financial autonomy as well as incorporating local people into that institutional framework. Likewise, the *millet* (a community defined by religion) system should not be a criterion for local government, since that system took religion as social identity, and therefore was not autonomous. The practice of local government was first introduced during the Tanzimat era by abolishing tax-farming. Collection councils were then set up, which included notables. There was, however, a dichotomy between commitment to decentralization and conservative centralization. What emerged was a limited degree of self-government (largely because of the shortage of trained personnel) within an 'essentially centralized framework'.

630 **Some notes on the *salyane* system in the Ottoman Empire as organized in Arabia in the sixteenth century.**
Salih Özbaran. *Osmanlı Araştırmaları*, vol. 6 (1986), p. 39-45.

This is a comparative study on the *salyane* (annual tax) system in some Arab provinces of the Ottoman Empire such as Yemen, Basra and Lahsa, showing that the system was not necessarily uniform.

631 **The müfti of İstanbul: a study in the development of the Ottoman learned hierarchy.**
R. C. Repp. London: Ithaca Press for the Board of the Oriental Studies, Oxford University, 1986. 325p. bibliog. (Oxford Oriental Institute Monographs, no. 8).

The book focuses on the *mufti* of İstanbul. It looks at the roots of this institution in the early 1400s, and follows its development until the late 1500s. This biographical research, which connects the evolution of the office with the careers of its occupants, is concerned with how, why and under which circumstances the office attained its pre-eminence among both the learned classes and in the political hierarchy.

632 **Ottoman political reform in the provinces: the Damascus advisory council in 1844-45.**
Elizabeth Thompson. *International Journal of Middle East Studies,* vol. 25, no. 4 (1993), p. 457-75.

The article reevaluates centre-periphery relations in the early Tanzimat period by focusing on the Damascus council during the period 1844-45. The councils were reorganized across the Ottoman Empire in 1840 as a part of the Tanzimat reform. The author concludes that like many of the European cases, compromising deals were made between the Ottoman state and the elite landowning class, which dominated peasants and treated them as unequal parties.

633 **An analytical study of the administrative and social policy of the Ottoman state (16th and 17th centuries).**
Gülgün Üçel-Aybet. *Varia Turcica,* vol. 4 (1987), p. 159-70.

The Islamic law, state laws and the army comprised the backbone of the Ottoman centralized state system. The social order, that is, the welfare and security of the *reaya*, also depended on the smooth functioning of laws and the military. While social mobility was severely curtailed – with few exceptions – occupational mobility was allowed as long as the individual's family remained in the class to which they belonged. Political mores dictated that injustices be redressed swiftly. In the newly conquered lands, the Ottomans secured the allegiance of the population by returning their possessions and by systematically alienating them from the aristocrats whom they formerly served. The native landed nobility was not permitted 'to use the services of the native people of the same region but had to purchase slaves'.

634 **The role of *ayan*s in regional development during the pre-Tanzimat period in Turkey: a case study of the Karaosmanoğlu family.**
Nagata Yuzo. In: *The proceedings of the international conference on urbanism in Islam (October 22-28, 1989).* Tokyo: Middle Eastern Culture Centre in Japan, 1989, p. 166-91.

This study depicts the term *ayan* as a social class which derived power from taxes, farming, a large estate, and a local office. The Karaosmanoğlu family from Manisa was an example of this class. In the 18th century respective members of the family tenaciously held onto power and wealth, even when confronted with Sultan Mahmud II's efforts at centralization in the first part of the 19th century. The pious foundations which the family endowed were not only another source of power, but also contributed to the urbanization of the Saruhan province, beginning with İzmir. The Karaosmanoğlu *ayan*s were agents of local/self government.

Turkish Republic

635 **The politics of rapid urbanization: government and growth in Modern Turkey.**
Michael N. Danielson, Ruşen Keleş. New York; London: Holmes & Meier, 1985. 286p.

The book describes the role of the government in Turkish urban growth and examines the impact of government on patterns of urbanization, including migration, settlement patterns, distribution of jobs, housing, and location of facilities such as transport. The authors conclude that centralization of authority leads to fragmentation of function. Hence, attempts to deal with uncontrolled urban growth have been largely ineffective.

636 **Relations between central and local governments in Turkey: an historical perspective.**
Melih Ersoy. *Public Administration and Development*, vol. 12, no. 4 (1992), p. 325-41.

The article presents an analysis of the administration of Turkish municipalities since the mid-19th century. It covers political, administrative, financial as well as historical developments with respect to the legal and institutional framework of urban planning, which is essentially paternalistic and authoritarian. The author also assesses the authenticity of the recent liberalization policies, and the subsequent implementation mechanisms devised since 1984.

637 **Organizational socialization as reality-testing: the case of the Turkish higher civil servants.**
Metin Heper, Ersin Kalaycıoğlu. *International Journal of Political Education*, vol. 6, no. 2 (1983), p. 175-98.

The authors examine the role of the family, school, and organization, in the political socialization of the Turkish bureaucratic elite. The results show that the elitist attitude is usually acquired through direct socialization at school, and not as a direct recipient of values from the parents. This is dysfunctional in a polity which since the mid-1940s has adopted competitive politics. The bureaucrat who faces this reality tempers his elitist attitude.

638 **Dilemmas of decentralization: municipal government in Turkey.**
Edited by Metin Heper. Bonn: Friedrich Ebert Stiftung, 1986. 128p.

A useful survey of the subject, though rapid changes in this field have now rendered it rather out-of-date. Papers (by Ruşen Keleş, Ayşe Öncü, Hans F. Illy, and the editor) include an overview of Turkish local government between 1923 and 1980, municipal finance with special reference to İstanbul, the potential and limitations of local government, especially in İstanbul, directions for reform, and decentralization as a tool for development.

639   **The state and public bureaucracies: a comparative perspective.**
Edited by Metin Heper. New York: Greenwood Press, 1987. 201p.
This volume contains global theoretical chapters as well as country studies, including the United States, Great Britain, Germany, France and Turkey.

640   **Democracy and local government: İstanbul in the 1980s.**
Edited by Metin Heper. Huntingdon, England: The Eothen Press, 1987. 64p.
A useful short collection of papers on the reform of local government in the 1980s as it affected İstanbul. The volume includes papers by Üstün Ergüder, Ruşen Keleş, and the editor, on the decentralization of local government, Turkish political culture, a grassroots perspective of municipal government in İstanbul, and developments in municipal finance.

641   **Local government in Turkey: governing greater İstanbul.**
Edited by Metin Heper. London: Routledge, 1989. 92p.
The book discusses the scope for political and administrative decentralization within the İstanbul metropolitan municipality.

642   **The state debureaucratization: the Turkish case.**
Metin Heper. *International Social Science Journal,* no. 126 (1990), p. 605-15.
The author first discusses the concept of state and its institutionalization as a bureaucratic structure in a number of countries, and then exposes the development and the characteristics of the state in Turkey. He argues that the post-1980 Turkish state was restructured in the office of the presidency and the National Security Council with a ruler-dominated government, which was isolated from civil societal elements. Consequently, the rest of the administration was debureaucratized and became insignificant.

643   **The restructuring of local administration in Turkey.**
Korel Göymen. In: *Local administration: democracy versus efficiency?* Edited by Korel Göymen, Hans F. Ily, Winfried Veit.
Bonn: Friedrich Ebert Stiftung, 1982, p. 137-52.
This paper contains the basic proposals and suggestions which help in the preparation of pertinent legislation, and the administrative restructuring process which was expected to commence after the new Constitution (1982) had been accepted by a referendum. Two sections precede the actual body of proposals, which contain a short historical background of Turkish local administration, including recent developments and the nature of central government domination of municipalities in Turkey, which is useful for readers not intimately acquainted with Turkey.

644 **Perspectives in the centre-local relations: political dynamics in the Middle East.**
Takeji Ino. Tokyo: Institute of Developing Economies, 1991. 204p.

Although the book is not specifically on Turkey, it is nevertheless an important source for comparative studies. The first three chapters deal with Egypt, and the fourth chapter covers Sudan. The final chapter focuses on mayors and party elites in post-1983 Turkey, analysing the dynamics of intergovernmental relations.

645 **Decentralization: experience and prerequisites.**
Ruşen Keleş. In: *Local administration: democracy versus efficiency?*
Edited by Korel Göymen, Hans F. Illy, Winfried Veit. Bonn:
Friedrich Ebert Stiftung, 1982, p. 69-82.

The author claims that the concepts of territorial decentralization and functional decentralization were incorporated into Turkey's administrative structure in the late 19th century. He also asserts that proposals which aimed at creating a highly decentralized administrative set-up based on a semi-federalist model were not found acceptable simply because of the need for preserving the territorial integrity of the Ottoman Empire, which was a multinational state. The paper proceeds to discuss, in a comparative framework and with reference to the legal context within which this evolution took place, the evolution of the municipal administration in Turkey, and its present state.

646 **The metropolitan administration in Turkey.**
Ruşen Keleş. *Turkish Public Administration Annual*, vol. 12
(1985-86), p. 91-110.

The article gives a brief history of urbanization in Turkey since 1923, together with an overview of the development of municipalities in the Ottoman-Turkish context. Other parts of the work cover the constitutional-legal basis and practices of the metropolitan administration model in Turkey, which was introduced after 1984. The author discusses the successes and failures of the model and the prospects for the future.

647 **Local politics and democracy in Turkey: an appraisal.**
Levent Köker. *Annals of the American Academy of Political and Social Science*, vol. 540 (1995), p. 51-62.

Argues that local governments in Turkey were created by and for the central state. In the first place a social, democratic municipal movement emerged to put an end to central government tutelage. This was followed by a new conservatism, a synthesis of technical reason and traditional nationalism, which identified local political problems with technical problems of urban management. Recently, Islamic political parties have adopted this synthesis. The author elaborates on the respective capabilities of major trends in local government.

648   **Some basic problems of local administration.**
Turgut Tan.   In: *Local administration: democracy versus efficiency?*
Edited by Korel Göymen, Hans F. Illy, Winfried Veit.   Bonn:
Friedrich Ebert Stiftung, 1982, p. 131-36.

The paper aims to discuss the basic problems concerning local administration in
Turkey in the light of constitutional principles. The author discusses the local administration in the Constitution of 1961 and the 1982 Constitutional Draft (which later
became the Third Constitution of the Republic).

**Can municipalities in Turkey be considered as institutions of civic
society with a broad social base?**
See item no. 896.

**The development of the İstanbul metropolitan area: urban administra-
tion and planning.**
See item no. 900.

Turkish Public Administration Annual.
See item no. 1379.

Foreign Relations

General

649 **Étatism and diplomacy in Turkey: economic and foreign policy strategies in an uncertain world, 1929-1939.**
Dilek Barlas.   Leiden, the Netherlands: E. J. Brill, 1998. 256p.
bibliog. (The Ottoman Empire and Its Heritage: Politics, Society and Economy, no. 14).

The volume deals with Turkey's étatist policy and foreign relations in the early years of the Turkish Republic. It elucidates the symbiotic relationship between Turkey's internal developments and its international strategies. The first part of the book examines the theory and politics of étatism, while the second part looks at the diplomacy of the interwar period.

650 **View from Turkey: Turkey's new security environment, nuclear weapons and proliferation.**
Duygu Bazoğlu Sezer.   *Comparative Strategy*, vol. 14, no. 2 (1995), p. 149-72.

A brief study on Turkish perceptions of the changing security environment at the end of the Cold War. Turkey's views on nuclear energy, the nuclear option and the potential for proliferation in neighbouring states are presented. The author pays particular attention to the dissolution of the Soviet Union and its impact on Turkey's perceptions and policies.

651 **Turkey's strategic position at the crossroads of world affairs.**
S. J. Blank , S. C. Pelletiere, W. T. Johnson.   Carlisle, Pennsylvania:
Strategic Studies Institute, U.S. Army War College, 1993. 133p.
The authors analyse the effects of Turkish policies in Europe, the Middle East and the
former Soviet Republics, and discuss the implications of these policies for US policy
formation.

652 **Turkish foreign policy during the Second World War: an 'active'**
neutrality.
Selim Deringil.   Cambridge, England: Cambridge University Press,
1989. 238p. bibliog. (LSE Monographs in International Studies).
The first section of the book examines the historical legacy of the Ottoman Empire and
in particular the social, economic and military factors that influenced foreign policy
making in republican Turkey. The following chapters concentrate on Turkish policy
between 1940 and 1945, concluding with an account of the Soviet demands on Turkey at
the end of the war. The study is based on British government archives as well as Numan
Menemencioğlu's (then Turkey's Minister of Foreign Affairs) unpublished memoirs.

653 **Turkish foreign policy: new prospects.**
Edited by Clement H. Dodd.   Huntingdon, England: The Eothen
Press, 1992. 117p. (Modern Turkish Studies Programme, SOAS.
Occasional Papers, no. 2).
This collection of papers provides an overview of Turkey's foreign relations in the
changing external environment of the 1990s against the background of Turkey's belief
in its European destiny and aspiration to become a member of the European Union.
The titles are: 'The Turco-Greek dispute', Süha Bölükbaşı; 'Turkish foreign policy
since Atatürk', Selim Deringil; 'EC and Turkey', Michael Cendrovitz; 'Turkish for-
eign policy in the Middle East', Andrew Mango; 'Turkish foreign policy in the Gulf
Crisis', Philip Robins; and 'Turkey's expanding relations with the CIS and Eastern
Europe', Türkkaya Ataöv.

654 **The political and socioeconomic transformation of Turkey.**
Edited by Atilla Eralp, Muharrem Tunay, Birol Yeşilada.   Westport,
Connecticut: Praeger, 1993. 244p. bibliog.
The chapter on 'Turkish foreign policy towards the Middle East' by Birol Yeşilada
(p. 169-92) is a critical analysis of Turkey's policies. Duygu Sezer's contribution to
the volume, entitled 'Turkey and the Western Alliance in the 1980s' (p. 215-29), provides a summary and analysis of Turkey's troubled relations with NATO during the
1980s.

655 **Turkey's new geo-politics: from the Balkans to western China.**
Graham E. Fuller, Ian O. Lesser, with Paul B. Henze, J. F. Brown.
Boulder, Colorado: Westview, 1993. 197p. bibliog.
This is a useful study, though some of the contributors may have overestimated
Turkey's international role. The opening section, by Paul B. Henze, discusses overall
trends in Turkey's international relations since the end of the Cold War. This is
followed by a discussion of Turkey's relations with the Middle Eastern states and the

CIS by Graham E. Fuller. In the following section, Ian O. Lesser considers Turkey's strategic relationships with Europe and the United States. J. F. Brown discusses Turkey's relations with the Balkan countries; however, it tells the reader little about Turkish policy towards this region.

656 **Turkey: toward the twenty-first century.**
Paul B. Henze. Santa Monica, California: RAND, 1992. 42p. (RAND, no. 3558).

Discusses the most important trends in Turkey's political, economic and social development in the 1980s, and presents projections for the 1990s.

657 **Turkish democracy and the American alliance.**
Paul B. Henze. Santa Monica, California: RAND, 1993. 52p. (RAND, no. 7796).

After a brief survey of American relations with the Ottoman Empire, the publication describes the establishment of relations between the United States and the Turkish Republic, and their development from the proclamation of the Truman Doctrine in 1947 to date.

658 **Turkey and Atatürk's legacy: Turkey's political evolution, U.S relations and prospects for the 21st century.**
Paul B. Henze. Haarlem, the Netherlands: SOTA, 1998. 186p.

Written by a sympathetic and knowledgeable observer of Turkey for many years, this work offers an up-to-date review and interpretation of Turkish-American relations over the years, and Henze's own views about Turkey's prospects for the future. In 'Turkey and Atatürk's legacy', Henze also provides a brief history of the Republic, and the book has chapters on the Özal era and on Turkey in the 1990s.

659 **Turkey and the Southern Flank: domestic and external contexts.**
Ali Karaosmanoğlu. In: *NATO's Southern Allies: internal and external challenges.* Edited by John Chipman. London; New York: Routledge, 1988, p. 287-353.

Analyses the impact of internal and external factors on Turkey's security policy-making. The author emphasizes the role played by domestic factors such as religion, civil and military bureaucracy, political parties and public opinion in the formulation and implementation of Turkey's security policies.

660 **Turkish foreign policy: recent developments.**
Edited by Kemal H. Karpat. Madison, Wisconsin: University of Wisconsin Press, 1996. 218p.

The volume contains an introduction by the editor, followed by twelve essays which present a survey of contemporary Turkish foreign policy towards the following regions and organizations: Europe (Ali L. Karaosmanoğlu, Brock Millman, Birol A. Yeşilada); New Independent States (Umut Arık); the Organization for Black Sea Economic Cooperation (Oral Sander); the Organization of the Islamic Conference (Ekmeleddin İhsanoğlu); Greece (Baskın Oran); the Middle East (Erol Manisalı); and Cyprus (Faruk Sönmezoğlu, Necati M. Ertekün).

661 **An analysis of Atatürk's foreign policy, 1919-1938.**
Ömer Kürkçüoğlu. *The Turkish Yearbook of International Relations 1980-81*, vol. 20 (1986), p. 133-89.
In this comprehensive analysis of Turkey's foreign policy during the Atatürk era, the author focuses on the foreign policy principles set by Atatürk in his time. By placing these principles into their historical context, he brings a new dimension to the subject.

662 **Turkey between East and West: new challenges for a rising regional power.**
Edited by Vojtech Mastny, R. Craig Nation. Boulder, Colorado: Westview Press, 1997. 296p.
The authors of this volume address aspects of Turkey's role in the changing international arena, including its historical and contemporary place in Europe, the Cold War legacy, and strategies for future political and economic development. After an introductory historical chapter on Ottoman rule in Europe (K. H. Karpat), and the development of Turkey's relations with the West since the Second World War (B. R. Kuniholm), the following chapters look at: Turkey's new security environment in the Balkans and the Black Sea region (Duygu Bazoğlu Sezer); the Turkic and other Muslim peoples of Central Asia, the Caucasus and the Balkans (R. Craig Nation); developments in Turkish democracy (C. H. Dodd); and state, society and democracy in Turkey (İlkay Sunar). There are also contributions on Turkey's economic development (Ziya Öniş) and on the Black Sea Economic Cooperation (N. Bülent Gültekin and Ayşe Mumcu). Relations between Turkey and the European Union are discussed by Henz Kramer, and Turkish communities in western Europe by Faruk Şen.

663 **The US-Turkish-NATO Middle East connection: how the Truman doctrine and Turkey's NATO entry contained the Soviets.**
George McGhee. London: Macmillan, 1990. 224p. bibliog.
This book offers an original first-hand account of Turkish-United States relations during the post-war years by a Cold War warrior who, besides serving other senior State Department appointments, was Assistant Secretary of State for the Near East before becoming the US Ambassador to Turkey between 1951 and 1953. The book contains valuable information, although it could have been organized better.

664 **Daring and caution in Turkish foreign policy.**
Malik Mufti. *Middle East Journal*, vol. 52, no. 1 (1998), p. 32-50.
The article outlines the main features of Turkey's new post-Cold War security environment, and assesses the role of historical legacies, institutional structures and normative pressures in shaping the contemporary debate about Turkey's foreign policy orientation.

665 **Israel, Turkey and Greece: uneasy relations in the East Mediterranean.**
Amikam Nachmani. London: Frank Cass, 1987. 130p.
The author focuses on the tripartite relations between Israel, Turkey and Greece. He describes the bones of contention which exist among the three states, while analysing the areas and periods of understanding and agreement. Through his use of Israeli state

archives, the author adds valuable insight into Israeli-Turkish relations between 1948 and 1958, during the formative years of the state of Israel.

666 **Nationalism and peace: the significance of Atatürk's movement.**
Oral Sander. *The Turkish Yearbook of International Relations,*
1980-81, vol. 20 (1986), p. 245-63.
A brief article on Turkey's foreign policy during the Atatürk era (1923-38). The author emphasizes the significance of Atatürk's motto 'Peace at home peace abroad'; he claims that Atatürk's foreign policy can only be understood if the two parts of the sentence 'peace at home' and 'peace abroad' are taken as interdependent.

Turkey and the West

667 **Turkey's foreign policy and its implications for the West: a Turkish perspective.**
Gülnur Aybet. London: Royal United Services Institute for Defence Studies, 1994. 60p.
The book gives an outline of Turkish foreign policy after 1991, and points out that despite policies which may appear to be a radical departure, Turkey's stance is a continuation of a strategy adopted a decade ago.

668 **Turkey and Europe.**
Edited by Canan Balkır, Alan M. Williams. London; New York: Pinter Publishers, 1993. 247p.
Concentrates on relations between Turkey and the European Union. The contributors are Atila Eralp, Gülten Kazgan, Ayşe Kadıoğlu, Şükrü S. Gürel, Türkkaya Ataöv, Feride Acar and the editors. Part one places this theme into the broader context of changes in the international system; part two focuses on economic relations; and part three concentrates on political and cultural factors such as the role of Islam, and Turkey's relations with the Commonwealth of Independent States, Eastern Europe and Greece. The concluding chapter provides an overall assessment of Turkey's role in the area in the aftermath of the Gulf Crisis.

669 **Turkey and the European Community.**
Edited by Ahmet Evin, Geoffrey Denton. Opladen, Germany: Leske & Budrich, 1990. 204p. bibliog. (Schriften des Deutschen Orient-Instituts).
Due to publication delays, this collection of papers was already rather out-of-date when it was first published in 1990, and is more so now. Nevertheless, it offers a useful survey of the topic, as it appeared in the early 1980s. It begins with a discussion of cultural issues (Şerif Mardin, Ahmet Evin), and continues with some historical background on the relationship (Selim İlkin, Roswitha Bourgignon) and options for future relations (Bernard Burrows, Seyfi Taşhan, Geoffrey Denton). The following chapters

deal with the constitutional and legal implications of a possible Turkish membership of the EC/EU (Tuğrul Ansay), and Greek-Turkish relations (Andrew Mango, Matthias Esche). The final section deals with economic issues (William Hale, Harun Gümrükçü, İsmet Ergün, Geoffrey Denton).

670 **Four centuries of Turco-British relations. Studies in diplomatic, economic and cultural affairs.**
William Hale, Ali İhsan Bağış.   Huntingdon, England: The Eothen Press, 1984. 141p.

A collection of studies by Turkish and British scholars which provides an understanding of the course of Turco-British relations against a background of significant events in European history.

671 **Turkish economic liberalization and European integration.**
Meltem Müftüler (Bac).   *Middle Eastern Studies*, vol. 31, no. 1 (1995), p. 85-98.

A study on the mutual impact of Turkey's relations with the European Union and its economic and foreign policy making. The author discusses the extent to which economic reforms undertaken in the 1980s were shaped by Turkish policy makers' concerns regarding the potential ramifications of these reforms on Turkey's relationship with, and bid to join, the European Union.

672 **Turkey's relations with a changing Europe.**
Meltem Müftüler-Bac.   Manchester, England: Manchester University Press, 1997. 208p. bibliog.

The author analyses the impact of the end of the Cold War on Turkey's internal and external policies with special reference to the new European order.

673 **Turkey in Europe and Europe in Turkey.**
Turgut Özal.   Nicosia: K. Rüstem & Brother, 1991. 371p. bibliog.

This book is interesting because it is the only book-length work in English which, at least nominally, comes from the pen of the late Prime Minister and President of Turkey. In a generally lucid and readable style, Turgut Özal reviews the history of relations between Turkey and Europe, in support of the case for Turkey's admission as a full member of the European Union. Chapter twenty-one is particularly important as it outlines the broader policies of Özal's Motherland Party, and thus also has relevance to Turkish domestic politics.

674 **The next Mediterranean enlargement of the European Community: Turkey, Cyprus and Malta?**
John Redmond.   Aldershot, England; Brookfield, Vermont: Dartmouth Publishing Company, 1993. 157p. bibliog.

Books on Turkey's relations with what is now the European Union run the risk of becoming outdated rapidly due to the constantly changing institutional and political environment. Nonetheless, the chapter on Turkey provides a refreshingly objective and well informed analysis of the relationship as it was in the early 1990s, much of which still holds good.

675 **Turkey: the changing European security environment and the Gulf Crisis.**
Sabri Sayarı. *Middle East Journal*, vol. 46, no. 1 (1992), p. 9-21.
In this essay on Turkey's foreign policy in the aftermath of the Cold War, the author focuses on what he terms the 'new thinking' that shaped Turkish foreign policy during Turgut Özal's presidency. The period covered is 1989-92. The author touches upon some of the major issues in European security, the Gulf Crisis, and the policies Turkey adopted during this short time span.

Turkey: the challenge of a new role.
See item no. 14.

Türkiye-Avrupa Topluluğu bibliyografyası, I: 1957-1990. (Turkey-European Community bibliography, I: 1957-90.)
See item no. 1402.

Türkiye-Avrupa Topluluğu bibliyografyası, II: 1990-1992. (Turkey-European Community bibliography, II: 1990-92.)
See item no. 1403.

Turkey and the Balkans

676 **Greece and Turkey, adversity in alliance.**
Edited by Jonathan Alford.   Aldershot, England: Gower Press for the International Institute for Strategic Studies, 1984. 151p. maps.
(Adelphi Library, no. 12).
After a general introduction, this book contains five chapters which focus on Turkish and Greek security policies, and on the Aegean dispute. Two of the chapters comprise the texts of speeches delivered by the Greek politician Ioannis Pesmazoglu, and the Turkish Prime Minister Bülent Ecevit to the International Institute for Strategic Studies.

677 **The Mediterranean feud.**
Andrew Borowiec.   New York: Praeger, 1983. 190p. bibliog.
This is a partly journalistic account of problems in Turkish-Greek relations and their impact on NATO and the United States specifically. The author makes use of interviews conducted in Turkey, Greece and Cyprus. The significance of domestic developments in Turkey and Greece are examined, and recommendations are given for a possible solution to the Cyprus question.

678   **The United States, Greece and Turkey: the troubled triangle.**
Theodore A. Couloumbis.   New York: Praeger, 1983. 232p. bibliog.
(Praeger Special Studies, Studies of Influence in International
Relations).
The author examines Greek and Turkish relations with the United States, and the
impact of these relations on bilateral ties between Athens and Ankara. The focus on
this triangular relationship is on events after the 1960s, with particular attention paid
to the Cyprus question, the Aegean issue, and United States military installations in
Greece and Turkey.

679   **Balkans: a mirror of the new international order.**
Edited by Günay Göksu Özdoğan, Kemali Saybaşılı.   İstanbul: Eren,
1995. 351p.
Contains the published papers of an international symposium on Turkey and the
Balkans held in April 1993, organized by the Department of International Relations,
Marmara University, İstanbul. The papers, which specifically focus on Turkey, discuss
Ottoman foreign policy in the Balkans and the Ottoman legacy in the region, Turkish
nationalism and the Balkan question, regional security and Turkey's role, and
Turkey's diplomatic initiatives in the Bosnian crisis.

680   **Balkan triangle: birth and decline of an alliance across ideological
boundaries.**
John O. Iatrides.   The Hague: Mouton, 1968. 211p. map.
Discusses the origins, background and development of the February 1953 Treaty of
Friendship and Collaboration between Turkey, Yugoslavia and Greece (the Treaty of
Ankara), which aimed for regional cooperation in the Balkans. The book also examines the Treaty of Bled of August 1954, concluded between the three states, which
referred to joint defence against aggression. An analysis is given of the ineffectiveness
of the two treaties.

681   **The implications of the Yugoslav crisis for Western Europe's
foreign relations.**
Edited by Mathias Jopp.   Paris: Institute for Security Studies, Western
European Union, 1994. 91p. (Chaillot Papers, no. 17).
In this work scholars from various countries analyse the perceptions of their states,
and of Western Europe's handling of the Yugoslav crisis. Duygu B. Sezer's chapter,
entitled 'Implications for Turkey's relations with Western Europe', notes that the negative public image in Turkey of Western Europe's role in the Bosnian crisis may
ultimately undermine the basis of support for the Turkish government's traditional
pro-Western policy.

682 Post Second World War immigration from Balkan countries to Turkey.

Kemal Kirişçi. *New Perceptions on Turkey*, no. 12 (1995), p. 61-77.

The author argues that Turkey may be considered as an 'immigration country' for Turks and Muslims from Romania, Greece, Yugoslavia and Bulgaria. Muslim immigrants who fled ethnic and religious persecution came to be regarded, in effect, by the authorities in Ankara as immigrants of Turkish origin.

683 The volatile powder keg: Balkan security after the Cold War.

Edited by F. Stephen Larrabee. Washington, DC: The American University Press for the RAND, 1994. 320p.

This collection of papers was originally presented at a conference in Rhodes in September 1991. The contributions focus on Turkey's policies and interests in the Balkans, and include: Ian O. Lesser, 'The strategic environment in the Balkans and the Mediterranean'; F. Stephen Larrabee, 'Washington, Moscow and the Balkans: strategic retreat or re engagement?'; and Graham E. Fuller, 'Turkey in the new international security environment'.

684 Turkey and the Balkans: economic and political dimensions.

Edited by Erol Manisalı. İstanbul: Middle East Business and Banking Publications, 1990. 96p.

Brings together the published papers of one of the International Girne Conferences held in northern Cyprus, where scholars and commentators from Turkey and other countries presented papers on a range of topics, including Greek-Turkish and Turkish-Bulgarian relations, Turkey's economic role in the region, and the impact of developments in the Soviet Union and eastern Europe.

685 The Eastern Question: the last phase: a study in Greek-Turkish diplomacy.

Harry J. Psomiades. Thessaloniki, Greece: Institute for Balkan Studies, 1968. 145p. 3 maps. bibliog.

The author discusses developments in Greek-Ottoman/Turkish relations immediately before and after the foundation of the Turkish Republic. The negotiations conducted at the Conference of Lausanne are examined. Individual chapters analyse, from a Greek perspective, the exchange of the minority Greek and Turkish populations, and focus on the status of the ecumenical Patriarchate based in İstanbul.

686 Entangled allies: US policy toward Greece, Turkey and Cyprus.

Monteagle Stearns. New York: Council of Foreign Relations Press, 1992. 185p.

Contains the views of a former US ambassador to Greece. The book emphasizes the need to 'disentangle' the various problems in Turkish-Greek relations before the Cyprus issue may be resolved. Stearns believes that the ending of the Cold War presents an opportunity to establish a new foundation in the relationship between the two states, and recommends the signing of a Treaty of Friendship and Non-Aggression.

687   **The Western question in Greece and Turkey: a study in the contact
of civilisations.**
Arnold Joseph Toynbee.   London: Constable, 1992; New York:
Howard Fertig, 1970. 420p. maps. bibliog.

The author had the opportunity to study Greek and Ottoman/Turkish affairs at first-
hand during his travels to both countries in 1921. He discusses western diplomacy,
and the policies of the Greeks and the Turks in detail, and provides background information on Anatolia. The book focuses on developments in Greek-Ottoman/Turkish
relations after the First World War.

688   **The Turkish presence in Bulgaria: communications 7 June 1985.**
Turkish Historical Society.   Ankara: Turkish Historical Society, 1986.
90p. maps. (Serial VII, no. 87a).

The four chapters of this book cover the use of the Turkish language in Bulgaria,
Turkish settlement in the Balkans at the time of the Ottoman Empire, the immigration
of Turks from Bulgaria in the 19th and 20th centuries, and 'The question of the
Turkish minority in Bulgaria from the perspective of international law'.

689   **Where East meets West: Turkey and the Balkans.**
Gareth Winrow.   London: Alliance Publishers for the Institute for
European Defence and Strategic Studies, 1993. 38p. (European
Security Study, no. 18).

The author provides an overview of Turkish policy in the Balkans, tracing developments from the final years of the Ottoman Empire to the crisis in Bosnia following the
break-up of Yugoslavia. The position of the Turks in other Balkan states is also discussed. Winrow also considers the possible role of Turkey in the furthering of Balkan
cooperation, taking into account Ankara's sponsoring of the Black Sea Economic
Cooperation process.

Turkey and the Soviet Union, Russia and the former Soviet Republics

690   **The importance of Turkey to relations between Europe and the
Turkic Republics of the former Soviet Union.**
Bülent Aras.   *UCLA Journal of International Law and Foreign
Affairs*, vol. 2, no. 1 (1997), p. 91-112.

The author discusses the relations of European countries with the Turkic Republics,
and Turkey's position with respect to both. He details Europe's economic relations
with each country in the region, and analyses Turkey's role as a facilitator in these
relations. Useful tables and figures accompany the text.

691   **The new geopolitics of Central Asia and its borderlands.**
Edited by Ali Banuazizi, Myron Weiner.   Bloomington, Indiana:
I. B. Tauris, 1994. 284p. map.

Assesses the recent developments in the six post-Soviet Muslim Republics of Central
Asia and Transcaucasus within a geopolitical framework. Chapter five by Tadeusz
Swietochowski, 'Azerbaijan's triangular relationship: the land between Russia,
Turkey and Iran', and chapter seven by Sabri Sayarı, 'Turkey, the Caucasus and
Central Asia', examine Turkey's role in the region, giving some historical background
and focusing on current issues of relevance to regional security.

692   **Black Sea Economic Cooperation. Handbook of Documents.**
Volume one.
Permanent International Secretariat of Black Sea Economic
Cooperation (BSEC).   İstanbul: BSEC Permanent International
Secretariat, 1995. 544p.

This volume covers a three-year period beginning with the İstanbul summit of 25 June
1992. It gives the details of the Bucharest High Level Meeting of 30 June 1995,
reports of the five meetings of the Ministers of Foreign Affairs of the BSEC participating states, as well as the reports of the meetings of the BSEC Subsidiary Bodies, and
the text of the Agreement Establishing the Black Sea Trade and Development Bank.

693   **Black Sea Economic Cooperation. Handbook of Documents.**
Volume two.
Permanent International Secretariat of Black Sea Economic
Cooperation (BSEC).   İstanbul: BSEC Permanent International
Secretariat, 1996. 219p.

Contains the reports of the sixth and seventh meetings of the Ministers of Foreign
Affairs of the BSEC participating states, as well as the reports of the meetings of the
Subsidiary Bodies – Working Groups of Experts, held between July 1995 to
September 1996.

694   **Turkey faces East: new orientations toward the Middle East and**
the old Soviet Union.
Graham E. Fuller.   Santa Monica, California: RAND, 1992. 70p.
bibliog. (R-4232-AF/A).

The book explores the origins of Turkey's interest in 'the East' and discusses the long-
term prospects of Turkey's relations with the Middle East and predominantly with the
ex-Soviet Muslim Republics. The impact of domestic developments on Turkish foreign policy is analysed. The author examines the possible significance of the 'new
Turkish nationalism' and the so-called 'neo-Ottomanism' on Turkey's external
relations.

695   **Turkey: a new actor in the field of energy politics?**
Temel İskit.   *Perceptions*, vol. 1, no. 1 (1996), p. 58-82.

This article, which is written by a deputy undersecretary in the Turkish Ministry of
Foreign Affairs, provides a detailed account of oil pipeline politics, noting the extensive petroleum reserves of Azerbaijan and Kazakhstan. It argues that Turkey is an

important player, although it will be difficult to construct a new Caspian-Mediterranean oil pipeline given Russian interest in energy politics.

696 Will Central Asia become Turkey's sphere of influence?

Heinz Kramer.   *Perceptions*, vol. 1, no. 1 (1996), p. 112-27.

Although Ankara has developed important cultural and scientific relations with the Turkic Republics of the former Soviet Union, Turkey is not likely to establish a politically dominant position in Central Asia given continued Russian influence in the area. The author recommends that Turkish officials downplay the issue of 'ethno-linguistic nearness' and instead encourage the formation of 'regional functional regimes' such as ECO and other multilateral and bilateral arrangements.

697 Central Asia meets the Middle East.

Edited by David Menashri.   London: Frank Cass, 1997. 234p. bibliog.

The book contains essays by authors who dwell on the impact of the formation of independent states in Central Asia and the Transcaucasus on the Middle East, with special emphasis on Turkey and Iran. Contributors include D. Menashri, R. D. McChesney, F. Kazemi and Z. Ajdari, S. T. Hunter, P. Robins, W. Hale, S. J. Blank, P. Clawson, G. E. Fuller and B. Shaffer.

698 The Third World and the Soviet Union.

Edited by Zaki Laidi, translated from the French by A. M. Berrett.
London; Atlantic Highlands, New Jersey: Zed Books, 1988. 125p.

The book focuses on Third World perspectives on the USSR. Chapter three by Semih Vaner, 'Turkey between its Western patron and the "Big Neighbour to the North"', examines the Turkish perception of the USSR, and also of Russia, placing special emphasis on the geostrategic context.

699 The Soviet Union and the Middle East: the post World War II era.

Edited by Ivo J. Lederer, Wayne S. Vucinich.   Stanford, California: Hoover Institution Press, 1974. 302p. map. bibliog. (Publication Series, no. 133).

Chapter three of this volume, 'The Soviet Union and Turkey', George S. Harris, analyses relations between Turkey and the Soviet Union since the Second World War. The causes of friction in Turco-Soviet relations, and issues of concern between the two states during the Stalin, Khrushchev and Brezhnev eras are discussed with particular reference to the Straits question and the Cyprus dispute.

700 Soviet advances in the Middle East.

George Lenczowski.   Washington, DC: American Enterprise Institute for Public Policy Research, 1972. 176p. (United States in the Middle East. Foreign Affairs Study, no. 2).

The author analyses Soviet policy in the Middle East. Chapter three, 'Turkey: toward normalization', discusses the development of Turco-Soviet relations from the aftermath of the First World War to an improvement in ties in the 1960s. Issues such as pan-Turkism, Soviet territorial demands, Cyprus, and friction in relations between Turkey and the United States are examined.

Foreign Relations. Turkey and the Soviet Union, Russia and the former Soviet Republics

701 **Turkey's relations with the Soviet Union and East Europe.**
Edited by Erol Manisalı. İstanbul: Middle East Business and Banking Publications, 1991. 116p.

Brings together the papers of one of the International Girne Conferences held in northern Cyprus. The contributors discuss, *inter alia*, economic relations between Turkey and the Soviet Union, Turkey-USSR cultural ties, the Turks in the Soviet Union, Azerbaijani-Turkish economic and cultural problems and the impact of Soviet-Turkish relations on developments in the Middle East and the Gulf.

702 **Russia's south flank: Soviet operations in Iran, Turkey and Afghanistan.**
Gunther Nollau, Hans Jurgen Wiehe. New York; London: Frederick A. Praeger, 1963. 171p. bibliog.

This book is based on subjective observations and generalizations, rather than being a scholarly work. It is largely the result of trips made by the authors to Iran, Turkey and Afghanistan. Chapter two on Turkey covers topics such as the principles of Atatürk, Mustafa Subhi, Turkish communism between 1919 and 1945, and Turco-Soviet relations.

703 **The political economy of Turkey in the post-Soviet era: going West and looking East?**
Edited by Libby Rittenberg. London: Praeger Publishers, 1998. 296p. bibliog.

The articles in the book explore the ways in which the economic and political fortunes of Turkey have changed since the end of the Cold War. Two sections of the book examine Turkey's relations with the European Union and with the former Soviet Union and the Soviet Bloc countries. The contents include: 'Introduction', L. Rittenberg; 'A brief account of the Turkish economy 1987-1996', Faruk Selçuk; 'Turkey and the European Union in the aftermath of the Cold War', Atilla Eralp; 'The Customs Union and beyond', Canan Balkır; 'International competitiveness of Turkey to the EU', Bahri Yılmaz; 'Prospects for new linkages', G. Winrow; 'The Black Sea Economic Corporation Project', Serdar Sayın and Osman Zaim; 'The political economy of relations between Turkey and Russia', Gülten Kazgan; 'Turkey and the changing oil market in Eurasia', Meliha Altunışık; and 'Turkey's emerging relationship with other Turkish Republics', Gül Turan and İlter Turan.

704 **Between sentiment and self-interest: Turkey's policy toward Azerbaijan and the Central Asian States.**
Phillip Robins. *Middle East Journal*, vol. 47, no. 4 (1993), p. 593-610.

In spite of the initial enthusiasm about Turkey's relations with the Turkic states of the former Soviet Union, 'hard decisions based on interests rather than fanciful notions of ethnic solidarity are informing decisions on both sides'. However, although the lack of geographic contiguity places Turkey at a disadvantage in comparison to Russia and Iran, Turkish influence on Azerbaijan and on the western part of Central Asia should not be discounted.

705 **Regional power rivalries in the new Eurasia: Russia, Turkey and
Iran.**
Edited by Alvin Z. Rubinstein, Oles M. Smolansky.   New York;
London: M. E. Sharpe, 1995. 304p. map.

The work includes contributions by George S. Harris, 'The Russian Federation and
Turkey' and Patricia M. Carley, 'Turkey and Central Asia: reality comes calling'.
Harris provides a largely chronological account of Turkish-Russian relations from
Atatürk to the CIS era, while Carley stresses that the importance of common ethnic
Turkic links has been overplayed with regard to Turkish policy in Central Asia.

706 **Peaceful coexistence: Turkey and the Near East in Soviet foreign
policy.**
Duygu B. Sezer.   *The Annals of the American Academy of Political
and Social Science*, vol. 481 (1985), p. 117-26.

The author concentrates on the improved relations between Turkey and the Soviet
Union since the 1960s as part of Moscow's policy of 'peaceful coexistence' with
Turkey and Greece. Turco-Soviet ties are examined within the wider context of Soviet
interests in the Near East, and particular attention is given to Soviet views on Turkish-
Greek rivalry and the Cyprus problem.

707 **The Caucasus and Central Asia: strategic implications.**
Seyfi Taşhan.   *Dış Politika – Foreign Policy*, vol. 18, no. 3-4 (1993),
p. 44-63.

This article, written by the head of the Foreign Policy Institute in Ankara, provides an
overview of the policies of Turkey, Russia, Iran and other states in the Caucasus and
Central Asia. Turkey promotes peace and stability in the Caucasus, which constitutes
a passageway between Turkey and Central Asia. Ankara aims to help the Turkish
Republics in Central Asia to become pluralist secular democracies with market
economies.

708 **Turkey and former Soviet Central Asia: national and ethnic
identity.**
Gareth M. Winrow.   *Central Asian Survey*, vol. 11, no. 3 (1992),
p. 101-11.

The author argues that Turkey may have an important role to play in stabilizing the
Central Asian region by emphasizing its common ethnic ties with the peoples of the
region. Interestingly, Ankara's concern to develop and expand cultural and educational links with the newly independent Turkic states is strikingly reminiscent of the
ideas promulgated at the turn of the century by Ismail Gasprinsky, who is regarded as
one of the most prominent Pan-Turkists.

709 **Turkey in post-Soviet Central Asia.**
Gareth Winrow.   London: The Royal Institute of International Affairs,
1995. 53p. (Former Soviet South Project, no. 1).

The author provides an overview of Turkish involvement in the predominantly Turkic
Republics of post-Soviet Central Asia. He gives some historical background, which is
followed by an examination of Turkey's reactions to the break-up of the Soviet Union.

The importance of common ethnic Turkic bonds is emphasized, although decision-makers in Ankara are motivated by economic and political self-interest as well as sentiment.

710 **Turkey's relations with the Transcaucasus and the Central Asian Republics.**
Gareth M. Winrow. *Perceptions*, vol. 1, no. 1 (1996), p. 128-45.

Given the geographic distance, post-Soviet Central Asia is of less strategic importance for Turkey than the Transcaucasus. However, the possible construction of new oil and gas pipelines across the Transcaucasus and the Caspian Sea from Central Asia to Turkey would interconnect the two regions. Given their oil and gas reserves, Turkey's economic and political ties with Kazakhstan and Turkmenistan could assume much greater importance.

711 **Transcaucasian boundaries.**
Edited by John F. R. Wright, Suzanne Goldenberg, Richard Schofield. London: UCL Press, 1996. 237p. map. (SOAS/GRC Geopolitics Series).

A collection of conference papers examining the geopolitical and territorial problems of the Caucasus and Transcaucasia. The third chapter by William Hale, 'Turkey, the Black Sea and Transcaucasia', examines the aims, experience and prospects of the Black Sea Economic Cooperation, which was initiated by Turkey. Turkey's relations with Azerbaijan, Armenia and Georgia are closely analysed, and the authors note the relevance of the Nagorno-Karabakh conflict and pipeline politics.

712 **Challenges to Turkey: the new role of Turkey in international politics since the dissolution of the Soviet Union.**
Bahri Yılmaz. New York: St. Martin's Press, 1998. 256p. bibliog.

The book evaluates and discusses the economic and political role of Turkey in the region. The author analyses the political and economic relations between Turkey and the European Union, the Black Sea Economic Cooperation Organization, the Near and the Middle East, the Balkans, and the new Central Asian states.

Turkey and the Middle East

713 **The place of the Palestinian-Israeli process in Turkish foreign policy.**
Bülent Aras. *Journal of South Asian and Middle Eastern Studies*, vol. 20, no. 2 (1997), p. 49-72.

The author examines the historical evolution of Turkish foreign policy behaviour towards the Palestinian-Israeli peace process in the context of the changing patterns of Turkish foreign policy. The first section of the article gives a brief summary of the trends in Turkish foreign policy from the 1940s to the present. The author sees Turkey as being important in the Middle East, and believes that it can play a positive role in the peace process.

714 **Turkey's role in the organization of the Islamic Conference, 1960-1992: the nature of deviation from the Kemalist heritage.**
Mahmut B. Aykan. New York: Vantage Press, 1994. 235p. bibliog.
Focuses on Turkey's evolving relations with the Muslim world from the 1960s onwards. Aykan analyses Turkey's membership to and role in the Organization of Islamic Conference against the backdrop of its troubled relations with the West – and in particular the United States – during the Cyprus crises. He discusses whether Turkey's membership in the OIC constitutes a deviation from the Kemalist heritage, and outlines the limits of *rapprochement* between Turkey and the Islamic world.

715 **Water as an element of cooperation and development in the Middle East.**
Edited by Ali İhsan Bağış. İstanbul: Sita Yayınları, 1998. 446p.
These are the papers of a conference organized in Ankara in 1994 by Hacettepe University and Friedrich Nauman Foundation in Turkey. Essays by international experts cover different aspects of the problem, and also views of different Middle Eastern nations. This volume is one of the few sources on the dispute over water in the Middle East.

716 **Reluctant neighbour: Turkey's role in the Middle East.**
Edited by Henri J. Barkey. Washington, DC: United States Institute of Peace, 1996. 243p.
Contains the papers of a conference held in June 1994. Contributors to the volume include: Phebe Marr, who discusses Turkey's involvement in Iraq; Alan Makovsky, who examines Turkey's policy towards Israel; and Patricia Carley, who looks at Turkey's place in the world.

717 **Turkey and Iran: limits of a stable relationship.**
John Calabrese. *British Journal of Middle Eastern Studies,* vol. 25, no. 1 (1998), p. 75-94.
The article scrutinizes Turco-Iranian relations throughout the 20th century. It claims that the stability and prosperity of the Middle East region depends on maintaining the stability of relations between these two countries, and that there is reason to be concerned about the state of their current relations.

718 **Turkish foreign policy toward the Middle East.**
Bilge Criss, Pınar Bilgin. *Middle East Review of International Affairs,* no. 1 (January 1997).
<http://www/biu.ac.il/SOC/besa/meria/criss.html>
This article examines Turkey's foreign policy toward the Middle East from the 1920s onwards. The authors take issue with the claims that Turkey's policy toward the Middle East changed during the Gulf Crisis (1990-91). They maintain that Turkey's policies during the Gulf Crisis did not constitute a deviation from the past, and that Turkey's traditional policy towards the region did not rule out an active role for

Turkey in the Middle East provided that this furthered its primary objective, which has always been moving closer to the West.

719 **Middle East, Turkey and the Atlantic Alliance.**
Edited by Ali L. Karaosmanoğlu, Seyfi Taşhan. Ankara: Foreign Policy Institute, 1987. 203p.

Analyses the dynamics of the relationship between Turkey and the Atlantic Alliance within the context of Middle Eastern politics. The nine essays that make up the volume analyse Turkey's security problems and explicate the implications of Turkey's strategic location between Europe and the Middle East on its foreign relations, and its role in the Atlantic Alliance.

720 **Cooperation or competition in the Islamic world: Turkish-Iranian relations from the Islamic revolution to the Gulf War and after.**
Nilüfer Narlı. *Cahiers d'Études sur la Méditerranée Orientale et le Monde Turco-Iranien (CEMOTI)*, no. 15 (1993), p. 265-93.

This article aims to show the complexity of Turkish-Iranian relations at both the sociological and the international level. Special attention is paid to the implications of the 1979 Iranian Revolution, the 1990-91 Gulf Crisis and the effects on both countries of new relationships in Central Asia. The author identifies a range of parallel trends and characteristics in the two countries, and makes substantial use of sources written in Turkish.

721 **The Kurdish question and Turkish-Iranian relations: from World War I to the present.**
Robert Olson. Costa Mesa, California: Mazda Publishers, 1998. 106p. bibliog. maps.

The book focuses on the trans-state aspects of the challenge of Kurdish nationalism on Turkish-Iranian relations, and on the domestic politics of both nations since the First World War, with emphasis on the period of the Iran-Iraq war (1980-88) and the Gulf War (1991). After a discussion of both countries, the author emphasizes that Turkey's and Iran's wider geopolitical and geostrategic interests in the Caucasus, the Balkans, Central Asia and the eastern Mediterranean compelled them to cooperate to prevent the emergence of a Kurdish state in northern Iraq after the Gulf War.

722 **Turkey and the Middle East.**
Philip Robins. London: Pinter Publishers, 1991. 130p. (The Royal Institute of International Affairs. Chatham House Papers).

This brief study examines Turkey's place in and relations with the Middle East. Robins analyses Turkey's relations with regional states and its policies towards major conflicts in the region, namely the Arab-Israeli conflict, the Iran-Iraq war, and the Gulf War (1990-91). He argues that the end of the Cold War and the ensuing erosion of Turkey's position *vis-à-vis* its European allies will require Turkey to reconsider its foreign policy priorities. Robins contends that Turkey's uncertain identity, caught between Islam and secularism, Europe and the Middle East, limits its foreign policy options.

723 **Rivers of discord: international water disputes in the Middle East.**
Greg Shapland. London: Hurst & Co., 1997. 187p.
The author analyses the water problem in the Middle East from different angles, principally geographical, historical, geopolitical, and legal. The section on the Tigris and the Euphrates rivers explains their past and present situation in Turkey, Syria, Iraq and Iran, and examines the geopolitical background of each river separately. The economic and strategic implications of the Turkish SEAP (GAP) plan (Southeast Anatolia Project) is discussed in detail.

The Cyprus issue

724 **Greek-Turkish relations since 1955.**
T. Bahçeli. Boulder, Colorado: Westview Press, 1990. 216p. maps. bibliog.
Bahçeli traces the deteriorating relations between Turkey and Greece since the days of Atatürk and Venizelos, dealing principally with the Cyprus issue.

725 **The genocide files.**
Harry Scott Gibbons. London: Charles Bravos Publishers, 1997. 494p.
A thorough research work into the Cyprus problem, but with a difference. The author attempts to explore the claim that Greeks and Turks had lived happily together from independence in 1960 to 1974 when the Turkish armed forces divided the island between the two communities. His research, together with his personal experiences on the island, convince him that Cypriot Greeks and Turks have never lived, and will never be able to live, in peace. The book also includes a fascinating account of the original Greek Colonels' Junta, from 1967 to 1973, the wars against Italy, Germany and the Greek Communists, and the reasons behind the decision for the military to take over Greece.

726 **The super powers and the Third World: Turkish-American relations and Cyprus.**
Süha Bölükbaşı. Lanham, Maryland; New York; London: University Press of America, 1988. 276p. bibliog. (Exxon Education Foundation Series on Rhetoric and Political Discourse, no. 15).
This is a study of the United States-Turkish relations as an example of 'influence relationship' between two unequal allies. The author focuses on the Cyprus crises of 1964, 1967 and 1974 in order to explore the influence of the relationship between the United States and Turkey. The book seeks to explain how geopolitical, domestic and functional factors affected the relationship, and secondly, to what extent the relationship between the two unequal allies had an impact on the outcome of the three Cyprus crises.

727 **Cyprus: the destruction of a Republic. British documents 1960-65.**
Salahi R. Sonyel. Huntington, England: The Eothen Press, 1977.
199p.

The author stresses that the problems associated with Cyprus stem from the events of the 1960s. He documents these events, using the recently released British documents, which also reveal the significant roles played by other powers in the decisions that led to the emergence of the Cyprus issue as it is today.

728 **The Cyprus issue. A current perspective.**
Clement H. Dodd. Huntingdon, England: The Eothen Press, 1995. 2nd ed. 37p.

A concise account of the Cyprus conflict, which refers to the implications of the inclusion of the Republic of Cyprus in the European Union.

729 **The political, social and economic development of Northern Cyprus.**
Edited by Clement H. Dodd. Huntingdon, England: The Eothen Press, 1993. 382p.

This book consists of research papers assessing the politics, society and economy of Northern Cyprus.

730 **The Cyprus imbroglio.**
Clement H. Dodd. Huntingdon, England: The Eothen Press, 1998. 218p.

The author addresses the issues which lie behind the Cyprus problem. He discusses how while the alleged injustices of history are etched every day more deeply into the minds of those embroiled in the struggle, the real problems of territory and the return of property to former owners on each side have become more intractable with the passage of time. He examines the legality and legitimacy of the Greek Cypriot claim of sovereignty over the whole of the island, the way in which the efforts of the international organizations have helped to intensify the conflict, and the rearmament that has taken place.

731 **Rauf Denktash at the United Nations. Speeches on Cyprus.**
Edited with an introduction by Michael Moran. Huntingdon, England: The Eothen Press, 1996. 378p.

The hundred-page introduction to the volume by the editor (based on original sources) explains how in 1964 the United Nations' Security Council set up a UN force in Cyprus, and began to treat the Greek Cypriot administration as the 'Government of Cyprus', and traces the subsequent effects of this recognition. The introduction is followed by the speeches of the leader of the Turkish Cypriot community, Rauf Denktash, to the United Nations. These documents serve as an informative primary source for historians.

732 **Turks and Greeks: neighbours in conflict.**
Vamık D. Volkan, Norman Itzkowitz.   Huntingdon, England: The
Eothen Press, 1995. 233p. maps. bibliog.
A psycho-political study of the historical legacy of suspicion and fear that underlies
Turkish-Greek relations, which inhibits solutions to present problems, such as the
Cyprus issue.

**Boğaziçi Journal. Review of Social, Economic and Administrative
Studies.**
See item no. 1319.

Central Asian Survey.
See item no. 1322.

Eurasian Studies.
See item no. 1330.

International Journal of Middle Eastern Studies.
See item no. 1333.

Journal of South Asian and Middle Eastern Studies.
See item no. 1337.

The Middle East Journal.
See item no. 1344.

Middle East Review of International Affairs (MERIA).
See item no. 1345.

Middle East Studies Association Bulletin.
See item no. 1346.

Middle Eastern Studies.
See item no. 1347.

New Perspectives on Turkey.
See item no. 1352.

Perceptions.
See item no. 1356.

Turkish Review of Balkan Studies.
See item no. 1380.

Turkish Review of Middle East Studies.
See item no. 1381.

Turkish Yearbook of Human Rights.
See item no. 1383.

The Turkish Yearbook of International Relations.
See item no. 1384.

Cyprus.
See item no. 1418.

Economy, Finance and Banking

733   **Fiscal imbalances, capital inflows, and the real exchange rate: the case of Turkey.**
Pierre Richard Agénor, C. John McDermott, E. Murat Uçer.
Washington, DC: IMF, 1997. 187p. (IMF Working Papers WP/97/1-EA).

Examines the links between fiscal policy, uncovered interest rate differentials, the real exchange rate and capital inflows in Turkey since the late 1980s.

734   **The political economy of Turkey: debt, adjustment and sustainability.**
Edited by Tosun Arıcanlı, Dani Rodrik.   Basingstoke, England: Macmillan, 1990. 278p. bibliog.

This detailed study brings together a number of essays on related issues ranging from public sector financing to investors' responses to the economic liberalization in Turkey since 1980. The articles question the validity of economic policies pursued throughout the 1980s.

735   **Banks in Turkey.**
The Banks Association of Turkey.   İstanbul: The Banks Association, 1995. 561p.

This publication carries general information about banks operating in Turkey. It also gives financial tables, which provide an overall evaluation of the performance of the Turkish economy and the banking sector in 1995.

736 **Stabilization and adjustment policies.**
Korkut Boratav.   Helsinki: WIDER, 1987. 80p. (United Nations
University, World Institute for Development and Economic Research,
Country Study, no. 5).
A critical and comprehensive study of stabilization and structural adjustment policies
in Turkey.

737 **Economic growth and structural change in Turkey.**
A. A. Çeçen, A. S. Doğruel, F. Doğruel.   *International Journal of
Middle East Studies*, vol. 26 (1994), p. 37-56.
The study offers a general discussion on the patterns of development in Turkey
between 1960 and 1988. The analysis concentrates on the macro developmental
aspects of the Turkish experience as well as referring to the historical specificity of the
underlying processes.

738 **Economic liberalization and labor markets.**
Edited by Parviz Dabir-Alai, Mehmet Odekon.   Westport,
Connecticut: Greenwood Press, 1998. 296p. bibliog. (Contributions in
Labor Studies, no. 51).
Focuses on how structural adjustment policies contribute to the overall development
effort by studying its impact on the labour markets of many regions and countries. The
contributors approach the subject from both theoretical and applied perspectives. The
first four chapters analyse the relationship between economic liberalization and labour
markets, and the following chapters provide case-studies of Greece, Chile, Argentina,
Mexico, Trinidad and Tobago, and Turkey. The chapter on Turkey, 'Economic liberalization and the Turkish labor market', is by Tevfik F. Nas and Mehmet Odekon.

739 **Big business and the state in Turkey: the case of TÜSİAD.**
Şebnem Gülfidan.   İstanbul: Boğaziçi University Press, 1993. 136p.
The book provides details on the organizational structure of the Turkish Industrialists'
and Businessmen's Association (Türkiye Sanayici ve İşadamları Derneği [TÜSİAD]),
and the influence of its members on the creation of the public policies of the Turkish
governments.

740 **The political and economic development of modern Turkey.**
William Hale.   London: Croom Helm, 1981. 279p. bibliog.
A comprehensive study on interrelations between the economic and political spheres
in Turkey. The book is divided into chapters which follow a historical periodization
since 1918, such as the étatism of the 1930s, the Democratic Party era, and the
planned economy regime of the 1960s.

741 **Turkey and the EU: the Customs Union and the future.**
William Hale.   *Boğaziçi Journal. Review of Social, Economic and
Administrative Studies*, vol. 10, no. 1-2 (1996), p. 243-62.
The author analyses the three aspects of the relationship between Turkey and the
European Union, namely: the complexity of the decision making process of the EU;

differences between the attitudes of member states; and the effects of the Customs Union between Turkey and the EU.

742 **Economic implications for Turkey of a Customs Union with the European Union.**
W. Glenn Harrison, T. F. Rutherford, G. David Tarr. Washington, DC: World Bank, International Trade Division, 1996. 24p. (Policy Research Working Paper, no. 1599).

The paper examines the implications of Turkey's customs integration with the EU countries and foreign economic relations.

743 **A theory of growth and its validation by the Turkish experience.**
Zeyyat Hatiboğlu. İstanbul: The Institute of Business Economics, İstanbul University, 1990. 128p.

Contains a summary of Turkish economic development, economic conditions and policy, and examines the applicability of the economic growth theories with reference to Turkey.

744 **Comments on conventional economics in the light of Turkish experience.**
Zeyyat Hatiboğlu. İstanbul: Institute of Business Economics, 1990. 312p.

This book complements *A theory of growth and its validation by the Turkish experience* (see item no. 743) by the same author. It contains a general theoretical introduction to macro-economics, and its implications for an economic policy in Turkey.

745 **The contemporary Turkish economy.**
Z. Y. Herschlag. London, New York: Routledge, 1988. 168p. bibliog.

This study deals with Turkey's economic performance and options in the 1980s and also gives a summary of the economic history of the Turkish Republic. This is a useful volume for all interested in Turkish politics and economy.

746 **The analysis of inflation: the case of Turkey.**
Metin Kıvılcım. Ankara: Capital Market Board, 1995. 238p. bibliog. (Publication no. 20).

A comprehensive econometric study of inflation in Turkey.

747 **A comparative analysis of the Turkish defence burden.**
Christos Kollias. *Boğaziçi Journal. Review of Social, Economic and Administrative Studies*, vol. 10, no. 1-2 (1996), p. 143-56.

The paper examines whether the Turkish defence burden is, in comparative terms, higher than that of other members of the NATO alliance given the country's comparative level of economic development and wealth.

748   **Turkey: recent economic developments.**
International Monetary Fund.   Washington, DC: IMF, November
1996. 143p. (Staff Country Report, no. 96/1922).
Prepared by an International Monetary Fund staff team, this detailed study of contemporary trends is comprehensively supported by fifty-eight tables and fifteen charts of statistical data, mostly from official Turkish sources. The four main sections of text cover the economy, public finances, money and banking, and external sector developments. The emphasis of this analysis is on the implications of the sharp fluctuations in growth and high and persistent inflation in recent years. A stabilization programme initiated in April 1994 led to a marked reduction in aggregate demand, output, and inflation. However, the Turkish economy rebounded in 1995, and continued this trend into 1996.

749   **State and class in Turkey: a study in capitalist development.**
Çağlar Keyder.   London; New York: Verso, 1987. 252p. bibliog.
The book develops an analysis of the Turkish economy in terms of class structures and class conflict. It examines the Turkish economy in historical perspective (from the last days of the Ottoman Empire to the late 1980s), and its integration into the world economic system, stressing the role of the bureaucracy in the establishment of the Republic and class formation in Turkey.

750   **The Euphrates River and the Southeast Anatolia Development Project.**
John F. Kolars, William A. Mitchell.   Carbondale, Illinois: Southern
Illinois University Press, 1991. 324p. maps. bibliog.
Gives a detailed account of Turkey's Southeast Anatolia Project (GAP), which is designed to irrigate more than 1.7 million hectares, doubling the country's energy production and yielding agricultural surpluses for sale to neighbours. However, the project will reduce the flow and quality of water in the Euphrates, and any outcome will be further exacerbated by major hydraulic projects downstream in Syria. This book gives a minutely detailed account of the hydrology of such developments, and considers their domestic and international political implications. The text is supported by 23 maps, 36 graphs and diagrams, and 109 statistical and other tables.

751   **Developmentalism and beyond.**
S. E. İbrahim, Ayşe Öncü, Çağlar Keyder.   Cairo: American
University in Cairo, 1994. 325p. bibliog.
Examines the economic policies and conditions in Turkey and Egypt since 1918.

752   **Liberalization and the Turkish economy.**
Edited by Tevfik F. Nas, Mehmet Odekon.   New York: Greenwood
Press, 1988. 221p. bibliog.
This volume contains articles on Turkish economy and finance which present views on financial liberalization and stability.

753 **Economic surveys: Turkey 1997.**
Organization for Economic Co-operation and Development (OECD).
Paris: OECD, 1997. 120p.
The Organization for Economic Co-operation and Development's annual survey of the Turkish economy.

754 **Energy policies of IEA countries: Turkey 1997 review.**
Organization for Economic Co-operation and Development (OECD).
Paris: OECD, 1997. 136p.
A comprehensive and in-depth assessment of the energy policies of Turkey, including recommendations on future policy developments. The publication includes a description of oil and gas pipeline projects in Turkey and the Caspian area.

755 **Economic crises and long-term growth in Turkey.**
Ziya Öniş, James Riedel.   Washington, DC: The World Bank, 1993.
133p. bibliog.
The authors explain why Turkey has experienced persistent macroeconomic instability punctuated by military intervention. They identify the sources of Turkey's macroeconomic problems, and explain why the governments responded to the crises in the ways they did. They discuss the effects of macroeconomic policy and crises management on long-term growth. The book, which includes tables and an index, starts with the 1950s and brings the reader to the present day.

756 **The political economy of Islamic resurgence in Turkey: the rise of the Welfare Party in perspective.**
Ziya Öniş. *Third World Quarterly,* vol. 18, no. 4 (1997), p. 743-66.
The author analyses how the mechanisms of economic globalization and the associated process of neoliberal restructuring have been instrumental in the rise of the pro-Islamic Welfare Party to a position of prominence in the mid-1990s, and furthermore how the cultural impulses associated with globalization have also prepared the way for the rise of political Islam in the Turkish context.

757 **State and market. The political economy of Turkey in comparative respective.**
Ziya Öniş. İstanbul: Boğaziçi University Press, 1998. 529p. bibliog.
The book contains twenty-seven essays written by the author between 1985 and 1996, in which he gives a detailed and critical evaluation of Turkey's experiment with neoliberalism during the post-1980 era. He discusses market reforms and the role of the government, interaction between globalization and the nation state, and asserts that for successful development an appropriate mix of state and market is necessary.

758 **Small firms and local economic development: entrepreneurship in southern Europe and Turkey.**
Gül Berna Özcan.   Aldershot, England: Avebury, 1995. 230p. bibliog.
This study dwells on the economics, anthropology, and entrepreneurial dynamics of small firms in the sectors of consumer durable retailers, foodstuffs wholesaling, machinery manufacturing, and housing construction, in three medium-sized cities in

Turkey. It provides background on local economic development in southern Europe, and the conditions of the Turkish economy.

759   **The economics of defense and the peace dividend in Turkey.**
Süleyman Özmucur.   İstanbul: Boğaziçi University Press, 1996. 76p. bibliog.

The book studies the economic effects of defence expenditure in Turkey going back to 1923 and provides a comparison of defence indicators of Turkey with Turkey's neighbours, and the historical pattern of defence expenditure. The relationship between defence expenditure, growth, and inflation is scrutinized.

760   **The impact of transnational banks on developing countries' banking sector: an analysis of the Turkish experience, 1980-89.**
Hatice Pehlivan, Colin Kirkpatrick.   *British Journal of Middle Eastern Studies*, vol. 19, no. 2 (1992), p. 186-201.

The number of foreign banks grew substantially in Turkey after restrictions on their operations in the country were removed in the financial liberalization programme after 1980. This article suggests that the improvements in the efficiency of the domestic banking sector, which were expected as a result of the liberalization, were not realized. The cost efficiency of domestic commercial banks did not improve although profitability increased because Turkish firms made productivity gains without being forced by effective competition into improving their cost-efficiency performance.

761   **Report about insurance activities in Turkey, 1995.**
Prime Ministry Undersecretariat of Treasury Insurance Supervisory Board.   İstanbul: Grafik Matbaacılık, 1995. 162p.

The annual publication of the Insurance Supervisory Board. The text is in Turkish and in English, and it gives detailed information about Turkish insurance companies.

762   **Exchange rate, inflation expectations and currency substitution in Turkey.**
Fabio Scacciavillani.   Washington, DC: IMF, 1995. 120p. (IMF Working Paper WP/95/111-EA).

The paper investigates the changes in the public's holding of foreign currency in Turkey in response to devaluations.

763   **State, society and privatization in Turkey, 1979-1990.**
Sallama Shaker.   Washington, DC: Woodrow Wilson Center Press, 1995. 101p. bibliog.

A study of Turkish economy, economic and industrial policies, and economic conditions since the 1960s.

764   **Defence spending in Turkey.**
        Selami Sezgin.   *Defence and Peace Economics*, vol. 8, no. 4 (1997),
        p. 381-409.
The paper gives a country survey of the Turkish defence economy. The first part provides a brief economic background of Turkey, its armed forces, the defence industry, its modernization and trends in Turkish defence expenditure. The rest of the paper focuses on the relationships between defence spending and economic growth.

765   **SEAP provincial statistics, 1950-1996.**
        State Institute of Statistics (SIS).   Ankara: State Institute of Statistics,
        1994- . annual.
This annual publication provides information on the provinces of Adıyaman, Diyarbakır, Gaziantep, Mardin, Şanlı Urfa, Siirt, Batman and Şırnak covered by the Southeast Anatolia Project (SEAP, or GAP in Turkish). The socio-economic structures of the eight provinces are presented through statistics on population, demography, health, education, justice, migration, elections, environment, agriculture, mining, energy, manufacturing, construction, transport, tourism, prices, finance, and income.

766   **Turkish Economy Statistics and Analysis.**
        State Institute of Statistics (SIS).   Ankara: State Institute of Statistics,
        1989- . monthly.
This monthly report brings together all the recent economic data produced by SIS. Since June 1994 it has been published in both Turkish and English. It covers national accounts, industry, agriculture, construction, foreign trade, prices, and income. Labour force statistics, annual statistics on research and development, environment, education, culture, health, and justice, as well as consumption statistics and population census data are included.

767   **Retail price statistics. Annual average prices by selected items,
        1993-1995.**
        State Institute of Statistics.   Ankara: State Institute of Statistics, 1996.
        618p.
This publication covers annual average retail prices of selected items covered by the consumer price indexes, including food, clothing, homes, furniture, health and personal care, transport, culture and entertainment, and household expenditure.

768   **Wholesale price statistics, 1996.**
        State Institute of Statistics.   Ankara: State Institute of Statistics, 1997.
        128p.
Contains annual average wholesale prices of selected items covered by the wholesale price index of both the public and the private sectors.

769   **Gross domestic product by provinces, 1987-1994.**
        State Institute of Statistics.   Ankara: State Institute of Statistics, 1998.
        762p.
The work comprises data on gross domestic product in current and constant prices by kind of activity in producer's value by provinces and regions.

770   **Gross domestic product by cost components, 1987-1995.**
State Institute of Statistics.   Ankara: State Institute of Statistics, 1998.
62p.
The work comprises data on cost components of the gross domestic product, compensation of employees by kind of economic activity, cost components of the gross domestic product, consumption of fixed capital, indirect taxes, subsidies, compensation of employees and operating surplus and national income at factor cost by current prices.

771   **Results of the household income distribution survey: income distribution by 20 per cent, 10 per cent, 5 per cent and 1 per cent groups in 19 selected province centers, 1994.**
State Institute of Statistics.   Ankara: State Institute of Statistics, 1998.
260p.
The volume presents a selection from data collected during the '1994 Household income distribution survey'.

772   **Results of the household income distribution survey: income distribution by 20 per cent, 10 per cent, 5 per cent and 1 per cent groups in Turkey, urban and rural areas and regions, 1994.**
State Institute of Statistics.   Ankara: State Institute of Statistics, 1998.
154p.
Presents data on disposable incomes of households, collected during the '1994 Household income distribution survey'.

773   **Household consumption expenditures survey: summary results of 19 selected province centers, 1994.**
State Institute of Statistics.   Ankara: State Institute of Statistics, 1998.
210p.
The volume contains information on disposable income, consumption expenditures, savings of households, average values per household, types of consumption expenditures of households, and subgroups of consumption expenditures on food, beverage and tobacco by employment status of household head.

774   **Household consumption expenditures survey results, 1994.**
State Institute of Statistics.   Ankara: State Institute of Statistics, 1998.
487p.
The volume contains data on types of consumption expenditures of households in Turkey, according to rural and urban areas, average household size, number of employed members, employment status, occupation, economic activity and educational status of household head.

775 **The economy of Turkey since liberalization.**
Edited by Sübidey Togan, V. N. Balasubramanyam. New York:
Macmillan Press Ltd, 1996. 200p.

Consists of an introduction and eight essays, which evaluate Turkey's liberalization experiment, in other words the impact of the 1980 economic reform package of the Özal government, and aim to draw lessons for the 1990s. Four of the chapters deal with trade liberalization, while other chapters address foreign aid, foreign direct investment, Turkey's relations with the European Union, and financial reform.

776 **Turkish standards catalogue, 1996.**
Turkish Standards Institution. Ankara: Turkish Standards Institution, 1996. 1024p.

This catalogue (in Turkish and in English) gives the standards classified according to the International Classification for Standards (ICS) system. There is an index in English.

777 **Liberalization and economic performance in Turkey.**
Ercan Uygur. Geneva: UNCTAD, 1993. 61p. (United Nations
Conference on Trade and Development, Discussion Papers, no. 65).

The paper examines Turkey's economic conditions and the impact of economic policies applied after 1980.

778 **Stabilization policy and structural adjustment in Turkey,
1980-1985.**
Peter Wolff. Berlin: German Development Institute, 1987. 196p.
(Occasional Papers of the German Development Institute, no. 87).

The report examines the role of the International Monetary Fund and the World Bank in an externally supported adjustment process.

779 **Turkey: informatics and economic modernization. A World Bank
country study.**
The World Bank. Washington, DC: World Bank Country Studies
Series, 1993. 270p.

An analysis of the role of informatics in economic development during 1980s in Turkey. It articulates a strategy for Turkey's transition to an information-based economy, and considers the potential for Turkish suppliers to enter international computer markets. It assesses the opportunity for Turkey to become an internationally competitive supplier of software services, and considers the policies and institutions needed to achieve that target. Educational policies for computer literacy, and modifications to the legal framework are also considered.

780 **Bureaucrats in business: the economics and politics of government ownership.**
The World Bank. Washington, DC: Oxford University Press, 1995. 350p. (Policy Research Report Series).
This study evaluates and analyses twelve countries including Turkey. It examines the economic problems that arise when government owned State Economic Enterprises are inefficiently operated.

Tea and the domestication of the Turkish state.
See item no. 457.

Supporting women owned business in Turkey.
See item no. 486.

Turkey: political, social and economic challenges in the 1990s.
See item no. 530.

Strong state and economic interest groups: the post-1980 Turkish experience.
See item no. 552.

Banka ve Ticaret Hukuku Dergisi. (Journal of Banking and Commercial Law.)
See item no. 1315.

Boğaziçi Journal. Review of Social, Economic and Administrative Studies.
See item no. 1319.

DEİK Bulletin.
See item no. 1326.

Menas Associates' Turkey Focus.
See item no. 1342.

METU Studies in Development.
See item no. 1343.

Monthly Bulletin.
See item no. 1349.

New Perspectives on Turkey.
See item no. 1352.

Quarterly Bulletin.
See item no. 1357.

Seventh Five-year Development Plan (1996-2000).
See item no. 1398.

Trade and Industry

781 Dimensions of service quality: expectations of Turkish consumers from services.
Perran Akan. İstanbul: Boğaziçi University Press, 1995. 157p.

The book contains an analysis of the results of a survey about the Turkish service industry (hotels, airlines, banking and insurance sector).

782 The state and the industrialization crisis in Turkey.
Henri J. Barkey. Boulder, Colorado; San Francisco, California; Oxford: Westview Press, 1990. 220p. bibliog. (Westview Special Studies on the Middle East).

The study evaluates the Import Substitution Industrialisation (ISI) strategy which was implemented before the structural adjustment policies of the 1980s in Turkey. The main argument of the book is that the ISI is not responsible for the failure of Turkey's industrialization effort. On the contrary, the main reason for the failure has been the state's inability to implement a successful development policy, and the state's lack of autonomy, which resulted from the emergence of powerful and competing vested interest among those segments of the private sector directly effected by import substitution.

783 The late coming tycoons of Turkey.
Ayşe Buğra. *Journal of Economics and Administrative Studies, Boğaziçi University,* vol. 1, no. 1 (1987), p. 143-55.

While reviewing the autobiographies written by three Turkish tycoons (V. Koç, N. F. Eczacıbaşı, and S. Sabancı), the author gives a brief history of business in republican Turkey. The article contains two interesting sections entitled 'The Turkish bourgeoisie as part of a social project' and 'Social legitimacy of business activity: change and continuity'.

784   **State and business in modern Turkey: a comparative study.**
Ayşe Buğra.   Albany, New York: State University of New York
Press, 1994. 328p. bibliog. (SUNY Series in the Social and Economic
History of the Middle East).
The central concern of the book is the relationship of the markets to the state and civil
society. It analyses the way in which state policy has shaped the business class, the
structure of business organizations, and the patterns of business associations.

785   **Facing the challenge: Turkish automobile, steel and clothing**
industries' responses to the post-Fordist restructuring.
Lale Duruiz, Nurhan Yentürk.   İstanbul: Ayhan Matbaası, 1992. 192p.
The authors investigate a Turkish firm in each of the following industries: automobile,
steel and clothing. They assess the use of microelectronics, chosen levels of automa-
tion, technological changes in production processes, projects and strategies. It appears
that flexibility, which is the watchword for the post-Fordian era, is still far from being
achieved, notably in the steel and automobile industries.

786   **A survey of foreign direct investment firms in Turkey.**
Deniz Erden.   İstanbul: Boğaziçi University Press, 1996. 228p.
An empirical country survey, which gives profiles of firms in terms of their structural,
strategic and performance characteristics.

787   **Policies for competition and competitiveness: the case of industry**
in Turkey.
Edited by Refik Erzan.   Vienna: United Nations Industrial
Development Organization, 1995. 278p.
This study contains twelve chapters on aspects of Turkish manufacturing in the context of the trade liberalization of the 1980s. It includes an overview of economic
developments in Turkey (Annex I) by C. Pazarbaşıoğlu, which sketches the background to recent developments in Turkish industry from the beginning of
comprehensive national planning in the early 1960s. References accompany each contribution, and there are forty-seven tables of data and trends.

788   **Competitiveness of Turkish SMSEs in the Customs Union.**
Refik Erzan, Alpay Filiztekin.   *European Economic Review*, vol. 41,
no. 3-5 (1997), p. 88-92.
In order to assess the impact of Customs Union, the paper analyses the impact of
changes on the small- and medium-scale enterprises (SMSEs) in terms of their levels
of protection, import penetration, wage levels, exchange rates and exchange rate
volatility, changes in domestic and foreign demand, and credit availability.

789   **Year book of companies.**
İstanbul Stock Exchange (ISE).   İstanbul: Mart Matbaası, 1997. 2 vols.
Consists of basic corporate information, financial statements, and the performance
charts of 237 companies, whose stocks are being traded on the Istanbul Stock
Exchange. The publication also provides information about new companies, and a list
of emerging markets as of April 1997.

Trade and Industry

790   **Swimming against the tide: Turkish trade reform in the 1980s.**
       Anne O. Krueger, Okan H. Aktan.   San Francisco: ICS Press, 1992.
       264p. bibliog. (An International Centre for Economic Growth
       Publication).

The main focus of this study is to analyse trade and payments liberalization of the
1980s, and its effects on Turkish economy and growth. In order to evaluate the effect
of the liberalization programme, the following issues are examined: the circumstances
of the Turkish economy, and Turkish economic policy before January 1980; the
macroeconomic environment and Turkish economic policy before January 1980; and
the macroeconomic development upon which the trade and exchange rate policy had
its effects after the January 1980 reforms.

791   **Small employers in Turkey: the OSTİM estate at Ankara.**
       Theo Nichols, Nadir Sugur.   *Middle Eastern Studies*, vol. 32, no. 2
       (1996), p. 230-52.

OSTIM (Middle Eastern Industrial and Commercial Centre) is the largest private
industrial estate in Turkey. This article reports on the results of fieldwork conducted
on small employers in this estate during the period 1992-93. It makes use of first-person reports from interviews conducted with the employers. It examines the meaning of
becoming a small employer, and the problems that small employers face in the context
of rural migration, and the industrial structure of Turkey.

792   **Turkey and world foreign trade, 1950-1993.**
       State Institute of Statistics (SIS).   Ankara: State Institute of Statistics,
       1995. 265p.

The publication gives information on Turkish foreign trade by country and commodity
groups, structural change in Turkish foreign trade, exports and imports of selected
countries by commodity groups and their shares in total foreign trade. It presents foreign trade statistics from 1950 to the present.

793   **Foreign trade statistics, 1996.**
       State Institute of Statistics.   Ankara: State Institute of Statistics, 1997.
       460p.

This annual publication contains statistics on the value (in US dollars and Turkish lira)
and quantity of exports and imports by year, month, major sector, commodity group,
source of financing, country of origin or destination, and international commodity
groups as defined by the standard international classification, and a classification of
broad economic categories.

794   **Foreign trade by transport system, 1996.**
       State Institute of Statistics.   Ankara: State Institute of Statistics, 1998.
       90p.

Contains statistics on the value and quantity of exports and imports by country and
transport system, Turkish and foreign carriers and chapters.

795 **Mining and quarrying statistics, 1995.**
State Institute of Statistics (SIS). Ankara: State Institute of Statistics,
1998. 148p.

This publication contains tables on selected minerals by years, number of establishments, annual average of persons engaged and employees, annual payments to
employees, total man-hours worked, total capacity of power equipment installed at the
end of the year, changes in stocks, gross additions to fixed assets during the year,
input, output and value added by commodity mined.

796 **Electricity, gas and water statistics, 1995.**
State Institute of Statistics (SIS). Ankara: State Institute of Statistics,
1998. 112p.

Covers detailed information on electricity, gas and water sectors in Turkey.

797 **Manufacturing industry quarterly: employment, payments,
production, and tendencies (provisional results),
1996 (IV)-1997 (IV).**
State Institute of Statistics (SIS). Ankara: State Institute of Statistics,
1998. 240p.

An annual publication which gives the results of quarterly surveys conducted in the
manufacturing industry establishments, and includes figures on employment, payments, production, sale values, and inventory as well as rate of utilization capacity by
sector.

798 **Small sized manufacturing industry statistics (1-9), 1995.**
State Institute of Statistics (SIS). Ankara: State Institute of Statistics,
1998. 176p.

The publication presents the data obtained by a survey in 1995. It contains data as to
number of establishments, annual average of number of persons engaged, wages,
investments, input, output and value added.

799 **Annual manufacturing industry statistics, 1994.**
State Institute of Statistics (SIS). Ankara: State Institute of Statistics,
1998. 176p.

Covers data on all public sector manufacturing enterprises and private sector establishments with ten or more employees. Information given includes employment and
payments, power equipment, changes in stock, gross additions to fixed assets during
the year covered, output, value added, sale and transfers by industry groups.

800 **Polities, technology and development: decision-making in the
Turkish iron and steel industry.**
Joseph S. Szyliowicz. London: Macmillan, 1991. 289p.

A detailed study of Turkey's Ereğli Iron and Steel Works (ERDEMIR), and the
process of technology transfer as it affects the industry.

801 **Recent industrialization experience of Turkey in a global context.**
Edited by Fikret Şenses. Westport, Connecticut: Greenwood Press,
1994. 219p. bibliog. (Contributions in Economics and Economic
History, no. 155).

The book traces 'the transition from import-substituting industrialization under strong
state direction to export-oriented industrialization with emphasis on market-based
policies' (p. 191) in the Turkish economy of the 1980s. The roles played by the
International Monetary Fund and the World Bank in Turkish economic decision-making
are explained. F. I. Nixson, A. H. Amsden, and J. Weiss focus on the importance
of industrialization, while Z. Öniş summarizes Turkey's experience with liberalization
and transnational corporations during the 1980s. M. Kaytaz, A. Eraydın, and H. K.
Ansal provide case-studies of particular Turkish industries.

802 **Technical change and efficiency in Turkish manufacturing
industries.**
Erol Taymaz, Gülin Saatçi. *Journal of Productivity Analysis*, vol. 8,
no. 4 (1997), p. 461-75.

The authors aim to measure and understand the extent and importance of technical
progress and efficiency in Turkish industries. The data used by the authors for the
plants in question (textile, cement, motor vehicles industries) are for the years
1987-92. The rate and direction of technical change for each industry is estimated by
introducing time-dependent variables in the production function. Sector-specific
factors which influence the technical efficiency of manufacturing plants are also
identified.

803 **Foreign trade regime and trade liberalisation in Turkey during the
1980s.**
Sübidey Togan. Aldershot, England: Avebury, 1994. 250p. bibliog.

This is an econometric approach to Turkey's transition to a market economy. The
book concentrates on foreign trade promotion in Turkey during the 1980s with particular reference to export credit regime and commercial policy. The author also provides
a detailed account of the legal framework of Turkey's foreign trade regime.

Turkey: political, social and economic changes in the 1990s.
See item no. 530.

**Strong state and economic interest groups: the post-1980 Turkish
experience.**
See item no. 552.

Agriculture

804 **Turkish agriculture and European Community policies, issues, strategies and institutional adaptation.**
Halis Akder, İlhan Akay, Allan Buckwell, Cemil Ertuğrul, Haluk Kasnakoğlu, John Medland, Nick Young.   Ankara: State Planning Organization, 1990. 148p. bibliog. (DPT: 2241-AETB: 25).
The book reports the findings of a study undertaken with the initiation of the Turkish government, and with the financial support of the United Nations Development Programme (UNDP). The research team was composed of scientists from Wye College (University of London), Middle East Technical University (Ankara) and the State Planning Organization of Turkey. The study employs a large-scale agricultural sector model to analyse the impacts of membership to the European Community (in particular the effects of the Common Agricultural Policy [CAP]) on the agricultural sector in Turkey. The study also looks at the costs of Turkey's full membership to the community budget.

805 **The agricultural development of Turkey.**
Oddvar Aresvik.   New York: Prager, 1975. 220p. maps. bibliog. (Prager Special Studies in International Economic Development).
The author has worked as an advisor and researcher for various international programmes. This study was partly based on his visits to Turkey, and partly on his reports on the agricultural development of Turkey when he worked as a Ford Foundation employee from 1963 to 1973. The contents analyse the natural resources, land use characteristics, agricultural production and income, production inputs, wheat marketing and floor pricing system, incentive policies and government involvement, agricultural development services, educational institutions, the rural community in relation to problems of development, agricultural projections, and the introduction of improved technology. The data in this study came from published material, as well as unpublished reports and personal interviews. Several tables and charts in the text and the statistical appendix give detailed figures on agriculture in Turkey. This is a technical book which is aimed at specialists.

806 **Food consumption and nutrition in Turkey.**
Hasan Gencağa.   Ankara: Turkish Development Research Foundation,
1985. 111p. bibliog. (Publication no. 6).

This publication reports the findings of a nutrition and food consumption survey carried out in 1981-82, on 1,480 families throughout Turkey by the Turkish Development Research Foundation in 1981-82 with the support of the Rockefeller Foundation. The survey's findings are broken down by rural/urban areas, regions, income groups, household size, and seasons related to calorie and protein intake, and consumption of main food items. The study attempts to identify and explain the determinants of malnutrition in Turkey, and relates it to income distribution and inflation. The book concludes with food demand, and production projection up to 1993. The sample design, sample characteristics and survey questionnaire are given in the annexes at the end of the book. The results of the survey are also compared with the results of a similar study conducted in 1974.

807 **The political economics of agricultural price support in Turkey: an empirical assessment.**
Arslan Gürkan, Haluk Kasnakoğlu.   *Public Choice*, no. 70 (1991),
p. 277-98.

The paper attempts to explain the variations in the extent of protection provided for producers of four selected agricultural crops in Turkey, using a set of factors representing various economic and political events of the 1962-83 period. The economic variables were selected in order to assess the divergence between the intentions of the policy makers, and their actions as reflected in the level of support actually provided. The political variables were chosen to assess the impact of elections, military takeovers and noticeable shifts in the underlying philosophy of the policy makers on the amount of support provided.

808 **Past trends and future prospects of Turkish agriculture.**
Haluk Kasnakoğlu, A. Arslan Gürkan.   *Yapı Kredi Economic Review*,
vol. 1, no. 2 (January 1987), p. 23-32.

A review of the developments in Turkish agriculture during the 1950-85 period, together with a discussion on the likely future developments. The variables considered are income, sources of growth, agricultural versus non agricultural prices, agricultural input versus output prices, and magnitudes and sources of income variability.

809 **Agricultural labor and technological change in Turkey.**
Haluk Kasnakoğlu, Halis Akder, A. Arslan Gürkan.   In: *Labor and rainfed agriculture in West Asia and North Africa.*   Edited by Dennis Tully.   Dordrecht, the Netherlands: Kluwer Academic Publishers, 1990, p. 103-34. maps. bibliog.

The book reports on the results of the first stage of the project on Agricultural Labor and Technological Change initiated by the International Center for Agricultural Research in the Dry Areas (ICARDA). It contains a review of literature on selected issues of regional importance, combined with more detailed analyses of the situations of eight countries with important rainfed agricultural sectors in West Asia and North Africa. Chapter six of the volume is devoted to Turkey. The paper starts with a description of temperature, rainfall and soil quality in Turkey, followed by a historical review of the agricultural sector and technology. The paper contains a rich set of mostly original empirical information on land and income distribution, ownership of machinery, production, income and expenditure composition, costs and profitability of important crops, technology use and farm size, decision making, support policies, structure of labor force, seasonal employment and migration in agriculture.

810 **Agriculture in Turkey: some key information for foreign investors.**
Ministry of Agriculture, Forestry and Rural Affairs. Ankara: Prime Ministry, 1987. 95p.

This document has been prepared with the purpose of giving general information about Turkish agriculture and its developments. The basic principles and policies of the government, and foreign economic relations concerning agriculture are indicated by citing passages from the Fifth Five-Year Development Plan. The work also discusses growth rate, crop and livestock production, agricultural trade and industry, the role of agriculture in Turkish economy, some of the important agricultural projects and activities, and possibilities for investment.

811 **Agriculture in Turkey.**
Maharaj K. Muthoo, Taylan Onul. Ankara: Ziraat Bankası, 1996. 73p. map. bibliog.

This book brings together under one cover the basic facts about, and prospects for, Turkish agriculture. The topics covered include a review of the agricultural sector in the economy, agricultural policy, research and training, crops, livestock, fisheries, forestry, irrigation, rural development, environment and globalization. At the time of the preparation and publication of the book, the authors were, respectively, the head of, and professional officer in, the Representation of Food and Agriculture Organization (FAO) in Turkey.

812 **Turkey.**
Hasan Olgun. In: *The political economy of agricultural pricing policy. Africa and the Mediterranean, volume 3.* Edited by Anne O. Krueger, Maurice Schiff, Alberto Valdes. Baltimore, Maryland: Johns Hopkins University Press, 1991, p. 230-67.

This is the third of five volumes summarizing the results of the World Bank research project 'A comparative study of the political economy of agricultural pricing policies'. The project consisted of eighteen country studies that employed a common analytical framework. The country study on Turkey is summarized in this article. It contains an overview of the economy and agriculture, history of interventions, effects of intervention on consumers, producers, government budget, income distribution, price stability and finally attempts to develop hypotheses towards the determinants or the political economy of agricultural policies. The analysis covers the period between 1950 and 1983.

813 **National policies and agricultural trade. Country study: Turkey.**
Organization for Economic Co-operation and Development (OECD). Paris: OECD, 1994. 243p. map. bibliog.

This publication presents an analysis of the support given to agriculture in Turkey for the period 1979-93. It contains detailed measurements of the levels of assistance granted for the main agricultural commodities using the concepts of Producer and Consumer Subsidy Equivalents. It examines the development and effects of national policies on agricultural production, consumption and trade in light of the principles for agricultural reform laid down by the OECD. The book also contains a compact summary of the main features of Turkish agriculture such as population growth and rural-urban migration, economic growth, prices and incomes, labour force, employment, external trade and balance of payments, land use, yields and output, geographical patterns, type, number and size of farm holdings, rural and regional development, agricultural institutions and agricultural policy.

814 **Food, states, and peasants. Analyses of the agrarian question in the Middle East.**
Edited by Alan Richards. Boulder, Colorado: Westview Press, 1986. 283p. bibliog. (Westview Special Studies on the Middle East).

This volume is based on papers presented at an international workshop sponsored by the Social Science Research Council (SSRC) and hosted by the International Fund for Agricultural Development (IFAD) in 1994. The volume is organized around four topics: the history of states, landlords and peasants; the political economy of supply; the political economy of demand; and the transformation of the agricultural labour force. The volume contains the following four contributions on Turkey: 'Agrarian relations in Turkey: A historical sketch' by Tosun Arıcanlı (p. 23-68); 'Agricultural support policies in Turkey, 1950-1980: an overview' by Kutlu Somel (p. 97-130); 'Agricultural price support policies in Turkey: an empirical investigation' by Haluk Kasnakoğlu (p. 131-58); and 'Migration and labor transformation in rural Turkey' by Sunday Üner (p. 225-64).

815 **Agricultural commodities marketing survey: planning of crop pattern and integration of marketing and crop pattern studies.**
The Southeast Anatolia Project (GAP/SEAP), Regional Development Administration. Ankara: Prime Ministry, 1992. 6 vols. bibliog.

This study reports the findings of a reset project initiated by the Southeast Anatolia Project Regional Development Administration, to study the likely crop patterns throughout the different phases of the irrigation investments, and at the end of project completion (2010). The study also examines the marketing sector and develops recommendations for the marketing infrastructure and system. The study was conducted by a large group of scientists from Turkey, the Netherlands and Germany. The findings are reported in six volumes: the first volume is an executive summary, the second provides a description of the agricultural sector in the world, Turkey and the Southeast Anatolia Project region, the third discusses the present marketing systems and recommendations for the future, and the fourth describes the analytical tools employed in the study and presents the present and predicted crop patterns in the project region. Volumes five and six comprise the technical appendices on models and data used, as well as detailed model results.

816 **Agricultural structure: production, price, value, 1996.**
State Institute of Statistics (SIS). Ankara: State Institute of Statistics, 1998. 612p.

This annual publication includes agricultural statistics on area sown, animal stock, number of trees, production, yield, prices received by farmers, value of production, agricultural equipment and machinery by regions and provinces, and the value and quantity of agricultural exports and imports. This publication has replaced the two separate publications entitled *Agricultural structure and production* and *Prices received by farmers* which were also published by the State Institute of Statistics.

817 The summary of agricultural statistics, 1996.
State Institute of Statistics (SIS).   Ankara: State Institute of Statistics, 1998. 68p.

This publication, produced annually since 1957, provides an overview of Turkey's agricultural sector and includes statistics on: area sown; production and yield of field crops; production of vegetables; number of fruit trees and production; agricultural equipment and machinery; livestock by type and breed; milk, meat, and hide production; and production of wool, hair, mohair, and apiculture and sericulture products. All statistics in this publication cover a period of twenty years.

818 Fisheries statistics, 1996.
State Institute of Statistics (SIS).   Ankara: State Institute of Statistics, 1998. 66p.

This annual publication covers a quantity of sea products by marketing methods, import and export, average prices of sea products and region, and number of fishing vessels (by region, tonnage, length, horsepower and operating type).

819 General agricultural census. Results of the agricultural holdings (households) survey, 1991.
State Institute of Statistics (SIS).   Ankara: State Institute of Statistics, 1994. 758p.

This publication reports on the second-stage findings of the agricultural census conducted in 1991. The census covered all villages and settlements with fewer than 5,000 inhabitants. The results presented in this publication are based on the detailed sample survey conducted on 32,000 agricultural holdings. Holdings in Turkey are given in terms of their legal status, type, size, land use, livestock owned as well as area sown and yields of main field crops, vegetables, fruits and numbers of livestock by kind. Also included are statistics on ownership of agricultural equipment and machinery, labour use and seasonal employment.

820 General agricultural census. Results of village information survey, 1991.
State Institute of Statistics (SIS).   Ankara: State Institute of Statistics, 1994. 146p.

This publication reports on the first-stage findings of the agricultural census conducted in 1991. The results presented are based on the data compiled from village heads in all of the 36,371 villages in Turkey. Information is given, at the regional and provincial level, for: numbers of settlements, locations of settlements, households, farmers, type of agricultural activity, size of agricultural land, number of livestock, land size distribution, land use, production of different agricultural products, numbers of equipment and machinery owned, irrigation, fertilization, use of chemicals, marketing channels, and use of seasonal workers.

Landholding and commercial agriculture in the Middle East.
See item no. 239.

Agricultural statistics of Turkey during the Ottoman period.
See item no. 253.

Turkey: political, social and economic challenges in the 1990s.
See item no. 530.

Women and household production: the impact of rural transformation in Turkey.
See item no. 844.

Assessment of rural landlessness in Turkey.
See item no. 876.

Settlement distribution and structural change in Turkish agriculture: a key to migration models and policy.
See item no. 878.

Boğaziçi Journal. Review of Social, Economic and Administrative Studies.
See item no. 1319.

METU Studies in Development.
See item no. 1343.

New Perspectives on Turkey.
See item no. 1352.

Yapı Kredi Economic Review.
See item no. 1391.

Transport and Communications

821 **1993 PTT statistics.**
General Directorate of PTT. Ankara: Research Planning
Coordination Department (APK), 1993. 351p.
The publication contains tables of statistics about postal services, telecommunication activities, telegraph, telephone, radio and television services.

822 **Approaches to regional transport problems: Middle East requirements. Papers and proceedings.**
Edited by Yücel Candemir with Nurhan Yentürk Çoban, N. Lerzan Özkale. İstanbul: İstanbul Technical University, Transportation and Vehicles Research Centre, 1989. 581p.
The proceedings of a conference held in İstanbul in May 1988. It contains thirty-five papers which examine transport problems in the Middle East, but most of the papers are about Turkey. Papers focus on the issues of highway network extension and maintenance management, comprehensive urban transport planning, transport safety, the relationship of transport to the rest of the national economy, traffic engineering and traffic management, international freight movement, institutional problems, project evaluation, and public transport.

823   **Evaluating transport movement systems in İstanbul metropolitan area: the case of the Bosphorus Tube Tunnel, metro alternatives and three combined alternatives.**
Cevat Karataş, Cem Payaslıoğlu.   *Boğaziçi Journal. Review of Social, Economic and Administrative Studies*, vol. 10, no. 1-2 (1996), p. 191-226.

In this detailed and informative paper, the authors compare the economics of several projects which are suggested in order to improve the transport system in İstanbul. Proposals involve connecting the two sides of the Bosphorus, the Bosphorus Tube Tunnel, two individual metro alternatives, and the combined alternative, which includes both the Tunnel and metro systems. The article contains four maps.

824   **Ankaray. Ankara Light Rail Transit System.**
Municipality of Greater Ankara, General Directorate of EGO (Electric, Gas, Autobus).   Ankara: Department of Transportation Planning and Rail System, 1992. 3 vols.

Ankara Light Rail Transit System covers the 8.5 kilometres between the Söğütözü and Dikimevi sections of the city. 5.5 kilometres of this distance is tunnelled, and sections were completed by 1996. These volumes explain the project in detail with tables, maps, and technical drawings.

825   **Postal statistics, 1996.**
Turkish Republic General Directorate of Posts.   Ankara: Research Planning Coordination Department (APK), 1996. 131p.

This annual publication of the Directorate presents activities and statistics regarding postal services for 1996.

826   **TCDDY annual statistics.**
Turkish Republic General Directorate of State Railways Administration.   Ankara: Devlet Demir Yolları, annual.

The publication gives detailed tables, statistics, and numbers related to Turkey's railways, distribution of lines by regions, and operational activities.

827   **Road motor vehicle statistics, 1997.**
State Institute of Statistics (SIS).   Ankara: State Institute of Statistics, 1998. 140p.

This annual publication provides statistics on motor vehicles registered (including motorcycles, special purpose vehicles, road construction and work machinery), by province, trademark, use, type, type of fuel used, horsepower, tyre size and carrying capacity. It also provides information on road motor vehicles withdrawn during the year by province.

828 **Sea vessels and sea transportation statistics, 1997.**
State Institute of Statistics (SIS). Ankara: State Institute of Statistics,
1998. 70p.
This has been published annually since 1994. It contains statistics on vessels by type,
tonnage group, ownership, kind of construction material, horsepower, year of construction, registration, registration office, country of construction, and passenger
capacity.

829 **Summary statistics on transportation and communication, 1996.**
State Institute of Statistics (SIS). Ankara: State Institute of Statistics,
1998. 48p.
The publication includes statistics on the transport of freight and passengers by mode
of transport, length of pipeline for petroleum and natural gas, and their transport volume, circulation and traffic volume on state and provincial roads, road motor vehicle
registration and withdrawal by use, kinds of fuel, road traffic accidents, length of railways, freight and passenger, rail transport, sea vessels, scheduled flights on domestic
and international airlines, and postal and telephone communications.

830 **Road traffic accident statistics, 1996.**
State Institute of Statistics (SIS). Ankara: State Institute of Statistics,
1998. 106p.
The publication provides data on road traffic accidents by time of day, month, and
year of occurrence; type of vehicle; place and type of accident; and persons killed or
injured by age group and sex.

831 **Türkiye'de büyük inşaat müeahhitlerinin doğuşunda
Cumhuriyet'in bayındırlık ve demiryolu programlarının etkisi.**
(The role of public works and railway construction programmes of the
Turkish Republic in the emergence of major building contractors in
Turkey.)
İlhan Tekeli, Selim İlkin. *Middle East Technical University Studies
in Development*, vol. 20, no. 1-2 (1993), p. 207-28.
The study looks at the development of building contractors in Turkey as a social stra-
tum for the period from the early 1930s to the post-Second World War years. The
information is mostly derived from the memoirs of the entrepreneurs.

832 **Türk Telekom. Telecommunication statistics.**
Türk Telekom Research Planning Coordination Department. Ankara:
MGB Matbaası, 1996. 348p.
In April 1995, Türk Telekomikasyon A.Ş. (Turkish Telecommunication Company)
took over some of the functions of the PTT (Post Telegraph Telephone) General
Directorate. This publication provides numerical data on the services and activities of
the new company.

Employment and Manpower

833　Turkish workers in Europe, 1960-1975: a social-economic
re-appraisal.
Edited by Nermin Abadan-Unat.　Leiden, the Netherlands: E. J. Brill,
1976. 425p. bibliog. (Social, Economic and Political Studies in the
Middle East, no. 19).
Presents an objective and diverse study of the problems of worker migration, taking
Turkey as a case-study. There are fifteen chapters grouped under specific areas such as
the factors influencing external migration, the economic impact of migration, social
issues related to migration, and the impact of Turkish migrants on European social
structures.

834　The labor movement in Turkey: labor pains, maturity,
metamorphosis.
Günseli Berik, Cihan Bilginsoy.　In: *The social history of labor in the
Middle East*.　Edited by Goldberg Ellis Jay.　Boulder, Colorado:
Westview Press, 1996, p. 37-64.
Labour developments during the periods 1923-45, 1946-60, 1960-80, and 1980-90s
are chronicled and analysed. The authors leave it open whether in the future worker
discontent may take on a reactionary colour and turn to individualistic solutions, or to
authoritarianism in its ultranationalist or Islamic fundamentalist forms.

835　Employment, unemployment and wages in Turkey.
Tuncer Bulutay.　Geneva: International Labour Office, 1995. 302p.
bibliog.
The work analyses the Turkish labour market, its evolution, mechanisms and structure
by matching data from various sources on different periods, and presents statistics on
employment, unemployment and wages from 1923 until 1988 in order to construct a
consistent database. The problems related to employment in Turkey are explained with
reference to the transformations that have taken place in the process of economic and

social development, in the geographic movement of labour and in the educational attainment of the population.

836   **Child labour in Turkey.**
Tuncer Bulutay.   Ankara: State Institute of Statistics, 1996. 102p.
This publication gives information on child labour and working children in Turkey, and discusses proposals for the prevention of child labour.

837   **Labour and state in Turkey: 1960-80.**
Ümit Cizre-Sakallıoğlu.   *Middle Eastern Studies*, vol. 28, no. 24 (1992), p. 712-28.
The author examines the three crucial periods in contemporary Turkish history (1950-60, 1960-70, and 1970-80) with reference to the relationship between labour and state in the governmental process.

838   **The development of Turkish trade unionism: a study of legislative and socio-political dimensions.**
Toker Dereli.   İstanbul: İstanbul University Press, 1968. 258p.
(İstanbul Üniversitesi Yayınları, no. 1348).
Although out-of-date, this is a useful book for historical comparative studies. Focusing on the legal aspects of trade unionism in Turkey, the book presents a structural-functional analysis. The first chapter is devoted to developing a theoretical framework, and the second chapter discusses the cultural environment in Turkey and the Republican reforms that surround the structure of the newly emerging industrial system. Trade union legislation in the periods before and after 1963 is presented and discussed in detail.

839   **1990'larda Türkiye işçi sınıfı: sosyal ve ekonomik göstergeler.**
Turkish working class in the 1990s: social and economic indicators.
DIAK Araştırma Enstitüsü.   İstanbul: DIAK, 1992. 82p.
The publication, in English and Turkish, carries tables and figures relating to the social and economic status of the working class in Turkey at the beginning of the 1990s.

840   **Patterns of child labour in rural Turkey.**
Yakın Ertürk.   Ankara, Turkey: International Labour Organization (ILO) Ankara Office, 1994. 96p. bibliog.
The aim of the study is to capture and analyse the dynamics and the patterns of child labour in order to build up a database for formulating policy measures and intervention strategies for an ILO led programme on the elimination of child labour (IPEC). Fieldwork for the study was carried out in the rural localities of three regions in Turkey. The underlying question posed by the study is whether rural households can secure family maintenance without the use of child labour under the conditions of the market economy.

841 **Türkiye'de memurlar ve sendikal haklar, 1926-1994.** (Civil servants
and union rights in Turkey, 1926-94.)
Mesut Gülmez. Ankara: Türkiye ve Orta Doğu Amme İdaresi
Enstitüsü, 1994. 251p. 2nd rev. ed. (Institute of Public Administration
for Turkey and the Middle East, no. 255).

The unionization of civil servants is a newer phenomenon than labour unions. Turkey
is one of the few countries which does not have legal regulations for the union rights
of civil servants. This unique book illustrates constitutional and legal developments,
dominant views and ideology concerning union rights for civil servants in Turkey
since the 1920s. The book uses primary sources, including parliamentary and High
Court records.

842 **Strong state and economic interest groups: the post-1980 Turkish
experience.**
Edited by Metin Heper. Berlin; New York: Walter de Gruyter, 1991.
198p.

The papers in this volume scrutinize the relations between the state and economic
interest groups in Turkey, including labour, agricultural, commercial and industrial
groups during the 1980s.

843 **Work and occupation in Modern Turkey.**
Edited by E. Kahveci, N. Sugur, T. Nichols. London: Cassell, 1996.
211p. bibliog.

Presents studies of work and occupation in Turkey, in the context of a rapidly changing society, the growth of a large informal sector, the emergence of an industrial
working class, and the declining economic and social position of the state employees.

844 **Women and household production: the impact of rural
transformation in Turkey.**
Deniz Kandiyoti. In: *The rural Middle East. Peasant lines and modes
of production.* Edited by Kathy Glavanis, Pandeli Glavanis.
London: Zed Books, 1990, p. 183-94.

Capitalist penetration into rural household organization and dynamics may produce
any of a variety of outcomes, partly because it builds on locally pre-existing patterns
of productive relations between the sexes. This chapter on Turkey identifies the range
of changes affecting rural women in the Anatolian household, traditionally built on
'classic' patriarchy, which appropriated the fruits of women's production.

845 **State and class in Turkey: a study in capitalist development.**
Çağlar Keyder. London; New York: Verso, 1987. 228p.

The book argues that Ottoman, and later Turkish, socio-economic development was
dominated by alternating contention and cooperation between the state bureaucracy
and the various segments of the commercial and industrial bourgeoisie.

846 **Manpower mobility across cultural boundaries. Social, economic and legal aspects: the case of Turkey and West Germany.**
Edited by R. E. Krane. Leiden, the Netherlands: E. J. Brill, 1975. 222p. bibliog. (Social, Economic and Political Studies in the Middle East, no. 16).

Organized in two sections, this work examines Turkish labour migration to West Germany, first in the German context and then from a Turkish point of view. It analyses problems related to Turkish workers at home and abroad, such as their learning behaviour, earning capacities, legal status, and family structures.

847 **The condition of mine labor in Turkey: injuries to miners in Zonguldak, 1942-90.**
Theo Nichols, Erol Kahveci. *Middle Eastern Studies*, vol. 31, no. 2 (1995), p. 197-228.

Studies the relationship between productivity and working conditions in Zonguldak coal mines until the 1990s. The authors argue that the increasing number of injuries can be related to the changes in the nature of political economy (i.e liberalization), but that ineffective trade unions are one of the major causes of poor working conditions.

848 **Exporting workers: the Turkish case.**
Suzanne Paine. Cambridge, England: Cambridge University Press, 1974. 227p. bibliog. (University of Cambridge, Department of Applied Economics, Occasional Paper, no. 41).

This book discusses foreign workers in European countries, their effect on European economic growth, and the consequences of the labour export on the home countries. Turkey is taken as a case-study, and is surveyed in detail for the 1960-73 period. The author assembles all the available data, and analyses the socio-economic characteristics of the immigrant workers, the fate of those who returned home, and the changes which have taken place over the decade.

849 **High level manpower in economic development: the Turkish case.**
Richard D. Robinson. Cambridge, Massachusetts: Harvard University Press, 1967. 134p. bibliog. (Harvard Middle Eastern Monographs, no. 17).

The book treats Turkey as a case-study for educational or manpower development. The contents describe political and military cycles; class roles and social change; social restraints on manpower development; income levels, and the balance of trade; high level manpower demand; manpower supply through education and training; formal, adult and military educational systems; and high level manpower in economic development. Although outdated, the book is important for historical comparative studies of manpower.

850 **Workers and the working class in the Ottoman Empire and the Turkish Republic, 1839-1950.**
Edited by Donald Quataert, Erik Jan Zürcher. London; New York: Tauris Academic Studies in Association with the International Institute of Social History, Amsterdam, 1995. 208p. bibliog. (Library of Modern Middle East Studies, no. 3).

A valuable collection of papers on the social history of Turkey. The titles of the contributions are: 'The emergence of the Ottoman industrial working class, 1839-1923', Y. S. Karakışla; 'Militant textile weavers in Damascus: waged artisans and the Ottoman labor movement, 1850-1914', S. Vatter; 'The workers of Slaonica, 1850-1912', D. Quataert; 'The development of class consciousness in Republican Turkey, 1923-45', F. Ahmad; 'The state of industrial workforce, 1923-40', E. Yavuz; 'Capital and labor during World War II', M. Ş. Güzel; and 'The current condition of the popular classes', Ç. Keyder.

851 **Household labour force survey results, October 1997.**
State Institute of Statistics (SIS). Ankara: State Institute of Statistics, 1998. 237p.

This is a semi-annual series (April and October) of household labour force surveys, published since 1988 with the assistance of the International Labour Organization. The State Institute of Statistics has been collecting data on the economically active population since 1955.

852 **Household income distribution survey, 1994.**
State Institute of Statistics (SIS). Ankara: State Institute of Statistics, 1998. 41p.

Contains the results of an income survey carried in nineteen selected provinces such as İstanbul, Bursa, İzmir, Adana, Samsun, Erzurum, Malatya, Diyarbakır, and Gaziantep.

853 **Labour statistics, 1996.**
State Institute of Statistics (SIS). Ankara: State Institute of Statistics, 1996. 456p.

The publication contains statistics on population by labour force and age group. It also covers average wages in manufacturing industry, service and mining sectors by size of establishments and their legal status.

854 **Child labour, 1994.**
State Institute of Statistics (SIS). Ankara: State Institute of Statistics, 1996. 142p.

The volume presents the results of a survey in 1994 on child labour involving children below the age of fifteen.

855 **Technology and employment, 10 December 1996.**
State Institute of Statistics (SIS). Ankara: State Institute of Statistics, 1998. 316p.
A collection of essays on the relationship between technological progress and the labour market in Turkey. It was prepared as part of the project 'Labour market information systems', financed jointly by the United Nations Development Program and International Labour Organisation. It includes the following essays: 'The nature of technological progress and general trends in technology', Tuncer Bulutay; 'International trade and technological progress: an appraisal of theoretical and policy issues', Oktay Türel; 'Implications of the Uruguay Round for the technology and employment in Turkish manufacturing industries', Erol Taymaz; and 'The relationship between employment and technical change: policy issues and the case of ICT', Ümit Efendioğlu.

856 **Labour market response to structural adjustment and industrial pressures: the Turkish case.**
Fikret Şenses. *Middle East Technical University Studies in Development*, vol. 21, no. 3 (1994), p. 405-48.
The author reviews the major structural characteristics of the Turkish labour market, and surveys its interaction with institutional forces and the economic policies implemented since 1980. The paper includes a detailed assessment of the main factors behind the sharp increase in real wages after 1989, and briefly discusses the draft bills on employment protection and unemployment insurance together with some recent steps towards increased labour market flexibility. It also provides a prospective evaluation of the main problems likely to face the labour market in the near future.

857 **Workers' participation and self-management in Turkey.**
Mehmet Nezir Uca. The Hague: Institute of Social Studies and Martinus Nijhoff, 1983. 254p.
This unique book describes and evaluates workers' participation and self-management in Turkey during the Ecevit administration between 1978 and 1979. The book, in seven chapters, describes the scope, nature, and circumstances surrounding the introduction of three different forms of workers' participation. It gives an overview of the main participatory institutions, including trade unions.

Money makes us relatives: women's labour in urban Turkey.
See item no. 506.

Strong state and economic interest groups: the post-1980 Turkish experience.
See item no. 552.

Turkey in transition: new perspectives.
See item no. 580.

Turkish Labor Law.
See item no. 610.

Statistics

858 **Publications and electronic services catalogue.**
State Institute of Statistics (SIS). Ankara: State Institute of Statistics, 1997. 95p.

The annual catalogue of the State Institute of Statistics presents the publications and services that the Institute provides. The catalogue, which is in Turkish and English, lists the publications of the Institute under the following headings: general, national accounts, agriculture, industry, building construction, prices and indexes, foreign trade, services, transport, finance, environment, population, labour force, demography, education and culture, justice, tourism, elections, and a list of the News Bulletins. Remote sensing studies, and explanations on the services of information and publications conclude the catalogue. The entries for publications provide information on the subject, format, language, number of pages, availability in magnetic form, and price of each item, together with a brief summary of its contents, and a colour photograph of the cover page. Other information includes the prices of services offered, ordering information, and contact addresses.

859 **Statistical Yearbook of Turkey.**
State Institute of Statistics (SIS). Ankara: State Institute of Statistics, 1928- . annual.

Contains a summary of all statistical data compiled by the State Institute of Statistics. Topics covered include: area, climate, environment, population, demography, health, education, justice, elections, social security, labour, income and consumption, agriculture, mining, energy, manufacturing, industry, construction, transport, communication, tourism, domestic trade, foreign trade, prices and indexes, money, banking and insurance, finance, national accounts, research and development, and purchasing power parity. The *Statistical yearbook* is also available on diskette and can be viewed (in Turkish and English) at: <http://www.die.gov.tr>.

860   **Turkey in statistics, 1997.**
      State Institute of Statistics (SIS).   Ankara: State Institute of Statistics,
      1998. 164p.
This publication is a shorter version of the *Statistical yearbook of Turkey*, and provides an overview of Turkey in statistics.

861   **Monthly Bulletin of Statistics.**
      State Institute of Statistics (SIS).   Ankara: State Institute of Statistics,
      1952- . monthly.
The publication covers statistical data for the preceding five years and thirteen months. It contains information on national accounts, industry, building construction, transport, environment, foreign trade, prices and indexes, finance, money and banking, companies, labour and social security.

862   **Statistical indicators, 1923-1995.**
      State Institute of Statistics (SIS).   Ankara: State Institute of Statistics,
      1997. 496p.
Published annually since 1991, this work provides a historical perspective on a number of key statistical indicators, including population, demography, health, education, culture, social security, agriculture, manufacturing industry, mining, energy, construction, transport, communication, tourism, domestic and foreign trade, prices and indexes, money and banking, finance and national accounts. The time series statistics in this publication cover the period from 1923 to date.

863   **Human Development Report Turkey 1996.**
      United Nations Development Programme.   Ankara: UNDP Office,
      1997. 125p. maps.
Like the Global Human Development Reports prepared for UNDP since 1990, this National Human Development Report has been prepared with the aim of exploring key problems of national and local development in Turkey with special focus on urban management and the eradication of poverty. The report provides an overall assessment of the country's human development performance. It offers an analysis of Turkey's standing *vis-à-vis* other countries, and within the country through a disaggregated analysis of data by region, province and gender. In-depth analyses of the key components of the human development index are also provided with particular emphasis on education and health delivery issues, and on gender disparities.

Provincial and regional statistics, 1994.
See item no. 113.

Ottoman foreign trade in the 19th century.
See item no. 252.

Agricultural statistics of Turkey during the Ottoman period.
See item no. 253.

Ottoman industry: industrial census of 1913, 1915.
See item no. 254.

Statistics

The first statistical yearbook of the Ottoman Empire.
See item no. 255.

The population of the Ottoman Empire and Turkey (1500-1927).
See item no. 291.

The first population census during the Ottoman Empire, 1831.
See item no. 292.

Genel nüfus sayımı. İdari bölünüş. 21.10.1990. (Census of population: administrative division).
See item no. 304.

1989 Turkish demographic survey.
See item no. 306.

Census of population. Social and economic characteristics of population, 1990.
See item no. 307.

The population of Turkey, 1923-1994. Demographic structure and development, with projections to the mid-21st century.
See item no. 308.

Death statistics from provincial and district centers, 1995.
See item no. 309.

Suicide statistics, 1996.
See item no. 310.

Marriage statistics, 1996.
See item no. 311.

Divorce statistics, 1996.
See item no. 312.

Women in statistics.
See item no. 489.

Women in statistics, 1927-1992.
See item no. 503.

Turkey. Demographic and health survey, 1993.
See item no. 519.

Judicial statistics, 1996.
See item no. 611.

SEAP provincial statistics, 1950-1996.
See item no. 765.

Turkish Economy Statistics and Analysis.
See item no. 766.

Retail price statistics. Annual average prices by selected items, 1993-1995.
See item no. 767.

Wholesale price statistics.
See item no. 768.

Gross domestic product by provinces, 1987-1994.
See item no. 769.

Gross domestic product by cost components, 1987-1995.
See item no. 770.

Results of the household income distribution survey: income distribution by 20 per cent, 10 per cent, 5 per cent and 1 per cent groups in 19 selected province centers, 1994.
See item no. 771.

Results of the household income distribution survey: income distribution by 20 per cent, 10 per cent, 5 per cent and 1 per cent groups in Turkey, urban and rural areas and regions, 1994.
See item no. 772.

Household consumption expenditures survey: summary results of 19 selected province centers, 1994.
See item no. 773.

Household consumption expenditures survey results, 1994.
See item no. 774.

Turkey and world foreign trade, 1950-1993.
See item no. 792.

Foreign trade statistics, 1996.
See item no. 793.

Foreign trade by transport system, 1996.
See item no. 794.

Mining and quarrying statistics, 1995.
See item no. 795.

Electricity, gas and water statistics, 1995.
See item no. 796.

Small sized manufacturing industry statistics (1-9), 1995.
See item no. 798.

Annual manufacturing industry statistics, 1994.
See item no. 799.

Agricultural structure: production, price, value, 1996.
See item no. 816.

The summary of agricultural statistics, 1996.
See item no. 817.

Fisheries statistics, 1996.
See item no. 818.

General agricultural census. Results of the agricultural holdings (households) survey, 1991.
See item no. 819.

General agricultural census. Results of village information survey, 1991.
See item no. 820.

Road motor vehicle statistics, 1997.
See item no. 827.

Sea vessels and sea transportation statistics, 1997.
See item no. 828.

Summary statistics on transportation and communication, 1996.
See item no. 829.

Road traffic accident statistics, 1996.
See item no. 830.

Household labour force survey results, October 1997.
See item no. 851.

Household income distribution survey, 1994.
See item no. 852.

Labour statistics, 1996.
See item no. 853.

Environmental statistics: municipal solid waste statistics, 1991.
See item no. 871.

Environmental statistics: manufacturing industry waste statistics, 1992.
See item no. 872.

Environmental statistics: household solid waste composition and tendency survey results, 1993.
See item no. 873.

Environmental statistics: air pollution, 1990-1993.
See item no. 874.

National education statistics: formal education, 1994-1996.
See item no. 973.

National education statistics: adult education, 1994-1995.
See item no. 974.

Cultural Statistics, 1996.
See item no. 975.

Environment

Environmental protection

864 Turkey towards the year 2000.
Cihan Dura, Mahir Fisunoğlu, Ergun Hiçyılmaz, Hakan Türkkuşu.
Ankara: Önder Matbaası, 1987. 64p. (Environmental Problems
Foundation of Turkey).

In 1986, the Foundation held a competition on the theme 'Turkey towards the year 2000' in order to encourage research into Turkey's environment, natural resources, population and energy sources. Three successful entries are published in this book. They discuss a variety of subjects such as the ecological tensions in Turkey and their results, population dynamics, the energy problem and clean energy sources, the supply of and demand for food in the Turkish economy, land and water resources, and Turkey's major environmental problems in the mid-1980s.

865 New and clean energy sources in Turkey.
Environmental Problems Foundation of Turkey.   Ankara: Önder
Matbaası, 1984. 200p. bibliog.

The book provides summaries of research about alternative energy sources in Turkey, and the services provided for new and clean energy sources by governmental organizations and Turkish universities. Information about private companies and voluntary organizations that take an interest in the subject is also given.

866 Cost analysis of alternative heating systems for Ankara.
Environmental Problems Foundation of Turkey.   Ankara: Önder
Matbaası, 1987. 223p.

Air pollution in Ankara was a topic of national debate for many years until the introduction of natural gas. This study was prepared with the purpose of evaluating different options for heating in Ankara: electricity, natural gas and solar energy.

867 **Environmental policy of Turkey.**
Environmental Problems Foundation of Turkey.   Ankara: Önder
Matbaası, 1987. 71p.

The result of a team effort, this book dwells on the concept of environmental policy,
and what Turkey's environmental policy is. The difference between politics in the nar-
row sense and policy in the broad sense constitutes the basis of the study. The aim is
to convey to general readers and concerned parties the attitudes, scientific currents,
and movements that influence environmental policies, and the importance of pressure
groups.

868 **Urbanization and environment conference.**
Environmental Problems Foundation of Turkey.   Ankara: Önder
Matbaası, 1987. 119p.

Contains papers presented at a conference organized by the Foundation in 1987. They
discuss the relationship between urbanization and economy, new settlement areas and
the environment, urbanization and environmental policies, developments in İstanbul
and the Golden Horn area, and environmental problems in İzmir.

869 **Environmental profile of Turkey.**
Environmental Problems Foundation of Turkey.   Ankara: Önder
Matbaası, 1989. 328p.

This book contains reports by experts on air, water and soil pollution. Chapters give
brief definitions of the problems, their effects on humans, and the extent of the problems on a national scale.

870 **Environmental policies in Turkey.**
Organisation for Economic Co-operation and Development (OECD).
Paris: OEDC, 1992. 176p. maps.

Turkey's rapid and dynamic change during the last decade has put severe pressures on
natural resources and the environment. This report by OECD's Environment Policy
Committee reviews the environmental policies in Turkey in the context of physical,
human, economic, institutional, and natural resources. It discusses the management of
water resources, urban pollution, coastal zone management, and includes suggestions
for improvements to foster environmental progress and sustainable development.

871 **Environmental statistics: municipal solid waste statistics, 1991.**
State Institute of Statistics (SIS).   Ankara: State Institute of Statistics,
1996. 420p.

The publication is based on a survey which was carried out in 2,033 provinces, districts and village municipalities in Turkey. The data includes information on
settlement location, seasonal population, garbage collection, amount of solid waste,
personnel engaged in garbage collection, disposal methods of garbage, amount of
recyclable garbage, and the status and frequency of road washing activities.

872 **Environmental statistics: manufacturing industry waste statistics, 1992.**
State Institute of Statistics (SIS).   Ankara: State Institute of Statistics, 1996. 324p.

The publication contains the results of a survey carried out in 2,548 establishments, and provides data on environmental pollution.

873 **Environmental statistics: household solid waste composition and tendency survey results, 1993.**
State Institute of Statistics (SIS).   Ankara: State Institute of Statistics, 1996. 462p.

The publication contains information about households by income group and solid waste collection method, destination of recyclable materials collected separately and preferred time for waste collection.

874 **Environmental statistics: air pollution, 1990-1993.**
State Institute of Statistics (SIS).   Ankara: State Institute of Statistics, 1996. 306p.

This annual publication, first published in 1991, gives information about air pollution in sixty-three provincial and ten district centres for the given period. It carries data on annual, monthly, and winter season (October-March) measurements on average concentrations of sulphur dioxide and particulate matter, minimum and maximum concentrations, and rates of change.

Environment law of Turkey.
See item no. 596.

Environment law and its application in Turkey.
See item no. 597.

Environmental legislation in EC and Turkey.
See item no. 598.

Turkish environment law and some other related legal provisions.
See item no. 599.

Rural planning

875 **Ankara Research Institute of Rural Services: summaries of final reports and activities (1962-1987).**
Republic of Turkey, Ministry of Agriculture, Forestry and Village Affairs, General Directorate of Rural Services, Ankara Research Institute. Ankara: Ministry of Agriculture, Forestry and Village Affairs, 1988. 115p. (Introductory Publications no. 2-14; General Publications, no. 12-8).
This useful publication contains summaries of research activities carried out since the Institute was established in 1962 to the end of 1987.

876 **Assessment of rural landlessness in Turkey.**
Ziya Gökalp Mülayim. Ankara: University of Ankara, Publication of Faculty of Agriculture, 1992. 128p. maps. bibliog.
The major focus of the book is to assess (as accurately as possible) the number of rural landless, and their socio-economic conditions, and to determine the multiple causes of landlessness with a view to developing policies which would improve access to land, income and employment in the rural areas of Turkey. There are twenty-one tables in the book, including those of the number of landless households in Turkey (1962-69).

877 **GAP: an irrigation and development project in Turkey.**
Duran Taraklı. *Journal of the Faculty of Architecture, Middle East Technical University*, vol. 9, no. 2 (1989), p. 161-76.
The paper discusses the Southeast Anatolia Project (GAP/SEAP) initiated in 1976. The article looks at the area in terms of its natural conditions, social structure, settlement patterns, land tenure, and the main features of the GAP. Using the results of the 'Devegeçidi Irrigation Scheme' (one of the small irrigation schemes within the GAP), the scope and framework of the GAP are discussed.

878 **Settlement distribution and structural change in Turkish agriculture: a key to migration models and policy.**
İlhan Tekeli, Leila Erder. In: *Why people move.* Edited by Jorge Balan. Paris: The Unesco Press, 1981, p. 122-39.
The article focuses on one aspect of rural-urban migration: land-ownership and technological change in agriculture. The urban view of rural exodus is based on the city-dweller's interpretation, and the slogan of 'rural push' has been created, reducing explanations of movement to mechanization in agriculture, and foisting the blame for urban overcrowding on to the rural areas. However, a rural view could equally well describe rural overcrowding. The authors conclude that the key to migration analysis and settlement policies is the pattern of land ownership in rural areas.

879   **The Southeastern Anatolia Project (GAP) master plan study.**
Republic of Turkey, Prime Ministry, State Planning Organization.
Ankara: GAP, 1988. 4 vols.
The Master Plan is composed of the main report which contains a complete regional
development master plan for the GAP region, and the appendices which contain more
detailed analysis of the present conditions by sectors, and specific aspects of the plan
with all the supporting data.

880   **Underdevelopment and rural structures in Southeastern Turkey:
the household economy in Gisgis and Kalhana.**
Zülküf Aydın.   London: Ithaca Press, 1986. 301p. bibliog. (Published
for the Centre for Middle Eastern and Islamic Studies, University of
Durham).
Deals with the relationship between household economy and the development of capitalism and capital accumulation in south-east Turkey. The author asserts that rural
development and transformation can be clarified best if studied within the context of
social formation and the world system of capitalism. Using data collected from south-
east Turkey in general, and from two villages of Gisgis and Kalhana in the province of
Diyarbakır in particular, the book shows which forces of capital operate in south-east
Anatolia, and illuminates the impact of their articulation in the structure of land ownership, and the nature of production relations, marketing and finance at village level.

Migration and reintegration in rural Turkey: the role of women behind.
See item no. 332.

Migration and urbanization in rural Turkey.
See item no. 333.

**From economic integration to cultural strategies of power: the study of
rural change in Turkey.**
See item no. 473.

Culture and economy: changes in Turkish villages.
See item no. 476.

Agriculture in Turkey: some key information for foreign investors.
See item no. 810.

Urban planning

881 **Regenerating the lost green of Ankara: a hard task ahead.**
Nazan Aydın-Wheater, Gaye Gülcüoğlu. In: *The urban experience. A people-environment perspective.* Edited by S. J. Neary, M. S. Symes, F. E. Brown. London: E & FN Spon, 1994, p. 279-88. (Proceedings of the 13th Conference of the International Association for People-Environment Studies held on 13-15 July 1994).
The paper discusses the development of a physically inadequate and desolate small Anatolian town into a capital city. It outlines the four major planning processes in the planning history of Ankara: the Jansen Plan (1932-57); the Uybadın-Yücel Plan (1957-69); the AMPO (Ankara Metropolitan Planning Office Plan) (1970-80); and the Ankara Green Belt Afforestation Project (AGBAP) for Ankara (1985-2015). Urban open/green space applications are discussed within the context of each plan period. The study ends with a discussion of the shortcomings of the provisional agenda.

882 **The politics of rapid urbanization: government and growth in modern Turkey.**
Michael N. Danielson, Ruşen Keleş. New York; London: Holmes & Meier Publishers, Ltd, 1985. 286p. bibliog.
The study explores the complex interplay between urban development and political structure in Turkey from the late 1940s to 1980. Focusing primarily on İstanbul and Ankara, the authors analyse several aspects of Turkish government and politics (including governmental structure, public finance, bureaucracy, intergovernmental relations, political participation, special interest groups and public policy) as they relate to the patterns of urban development. The article also explores the reciprocal consequences of urbanization on the political structure.

883 **The effect of popular culture on urban form in Istanbul.**
Aytanga Dener. In: *The urban experience: a people-environment perspective.* Edited by S. J. Neary, M. S. Symes, F. E. Brown. London: E & FN Spon, 1994, p. 73-84. (Proceedings of the 13th Conference of the International Association for People-Environment Studies held in 1994).
The paper aims to discuss how and why urban housing in Turkey has been deeply affected by popular culture. The early Republican period is characterized by the efforts to become industrialized through government control, which is symbolized by the luxurious apartments of the high-level civil servants and the bourgeoisie. However, the later years are characterized by liberalism, symbolized by small-scale businesses and cheap and cheerful (sic) buildings.

884   **The urbanization pattern in Turkey and its future development.**
Vedia F. Dökmeci.   In: *Urban problems and economic development.*
Edited by Lata Chatterjee, Peter Nijkamp.   Amsterdam: Proceedings
of the NATO Advanced Study Institute on Urban Problems and
Policies in a Spatial Context, 1981, p. 53-68.

The essay analyses the patterns of urbanization in settlements with over 10,000 inhabitants over a period of three decades (1945-75).

885   **An application of the Garin model-Istanbul model.**
Koray Gökan.   In: *Urban problems and economic development.*
Edited by Lata Chatterjee, Peter Nijkamp.   Amsterdam: Proceedings
of the NATO Advanced Study Institute on Urban Problems and
Policies in a Spatial Context, 1981, p. 263-80.

This study attempts to identify and evaluate the problems encountered during the
application of what is known as the Garin Model, on which the model created for
İstanbul is based. The theoretical basis of the model, its technical formulation, zones
of the model town-system, data necessary to calibrate the model, the calibration
process, the model town-system of İstanbul, a practical application of the model are
all discussed, and in the conclusion the limitations and problems encountered in the
model building process are listed.

886   **Housing and settlement in Anatolia: a historical perspective.**
HABITAT II.   İstanbul: The Economic and Social History
Foundation, 1996. 492p.

The 'Housing and settlement in Anatolia: a historical perspective' exhibition was
organized on the occasion of the HABITAT Conference in İstanbul to display the culture of housing and settlement which evolved in Anatolia over 12,000 years. This
volume was prepared to accompany the exhibition, with the collaboration of over forty
researchers and scholars. The authors of the first section of the book explore the subject in its historical continuity; the second section includes selected visual material
from the exhibition itself, along with conceptual articles exploring the dwelling and
settlement examples of various periods in a historical sequence.

887   **Urban experience in an Ottoman town in central Anatolia.**
Vacit İmamoğlu.   In: *The urban experience. A people environment
perspective.*   Edited by S. J. Neary, M. S. Symes, F. E. Brown.
London: E & FN Spon, 1994, p. 61-72. (Proceedings of the 13th
Conference of the International Association for People-Environment
Studies held on 13-15 July 1994).

The author explores dimensions of urban experience and general characteristics of the
architectural environment in Kayseri during the first half of the 20th century. He
attempts to explain how people lived, and what their attitudes and values were. Topics
discussed include: the historical evolution of the town; its physical, social and cultural
setting; summer-winter differentiation in town life; the concern for security;
dwellings, gender and privacy; living styles of different religious groups; and historical patterns of settlement in Central Anatolia.

888   **Economic development and social consciousness – Turkey under the developmentalism.**
      Ruşen Keleş, Hiromasa Kano.   Tokyo: Institute of Developing Economics, 1986. 197p.

The book gives the results of a research project entitled 'The Middle East', carried out by the Institute of Developing Economies. The contents include a discussion of development plans and policies, and development models in the Middle East and in Turkey, five development plans and changes in the development policies during the 1970s and 1980s, urban development and housing polices, urban problems of Turkish society, gaps between the capital city and local cities, and social attitudes of Turkish urbanites towards developmentalism. English translations of Turkish laws on *gecekondu* (squatter housing), outlines of a squatter housing survey conducted by the authors, and other data are presented in the 'Appendix'.

889   **Housing and the urban poor in the Middle East: Turkey, Egypt, Morocco and Jordan.**
      Ruşen Keleş, Hiromasa Kano.   Tokyo: Institute of Developing Economics, 1987. 320p.

The aim of the book is to improve the understanding of the urban poor's social conditions and to disseminate information about their social attitudes within the changing urban societies of the Middle East. The authors discuss the aims of the development plans of four non-oil exporting countries, their policies toward low income groups, and their continuous or changing housing policies during the late 1980s. Then, based on the research on the *gecekondu* areas of six Turkish cities, the authors dwell on the housing burdens of the urban poor, and their attitudes towards housing improvement and the development plans of the government.

890   **Structural change in Turkish society.**
      Edited by Mübeccel Kıray.   Bloomington, Indiana: Indiana University Turkish Studies, 1991. 193p. (Indiana University Turkish Studies Series, no. 10).

This collection of essays aims to conceptualize and capture the trends of structural change in various aspects of Turkish society. The main sections of the volume are depeasantization and urban settlement, ex-peasants in cities, ex-peasants in Europe and urban social stratification. After an introduction on the theoretical framework, this important volume contains the following essays: 'The squatter housing problem in İstanbul and in Cairo', Tansı Şenyapılı; 'Development of intra-urban trips and their organization in Ankara', İlhan Tekeli; 'The rationality of informal economy: the provision of housing in southern Turkey', Alan Duben; 'Individualistic vs. relational models of man: the case of intervention research', Çiğdem Kağıtçıbaşı; 'Of *türbe* and *evliya*: saints and shrines as environments that facilitate communication and innovation', Emelie Olson; 'A ghetto in welfare society: Turks in Rinkeby-Stockholm', Sema Köksal; 'Ethnic differentiation in France: Turks and Muslims', Riva Kastoryano; 'Industrial change and social stratification in the urban context', Sencer Ayata; 'The transformation of the bases of social standing in contemporary Turkish society', Ayşe Öncü; 'Social change and the 1983 governing elite in Turkey', Yeşim Arat; and 'Market research and public opinion polling in Turkey as an agent of social change', Nermin-Abadan Unat.

891   **Housing question of the 'Others'.**
Edited by Emine M. Komut.   Ankara: Chamber of Architects of
Turkey, 1996. 577p.
The book contains papers from an international symposium organized by the Chamber
of Architects in 1995. The motto of 'adequate housing for all' (one of the main themes
of HABITAT II) is discussed from the point of view of different disciplines, and using
the experiences of different countries. Topics include: women and housing, migrants
and housing, disabled and housing, elderly and housing, and children and housing.
There are papers from disciplines such as sociology, economics, geography, planning,
and architecture by participants representing a variety of countries.

892   **Tradition and change in a Turkish town.**
Paul J. Magnarella.   Cambridge, Massachusetts: Schenkman
Publishing Company, 1981. rev. ed. 209p. maps. bibliog. (Schenkman
Series on Socio-economic Change, no. 5).
This book, first published in 1974, provides an insight into the socio-political and eco-
nomic dynamics of Turkey in the 1970s. The author bases his research on Susurluk
(Balıkesir) where he lived for a time. He claims that Susurluk's experience fits a general pattern of change shared by many small urban communities throughout Turkey.
Formerly characterized by subsistence agriculture and a limited market economy, this
small town has been transformed, with the consent of its residents, into an industrial,
commercial and governmental centre, having a much greater degree of regional,
national, and international involvement. All major aspects of the society are examined
in a way that combines observation and insight. An 'Epilogue' has been added to the
revised edition, reviewing recent developments and prospects.

893   **Rural-urban migration and formation of squatters in Turkey.**
İsmail Hakkı Özsabuncuoğlu.   In: *Urban problems and economic
development.*   Edited by Lata Chatterjee, Peter Nijkamp.
Amsterdam: Proceedings of the NATO Advanced Study Institute on
Urban Problems and Policies in a Spatial Context, 1981, p. 201-14.
This is a study of the housing difficulties of the migrants from rural areas to urban
centres. The author uses data collected from Gaziantep city centre in 1970.

894   **Involuntary displacement and the problem of resettlement in
Turkey from the Ottoman Empire to the present.**
Seteney Shami.   In: *Population displacement and resettlement:
development and conflict in the Middle East.*   Edited by Seteney
Shami.   New York: Centre for Migration Studies, 1994, p. 202-26.
Discusses the displacement and the policy of population redistribution in the classical
era of the Ottoman Empire (the 16th century), resettlement problems and the involuntary settlement of tribes in the 18th century, resettlement in the 19th century,
large-scale displacement and population exchange during the ten-year period of wars
and crises between 1912 and 1922, and resettlement from 1950 to 1994.

895 **On the dynamics of experience of urbanization in Turkey.**
İlhan Tekeli. In: *Urban problems and economic development.*
Edited by Lata Chatterjee, Peter Nijkamp. Amsterdam: Proceedings
of the NATO Advanced Study Institute on Urban Problems and
Policies in a Spatial Context, 1981, p. 69-82.

After a general theoretical introduction, the study presents the Turkish experience in
terms of municipal administration, and the emergence of urban movements paralleling
the process of urbanization. The study ends with the conclusion that as the phenomenon of urbanization in a country evolves, theories explaining or accounting for it also
evolve and become more profound. Consequently, one must be fully aware that these
theories are only transitory explanations open to modifications and gross alterations as
the phenomenon itself evolves and changes.

896 **Can municipalities in Turkey be considered as institutions of civic
society with a broad social base?**
İlhan Tekeli. In: *Local administration: democracy versus efficiency?*
Edited by Korel Göymen, Hans F. Illy, Winfried Veit. Bonn:
Friedrich Ebert Stiftung, 1982, p. 69-82.

This paper discusses the historical development of municipal organization in Turkey
from the second half of the 19th century to the present. The paper questions why the
'municipality' failed to develop as a powerful civic social institution at the beginning,
and why a new concept of local government started to emerge only after 1973. The
authors conclude that the democratic municipality movement in Turkey emerged at a
time when the rate of urbanization was approaching the fifty per cent level, and when
the voting trends in the larger centres favoured social democracy, while the villages
and small towns voted for the conservative parties. The competition between central
and local governments created a favourable atmosphere for the development of a plu-
ralistic municipal movement, but the positive values and beliefs which Turkish
politics attached to monolithic power bases could not easily tolerate such plurality.

897 **Case study of a relocated capital: Ankara.**
İlhan Tekeli, Tarık Okyay. In: *Urban planning practice in developing
countries.* Edited by John L. Taylor, David G. Williams. New
York: Pergamon Press, 1982, p. 123-43.

The authors look at the reasons for the selection of Ankara as the new capital, and discuss its planning and development. According to the authors, the Ankara experiment
shows that the concentration of all resources into the development of one city may
create an orderly urban environment, but such an achievement is often short-lived, and
it is not possible to solve urban problems without tackling the basic and larger developmental issues of the country.

898 **Nineteenth century transformation of Istanbul metropolitan area.**
İlhan Tekeli. In: *Villes ottomanes à la fin de l'empire* (Ottoman
towns at the end of the Empire). Under the direction of Paul Dumont,
François Georgeon. Paris: L'Harmattan, 1991, p. 33-45.

The author dwells on the major problems of urban growth during the 19th-century
Ottoman Empire, and the legal framework and administrative organization developed
to solve them. He discusses projects, city-scale plans and local plans, their level of

success and their impact on successive periods, with emphasis on the patterning of the urban form in each period.

899 **Development of İstanbul metropolitan area and low cost housing.**
Edited by İlhan Tekeli. İstanbul: Turkish Social Science Association, Municipality of Greater İstanbul, IULA-EMME Publication, 1992. 235p.

A collection of essays based on a research project financed by the International Research Development Centre (IDRC) of Canada, and carried out by a group of Turkish academics from the Middle East Technical University, Ankara. The project tested the hypothesis that the division of labour in a workplace determines the type of housing and the life styles of the workers. The essays in the book also discuss the consequential reflection of this hypothesis on housing policies. After an analysis of the formation and patterning of the metropolitan İstanbul, the location and differentiation of industry in the metropolitan area are discussed. This is followed by chapters which deal directly with the housing issue based on three different surveys. The final section of the book covers the impact of work processes in factories on the housing and life styles of the workers.

900 **The development of the İstanbul metropolitan area: urban administration and planning.**
İlhan Tekeli. İstanbul: IULA-EMME, Kent Basımevi, 1994. 320p.

This book provides a detailed overall evaluation of 150 years of planning in İstanbul, starting with the administrative measures taken to control urban development during the 19th century up to the late 1980s.

901 **The patron-client relationship, land-rent economy and the experience of 'urbanization without citizens'.**
İlhan Tekeli. In: *The urban experience. A people-environment perspective.* Edited by S. J. Neary, M. S. Symes, F. E. Brown. London: E & FN Spon, 1994, p. 9-18. (Proceedings of the 13th Conference of the International Association for People-Environment Studies held on 13-15 July 1994).

The author concentrates on the mutual interaction of three variables: a dominant populist attitude in politics or the patron-client relationship; an urban land-rent economy; and a lack of formation of citizenship (or urbanization without citizens). The study ends with the optimistic claim that although the individuals may be forced to be alienated in society, the motivation for social solidarity cannot be regressed to such a point that it cannot be activated again.

902 **Housing finance in Turkey during the last decade.**
Ali Türel. In: *European housing finance.* Edited by Will Bartlett, Glen Bramley. Bristol, England: The Alden Press, 1994, p. 199-215.

In Turkey, housing finance has been provided predominantly by state-owned institutions. In addition to a state-owned bank which was established in 1926, social security institutions and pension funds have been engaged in housing finance since 1950. A radical change was introduced in 1984, which required much greater involvement of the state than before. Although substantial amounts of resources have been drawn into the housing sector during the last decade, most of the people who buy or build houses are still without credit support. In this essay, the housing credit system introduced in 1984 is evaluated in terms of its sources and the ways in which credits have been allocated.

Gecekondu: rural migration and urbanization.
See item no. 462.

METU Studies in Development.
See item no. 1343.

New Perspectives on Turkey.
See item no. 1352.

Architecture

General

903 **Varieties of tradition and traditionalism.**
Gül Asatekin, Aydan Balamir. *Traditional Dwellings and Settlements Review: Journal of the International Association for the Study of Traditional Environments*, vol. 1, no. 11 (1990), p. 61-70.
The authors attempt to resolve the argument of 'universal civilization versus national culture' by suggesting a simultaneous unfolding of the historical problems of the Anatolian house tradition, and the theoretical problems of presumed dichotomies, such as traditional versus modern.

904 **The wall in Anatolia through the ages.**
Nezih Başgelen. İstanbul: Grafbas Ajans, 1993. 113p.
This work narrates the 12,000-year history of the evolution of the wall in Anatolia. Başgelen discusses the incredible architecture of Çayönü, the mud-brick of Çatalhöyük, the unity of stone, adobe and wood which have lasted for centuries, the first Anatolian state and its walls, the beginning of city planning in western Anatolia, Roman architecture, and Byzantium, Anatolian and Turkish architecture. There are colour and black-and-white sketches, and photographs.

905 **Displaying the Orient: architecture of Islam at nineteenth-century world's fairs.**
Zeynep Çelik. Berkeley, California: University of California Press, 1992. 260p. bibliog. (Comparative Studies on Muslim Societies, no. 12).
Almost all of the international expositions held in the 19th century contained oriental exhibits. For the Europeans and the Americans, Islamic cultures were exotic, and the organizers of the fairs used Islamic attractions as yardsticks to measure the progress of

Western civilization. The author maintains that while the Islamic displays at the fairs were exercises in Orientalism, they also had consequences for the Islamic cultures themselves. For example, the Islamic elites set out to modernize their societies in accordance with the visions of the future as projected at European and American fairs.

906 **Muslim religious architecture.**
     Doğan Kuban.   Leiden, the Netherlands: E. J. Brill, 1974-85. 3 vols.

The author starts by illustrating that the religious content of mosque design retained a fundamental homogeneity throughout its history, but that its stylistic development became more and more diversified as it moved further in time and space from the centre of classical Islam. It underwent modifications induced by pre-Muslim traditions, which survived after the establishment of Islam. Kuban then follows the mosque architecture and its development by regions: Egypt during the Fatimid period, Mamluk architecture in Egypt, mosques in North Africa after the 9th century, mosque architecture in areas of Irano-Turkish culture and in the Indian sub-continent, and mosque design in the Anatolian-Turkish region. He also studies the religious architecture outside the mosques.

907 **Traditional Turkish arts: architecture.**
     A. Haluk Sezgin.   Ankara: Ministry of Culture and Tourism, 1992.
     78p. bibliog.

The book, prepared on the occasion of 'The age of Sultan Suleiman the Magnificent' exhibition, traces the development of Turkish art and architecture since its beginnings in Central Asia. Architecture among pre-Anatolian Turks and during the Ottoman period is traced through the prominent buildings of the period in question. The work includes colour photographs of most of the buildings discussed.

908 **The evolution of Turkish art and architecture.**
     Metin Sözen, translated from the Turkish by M. Quigley-Pınar.
     İstanbul: Haşet, 1987. 336p. bibliog. (Akşit Culture and Tourism
     Publications, no. 2).

The book traces the different architectural works of the Turkish dynasties in Central Asia and in Anatolia between the 10th and the 20th centuries.

Byzantine

909 **Chora: mosaics and frescoes.**
     Fatih Cimok.   İstanbul: Turizm Yayınları, 1987. 117p.

What is today called the Kariye Museum was originally the church of the monastery of the Chora, and later the Kariye Mosque. It is one of the most important examples of late Byzantine art. The book includes illustrations of most of the figural mosaic panels and frescoes (in the mortuary chapel of the church). The author follows the original iconographic sequence of dedicatory panels: the genealogy of Christ, the life of the Virgin, and the life cycle and miracles of Christ.

910   **Hagia Sophia: architecture, structure and liturgy of Justinian's great church.**
Rowland J. Mainstone.   London: Thames & Hudson, 1988. 288p.
The book offers an architectural analysis of the church of Hagia Sophia, which was constructed during the reign of Justinian, the Byzantine Emperor. Plans, drawings and photographs by the author complement the text.

911   **Studies on Constantinople.**
Cyril Mango.   Aldershot, England: Ashgate Publishing Group, 1993. 288p. (Collected Studies).
The essays in the book examine the history, monuments, and topography of Byzantine Constantinople. The author reconstructs different Byzantine buildings and sites in İstanbul.

912   **The church of Akdamar (Aght'amar).**
Gönül Öney.   Ankara: Ministry of Culture Publications, 1990. 73p.
A study of the Armenian monastery on the small island of Lake Van in eastern Turkey, which is well known for its relief carvings on stone on the facades of the church.

Ottoman and Seljuk

913   **An outline of Turkish architecture in the middle ages.**
Ara Altun.   İstanbul: Arkeoloji ve Sanat, 1990. 249p. maps.
A handbook of Turkish architecture in the Middle Ages. Footnotes and detailed explanations have been omitted to sustain fluency, but a number of selected sources are given at the end of the work. The book covers subjects such as the early Turkish-Islamic architecture and its influences outside Anatolia, early Turkish architecture in Anatolia, and the course of development in architectural types. The work has several black-and-white photographs and plans.

914   **Further observations on the 'Çoban Mustafa Paşa Mosque' at Gebze.**
Heba Nayel Barakat.   *Journal of the Faculty of Architecture, Middle East Technical University*, vol. 13, no. 1-2 (1993), p. 17-30.
The paper discusses the double controversy confronting researchers about the complex of Çoban Mustafa Paşa. The first problem is its attribution to an architect, and the second is the degree to which the marble work is of late Mamluk origin. Following an introduction, which presents the controversy, the patronage, plan, date, materials, building techniques and decorations of the mosque are discussed.

915 **The Ottoman city and its parts: urban structure and social order.**
Edited by Irene A. Bierman, Rifa'at A. Abou-El-Haj, Donald Preziosi.
New York: A. D. Caratzas, 1991. 256p. maps. (Subsidia Balcanica;
Islamica et Turcica, no. 3).

Contains six essays by historians, art and architectural historians, who analyse
Byzantine Constantinople and Ottoman İstanbul within the context of the evolution of
a millennial imperial iconography. Topics covered include: the Ottomanization of
Crete, power and social order, power structure and architectural function, administrative complexes, palaces and citadels, changes in the loci of medieval Muslim rule,
façades in Ottoman Cairo, Ottoman Sultans' mosques, and icons of imperial legitimacy. The book includes a glossary.

916 **Risāle – i mi'māriyye: an early seventeenth-century Ottoman
treatise on architecture.**
Cafer Efendi, facsimile edition with translations and notes by Howard
Crane. Leiden, the Netherlands: E. J. Brill, 1987. 136p. (Studies in
Islamic Art and Architecture, no. 1).

This is a rare architectural treatise from the Ottoman period. It was written in the 17th
century as a bibliography of Mehmed Aga, the architect of the 17th-century Sultan
Ahmed mosque in İstanbul, among other works. The manuscript is also a polyglot
(Arabic, Persian and Turkish) glossary of terms for architecture, the building trades
and music.

917 **Typical commercial buildings of the Ottoman classical period and
the Ottoman construction system.**
Mustafa Cezzar, translated from the Turkish by Ahmet E. Uysal.
İstanbul: Türkiye İş Bankası, 1983. 315p.

The commercial areas of Turkish cities were characterized by a concentration of commercial buildings (the *bedesten* and *han*s) and shops, which formed an integrated
system with other types of buildings in the neighbourhood. The location of these commercial buildings was determined by their function and proximity to other public
buildings, and by the residential quarters they were intended to serve. The development of commercial areas in cities affected their general architectural textures;
therefore, a careful assessment of the commercial area of a Turkish city from the point
of view of city development is essential for an understanding of its foundation, development and life. This study describes the architectural features of *bedesten*s, covered
bazaars and shops, which are now either in a state of ruin or maintain their functions
after being modified and adapted to serve present-day requirements. There are several
black-and-white and colour photographs, and plans.

918 **The remaking of İstanbul: portrait of an Ottoman city in the
nineteenth century.**
Zeynep Çelik. Seattle, Washington: University of Washington Press,
1986. 183p. bibliog. (Publications on the Near East, no. 2).

The book shows in great detail how modern İstanbul came into being. The contrast
between the old and the new is shown through many photographs, maps and drawings.

919 **Türk evi: Osmanlı dönemi. Turkish houses: Ottoman period.**
Sedat Hakkı Eldem. İstanbul: Türkiye Anıt Çevre Turizm Değerlerini
Koruma Vakfı, 1984-85. 5 vols.
This monumental work documents the rich material that Sedat Hakkı Eldem compiled
through a lifetime of research on the Turkish house. The text focuses on the evolution
of plan types and the uses of different architectonic elements. Volume one, entitled
'The classical Turkish house', traces the evolution of the Turkish house through urban
houses illustrated by measured drawings. It contains 541 photographs and 121 plans.
In volume two, 'Mansions, palaces, kiosks, vault and strong rooms', the author illustrates that although these buildings have been elaborately constructed when compared
to a modest house, similar principles of planning can be traced in all of them. The volume contains 380 illustrations and 385 plans. In the third volume, 'Architectural
elements', the author illustrates the skills of the craftsmen through the architectural
elements and decorations of the Turkish house. Volume four, 'Rumelian houses',
illustrates the vernacular domestic architecture from Ottoman times, and volume five,
'Anatolian houses', deals with the Anatolian architecture.

920 **Erken Osmanlı mimarlığında çok-işlevli yapılar: kentsel
kolonizasyon yapıları olarak zaviyeler. Cilt I: Öncül yapılar: Tokat
zaviyeleri. Cilt II: Orhan Gazi dönemi yapıları.** (Multi-functional
buildings in early Ottoman architecture: zawiyas as buildings of urban
colonization. Volume I: Early buildings: zawiyas of Tokat. Volume II:
Buildings of the Orhan Gazi period.)
Sedat Emir. İzmir: Akademi Kitabevi, 1994. 3 vols. bibliog.
This study deals with the multi-functional buildings of the early Ottoman period,
which are different from conventional types of Islamic architecture. The author looks
at these Ottoman buildings of the 14th and 15th centuries in terms of their specific features and their role in the formation of the Ottoman built environment. The word
zawiya, which meant 'the cell of a recluse' and was also used for 'the hostel of the Ahi
sect connected with the guilds and the Janissaries', came to be used for the lodgings of
travelling dervishes. In reality, the *zawiya*s, erected in areas away from the city centres, were intended for all travellers, and they also contained a prayer area. They were
the focal buildings of the early Ottoman complexes, which comprised at least a
madrasa and a bath. In time, these buildings came to serve as nuclei for settlement
units. The first part of the work analyses the buildings in detail, while the second deals
with the origins, evolution and the functions of these buildings. The volumes include
plates and plans.

921 **The Seljuks. A journey through Anatolian architecture.**
Edited by Ahmet Ertuğ. İstanbul: Ahmet Ertuğ Publications, 1991.
219p. map.
Caravanserais were relay buildings constructed by the Seljuk Sultans on commercial
routes in order to provide shelter, food and security for the tradesmen and other travellers. They were constructed in stone, and their portals were decorated with
magnificent stone-relief carvings in floral, geometrical and figural motifs, which
reflected the taste of their architectural patrons and the skills of the Seljuk craftsmen
in Anatolia. This is a magnificently illustrated book on the Seljuk caravanserais and
mosques, constructed in Anatolia between the 11th and 13th centuries.

922 **İstanbul: city of domes.**
Semavi Eyice, edited by Robert Bragner, photographs by Ahmet Ertuğ.
Milan, Italy: Ahmet Ertuğ Publications, 1992. 132p.

The skyline of İstanbul is distinguished by the world's richest clustering of domes with an ever-changing multiplicity of scale, varying from thirty-two metres in diameter to two metres. This book introduces the reader to the history of İstanbul through its domes. The illustrations are supported by text, which includes a discussion of the historical development of the city, and its architectural development and monuments. Black-and-white and colour photographs and sketches are also included.

923 **Sinan: architect of Suleiman the Magnificent, and the Ottoman golden age.**
J. Freely, A. R. Burelli.   New York: Thames & Hudson, 1992. 144p.

Contains A. Burelli's measured drawings in colour of some of 16th-century architect Sinan's buildings, mainly the mosque of Selimiye in Edirne. Also included are Ara Güler's photographs of the buildings, concentrating on the details of finesse accompanying the constructions.

924 **Sinan: Ottoman architecture and its values today.**
Godfrey Goodwin.   London: Saqi Books, 1993. 135p.

The book focuses on the works of the great 16th-century Ottoman architect Sinan, and how he revolutionized the inherited Ottoman building methods, a tradition based on structure, with an awareness of the psychology of space. Until Sinan, the Ottoman architecture had been a reading of parts. Sinan broke down the distinct forms which created a certain rigidity, thus freeing interior space and interior form simultaneously. Underlying his architectural concepts are the mathematical theories and practices of the classical period, which he shared with builders in the West. The author argues that the works of Sinan and that of Italian architects Bramante and Palladio must be seen as parts of the same intellectual revolution. The author bases his analysis on a detailed comparative study of several of Sinan's buildings, and the chapters on light and space, the dome, the minaret and the apsidal form, decoration and tiles are particularly important. The work includes 160 illustrations, photographs, plans and elevations of many of Sinan's works, together with a list of Sinan's buildings.

925 **A history of Ottoman architecture.**
Godfrey Goodwin.   London: Thames & Hudson, 1997. 3rd ed. 511p.
maps. bibliog.

The only comprehensive survey in English of Ottoman architecture. It is chronologically ordered, and places architecture in its historical and social setting. The Anatolian Baroque of the 17th century, which is a much neglected subject, is also extensively treated. The final chapter is concerned with domestic architecture, and the Ottoman concept of towns. The glossary explains the Turkish words, and there is a chronological table listing Ottoman rulers and relevant historical events, as well as an extensive bibliography. The book has 521 illustrations and 81 plans.

926 **Story of the Grand Bazaar.**
Çelik Gülersoy. İstanbul: İstanbul Kitaplığı, 1990. 104p. map. bibliog.
The Turkish title of the book is *Kapalı Çarşının romanı.* It provides a history of the
Grand Bazaar in İstanbul, and contains many illustrations, some in colour. A folded
map is included.

927 **The Çeragan palaces.**
Çelik Gülersoy. İstanbul: İstanbul Kitaplığı, 1992. 208p. bibliog.
(Publications of the İstanbul Library).
The name *çerağ* (or *çirağ*), meaning 'light, candle, torch', reflects the festivities during what is known as the Tulip Period in Ottoman history (1703-30). Different types
of lighting with candles and torches were used to admire the beauty of the tulips in the
evenings, in the gardens of water-front houses by the Bosphorus. The first Çiragan
Palace was built at the beginning of the 18th century in Beşiktaş, and after it burnt
down, a new one was constructed at the end of the 19th century in the eclectic style of
the period. This second building also burnt during the early 20th century, and a hotel
has been built on its site. The book traces the history of these palaces through engravings and photographs.

928 **İstanbul sinagogları.** (The synagogues of İstanbul.)
Naim Güleryüz. İstanbul: Naim Güleryüz, 1992. 125p.
After the 15th century İstanbul had a large Jewish population settled mainly around
the Golden Horn (Hasköy and Feriköy). The book illustrates the synagogues in İstan-
bul which are still in use.

929 **Splendours of the Bosphorus: houses and palaces of İstanbul.**
Chris Hellier, photographs by Francesco Venturi. London: I. B.
Tauris, 1993. 228p. map. bibliog.
The Bosphorus, which became a popular summer suburb in İstanbul especially after
the 18th century, was full of the water-front houses (*yalı* and *konak*) of the rich merchants and of high administrative classes. Palaces of the Sultans by the sea contributed
to the new landscape of the Bosphorus. This book documents both the social and the
architectural history of these buildings with contemporary photographs, and brief information about each site. It has 162 colour halftone illustrations, a glossary, and an index.

930 **İstanbul: a glimpse into the past.**
Ekmeleddin İhsanoğlu. İstanbul: Research Centre for Islamic
History, Art and Culture (IRCICA), 1987. 2nd ed. 126p.
The book is described by its compiler as an album, because it contains over 100 photographs of late 19th-century İstanbul and Bosphorus in a nostalgic and uncritical
way. The selection of photographs comprises the work of Vasiliki Kargopoulo,
Abdullah Frerés and Emile Römmler-Jonas, and includes general views of
Sarayburnu, Eminönü, Galata, and beauty spots along the Bosphorus. There are also
several studio portraits, and photographs depicting daily scenes at royal fountains, city
squares and streets, bridges and coffee-houses. The contents of each picture are
described in some detail. The photographs presented have the additional significance
of having been selected from the personal collection of the Sultans Abdül Aziz and
Abdülhamid II, both of whom were great patrons of photography.

931　**Terminology relating to buildings that have combined functions in Anatolian Seljuk architecture.**
Başak İpekoğlu. *Journal of the Faculty of Architecture, Middle East Technical University*, vol. 13, no. 1-2 (1993), p. 53-65.
This research paper assess the validity of a classification of architectural edifices, based on new terminology developed for groups of buildings from the Anatolian Seljuk period. These groups of buildings are often combinations of mosques and other official buildings, which carry distinct design characteristics of the Seljuk period, and which seem to have evolved later into the Ottoman period.

932　**Bodrum castle and its knights.**
E. L. Kalcas.　İzmir: Bilgehan Basımevi, 1984. 55p.
Bodrum Castle was constructed by the Knights of Rhodes, and is a smaller version of the original in Rhodes. It was taken over by the Ottomans during the reign of Sultan Suleiman the Magnificent. Today the site is a museum which specializes in underwater archaeology. This book offers a historical and architectural survey of Bodrum Castle during the time of the Knights.

933　**İstanbul'da Osmanlı dönemi Rum kiliseleri.** (The Greek Orthodox churches of İstanbul during the Ottoman period.)
Zafer Karaca.　İstanbul: Yapı Kredi Yayınları, 1995. 360p. (Sanat Dizisi, no. 7).
After the conquest of İstanbul by the Ottomans, most of the churches from the Byzantine era were transformed into mosques. The more modest churches continued to be used, and there were restrictions on the construction of new ones. After the proclamation of a constitutional monarchy in 1839, the non-Muslims in the Ottoman Empire were allowed to build more freely. The author has catalogued around 100 present-day Orthodox churches in İstanbul, which are preserved and administrated by the Greek Orthodox Patriarchate of İstanbul.

934　**Studies on the Ottoman architecture of the Balkans: a legacy in stone.**
Machiel Kiel.　Aldershot, England: Variorum, 1990. 350p.
In the Balkan countries monumental examples of all phases of Ottoman architecture can still be found, from late 14th-century mosques, hospices and baths, to the government buildings, schools and hospitals of the early 20th century. The author states that time, and especially men, have dealt harshly with the works of Ottoman architecture in the Balkans, and therefore the interaction between individual buildings will never be known in all their fullness. In the 19th century, and even more so in the 20th century, Ottoman buildings were destroyed to an amazing extent. The book is a collection of the author's previously published articles on Ottoman architecture in the Balkan countries, covering the oldest monuments of Ottoman-Turkish architecture in the Balkans, and including less well-known monuments of early and classical Ottoman architecture in Greek Thrace and in the Macedonian province, together with some singular Ottoman monuments in the Balkans. It contains thirteen plates, several photographs and plans.

935 **Ottoman architecture in Albania, 1385-1912.**
Machiel Kiel. İstanbul: Research Centre for Islamic History, Arts and Culture (IRCICA), 1990. 342p.

Ottoman architectural works in Albania are depicted together with their plans, and they are documented historically with archival material. The buildings covered include mosques, castles and bridges.

936 **The Turkish Hayat House.**
Doğan Kuban. İstanbul: Eren Publishers, 1995. 280p. bibliog.

The Turkish Hayat House, a building type which developed in Anatolia after the 16th century, has a highly complex cultural history. In provincial and rural Turkey, it survived as a relic of a pre-industrial pattern of life until the end of the Second World War. In the first part of the book, there is a discussion of what a Turkish Hayat House is, including its background, origin, evolution, plan, and early surviving examples. The second part deals with its morphology. The book contains 106 photographs, 28 illustrations, 167 sketches/plans, and a glossary.

937 **İstanbul: an urban history, Byzantion, Constantinopolis, İstanbul.**
Doğan Kuban. İstanbul: Economic and Social History Foundation of Turkey, 1996. 485p. maps.

A reference book for those who want to trace the urban development of İstanbul through its important periods: when it was first founded, when it became the capital of the East Roman Empire and then the Byzantine Empire, and when it became the capital of the Ottoman Empire.

938 **Sinan, the grand old master of Ottoman architecture.**
Abdullah Kuran. Washington, DC: Institute of Turkish Studies; İstanbul: Ada Press Publishers, 1987. 318p.

This book is about Sinan, who served as the chief court architect between 1538 and 1588 under three sultans, beginning with Suleiman the Magnificent. During this half-century, he created the finest examples of a distinct architectural style. Contemporary manuscripts ascribe 477 buildings to Sinan. Of these, some 200 have survived in their original form and character either fully or in part. The book discusses Sinan's personal and professional life, Ottoman architecture, as well as Sinan's buildings. The author has personally studied and measured the buildings discussed in the book, and prepared his own drawings. The appendix includes a chronological list of Sinan's buildings by location, and the present status of his buildings (not known or unidentified buildings; buildings that no longer exist; reconstructed, renovated buildings; buildings that survive as ruins; and buildings preserved in their original form and character).

939 **Turkish house in search of spatial identity.**
Önder Küçükerman. İstanbul: Türkiye Turing ve Otomobil Kurumu, 1991. 4th ed. 214p. bibliog.

After presenting the general characteristics of a traditional Turkish house, the author concentrates on the rooms. He meticulously studies the spatial conformation of 'the room' throughout its evolution within a designated system. The houses he writes about have been chosen from among hundreds of samples which he studied. Each page of the book includes colour and black-and-white photographs and plans.

940　The dervish lodge: architecture, art and sufism in Ottoman
　　　Turkey.
　　　Edited by Raymond Lifchez.　Berkeley, California; Oxford:
　　　University of California Press, 1992. 348p.
The contributors to the volume focus on different aspects of the culture associated
with the dervish lodges (*tekke, zaviye,* and *mevlevihane*) in the Ottoman Empire.

941　İstanbul: gateway to splendour. A journey through Turkish
　　　architecture.
　　　Ahmet Ertuğ.　İstanbul: Ahmet Ertuğ Publications, 1986. 224p.
This is a richly illustrated book (137 full colour plates) with Ertuğ's photographs of
Turkish architecture in İstanbul.

942　İstanbul: city of seven hills. A photographic journey through
　　　Byzantine and Ottoman monuments.
　　　Cyril A. Mango, A. Ertuğ, G. Kara, A. Güler.　İstanbul: Ertuğ &
　　　Kocabıyık Publications, 1994. 178p.
The author describes the classical and Byzantine antiquities of İstanbul. The text is
accompanied by aerial and interior colour photographs.

943　Architecture, ceremonial and power: the Topkapı Palace in the
　　　fifteenth and sixteenth centuries.
　　　Gülru Necipoğlu.　Cambridge, Massachusetts: The MIT Press; New
　　　York: The Architectural History Foundation, 1991. 336p. bibliog.
During the 15th and 16th centuries, which marked the height of Ottoman rule in İstan-
bul, the Topkapı Palace served both as the royal residence and as the seat of imperial
administration. Using the evidence provided by the existing buildings, together with
largely unpublished sources (including numerous descriptions and illustrations by
European visitors, and histories written in Ottoman, Arabic and Persian), the author
illustrates the role of the Palace as a vast stage that emphasized the Sultan's absolute
power. She leads the reader in a step-by-step tour of the Topkapı complex, and places
the Topkapı Palace in its original context by explaining not only the circumstances of
its patronage but also the complex interaction of cultural practices, ideologies and
socially constructed codes of recognition from which it is now removed. She draws
striking parallels between the Topkapı Palace and its prototypes like the classical and
post-Mongol Islamic palaces, and the Byzantine Great Palace of Constantinople. The
book includes plans, illustrations and detailed notes.

944　The Topkapı scroll: geometry and ornament in Islamic
　　　architecture.
　　　Gülru Necipoğlu, Mohammad al-Asad.　Santa Monica: Windsor
　　　Books International, 1996. 412p. (Sketchbooks & Albums Series).
The scroll in the Topkapı Palace museum library (MS H. 1956) is a Timuride album of
geometrical designs, which was acquired by the library during the Ottoman period.
Geometrical compositions which were drawn on the scroll without any textual explanation prompt new interpretations as to the function of the scroll. The scroll with its
114 individual geometrical patterns is reproduced in this volume.

945 **Architectural decoration and minor arts in Seljuk Anatolia.**
Gönül Öney, Ülker Erginsoy.   Ankara: Türkiye İş Bankası Yayınları,
1992. 291p.

Architectural decorations of the Seljuk buildings in Anatolia show a variety of
stonework in geometrical, figural and floral motifs, for which the portals of the buildings were reserved. Painted stucco carvings, tiles, glazed bricks, and woodwork ornate
the interiors. The authors discuss both the exteriors and the interiors of Seljuk buildings. Decorative art works, which include objects produced in ceramics, glass, metal
work and manuscripts conserved in various museums in Turkey, are treated in a separate chapter.

946 **The Topkapı Saray Museum architecture: the Harem and other
buildings.**
Translated from the Turkish and edited by J. M. Rogers, Kemal Çığ,
Sabahattin Batur, Cengiz Köseoğlu.   Boston, Massachusetts: Little,
Brown & Co., 1988. 216p.

The book deals with the riches and relics of the Topkapı Palace Museum, where six
centuries of Ottoman treasures are housed. The book offers a guided tour of the Palace
and its grounds. From its construction (1465-79) under Mehmed the Conqueror up to
the mid-19th century, Topkapı was occupied by a succession of Sultans, and therefore
it is a living gallery of Ottoman culture, reflecting the architectural and decorative
styles of many periods, and embracing buildings of state, places of worship, residential quarters and the Harem. The book includes opulent detail on every building of the
Topkapı complex. More than 100 colour plates show examples of the exteriors, and
the interiors of those sections which are open to the public. Three essays describe the
rooms and apartments within the Palace complex, revealing the history and development of the Palace as a whole, and the nature, structure and organization of the
traditional Harem in Ottoman palace life. The appendix includes a key plan of the
Harem.

947 **The role of the Balian family in Ottoman architecture.**
Pars Tuğlacı.   İstanbul: Yeni Çığır Bookstore, 1990. 2nd ed. 744p.

First published in 1981, the book discusses the Balian family of Kayseri, nine members of which served as imperial architects under six Ottoman sultans from the late
18th to late 19th centuries. These nine imperial architects of the Balian family built
prolifically in İstanbul and its environs, making their mark on an era of Turkish architecture. The book deals with the social, political and cultural factors on which the
Westernization movement in the Ottoman Empire was based, and discusses the nine
Balian architects, and their works. The book reflects extensive research, and contains a
rich collection of colour and black-and-white photographs, and plans.

948 **Tokat (Comana).**
Ersal Yavi.   İstanbul: Güzel Sanatlar Matbaası, 1987. 185p.

The author acquaints the reader with the works of art, culture and architecture of
Tokat and its districts, from the Bronze and Iron Ages to the mid-19th century. He discusses the state of hundreds of works of art which have not been protected adequately.
The book also covers the rulers, who created these works of art, and important events
in the history of the region. The book contains coloured plates.

949　Ottoman architectural works outside Turkey.
　　　Edited by Filiz (Çalışlar) Yenişehirlioğlu.　Ankara: Dışişleri
　　　Bakanlığı, 1989. 256p. bibliog.

A reference book which documents Ottoman architectural works outside Turkey, over
a large geographical area and covering long periods of history. It is not a comprehensive catalogue, but nevertheless contains general information about the works, the
countries of location and their Ottoman history. There is a list of preserved buildings,
classified according to a system based on 873 black-and-white and colour photographs
and slides of Ottoman architectural works, which are accepted as the precise examples
of the period of Ottoman rule, and of the native civilization.

950　Ali Saim Ülgen's drawings of Mimar Sinan buildings.
　　　Compiled and edited by Filiz Yenişehirlioğlu, Emre Madran.　Ankara:
　　　Türk Tarih Kurumu, 1989. 2 boxes, in folio.

The plans and elevations of the buildings attributed to Mimar Sinan (16th century),
compiled by Ali S. Ülgen and his architectural team, are conserved at the Turkish
Historical Society in Ankara. This work contains these drawings, prepared for publication with a fifty per cent reduction in scale. The publication is in two boxes, entitled
'Architectural complexes' and 'Single buildings'. Each drawing is a loose sheet which
can be used independently. The original drawings did not include orientation signs for
most of the elevations, sections and some of the plans. However, these have been
added to a schematic plan of the buildings which is reproduced in a separate catalogue, together with essential information about the buildings and a short bibliography
about the building in question.

951　Along ancient trade routes: Seljuk caravanserais and landscapes in
　　　Central Anatolia.
　　　Landscape Foundation of Belgium and the European Foundation of
　　　Landscape Architecture.　Brussels: Salvo nv., 1996. 156p.

The book reflects the Turkish contribution to the International Silk Road Project
(1993), including a multidisciplinary survey of the landscapes along the Silk Road
from Istanbul to China, which was carried out by the Landscape Foundation of
Belgium and the European Foundation of Landscape Architecture. In the course of ten
millennia, the inhabitants of Central Anatolia have been guided by the landscape, and
have helped to shape it. This is reflected in the pattern of the trade routes, the spreading of the settlements, the structure of the dwellings, the building material used for the
caravanserais, the rugs, embroideries, ceramics, carpets and kilims, the architecture of
the houses, and the way in which people live their daily lives in these regions. Each of
these aspects is discussed in the book by sixteen writers. The book includes several
colour plates and plans. This is an exceptional book on the magnificent caravanserais
of the Seljuk era (12th-13th centuries) which dot the unique and highly diverse landscapes of Central Anatolia.

Turkey: a traveller's historical and architectural guide.
See item no. 66.

Anadolu Selçuklu dönemi sanatı bibliografyası. (A bibliography of the
arts of the Anatolian Seljuk period.)
See item no. 1411.

Contemporary

952 **Sedat Eldem: architect in Turkey.**
Sibel Bozdoğan, Suha Özkan, Engin Yenal.   Singapore: Concept
Media Ltd with Butterworth Architecture, 1987. 175p.

Sedat Eldem, representative of modern Turkish architecture, has practised, taught, researched and written about architecture for over fifty years. In his works he not only made a personal architectural statement but also demonstrated an approach which can be adopted by others. The book contains a personal profile of Eldem, together with an account and evaluation of his works. The book contains several colour and black-and-white photographs of his works, plans, sketches, and a chronology of his works (1931-86).

953 **Contemporary mosque architecture in Turkey.**
Jale Erzen, Aydan Balamir.   In: *Architecture of the contemporary mosque.*   Edited by İsmail Serageldin, James Steele.   London:
Academy Group Ltd, 1996, p. 100-16.

The authors assert that the fast population growth in Turkey represents to a large extent the middle and lower income classes from the agrarian hinterland, who migrate to towns and cities. It is generally this section of the Turkish urban population, together with the rural population, who observe religion most zealously. The drastic change in environment and the confrontation with modernization meant that this new urban dweller was in need of a new cultural identity. Until recently, contemporary architects, who are the product of an education based on Modernist attitudes, designed buildings along the lines of international movements. However, during the last decade, the emphasis has shifted towards the past, locating cultural identity in architecture that descends from the classical Ottoman, or the vernacular tradition. Apart from any ideological connotations, the architects' choice of either 'modern' or 'traditional' forms has brought to the fore problems of function and meaning. The authors discuss their ideas with several examples of mosques recently built in Ankara and in Istanbul. The article is accompanied by photographs and plans.

954 **Modern Turkish architecture.**
Edited by Renata Holod, Ahmet Evin.   Pennsylvania: University of
Pennsylvania Press, 1984. 192p.

The papers in this collection discuss the social context of the development of architecture in Turkey. They trace the rise of architecture as a profession, and the transformation of the building industry in Turkey in the 20th century. The collection provides an opportunity to examine the processes which produced the newly built environment, and the terminology which was created to describe them. In these articles, individual buildings are evaluated primarily in terms of how they fit into a socio-political context, and their response to cultural ideas or ideologies.

955 **Architectural education in Turkey in its social context: underlying concepts and changes.**
Haluk Pamir. In: *Architecture education in the Islamic world.*
Singapore: Concept Media, 1986, p. 131-52. (The Aga Khan Award for Architecture).

Examines some of the changes in architectural education in terms of the space in which relations within and between two interrelated processes take place: the professionalization of architecture, and architectural education as social production. The article covers: the conceptual framework; social order and control; sources of multi-modal architectural services and their organization within an integrated educational system (1300-1700); unintegrated changes in technical and architectural education; facing reinterpretation problems of the effects of modernity; the search by Turkish architects for a new integration of architecture within an old schema of Turco-Islamic architecture in the context of Turkish nationalism, or Kemalism; and Turkish architecture and architecture education.

956 **Architecture and society.**
İlhan Tekeli. In: *Architecture education in the Islamic world.*
Singapore: Concept Media for 'The Aga Khan Award for Architecture', 1986, p. 65-74.

The author asserts that there are multi-dimensional and complex relations between architecture and society, which he examines on three different levels: ideology; the organizational mode of building activities and architectural services in a society; and the way in which architectural ideologies and skills are reproduced in a society. The emphasis in this chapter is on the organization of education. Finally, the mutually determinant aspects of the three levels are discussed.

957 **Problems of conservation and preservation of Ottoman-Turkish architectural heritage in Greece.**
Turkish Cultural Foundation. İstanbul: Turkish Cultural Foundation, 1994. 185p.

The preservation of the Ottoman architectural heritage in the Balkans is problematic. This book illustrates examples of Ottoman-Turkish architectural heritage in Greece which are not preserved and conserved in accordance with the European Community regulation for the preservation of the European heritage.

958 **Ten years with seventeen-ten: a decade in the conservation of traditional vernacular houses, 1973-1983.**
Okan Üstünkök. *Journal of the Faculty of Architecture, Middle East Technical University,* vol. 9, no. 2 (1989), p. 117-24.

The author discusses the statutory framework within which the Antiquities Law 1710 functions in Turkey; how legislation on planning and Law 1710 interact; and whether Law 1710 is really to be blamed for the existing problems of conservation. The study ends on a pessimistic note, claiming that in the near future there will be fewer buildings to conserve, and less time in which to do it.

**Journal of Faculty of Architecture of Middle East Technical University.
Orta Doğu Teknik Üniversitesi Mimarlık Fakültesi Dergisi.**
See item no. 1336.

Muqarnas. An Annual on Islamic Art and Architecture.
See item no. 1350.

Education

959 **University teaching around the world.**
Jeanne Ballantine. *Teaching Sociology*, vol. 17, no. 3 (1989),
p. 291-96.
The author explores the concept of good teaching by interviewing university teachers
and exchange students from different countries, including Turkey. The results show
that teaching receives low priority in elite research institutions while universities with
open access consider good teaching important.

960 **Higher education in Turkey. Monographs on higher education.**
Edited by Leland Barrows. Ankara: UNESCO, 1990. 70p. (Student
Selection and Placement Centre, Ankara & European Centre for Higher
Education, Bucharest).
The monograph examines higher education in Turkey. It contains general information
about Turkey, the historical development of higher education, the administrative structure, the teaching staff, the content and organization of course programmes, diplomas
and degrees, and other necessary and useful information. Appendices contain a list of
universities and programmes offering instruction in English, course programmes for
eight recognized broad fields of study, and addresses of universities and higher education administrative bodies. Since the number of universities and regulations have
changed in Turkey since 1990, the reader is advised to be cautious.

961 **Educational problems in Turkey, 1920-1940.**
İlhan Başgöz, Howard E. Wilson. Richmond, England: Curzon Press,
1998. 268p. bibliog. (Indiana University Uralic and Altaic Series,
no. 86).
Originally published in 1968, this book presents a history of education in Turkey,
starting with the Ottoman Empire, the War of Liberation, up to 1940. It discusses the
social foundations of Turkish education under the Republic, providing general infor-

mation on the factors and problems which affected the search for a new educational system. It is one of very few books in English to give a history of Ottoman/Turkish education.

962 Alternative to the available: home based vs centre based programs.
Sevda Bekman. *Early Child Development and Care*, vol. 58 (1990), p. 109-19.
The author studies children in pre-school education, custodial pre-school, and home care, and discusses the effects of early childhood education on children's development.

963 Pre-school education system in Turkey: revisited.
Sevda Bekman. *International Journal of Early Childhood*, vol. 25, no. 1 (1993), p. 13-19.
Describes Turkey's pre-school educational system, and discusses the outcome of an investigation on the effects of social class and pre-school centre type on child and staff behaviour. The article also outlines a project to develop an intervention model for disadvantaged environments.

964 Impressions of Soviet Russia and the new revolutionary world: Mexico, China, Turkey.
John Dewey. New York: Columbia University Teachers College, 1964. 178p.
Education in Turkey was deeply affected by Dewey's ideas. He was invited to Turkey in 1924 by the Ministry of Education, and part of this book includes the observations he made during this visit.

965 Higher education reform in Turkey – the university in the service of the community: results after three years of application.
İhsan Doğramacı. *Higher Education in Europe,* vol. 9, no. 4 (1984), p. 74-82.
The article discusses the higher education law of 1981, its background, the immediate response to its implications for institutional autonomy and academic freedom, and the changes and progress made in the three years following its implementation.

966 Cost and economies of scale in Turkey's post-secondary vocational schools.
Halil Dündar, Darrell R. Lewis. *Higher Education*, vol. 30, no. 4 (1995), p. 369-87.
An analysis of the institutional cost structures of Turkey's post-secondary vocational schools, which deals with appropriate controls for institutional quality, discretionary allocation of staffing resources, degree of technical instruction in the curriculum, and regional variations. Average and marginal costs per institution are examined over various ranges of student enrolment in order to determine prospective economies of scale.

Education

967   **The People's Houses in Turkey, establishment and growth.**
       Kemal H. Karpat. *Middle East Journal,* vol. 17, no. 1-2 (1963),
       p. 55-67.
Cultural centres, called the People's Houses, were opened in 1932 to teach the principles of the new Republic to the masses, and to close the gap between the people and
the intelligentsia. This article discusses their history, purpose, policies, organization,
and their influence on society. The reasons behind their abolition in 1951 are also
summarized.

968   **The Village Institutes experience in Turkey.**
       M. Asım Karaömerlioğlu. *British Journal of Middle Eastern Studies,*
       vol. 25, no. 1 (1998), p. 47-73.
The article analyses the historical and intellectual context of the period between 1930
to the mid-1940s, describes the development of the concept of Village Institutes, and
assesses their most important and controversial characteristics.

969   **Teacher education reform in Turkey.**
       Galip Karagözoğlu. *Action in Teacher Education,* vol. 13, no. 3
       (1991), p. 26-29.
The article describes the problems of teacher training practices and reforms in the
Turkish educational system. The author concludes that Turkey faces problems in the
training, recruitment, employment, and professional development of its teachers.

970   **Economies of scale and scope in Turkish universities.**
       Darrell R. Lewis, Halil Dündar. *Education Economics,* vol. 3, no. 2
       (1995), p. 133-57.
Examines the production and cost structures of twenty-eight Turkish universities in
order to estimate their economies of scale and scope. The authors estimate multi-prod-
uct cost functions for teaching and research, by examining social, health and
engineering departments across 186 faculties.

971   **Teaching drama in Ankara.**
       Nellie McCaslin. *Youth Theatre Journal,* vol. 7, no. 2 (1992),
       p. 25-26.
The author describes the experiences of an American professor of educational theatre
who spent a week teaching post-graduate courses at Ankara University.

972   **Nursing education in modern Turkey.**
       Julie Fisher Robertson. *Nursing Outlook,* vol. 40, no. 3 (1992),
       p. 127-32.
The author discusses how nursing education and the nursing profession in Turkey are
closely related to women's rights and social status. She claims that the complexity of
educational programmes and heavy state involvement are obstacles to change in this
field.

973 **National education statistics: formal education, 1994-1996.**
State Institute of Statistics (SIS). Ankara: State Institute of Statistics,
1998. 578p.
The publication includes data on: pre-school education; primary schools; general,
technical and vocational high schools; enrolment numbers in these institutions by
province; data about students, such as date of birth, success rate and graduation status;
and number of teachers by province and kind of school.

974 **National education statistics: adult education, 1994-1995.**
State Institute of Statistics (SIS). Ankara: State Institute of Statistics,
1998. 136p.
The publication contains data on the educational institutions active in adult education,
including those offering Koranic courses and private courses.

975 **Cultural statistics, 1996.**
State Institute of Statistics (SIS). Ankara: State Institute of Statistics,
1998. 174p.
The publication contains information (by province) on printed media, the National
Library and other provincial libraries, museums, theatres and the film industry.

976 **Wage employment, earnings and return to schooling for men and
women in Turkey.**
Ayşit Tansel. *Economics of Education Review*, vol. 13, no. 4 (1994),
p. 305-20.
This article estimates an earnings function for urban wage earners in Turkey, and
defines 'wage earner choice education'. Returns to education, and probability of wage
earner participation increase as the previous levels of schooling of the candidates
increase, although this number is smaller for women wage earners. The highest
returnees to education are younger men, particularly vocational and technical high
school graduates.

977 **The 'Village Institutes' in Turkey.**
Alexandre Vexliard, Kemal Aytaç. *Comparative Education Review*,
vol. 8, no. 1 (1964), p. 41-47.
This brief article describes how Village Institutes (*Köy Enstitüleri*) were created and
organized, how they functioned between 1930 and the mid-1940s, and what the results
of the experiment were.

978 **International handbook of early childhood education.**
Edited by Gary A. Woodill, J. Bernhard, L. Procher. New York:
Garland Publishing Inc., 1992. 950p. bibliog.
The book provides a cross-national analysis of themes in late 20th-century child-care
and early education.

979 **Handbook of world education. A comparative guide to higher education and educational systems of the world.**
Edited by Walter Wickremasinghe. Houston, Texas: American Collegiate Service, 1991. 898p.
Provides individual overviews of the major aspects of the educational systems of around 100 countries, including Turkey, a descriptive overview of the country's educational system, and its history.

980 **Education and social change in Egypt and Turkey: a study in historical sociology.**
Bill Williamson. Basingstoke, England: Macmillan, 1987. 242p. bibliog.
Using secondary sources, the author compares the historical and socio-economic aspects of education in Turkey and in Egypt.

981 **Use of computers at high schools in Turkey.**
Ömer A. Yedekçioğlu. *T.H.E. Journal*, vol. 23, no. 6 (1966), p. 64-69.
The article describes the initiatives taken by the Ministry of Education of Turkey between 1984 and 1994 to increase computer literacy and the use of computers in Turkish schools.

Architectural education in Turkey in its social context: underlying concepts and changes.
See item no. 955.

Hacettepe Journal of Education.
See item no. 1332.

Science and Technology

982 **Scientific and technological responses to structural adjustment: human resources and research issues in Hungary, Turkey, and Yugoslavia.**
Charles Weiss. *Technology in Society*, vol. 15, no. 3 (1993), p. 281-99.

The author claims that before the 1980s, a lack of competition had suppressed the demand for improved technology in Hungary, Turkey and Yugoslavia, and that investments in civilian science and technology led to the development of enclaves of technological capacity that were largely cut off from the rest of the country. When Turkey emerged from this situation in the 1980s, it expanded rapidly. The article shows that a decade later Turkey's private and public sectors are contemplating substantial investments in the areas of human resources and research.

983 **Scientific research and science policy in Turkey.**
Regine Erichsen. *Cahiers d'Etudes sur la Méditerranée Orientale et le Monde Turco-Iranien* (CEMOTI), no. 25 (1998), p. 197-227.

This is a carefully assembled and detailed account of the organization of science in Turkey. A brief historical introduction is followed by an overview of institutions linked with the Prime Minister's Office, the ministries, universities, and non-governmental organizations (NGOs). Turkey is then compared with other countries in terms of its financial commitments to state or industry-financed science. The author notes that Turkish research and development generates a relatively high level of publication activity despite investment levels which compare unfavourably with those of European countries. Ankara aims to develop applied research and technical education, although this has yet to have a significant effect on the brain drain from Turkey.

984 **Reviews of national science and technology policy: Turkey.**
Organization for Economic Co-operation and Development (OECD).
Paris: OECD, 1996. 152p.

This publication reviews the recent reforms in Turkey undertaken in order to strengthen its science and technology systems. The recommendations made by the authors of this report include: increasing the research and technology budget; creating better synergy between the universities, research institutions, and businesses; and establishing support mechanisms for technological innovation in small- and medium-sized enterprises.

985 **Transfer of modern science and technology to the Muslim world.**
Edited by Ekmeleddin İhsanoğlu. İstanbul: Research Centre for Islamic History, Art and Culture (IRCICA), 1992. 442p. (Studies and Sources on the History of Science Series, no. 5).

Contains twenty-four papers presented at an international symposium held in İstanbul (1987) on science and technology transfer from the West to the Muslim world, from the Renaissance to the beginning of the 20th century. The papers focus on the changes in the 16th and 17th centuries that led to the dependence of the Islamic world on western technologies. The contributions cover a wide range of topics, including statistics, medicine, anatomy, architecture, urban planning, printing, minting money, manufacturing arms, and business partnership.

986 **Research and development statistics, 1990-1995.**
State Institute of Statistics (SIS). Ankara: State Institute of Statistics, 1998. 142p.

The volume contains data on scientific and technological research and development activities in the private and public sectors and in higher education.

Bilim ve Teknik. (Science and Technology.)
See item no. 1300.

Turkish Journal of Agriculture & Forestry.
See item no. 1367.

Turkish Journal of Biology.
See item no. 1368.

Turkish Journal of Botany.
See item no. 1369.

Turkish Journal of Chemistry.
See item no. 1370.

Turkish Journal of Earth Sciences.
See item no. 1371.

Turkish Journal of Electrical Engineering and Computer Sciences.
See item no. 1372.

Turkish Journal of Engineering and Environmental Sciences.
See item no. 1373.

Turkish Journal of Mathematics.
See item no. 1374.

Turkish Journal of Medical Sciences.
See item no. 1375.

Turkish Journal of Physics.
See item no. 1376.

Literature

Reference works and special issues

987 **Special issue on Yaşar Kemal.**
Edited by Ahmet Ö. Evin. *Edebiyāt*, vol. 5 (1980), p. 1-237.
This special issue is a handy companion volume which takes stock of Yaşar Kemal's broad international appeal as a novelist, and examines his contribution to the development of Turkish literature.

988 **Turkey: from empire to nation.**
Special editor Talat S. Halman. *Review of National Literatures*, vol. 4, no. 1 (1973), p. 1-142.
Even though slightly outdated, several of the articles in this special issue provide useful overviews. John Walsh's article, 'Turkey: bibliographical spectrum', is one of the best, though brief, tours of Ottoman literature available in terms of main authors and works, while Richard Clark's article, 'Is Ottoman literature Turkish literature?', is limited to a discussion of E. J. W. Gibb's work. The other contributions are as follows: Kathleen Burrill, 'Modern Turkish literature'; Talat S. Halman, 'The ancient and Ottoman legacy'; Metin And, 'Origins and the early development of the Turkish theatre'; Bedia Turgay-Ahmad, 'Modern Turkish theatre'; Süheyla Artemel, 'Turkish imagery in Elizabethan drama'; and İlhan Başgöz, 'Love themes in Turkish folk poetry'.

989 **Turkey.**
Guest edited by Talat S. Halman. *The Literary Review: An International Journal of Contemporary Writing*, vol. 15, no. 4 (1972).
This special issue starts with the essay 'Turkish literature in the 1960s' by Halman, which sets the scene. It is followed by translations of a selection of short stories by Oktay Akbal, Fakir Baykurt, Bilge Karasu, and Orhan Kemal, and poems by S. K. Aksal, Ö. Asaf, M. C. Anday, M. Başaran, İ. Berk, S. Birsel, E. Cansever, M. Çınarlı,

N. Cumalı, F. H. Dağlarca, A. Damar, M. Eloğlu, N. Hikmet (Ran), Ö. İnce, C. Irgat, C. A. Kansu, B. Necatigil, O. Rifat, C. Süreyya, Ü. Tamer, Ö. F. Toprak, O. Türkay, N. Üstün and T. Uyar.

990 **Ottoman Turkish writers. A bibliographical dictionary of significant figures in pre-Republican Turkish literature.**
Louis Mitler. New York: Peter Lang, 1988. 203p. (American University Studies: Series XIX, General Literature, no. 15).

Provides brief bio-bibliographical entries of Ottoman Turkish writers, mostly poets and historians. The authors are cited according to the prevailing modern Turkish forms of their names.

991 **Contemporary Turkish writers. A critical bio-bibliography of leading writers in the Turkish Republican period up to 1980.**
Louis Mitler. Richmond, England: Curzon Press, 1997. 325p. (University of Indiana Uralic and Altaic Series, no. 146).

Originally published in 1988, this book contains brief bio-bibliographical entries of 192 modern Turkish writers (excluding those who died before 1923). Besides poets and novelists, journalists, scholars of language and literature, and historians are covered. The entries are ordered by surname (wherever possible), and include full name, dates of birth and death, a biographical sketch, an evaluation of the author's main achievements, and a list of works in Turkish and in English translation (these citations are frequently incomplete).

Anthologies and collections

992 **Ottoman lyric poetry. An anthology.**
Walter G. Andrews, Najaat Black, M. Kalpaklı. Austin, Texas: University of Texas Press, 1997. 312p. bibliog.

This anthology contains free translations of seventy-five lyric poems from the 14th to the early 20th centuries. The original Ottoman texts of the poems are also included, and the authors provide concise background information on Ottoman history and literature, informative notes about the poems, and biographies of the poets.

993 **Modern Turkish poetry.**
Edited, translated from Turkish and introduced by Feyyaz Kayacan Fergar, with additional translations by Richard McKane, Ruth Christie, Talat S. Halman, Mevlüt Ceylan. Ware, England: The Rockingham Press, 1992. 189p.

A remarkable anthology, mainly for the excellent quality and fluency of the translations (most of them by the late Fergar) and for the entertaining introduction (also by Fergar) which is full of perceptive observations. The editor/translator has concentrated on shorter poems, and therefore has managed to offer a representative sample of the entire spectrum of modern Turkish poetry, making this one of the most readable anthologies available. There are excellent biographical and critical entries on all the fifty-nine poets represented.

994   **Modern Turkish drama: an anthology of plays in translation.**
       Edited by Talat S. Halman.   Minneapolis, Minnesota: Bibliotheca
       Islamica, 1976. 415p.

The volume contains a fifty-one page introduction by Halman on Ottoman and modern Turkish theatre, tracing its 19th-century origins and surveying major trends in the Republican period. It includes translations of four modern plays: 'İbrahim the mad', by Turan Oflazoğlu; 'Dry summer', by Necati Cumalı; 'The ears of Midas', by Güngör Dilmen; and 'The ballad of Ali of Keshan', by Haldun Taner.

995   **Contemporary Turkish literature: fiction and poetry.**
       Edited by Talat S. Halman.   London: Associated University Press,
       1982. 458p.

Contains a comprehensive selection of fiction and poetry from the Republican period. The translations are by forty-six contributors, in addition to the editor, and are of high quality. The introductory essay focuses on general trends and key writers. The selections are presented in an alphabetical order by author's name.

996   **An anthology of modern Turkish short stories.**
       Edited by Fahir İz.   Minneapolis, Minnesota: Bibliotheca Islamica,
       1978. 287p.

The volume contains an introduction by the editor that covers the pre-Ottoman (very brief), Ottoman, pre-Republican and Republican periods. This is followed by translations of stories by major authors such as Halit Ziya Uşaklıgil, Ahmet Hikmet Müftüoğlu, Memduh Şevket Esendal, Ömer Seyfettin, Halide Edip Adıvar, Halikarnas Balıkçısı, Refik Halit Karay, Yakup Kadri Karaosmaoğlu, Reşat Nuri Güntekin, Ahmet Hamdi Tanpınar, Sabahattin Ali, Sait Faik, Kemal Tahir, Orhan Kemal, Haldun Taner, Aziz Nesin, Samim Kocagöz, Necati Cumalı, Oktay Akbal, Talip Apaydın, Fakir Baykurt, Sevim Burak, Bekir Yıldız, Füruzan and Vüs'at O. Bener.

997   **Short dramas from contemporary Turkish literature.**
       Edited by Suat Karantay.   İstanbul: Boğaziçi University Press, 1993.
       223p.

The compilation contains one-act plays written for the stage, radio plays and 'tales for the radio' by the following prominent Turkish writers: Güner Sümer, Adalet Ağaoğlu, Melih Cevdet Anday, Behçet Necatigil and Nazlı Eray. The students of Boğaziçi University provided the translations, which have been edited by their lecturer Suat Karantay. Short biographies of the writers are also provided.

998   **The Penguin book of Turkish verse.**
       Edited by Nermin Menemencioğlu with Fahir İz.   Harmondsworth,
       England: Penguin, 1978. 416p.

An almost comprehensive anthology of Ottoman and Modern Turkish poetry until 1975. The Ottoman section is divided into *divan* (Ottoman court literature), popular mystic, folk and transition (1850-1923) poetry. The usefulness of this volume lies in the good quality of the translations throughout.

999 **Short stories by Turkish women writers.**
Translated from Turkish by Nilüfer Mizanoğlu Reddy. Bloomington, Indiana: Indiana University Turkish Studies, 1988. 130p. (Indiana University Turkish Studies Series).

This volume contains meticulous translations from twenty women writers which respect their divergent styles. The writers are: Nezihe Meriç, Sevim Burak, Selçuk Baran, Leyla Erbil, Füruzan, Sevgi Soysal, Gülten Dayıoğlu, İnci Aral, Adalet Ağaoğlu, Tezer Özlü, Nursel Duruel, Pınar Kür, Işıl Özgentürk, Ayla Kutlu, Aysel Özakın, Erendiz Atasü, Ayşe Kilimci, Latife Tekin, Tomris Uyar and Nazlı Eray.

1000 **Contemporary Turkish poetry.**
Translated from Turkish by Murat Nemet-Nejat. *Talisman: A Journal of Contemporary Poetry and Poetics*, no. 14 (1995), p. 32-59.

The introductory essay by Nemet-Nejat reinstates Sufism as a source for the literary identity to which Nazım Hikmet and the poets of the *Garip* (otherwise known as the *First new*) movement turned. It then identifies two underlying ideas behind the *Second new* movement: *eda,* an alluring term with Sufi connotations derived from folk poetry, which means the tone, sound and style which every poem must have; and the centrality of İstanbul and its topography. The selection contains poems by Cemal Süreya, Ece Ayhan, İlhan Berk, Behçet Necatigil, Özdemir İnce, Nilgün Marmara, Mustafa Ziyalan and Melisa Gürpınar.

1001 **An anthology of Turkish literature.**
Edited by Kemal Sılay. Bloomington, Indiana: Indiana University Turkish Studies, 1996. 648p. bibliog. (Indiana University Turkish Studies & Turkish Ministry of Culture Joint Series, no. 15).

This anthology provides a selection of translated texts and explanatory essays covering the entire span of Turkish literature. It starts with a section from the early Turkic Orkhon inscriptions ('Kül Tigin'), and Uygur Manichean literature (one hymn and one poem), and continues with the Karakhanid (middle Turkic) Islamic literature ('Ḳutaḏġu Bilig'), followed by longer excerpts from Anatolian Turkish literature. These are selected from *divan* literature (Ottoman court literature), medieval popular literature, and literature of the 19th and 20th century. The anthology is sprinkled with introductory or critical essays between selections, and includes brief biographies of the authors, and a selected bibliography of works on Turkish literature written in English. It is the first anthology of its kind, and is enhanced with illustrations and photographs.

Studies

Pre-Ottoman and Ottoman

1002 Candid penstrokes. The lyrics of Meʾālī, an Ottoman poet of the 16th century.
Edith Ambros. Berlin: Klaus Scharwz, 1982. 520p.

This book deals with a charming and humorous minor (and therefore perhaps more interesting) poet, and includes a critical edition of his *divan* (collection of poems) in transcription, and a discussion of his style and language, illustrated with several examples of translated verses. The poems are conveniently numbered, facilitating further study.

1003 An introduction to Ottoman poetry.
Walter G. Andrews. Minneapolis, Minnesota: Bibliotheca Islamica, 1976. 195p. bibliog. (Studies in Middle Eastern Literatures, no. 7).

This introduction to the nitty-gritty of Ottoman poetry deals with prosody and scansion, rhyme, rhetoric and formal aspects. The inclusion of references to selected texts (in transcription and translation) makes this work very accessible.

1004 Poetry's voice, society's song: Ottoman lyric poetry.
Walter G. Andrews. Seattle, Washington: University of Washington Press, 1985. 219p. bibliog.

A study of the Ottoman *gazel* (lyric poem) genre. The author's main concern is to demonstrate the three voices (contexts) in which this genre and all *divan* poetry speak: the religious-mystical, torn between the material and the spiritual; the political-authoritative, reflecting power structures; and the psychological-emotional, where the poet shares with his audience. The author challenges the received wisdom advocated by late 19th- and early 20th-century English Orientalists and Turkish scholars alike, namely that Ottoman poetry was restricted exclusively to a small elite audience, and had little connection with the wider community and its ideological or human concerns.

1005 The quatrains of Nesimī, fourteenth-century Turkic hurufi. With annotated translations of the Turkic and Persian quatrains from the Hekimoğlu Ali Paşa MS.
Kathleen Burrill. The Hague: Mouton, 1972. 391p. bibliog.

This is a well-rounded study of Nesimī, a mystic poet who is frequently considered as an Azerbaijani rather than an Ottoman poet because of certain Azerbaijani traits of his language, despite the fact that the two languages were hardly differentiated as separate literary languages at the time. Part one deals with the poet's life and creed and the literary style of the quatrains. Part two comprises an edition of the text of the Turkic and Persian quatrains (in Arabic script), followed by a translation and annotations. The appendices include brief remarks on orthography and vocabularies (Turkic and Persian), together with a facsimile of the manuscript used.

1006 **Origins and development of the Turkish novel.**
Ahmet Ö. Evin. Minneapolis, Minnesota: Bibliotheca Islamica,
1983. 224p. bibliog.
This book traces the emergence of the Turkish novel during the 19th century. The
introduction of Western genres like drama and the novel in the wake of the *Tanzimat*
reforms was linked to a reformist movement which saw the novel, rather than the genres of Ottoman *divan* poetry, as a means towards educating the public in progressive
values. The adaptation of the genre by writers who admired the West but also
respected the Ottoman past and present is the focus of Evin's study.

1007 **The development of Ottoman rhetoric up to 1882. Part I: the**
medrese **tradition.**
Christopher Ferrard. *Journal of Ottoman Studies*, vol. 3 (1982),
p. 165-88.
Provides a succinct survey of the development of rhetoric curriculum before the
Ottomans. The author goes on to examine the major textbooks used in the *medrese*
curriculum in the Ottoman period for the study of the Arabic science of literary
rhetoric, which was an ancillary Q'uranic science.

1008 **The development of Ottoman rhetoric up to 1882. Part II:**
contributions from outside the *medrese*.
Christopher Ferrard. *Journal of Ottoman Studies*, vol. 4 (1984),
p. 19-34.
This article discusses an alternative tradition of rhetoric, which developed outside the
medrese curriculum, the most forceful expression of which was given by Recāʿīzāde
Maḥmūd Ekrem in *Taʿlīm-i edebīyāt* (1882). Namık Kemal's literary manifesto, based
on the French model, called for a national literature and a national rhetoric, which
would avoid the Arabic style that obfuscated the message and made communication
difficult. Ekrem responded to Namık Kemal's appeal by accepting French literary theory. Ferrard offers a detailed analysis of Ekrem's work, and concludes that its main
value was the emphasis it placed on ideas rather than outward forms.

1009 **Recāʿīzāde Maḥmūd Ekrem's *Taʿlīm-i edebīyāt*. Parts I and II.**
Christopher Ferrard. *Türk Dili ve Edebiyatı Dergisi*, vol. 14-15
(1986), p. 215-33; *Journal of Ottoman Studies*, vol. 6 (1986),
p. 139-61.
In this article the author discusses Aḥmed Cevdet Paşa (1822-95). *Belāġat-i
ʿOsmanīye* was one of the many textbooks he wrote, in which he rendered the classical Arabic theory of rhetoric applicable to Ottoman Arabic. Ferrard examines selected
passages in detail before proceeding to consider the debate it generated and the opposition it received.

1010 **The *Belāġat-i ʿOsmanīye* of Aḥmed Cevdet Paşa and its critics.**
Christopher Ferrard. *Journal of Ottoman Studies*, vol. 7-8 (1988),
p. 309-46.
Ferrard discusses one of the many textbooks written by Cevdet Paşa, in which he rendered the classical Arabic theory of rhetoric applicable to Ottoman. He also examines

selected passages in detail, before proceeding to consider the debate it generated and the opposition it provoked.

1011   The early Turkish novel: 1872-1900.
Robert Finn.   İstanbul: The Isis Press, 1984. 196p. bibliog.
This study examines the emergence and evolution of the Ottoman Turkish novel. The author examines thirteen novels in detail, and investigates the depiction of society in them, focusing on familial relations, the treatment of women, and the Europeanization of İstanbul society.

1012   A history of Ottoman poetry.
Translated from Turkish and introduced by E. J. W. Gibb, Edward G. Browne.   London: Luzac, 1900-09. 6 vols.
When Gibb died before he could complete the major part of his massive work, his drafts were published by a colleague, whose knowledge of Ottoman Turkish was certainly not as great as his dislike of Ottoman poetry, which is hardly concealed throughout the work. Nevertheless, almost a century later, this remains a serious attempt to describe the development of Ottoman poetry. Unfortunately, Gibb's translation of Ottoman into English verse remained faithful to the metres and rhymes of the original (composed in quantitative metre), and therefore his translations are frequently impenetrable.

1013   The unreachable shores of love: Turkish modernity and mystic romance.
Victoria Rowe Holbrook.   Austin, Texas: University of Texas Press, 1994. 256p. bibliog.
A pioneering and original work, which presents a post-modernist introduction to the poetics of Ottoman Turkish romance through the study of Sheykh Galib's *mesnevi* (romance) *Ḥüsn ü ʿİşq* (Beauty and love), composed in 1783.

1014   Superwesternization in urban life in the Ottoman Empire in the last quarter of the 19th century.
Şerif Mardin.   In: *Turkey: geographical and social perspectives.* Edited by P. Benedict, E. Tümertekin.   Leiden, the Netherlands: E. J. Brill, 1974, p. 403-46.
This substantial article looks at the 19th-century novel as a source for the study of Ottoman modernization. Most of the principal writers are discussed, but a leitmotif is made out of Bihruz Bey, the archetypal westernized fop of Recāʿīzāde Maḥmūd Ekrem's *Araba sevdası* (1896).

1015   Eremya Chelebi Kömürjian's Armeno-Turkish poem 'The Jewish bride'.
Edited by Avedis K. Sanjian, Andreas Tietze.   Wiesbaden, Germany: Otto Harrassowitz, 1981. 198p. bibliog.
A critical edition and English translation of the Armeno-Turkish version (Turkish language in Armenian script) of the *Jewish bride*, composed by the well-known

Armenian author Eremya Chelebi (1637-95). Eremya Chelebi also wrote an Armenian version, and there exists a contemporary anonymous Greek version. The introductory chapters provide some background on Armeno-Turkish literature and an analysis of the literary and linguistic aspects of the work.

1016 **Nedim and the poetics of the Ottoman court: medieval inheritance and the need for change.**
Kemal Sılay. Bloomington, Indiana: Indiana University Turkish Studies, 1994. 183p. bibliog. (Indiana University Turkish Studies Series, no. 13).
Sılay argues that the social and literary environment in which Nedim operated saw the blurring of the boundaries between different genres and literary traditions, particularly between court and folk poetry. Nedim's influential creativity and literary orientation detected in folk poetry a source of vitality as the court tradition was becoming moribund. The author sees Nedim as a precursor of Turkish nationalist modernism.

Republican Turkey

1017 **The image of woman in Turkish literature.**
Füsun Akatlı (Altıok). In: *Women in Turkish society.* Edited by Nermin Abadan-Unat. Leiden, the Netherlands: E. J. Brill, 1981, p. 223-32. (Social, Economic and Political Studies of the Middle East, no. 30).
This short article provides a good, brief overview of a topic covered more extensively elsewhere. It is particularly attractive, however, because it offers a summary of an essay (entitled 'The state of the beloved') by a well-known poet, Cemal Süreya, on the evolution of the image of women in Ottoman and Modern Turkish literature.

1018 **The Turkish peasant novel, or the Anatolian theme.**
Güzine Dino. *World Literature Today*, vol. 60 (1986), p. 266-75.
This article is packed with information and ideas, and begins by asking the question: 'Is there a peasant-novel genre, or are there simply novels with a dominant peasant theme?' The article discusses, with examples, the fairly simple plot but diverse narrative influences of the peasant novel, covering all the major writers.

1019 **Sexual discourse in Turkish fiction: return of the repressed female identity.**
Sibel Erol. *Edebiyāt. New Series*, vol. 6 (1995), p. 187-202.
Taking the female body and female sexuality as the critical criteria, Erol examines three authors from a feminist stance: Adalet Ağaoğlu, Halid Ziya Uşaklıgil and Duygu Asena.

1020   **The novels of A. Ağaoğlu: narrative complexity and feminist**
        social consciousness in Modern Turkey.
        Ellen Ervin.   New York: Columbia University Press, 1988. 437p.
        bibliog.

The author gives a close contextual reading of the novels *Lying down to die*, *Slender rose of my desire*, *A wedding party*, *Summer's end*, and *Four or five people* within the context of Ağaoğlu's personal experience as a Turkish woman.

1021   **Novelists: new cosmopolitanism versus social pluralism.**
        Ahmet O. Evin.   In: *Turkey and the West: changing political and*
        cultural identities.   Edited by Metin Heper, Ayşe Öncü, Heinz
        Kramer.   London: I. B. Tauris, 1993, p. 92-115.

In this illuminating essay, the author examines the social and literary history of contemporary Turkey. This is essential reading for anyone interested in Turkish literature.

1022   **Reinventions of Turkey: Emine Sevgi Özdamar's *Life is a***
        Caravanserai.
        Margrit Frölich.   In: *Other Germanies: questioning identity in*
        women's literature and art.   Edited by Karen Jankowsky, Carla
        Love.   New York: State University of New York Press, 1997, p. 56-73.

This essay is concerned with issues of identity and cultural diversity in German literature, and, *inter alia*, it illustrates that Turkish-German author Emine Sevgi Özdamar writes against the usual conception of 'migrants' literature' because she places Turkish society at the centre of her narrative, whereas Germany appears only on the periphery.

1023   **Nazım Hikmet: romantic communist. The poet and his work.**
        Saime Göksu, Edward Timms.   London: Hurst & Co., 1998. 375p.
        bibliog.

This is the first biography of Nazım Hikmet, who was described by Stalin's daughter Stevlana as a 'romantic communist' because of his political idealism. The text examines his life and work.

1024   **The woman in the darkroom: contemporary women writers in**
        Turkey.
        Güneli Gün.   *World Literature Today*, vol. 60 (1986), p. 275-79.

In an absorbing article that pulls no punches, Gün takes a critical look at female contemporary Turkish authors.

1025   **Some Jewish characters in modern Turkish literature.**
        Nedim Gürsel.   In: *The Jews of the Ottoman Empire.*   Edited by
        Avigdor Levi.   Princeton, New Jersey: Darwin Press, 1994,
        p. 647-65.

Jews did not figure among the typical characters of the earliest Turkish novelists, and in the Republican era Jewish characters played only a limited and secondary role.

Gürsel analyses the characters of Torlak Kemal (Samuel), Raşel and Mardanapal in the works of Nazım Hikmet; Maria Pruder in Sabahattin Ali's *Kürk mantolu madonna* (Madonna in the fur coat); Ester and Roza in Oktay Akbal's *Ester ile Roza* (Ester and Roza); Sara in Necati Cumalı's *Yakub'un koyunları* (Jacob's sheep); Moiz in Mithat Cemal Kuntay's *Üç İstanbul* (Three İstanbuls); and Zembul Allahanati in Sevim Burak's *Ah ya'rab Yehova* (Oh God Jahve).

1026 **Social themes in contemporary Turkish literature.**
Kemal Karpat. *The Middle East Journal*, vol. 14 (1960), p. 29-44; vol. 14 (1961), p. 153-68.
Despite its age, this article remains very useful in providing a general background to and a brief survey of major trends and authors of Turkish literature from the mid-19th century to the late 1950s.

1027 **Semantic structuring in the modern Turkish short story: an analysis of the *Dream of Abdullah Effendi* and other short stories by Ahmed Hamdi Tanpınar.**
Sarah Moment-Atış. Leiden, the Netherlands: E. J. Brill, 1983. 205p. bibliog.
Atış embarks on a 'practical analysis' of the narrative structure of five of Tanpınar's stories, and concludes, confirming an intuitive reaction, that the stories all share a fundamental thematic pattern: ' . . . the plight of a man unable to function successfully because of his awareness of a basic contradiction inherent in his own nature or in that of the world surrounding him'.

1028 **Modern literatures of the Near and Middle East, 1850-1970.**
Robin Ostle. London: Routledge, 1991. 248p. bibliog.
A survey volume which contains three chapters on Turkish literature. The chapter by Saliha Paker (p. 17-32) in the section 'The age of translation and adaptation, 1850-1914' focuses on the translations of Western genres during the 19th century, including the rise of drama. The chapter by Geoffrey Lewis (p. 90-103) in the section 'From romantic nationalism to social criticism, 1914-1950' discusses Halide Edib, Yakup Kadri and Haldun Taner as representative authors of prose, and Yahya Kemal, Nazım Hikmet, Orhan Veli and Fazıl Hüsnü Dağlarca as representative poets of the period up to 1950. The chapter by Cevat Çapan (p. 170-79) in the section 'The age of ideology and polarization since 1950' is mainly a survey of the poets of the *Second new* movement, with a brief mention of prose writers after 1950.

1029 **Unmuffled voices in the shade and beyond: women's writing in Turkish.**
Saliha Paker. In: *Textual liberation: European feminist writing in the twentieth century*. Edited by Helena Forsas-Scott. London: Routledge, 1991, p. 270-300. bibliog.
A survey of women's writing in Turkey from the late 19th century to the 1980s, organized under the following subheadings: 'The present context of feminist consciousness'; 'Pioneers in early feminist writing: Fatma Aliye and Halide Edip'; and 'The upsurge in women's fiction: 1960 to the present'.

1030 **The village in the Turkish novel and short story, 1920 to 1955.**
Carole Rathbun. The Hague: Mouton, 1972. 192p. bibliog.
The book provides a useful overview of the portrayal of village life in fiction, concentrating mainly on the writers of the early Republic who, despite being urban intellectuals, explored the village theme.

1031 **Finding a voice: identity and the works of German-language Turkish writers in the Federal Republic of Germany to 1990.**
Marilya Veteto-Conrad. New York: Peter Lang, 1996. 92p. bibliog. (American Studies. Series III. Comparative Literature, no. 48).
The book deals with the perspective and experience of the Turks in Germany, discussing works by Turkish authors, and the perception of and reception by native German readers to those works.

Translations from single authors

1032 **Sea rose.**
Necati Cumalı, translated from the Turkish by Nilbahar Ekinci.
Ankara: Ministry of Culture, 1991. 90p.
The *Derya gülü* (The sea rose), first staged in 1963-64, is one of Cumalı's most popular plays about a domestic triangle between a fisherman, his wife and her lover.

1033 **Selected poems.**
Fazıl Hüsnü Dağlarca, translated from the Turkish by Talat S.
Halman. Pittsburgh, Pennsylvania: University of Pittsburgh Press, 1969. 195p. (Pittsburg Poetry Series, no. 46).
With most of the poems selected or approved for inclusion by Dağlarca himself, this selection offers a panoramic view of the famous poet's career, and includes poems from each of his thirty-one collections published between 1935 and 1968. There is a useful introduction by Yaşar Nabi Nayır (translated by Halman).

1034 **I, Anatolia. A play for one actress.**
Güngör Dilmen, translated from the Turkish by Talat S. Halman.
Ankara: Ministry of Culture, 1991. 70p.
The idea of a play where one actress portrays famous Anatolian women from mythological ages to the present was originally conceived by Talat Halman. Part one of the play portrays women such as Cybele (the Mother Goddess), Puduhepa (Queen of the Hittites), Lamassi (a temple harlot), Andromache (wife of Hector), Niobe (an Amazon), Queen of Caria, Artemis of Ephesus, Theodora (Byzantine empress), and Anna Comnena (Byzantine historian). Part two portrays Ottoman Turkish women, such as Nilüfer Hatun (Byzantine princess and wife of Sultan Orhan), the wife of Nasrettin Hodja, Ayşe Sultan (the daughter of Sultan Ahmed I), Nakşıdil Sultan (the foster mother of Sultan Mahmud II), Nigār (a poetess), and finally Halide Edib (writer and Republican nationalist), and the actress herself.

1035 **The poetry of Can Yücel. A selection. Can Yücel'in şiirleri. Seçmeler.**
Edited, translated from the Turkish and introduced by Feyyaz
Kayacan Fergar (with supplementary translations by Richard
McKane, Ruth Christie, Talat S. Halman). İstanbul: Papirüs
Yayınları, 1993. 177p.

In this selection of Yücel's poetry, the poems appear as parallel texts in English and in
their original Turkish. The reader should be aware that the quality of translation varies
somewhat between poems, and that not all of the translations fully reflect the satire of
Yücel's poetry.

1036 **Leylā and Mejmūn.**
Fuzūlī, translated by Sofi Huri, with a history of the poem, notes, and
bibliography by Alessio Bombaci (translated from the Italian by
Elizabeth Davies). London: George Allen & Unwin, 1970. 350p.
bibliog. (Unesco Collection of Representative Works, Turkish
Translation Series).

In part one of this book, Alessio Bombaci deals competently with the life, works and
literary style of Fuzūlī in general, and with the Arabic and Persian literary antecedents
to his work. There is also a useful annotated bibliography. Part two includes a reasonably faithful translation of the work from its lithograph Ottoman edition.

1037 **A last lullaby.**
Talat S. Halman. Merrick, New York: Cross Cultural
Communications, 1990. 48p.

This short selection includes poems in their original Turkish and in English translation. Halman's main poetic thrust is towards a synthesis of modern 'international
surrealism' and the so-called 'nonsense poetry' of the medieval Sufi tradition, which
is best exemplified by Yunus Emre.

1038 **Night: a novel.**
Bilge Karasu, translated from the Turkish by Güneli Gün. Baton
Rouge, Louisiana: Louisiana State University Press, 1994. 142p.

Winner of the Mobil Corporation Pegasus prize (1991), *Night* was originally published
in 1984 in Turkish under the title *Gece*. Gün's translation was prepared in collaboration with the late author, and is very successful. This is an allegorical, postmodernist
political novel about life in a world of violence, paranoia, and deception.

1039 **The epic of Sheikh Bedreddin and other poems.**
Nazım Hikmet, translated from the Turkish by Randy Blasing, Mutlu
Konuk. New York: Persea Books, 1977. 141p.

Nakim Hikmet (Ran) (1902-63) was one of Turkey's most exciting and controversial
poets, who remained an avowed communist all his life, much of which he spent in
prison or in exile. His works have been translated into more than fifty languages, and
the translations cited here (see item nos. 1039-43) are some of the more recent
editions of his works in English. This volume, originally published in Turkish in 1963,

is a dramatic account of the early 15th-century uprising of Sheikh Bedreddin and his followers, and how the rebellion was crushed by the Ottoman armies.

1040 Human landscapes.
Nazım Hikmet, translated from the Turkish by Randy Blasing, Mutlu Konuk. New York: Persea Books, 1983. 294p.

Originally published in 1963 after the poet's death in Moscow, this is an epic saga of the 20th century, written in prison and treating several themes, ranging from the decadence of the Turkish aristocracy to the Second World War.

1041 Nazım Hikmet: selected poetry.
Nazım Hikmet, translated from the Turkish by Randy Blasing, Mutlu Konuk Basing. New York: Persea Books, 1986. 178p.

A selection of fine verse in fine translation, containing most of Hikmet's best shorter poems and a number of previously uncollected poems.

1042 Nazım Hikmet. A sad state of freedom.
Nazım Hikmet, translated from the Turkish by Taner Baybars, Richard McCane. Warwick, England: Greville Press Pamphlets, 1990. 23p.

A selection of famous prison poems by Hikmet.

1043 Poems of Nazım Hikmet.
Nazım Hikmet, translated from the Turkish by Randy Blasing, Mutlu Konuk Blasing. New York: Persea Books, 1994. 242p.

Contains a selection of poems by Hikmet.

1044 Turkish stories from four decades.
Aziz Nesin, translated from the Turkish by Louis Mitler.
Washington, DC: Three Continents Press, 1991. 200p. bibliog.

Aziz Nesin is one of Turkey's most prolific and internationally acclaimed writers. He was a political satirist, and wrote several hundred stories, all of them full of frequently untranslatable colloquial humour. This volume includes competent translations of twenty short stories; seven from the 1950s, eight from the 1960s, three from the 1970s and two from the 1980s.

1045 Please, no police.
Aras Ören, translated from the Turkish by Teoman Sipahigil.
Austin, Texas: University of Texas, 1992. 136p. bibliog.

This was written in Turkish (from which it is translated here) and originally published as *Bitte nix Polizei* (1980). This novella is set in Berlin where the hero, Ali, a recently arrived Turkish migrant worker, is seeking illegal employment. The introduction is written by Akile Gürsoy Tezcan.

1046 **The prizegiving.**
Aysel Özakın, translated from the Turkish by Celia Kerslake.
London: Women's Press, 1988. 177p.
Aysel Özakın's partly autobiographical novel, *The prizegiving*, is about three critical days in the life of Nuray İlkin, a female writer in her forties who is on her way to Ankara to receive a prize for her autobiographical novel.

1047 **Mother tongue.**
Emine Sevgi Özdamar, translated from German by Craig Thomas.
Toronto: Coach House Press, 1994. 157p. (Passport Books, no. 3).
This volume by Özdamar, an award-winning Turkish-German author, contains four texts, all of them stories of exile, identity and confrontation between German and Turkish cultures. They are *Mother tongue, Grandfather tongue, Karagöz in Alamania,* and *A charwoman's career,* followed by an afterword by Alberto Manguel.

1048 **I, Orhan Veli: poems.**
Orhan Veli, translated from the Turkish by Murat Nemet-Nejat.
New York: Hanging Loose Press, 1989. 116p.
Orhan Veli Kanık (1914-50), writing at a time when Turkish was undergoing great changes, is one of Turkey's greatest poets. This book brings together a considerable collection of Orhan Veli's poetry, which was innovative fifty years ago and has lost little of its freshness today. The success of the present volume is due to the translator's good command of idiomatic English (he is a poet who writes in English himself), which is reflected throughout. The introduction, entitled 'Translating clarity', discusses Orhan Veli's aesthetics, and includes a detailed account of the transformation of the language from Ottoman to modern Turkish.

1049 **The white castle.**
Orhan Pamuk, translated from the Turkish by Victoria Holbrook.
Manchester, England: Carcanet Press, 1990. 161p.
The first novel of Orhan Pamuk to be translated into English, *The white castle* takes place in the İstanbul of the 17th century. A young Italian scholar sailing from Venice to Naples is taken prisoner and falls into the custody of a scholar known as Hoja, who is his exact physical double. The action is in the interplay of the two figures, who may on an easy reading be taken to represent Muslim and Western worldviews. Likewise, on a superficial level, the novel is a search for personal identity. It is laden with symbolism and metaphors, such as the 'white castle', a Polish fortress besieged by the Turks, which appears towards the end of the book.

1050 **The black book.**
Orhan Pamuk, translated from the Turkish by Güneli Gün.   London: Faber & Faber, 1994. 400p.
This is a translation of *Kara kitap,* Pamuk's fourth and complex postmodernist novel, written in the form of a detective story. İstanbul lawyer Galip begins a search for his missing wife, whom he suspects to be hiding with her famous journalist half-brother, also missing. During the search, Galip begins to read the journalist's old columns in search of clues, and the search becomes both a realistic and metaphysical process,

where Galip is obsessed with the nature of identity. He then assumes the journalist's identity by wearing his clothes, answering his phone, and even writing his columns.

1051 **The new life.**
Orhan Pamuk, translated from the Turkish by Güneli Gün. New York: Farrar, Straus & Giroux, 1997. 296p.

A translation of the author's postmodernist novel *Yeni hayat*. The novel begins with the sentence 'I read a book one day and my whole life was changed'. That book leads the narrator on a journey in the company of a mysterious young woman, who is searching for her lover, Mehmet, who had managed to enter and escape the world of the book.

1052 **Voices of memory: selected poems of Oktay Rifat.**
Oktay Rifat, translated from the Turkish by R. Christie, R. McCane. Ware, England: The Rockingham Press & Yapı Kredi Yayınları, 1993. 120p.

Oktay Rifat's influential career covered around half a century until his death in 1988. Setting out as a young poet rebelling against traditional forms, together with Orhan Veli and Melih Cevdet Anday, he went on to lead a very private life as a bureaucrat, publishing some fifteen collections of poems, three novels and eight plays. After the mid-1950s Rifat left realist poetry and started composing poetry by decomposing language. Since the 1970s, Rifat's work has been described as universal, idyllic and pastoral but with modern sensibilities. The selections in this volume amply represent all of the above periods through impressive translations. The introduction by Halman does justice to Rifat's achievements.

1053 **A dot on the map. Selected stories and poems of Sait Faik.**
Edited by Talat S. Halman. Bloomington, Indiana: Indiana University Turkish Studies, 1983. 308p. (Indiana University Turkish Studies Series, no. 4).

Sait Faik Abasıyanık has a special place in Turkish literature. His tales are written in a colloquial style, and offer vignettes of odd İstanbul characters, whom he either describes or allows to present their own case in autobiographical monologues. This volume contains translations of fifty of his stories, and several useful introductory essays.

1054 **The ballad of Ali of Keshan: an epic play.**
Haldun Taner, music by Yalçın Tura, translated from the Turkish by Nüvit Özdoğru. Ankara: International Theatre Institute, 1970. 111p.

Keşanlı Ali destanı (1964) is, typically for Haldun Taner, a satirical musical play about a man from one of the shantytowns of İstanbul who is jailed for a crime he did not commit. He becomes a hero because his alleged victim was a hated bully, assumes the personality forced upon him, and ends by committing an actual murder. The translation is remarkably successful given the richness of Haldun Taner's Turkish.

1055   **Thickhead, and other stories.**
Haldun Taner, translated from the Turkish by Geoffrey Lewis.
London: Forest Books/Unesco, 1988. 160p. (UNESCO Collection of
Representative Works: European Series).

Geoffrey Lewis' masterful translation introduces Haldun Taner's ten best short stories
to the English-speaking world. Taner was a gentle but devastating satirist who wrote
with compassion and empathy despite conveying a clear pessimism about the chances
of human personalities to improve. His use of good, rich Turkish is rendered great justice by Lewis' translations.

1056   **The neighbourhood. A play in three acts.**
Ahmet Kutsi Tecer, translated from the Turkish by Nüvit Özdoğru.
Ankara: Ministry of Culture, 1991. 127p.

Köşebaşı (1947) is a play of 'heightened realism' by a well-known Turkish author,
Ahmet Kutsi Tecer (1901-67). The play presents the daily problems of a wide cross-
section of a neighbourhood in İstanbul.

1057   **Berji Kristin: tales from the garbage hills.**
Latife Tekin, translated from the Turkish by Ruth Christie, Saliha
Paker.   London; New York: Marion Boyars, 1992. 160p.

A translation of *Berci Kristin çöp masalları* (1984) by one of Turkey's talented female
writers. The book is a tapestry of tales, full of black humour, where there are no central characters. The tales tell of a squatter community on the outskirts of a big city,
where there are to be found women of easy virtue, gamblers, pimps, anarchists, scam
artists, wife-beaters and exploiters. The author treats every character with impartiality
and good humour, and she portrays a world in which reality and fantasy are blurred as
the characters try to cope with the harsh realities of their environment.

1058   **Memed, my hawk.**
Yashar Kemal, translated from the Turkish by Edouard Roditi.
London: The Harvill Press, 1998. 352p.

A translation of Yaşar Kemal's *İnce Memed* (1955), his first and best known novel,
where he takes as his hero a modern version of the traditional folk tale bandit hero,
and follows him in his struggles on behalf of his oppressed fellow peasants against the
corrupt authorities. The first edition of the English translation was published in 1961
by Pantheon.

1059   **The wind from the plain.**
Yashar Kemal, translated from the Turkish by Thilda Kemal.
London: The Harvill Press, 1997. 288p.

A translation of *Ortadirek* (1960), the first book of the trilogy *The other face of a
mountain* (see also item nos. 1060 and 1061). In these novels societal change and the
conflicts it generates play a large part. Ordinary people have to struggle with every-
thing and everyone: nature, an array of bureaucrats, businessmen, bullies, and above
all insatiable feudal lords, who constantly deprive people of any chance for happiness.
The first edition of the English translation was published in 1963.

1060 **Iron earth, copper sky.**
Yashar Kemal, translated from the Turkish by Thilda Kemal.
London: The Harvill Press, 1997. 224p.

A translation of *Yer demir, gök bakır* (1963), the second part of Kemal's trilogy (see also item nos. 1059 and 1061). The novel features a Kurdish minstrel, Abdale Zeyniki, thereby allowing Yaşar Kemal to draw upon the rich heritage of lyrical and folk songs. The first edition of the translation was published in 1974.

1061 **The undying grass.**
Yaşar Kemal, translated from the Turkish by Thilda Kemal.
London: The Harvill Press, 1997. 328p.

A translation of *Ölmez otu* (1968), the third part of Kemal's trilogy (see also item nos. 1059 and 1060), where the defence systems of society are at work against the insecurity of change and struggle with the authorities. The first edition of the translation was published in 1977.

1062 **The sea-crossed fisherman.**
Yashar Kemal, translated from the Turkish by Thilda Kemal.
London: Random House UK, 1990. 288p.

This work exemplifies the author's shift of attention from peasant life in Anatolia to life in the fishing villages of the Bosphorus, and the Sea of Marmara. There are several lyrical passages amongst the many which describe the devastating effects of urbanization on traditional lifestyles. The first English translation was published in 1985.

1063 **The birds have also gone.**
Yashar Kemal, translated from the Turkish by Thilda Kemal.
London: Random House, 1989. 128p.

Kuşlar da gitti (1978) is the first novel of Yaşar Kemal not to be set in his homeland, Çukurova. Amid the chaos and cynicism of modern İstanbul, a gang of boys resort to trapping migratory birds to sell outside mosques, churches and synagogues. The suffering and exploitation of the Bosphorus low-life is, as always, portrayed in Dickensian colour. As with many of Kemal's novels, it is a statement on how ordinary people ultimately survive and prevail. The first English translation was published in 1987.

1064 **To crush the serpent.**
Yashar Kemal, translated from the Turkish by Thilda Kemal.
London: The Harvill Press, 1988. 108p.

Yılanı öldürseler (1976) is a story of revenge: a boy is slowly incited to kill his mother in order to avenge his father's death at the hands of his mother's lover. This violent act follows earlier dark events of drugging, rape, abduction and murder. As always, the style is lyrical, with a heavy dose of hyperbole when describing the conflicts of the peasants against cash-crop economy; however, the village life which Kemal depicts here is rapidly outdated.

1065 **Salman the solitary.**
Yashar Kemal, translated from the Turkish by Thilda Kemal.
London: The Harvill Press, 1997. 352p.
Another semi-autobiographical novel from Kemal, this is the touching story of İsmail Agha's household. İsmail Agha has been driven from his village in eastern Anatolia by the invading Russian armies. He builds himself a new life in a different part of Anatolia. In his household is Salman, his adopted son, whom he has saved from death as a child. The story turns into tragedy as the rivalry for the love of the father intensifies between the real son and Salman.

1066 **Wisdom of royal glory (Ḳutaḏġu bilig): a Turko-Islamic mirror for princes.**
Yūsuf Khāṣṣ Ḥājib, translated from the Karakhanid Turkish with an introduction by Robert Dankoff. Chicago: The University of Chicago Press, 1983. 281p.
A critical edition of *Ḳutaḏġu bilig* written in 1069 in Karakhanid Turkish, and hence the oldest monument of Islamic Turkish literature. It is meant to be a mirror of the political and cultural life of the Central Asian Turks at the outset of their lives as Muslims. It is written as a long didactic poem, consisting of dialogues set within a frame story. The aim of the author was to show that Turkish traditions of royalty and wisdom were comparable, if not superior, to Arab and Iranian counterparts, and that they were equally compatible with Islam. The major theme of the work is the conflict between individual conscience and communal obligation.

İstanbul boy: böyle gelmiş, böyle gitmez (that's how it was but not how it's going to be). The autobiography of Aziz Nesin, part I.
See item no. 281.

İstanbul boy: yol (path). The autobiography of Aziz Nesin, part II.
See item no. 282.

İstanbul boy: yokuşun başı (the climb). The autobiography of Aziz Nesin, part III.
See item no. 283.

Edebiyāt. New series. A Journal of Middle Eastern and Comparative Literature.
See item no. 1329.

International Journal of Middle Eastern Studies.
See item no. 1333.

Journal of Turkish Literature.
See item no. 1338.

Journal of Turkish Studies. Türklük Bilgisi Araştırmaları.
See item no. 1339.

Kitap-lık.
See item no. 1341.

Middle East Studies Association Bulletin.
See item no. 1346.

The Turkish P.E.N.
See item no. 1378.

Turkish Studies Association Bulletin.
See item no. 1382.

Oral tradition

1067 **Dream motif in Turkish folk stories and shamanistic initiation.**
İlhan Başgöz. *Asian Folklore Studies*, vol. 26, no. 1 (1967), p. 1-8.
The author discusses the 'dream motif' in Turkish folk stories, relates it to shamanistic rites, and explains the role of Sufism in the transformation of shamanistic rites into a fiction motif.

1068 **Turkish folklore reader.**
İlhan Başgöz. Richmond, England: Curzon Press, 1997. 147p.
bibliog. (Indiana University, The Uralic & Altaic Series, no. 120).
First published in 1971, this volume is a compilation of selections from Turkish folklore, and is designed as reading practice for those who have mastered basic Turkish. All genres of folk literature are represented in the book except for the epic. It also includes biographical notes on the poets, minstrels and writers, a dictionary, and grammatical notes which refer to the texts.

1069 **Bilmece: a corpus of Turkish riddles.**
İlhan Başgöz, Andreas Tietze. Berkeley, California; Los Angeles:
University of California Press, 1973. 1,063p. map. bibliog.
(University of California Publications, Folklore Studies, no. 22).
This is the most comprehensive and thorough study of Turkish riddles available in English. It was realized over a period of twenty years as a result of the collaboration of many scholars. The material was first collected by Pertev Naili Boratav, and later by Wolfram Eberhard. It is an unparalleled reference work for Turkish folklore studies.

1070 **Studies in Turkish folklore in honor of Pertev N. Boratav.**
Edited by İlhan Başgöz, Mark Glazer. Bloomington, Indiana:
Indiana University Turkish Studies, 1978. 232p. bibliog. (Indiana
University Turkish Studies, no. 1).
The book contains fifteen essays on various topics of Turkish folklore, such as dramatic fertility rituals, epithets in the prose of the epic *Dede Korkut*, folk theatre, riddles and legends.

1071   **Folklore studies and nationalism in Turkey.**
İlhan Başgöz.   In: *Folklore: nationalism and politics.*   Edited by
Felix Onias.   Columbus, Ohio: Slavica, 1978, p. 125-37.
In this essay the author has two specific points of emphasis. First he argues that any
interest in the study of Turkish literature and folklore is tied to national, internal, academic or political causes. Secondly, he provides a historical sketch of the ups and
downs in Turkish folklore studies during the mid-20th-century political turmoil.

1072   **Köroğlu's Tekgözler story.**
İlhan Başgöz.   *Wiener Zeitschrift für die Kunde des Morgenlandes,*
no. 76 (1986), p. 49-56.
An article of interest for the dissemination of the Polyphemus motif in Turkey where
it has already been collected in various non-epic forms.

1073   **The structure of the Turkish romances.**
İlhan Başgöz.   In: *Folk groups and folklore genres: a reader.*
Edited by Elliott Oring.   Logan, Utah: Utah State University Press,
1989, p. 197-208.
The author outlines the plot structure of Turkish romances, and discusses the relation-
ship which exists between that structure and the Turkish minstrels who perform them.

1074   **Minstrel tales from southeastern Turkey.**
Wolfram Eberhard.   Berkeley, California; Los Angeles: University
of California Press, 1955. 92p. bibliog. (University of California
Publications. Folklore Studies).
The material presented in this volume is important for historical or comparative studies, since it was collected by the author in the Çukurova region during 1951. Five
different tales are discussed in the book, which also contains a section on the biographies of the minstrels.

1075   **The song contests of Turkish minstrels.**
Yıldıray Erdener.   New York: Garland Publications, 1995. 222p.
(Milman Parry Studies in Oral Tradition).
A study of the tradition of song contests among Turkish minstrels. Specific topics
include the home of song duelling, the creators of song duels, the structure of the song
duels and their role in the oral transmission of culture, and strategies of minstrels to
gain fame, prestige and recognition. Although the book reflects valuable research in an
area where there are few sources in English, readers are advised to read its review by
Walter G. Andrews in *The Turkish Studies Association Bulletin* (vol. 19, no. 2 [1995],
p. 91-95).

1076 **Yunus Emre and his mystical poetry.**
Edited and translated from the Turkish by Talat S. Halman, İlhan Başgöz. Bloomington, Indiana: Indiana University Turkish Studies, 1981. 199p. bibliog. (Indiana University Turkish Studies Series, no. 12).

This important book contains several important essays by leading scholars on Turkish mystical literature, and includes English translations of over forty of Yunus Emre's poems by Halman, as well as a selected bibliography of studies on Yunus.

1077 **Poems by Karacaoğlan: a Turkish bard.**
Karacaoğlan, translated from the Turkish by Seyfi Karabaş, Judith Yarnall. Bloomington, Indiana: Indiana University Turkish Studies, 1996. 71p. (Turkish Studies Series, no. 14).

Contains translations of poems by Karacaoğlan, a 17th-century Turkish folk poet.

1078 **Turkish fairy tales and folk tales.**
Ignácz Kunos, translated from the Hungarian by R. Nisbet Bain. New York: Dover; Magnolia, Massachusetts: Peter Smith, 1969. 275p.

The tales were collected during the author's travels in Anatolia in the late 19th century and were originally published in 1901. The collection also includes four partly Turkish tales translated from Romanian, which carry elements of Romance, Slavonic, Magyar and Turkish traditions (p. 209-75).

1079 **The Book of Dede Korkut.**
Translated from the Turkish with an introduction and notes by Geoffrey Lewis. Harmondsworth, England: Penguin, 1988. 2nd ed. 213p.

This is an eminently successful English translation of the *Book of Dede Korkut*, which is not only enjoyable to read but is also scholarly. The first fully fledged epic tale to be recorded in any Turkic language, the Anatolian Turkish *Book of Dede Korkut* (extant in two 16th-century manuscripts) is a collection of tales (each called an *oghuzname*) about the early history of the Oghuz, from the time they lived around the Syr Darya river to their migration to Byzantine Anatolia. Lewis consults both extant manuscripts, but wisely does not follow the standard Turkish edition which collates them, despite the obvious fact that they do not derive from the same copy. The introduction discusses the historical and literary character of the collection and examines the main characteristics of each tale. Lewis deals succinctly with a number of difficult literary and philological points.

1080 **The Turkish minstrel tale tradition.**
Natalie K. Moyle. New York: Garland Publications, 1990. 267p. bibliog. (Harvard Dissertations in Folklore and Oral Tradition).

The book dwells on the structure and composition of minstrel (*aşık*) songs of north-eastern Turkey.

1081　**Individuals and institutions in the early history of Turkish folklore, 1840-1950.**
Arzu Öztürkmen.　*Journal of Folklore Research*, vol. 29, no. 2 (1992), p. 177-92.

The author believes that the idea of folklore was born and flourished during a period of transition, in which folklore constituted one of the many ways to imagine the new Turkish national identity during and after the 19th century. In order to expose the different faces through which folklore has been apprehended in Turkey, the article presents the story of individuals who actively took part in Turkish folklore studies, and the institutions which sheltered them between 1840 and 1950.

1082　**Tales from Turkey.**
Translated from the Turkish and compiled by Allan Ramsay, Francis McCullagh.　London: Simpkin, 1914. 282p.

The tales were collected by Ramsay during his long stay in Constantinople. These popular tales act as a mirror to the minds and everyday lives of the common people. The long preface by McCullagh gives information about the tales, and relates them to social life in Turkey during the first part of the 20th century.

1083　**Turkic oral epic poetry. Traditions, forms, poetic structure.**
Karl Reichl.　New York: Garland, 1992. 395p. bibliog.

A methodologically (from the point of view of Albert Lord's 'oral traditional poetry') solid and down-to-earth book on the Turkic oral epic traditions. The approach is descriptive and Reich provides a linguistic and historical background to the earliest extant works and the performers of the tales. He examines the issues of genre, story-patterns, formulaic diction, composition-in-performance, rhetoric, narrative technique, and finally, variation and diffusion.

1084　**Yunus Emre: the wandering fool. Sufi poems of a thirteenth century Turkish dervish.**
Edouard Roditi, Güzine Dino.　San Francisco: Cadmus Editions, 1987. 58p.

This small book contains readable and fluent translations of twenty poems and two stimulating essays by Dino and Roditi.

1085　**The book of Dede Korkut, a Turkish epic.**
Translated from the Turkish by Faruk Sümer, Ahmet E. Uysal, Warren S. Walker.　Austin, Texas: University of Texas Press, 1972. 212p.

This English translation of the anonymous *Book of Dede Korkut* follows the standard Turkish critical edition, which collates two manuscripts. In the introduction the editors take up the issues of historical setting, the legendary aspect of the characters, authorship, form and style.

1086   **The Koman riddles and Turkic folklore.**
        Andreas Tietze.   Los Angeles; Berkeley, California: University of
        California Press, 1966. 160p. bibliog. (University of California Near
        East Studies, no. 8).

The Koman riddles occupy a unique place in the Turkic riddling tradition. The book explores the similarities between the Koman riddles and Turkish riddles in general, and gives the texts of the riddles in their original language with English translations, explanations and notes on each one. There are indexes of Koman words and answers to the riddles at the end of the book.

1087   **The art of the Turkish tale.**
        Retold by Barbara K. Walker, illustrated by Helen Siegl.   Lubbock,
        Texas: Texas Technical University Press, 1990. 2 vols.

A translation into colloquial English of 131 tales recorded in Turkey between 1960 and 1990. The volumes include anecdotes, fables, tongue twisters, a heroic romance and wonder tales. There is a foreword by Talat Halman and an introduction by Barbara Walker on Turkish folk literature. Besides its value for folklorists, this is an important source for students of oral literature, despite the absence of any original texts.

1088   **Tales alive in Turkey.**
        Edited and translated from the Turkish by Warren S. Walker, Ahmet
        E. Uysal.   Lubbock, Texas: Texas Technical University Press, 1990.
        reprint. 310p. map. bibliog.

For over thirty-five years, Warren and Barbara Walker recorded and collected folk-tales from all over Turkey. This book contains English translations of folk-tales which were collected by the authors between the years 1961-64 during their visits to more than 200 locations in Turkey.

1089   **More tales alive in Turkey.**
        Warren S. Walker, Ahmet E. Uysal.   Lubbock, Texas: Texas
        Technical University Press, 1992. 326p. bibliog.

This volume is a sequel to *Tales alive in Turkey* (see item no. 1088), and it contains English translations of oral performances of Turkish folktales recorded for the Archive of Turkish Oral Narrative (ATON) at Texas Technical University.

1090   **A Turkish folktale: the art of Behçet Mahir.**
        Edited by Warren S. Walker.   New York: Garland, 1996. 136p.
        (World Folktale Library, no. 4).

The tale (actually two stories sharing the same hero) told in this volume is an English translation of a recording, made in 1977 in a coffee-house near Erzurum, of Behçet Mahir (1909-88), who may well have been 'Turkey's greatest storyteller of the twentieth century'. The translation is presented with a detailed and footnoted (and therefore easy to consult) commentary. There is also a useful index of motifs.

276

1091   **The drop that became the sea: lyric poems of Yunus Emre.**
Yunus Emre, translated from the Turkish by Kabir Helminski, Refik
Algan.   Putney, Vermont: Threshold Books, 1989. 96p.
The volume contains fifty-two poems of Yunus Emre, most of them previously
untranslated. These translations are appealingly lucid, even bordering on
oversimplification, partly because they do not employ rhyme or metre. The translators
are, for the most part, faithful to the text of the Gölpınarlı edition.

1092   **The city of the heart: Yunus Emre's verses of wisdom and love.**
Yunus Emre, translated from the Turkish by Süha Faiz.
Shaftesbury, England: Element Books, 1992. 135p.
A translation of 157 poems of Yunus Emre in which an effort has been made to maintain the original metrical rhythm and images. This faithfulness to the structure of the
original Turkish may trouble the unsuspecting reader, but the 'Foreword' serves as a
good introduction to the poet.

1093   **Yunus Emre: selected poems.**
Yunus Emre, translated from the Turkish by Talat S. Halman.
Ankara: Ministry of Culture, 1993. 2nd ed. 183p. bibliog. (Turkish
Classics Series, no. 21).
A collection of Yunus Emre's poems with parallel texts in Turkish and in English
translation. Halman's introduction to the work is entitled 'Yunus Emre's humanism'
(p. 13-37).

1094   **The poetry of Yunus Emre, a Turkish sufi poet.**
Yunus Emre, translated from the Turkish by Grace Martin Smith.
Berkeley, California: University of California Press, 1993. 146p.
(University of California Publications in Modern Philology, no. 127).
This book contains literal translations of about eighty poems by Yunus, which are
helpful in their clarity of interpretation but not entirely reliable in matters of transcription and prosody. The introduction and annotations are adequate and clear, but
surprisingly the selected bibliography is far too selective at the expense of earlier
translations and Yunus scholarship.

Archive of Turkish oral narrative: preliminary catalogue II.
See item no. 1265.

Türk folklor ve etnografya bibliyografyası. (Bibliography of Turkish
folklore and ethnography.)
See item no. 1420.

The Arts

General

1095 The Anatolian civilizations: the Council of Europe XVIIIth European art exhibition.
Edited by Ferid Edgü. İstanbul: T. C. Kültür ve Turizm Bakanlığı, 1983. 3 vols. (St. Irene -Topkapı Palace Museum, May 22-October 30, 1983).

This is the catalogue of an exhibition that brought together for the first time examples from Turkish museums in a single exhibition in order to illustrate through objects of art the variety of cultures hosted in Anatolia from Palaeolithic to contemporary times.

1096 Turkish traditional art today.
Henry Glassie. Bloomington, Indiana: Indiana University Press, 1993. 962p. maps. bibliog. (Indiana University Turkish Studies, no. 11).

This is probably the most comprehensive study on contemporary Turkish art written in English. With over 1,000 illustrations (photographs, maps, drawings and plans), the book shows the artists of Turkey and their creations. The author concentrates on calligraphy, woodworking, pottery, and carpet weaving. The book crosses over the boundaries of folklore, cultural geography, art history and anthropology, and depicts with accuracy the nature of human relationships in an Islamic Turkish context.

1097 Islamic art.
David Talbot Rice. London: Thames & Hudson; New York: Scribner, 1975. 152p. maps. bibliog.

The chapters on the Seljuks of Rum and the Ottoman Turks (p. 163-209) review the art of Anatolia during the period of the Seljuks and the Ottomans. The book contains illustrations in colour and black-and-white, which give examples of various forms of art (tiles, carpets and decorative pieces) and architecture.

1098   **Fifth International Congress of Turkish Art (September 21-27, 1975).**
Edited by Géza Fehér, Magyar Nemzeti Museum.   Budapest: Akadémiai Kiadó, 1978. 942p. (Proceedings of the conference held September 21-7, 1975 in Budapest, sponsored by the Hungarian National Museum).
The first International Congress of Turkish Art was held in Ankara in 1961. Since then academics, museum curators and researchers have come together every four years to discuss recent research on all aspects of Turkish art from the pre-Islamic to the contemporary period. This volume contains the papers from the Fifth Congress.

1099   **Ars Turcica: Akten des VI. Internationalen Kongresses für Türkische Kunst, München, vom 3. bis 7. September 1979.** (Ars Turcica: proceedings of the Sixth International Congress of Turkish Art, Munich, from 3 to 7 September 1979.)
Edited by Klaus Kreiser.   Munich, Germany: Maris, 1987. 3 vols. bibliog.
Contains the proceedings of the Sixth International Congress of Turkish Art.

1100   **Seventh International Congress of Turkish Art.**
Edited by Tadeusz Majda.   Warsaw: Polish Scientific Publishers, 1990. 292p.
Contains the proceedings of the Seventh International Congress of Turkish Art.

1101   **Eighth International Congress of Turkish Art: Cairo, 26th September-1st October 1987.**
International Congress of Turkish Art.   Cairo: Ministry of Culture, Egyptian Antiquities Organization, 1987. 148p.
Contains the papers presented at the Eighth International Congress of Turkish Art.

1102   **9. Milletlerarası Türk Sanatları Kongresi: bildiriler: 23-27 Eylül 1991, Atatürk Kültür Merkezi, İstanbul. 9th International Congress of Turkish Art: contributions: 23-27 September 1991, Atatürk Cultural Centre, İstanbul.**
International Congress of Turkish Art.   Ankara: Kültür Bakanlığı, 1995. 3 vols. bibliog.
Contains the papers presented at the Ninth International Congress of Turkish Art.

Turkey: a portrait.
See item no. 13.

The transformation of Turkish culture.
See item no. 16.

The evolution of Turkish art and architecture.
See item no. 908.

Nine thousand years of the Anatolian woman.
See item no. 1233.

Cornucopia. Turkey for Connoisseurs.
See item no. 1323.

Muqarnas. An Annual on Islamic Art and Architecture.
See item no. 1350.

Ottoman decorative arts

1103 **Treasury of Turkish designs: 670 motifs from İznik.**
Azade Akar.   New York: Dover Publications, 1988. 128p. (Dover
Pictorial Archive Series).
An illustrated book of Turkish pottery from İznik. The author dwells on the themes of
the motifs and the decorative value of the pottery.

1104 **The story of Ottoman tiles and ceramics.**
Edited by Ara Altun.   İstanbul: Creative Yayıncılık, 1997. 320p.
This volume traces the development of tile and ceramic manufacturing in the world,
the materials used, the techniques of glazing and the styles of decoration. It provides a
history of Ottoman tiles from their origins in the Seljuk period. The techniques,
designs and architectural uses of tiles are analysed and illustrated by photographs. The
final chapter discusses modern potters and their contribution to the preservation of this
art form.

1105 **Turkish miniature painting.**
Metin And.   İstanbul: Dost Yayınları, 1987. 146p. bibliog.
Provides a historical outline of Turkish miniature painting, and discusses its style and
technique, the social position of the artist, and the iconographical themes. The book
contains illustrations of miniatures.

1106 **The İznik tile kiln excavations (the second round: 1981-1988).**
Oktay Aslanapa, Serare Yetkin, Ara Artun, translated from the
Turkish by Robert Bragner, edited by Tülay Duran.   İstanbul: Önder,
1989. 326p.
The book illustrates, with measured drawings, sections and elevations, the different
kilns excavated in various parts of İznik, and a selection of the kiln material found on
the excavation sites.

1107 **Turkish miniature painting.**
Nurhan Atasoy, Filiz Çağman. İstanbul: Doğan Kardeş Matbaacılık, 1974. 107p. bibliog.
The first part of this book is a study of Turkish miniature painting from the 15th to the 19th centuries. The second section includes fifty plates, for which the following information is given: the subject, where the item is kept, the size and the artist.

1108 **İznik: the pottery of Ottoman Turkey.**
Nurhan Atasoy, Julian Raby. London: Thames & Hudson, 1994. 2nd ed. 352p.
The book, containing 991 illustrations, discusses a huge number of Ottoman ceramics conserved in various museums around the world, and classifies them according to theme or style.

1109 **Süleymanname: the illustrated history of Süleyman the Magnificent.**
Esin Atıl. Washington, DC: National Gallery of Art; New York: Abrams, 1986. 271p.
This is the reprint of the original manuscript conserved in the Topkapı Palace library. The text recounts the good deeds of Sultan Suleiman as written by the palace historiographer, and is illustrated with miniatures.

1110 **The age of Sultan Süleyman the Magnificent.**
Esin Atıl. Washington, DC: National Gallery of Art; New York: Harry N. Abrams, 1987. 416p. map. bibliog.
The catalogue of an exhibition of the same name, of which the author was curator. It contains 210 colour photographs of objects from museums around the world, assorted black-and-white photographs of various examples and details, an object list, and appendices which include transactions listed in several art records for 16th-century artisans. The text of the catalogue focuses on Suleiman and the historical setting, followed by a discussion of the royal ateliers, treasury, the imperial wardrobe, and the royal kilns.

1111 **Konuşan maden: tombak ve gümüş madeni eserler kolleksiyonu. (Gilding copper [*tombak*] and silver metalwork collection).**
Fulya Eruz, Robert Bragner. İstanbul: Yapı Kredi Yayınları, 1993. 157p. bibliog. (Yapı Kredi Koleksiyonları, no. 4).
Gilding copper and silverwork were used for luxury objects during the Ottoman period, and were also used on ceremonial military helmets. This work, written in English and Turkish, serves as a catalogue of collections where such works can be found.

1112   **The art of the Saljūqs in Iran and Anatolia. Proceedings of a symposium held in Edinburgh in 1982.**
Edited by Robert Hillenbrand.   Costa Mesa, California: Mazda Publishers, 1994. 319p. maps.

The book contains thirty-seven short essays on a wide range of topics on Seljuk art and architecture. The essays are illustrated with prints and drawings.

1113   **Islamic tiles.**
Venetia Parker.   New York: Interlink Publishing Group, 1995. 128p. bibliog.

The book documents tile production from Iran to Turkey. Beginning with a discussion of craftsmen and techniques, the author traces the development of tile production from 9th-century Iraqi to 19th-century Turkish styles. The 114 illustrations which complement the text are principally from the British Museum collection.

1114   **Tulips, arabesques and turbans: decorative arts from the Ottoman Empire.**
Edited by Y. Petsopoulos.   London: Alexandria Press, 1982. 200p.

Ottoman art is characterized by homogeneity of style, which changes according to period. Similar motifs and decorative compositions can be found on different types of material (textiles, carpets, ceramics, metal work, wood carvings, wall paintings). The articles in this book contribute to a chronological and stylistic introduction to decorative arts in the Ottoman Empire, drawing samples mainly from the works produced for the Palaces.

1115   **Turkish bookbinding in the 15th century: the foundation of an Ottoman court style.**
Julian Raby, Zeren Tanındı.   London: Azimuth Editions Ltd for the Association internationale de Bibliophilie, 1993. 245p.

The authors study manuscripts and their patrons through the catalogue of book bindings in the Topkapı Palace. Relevant archival material and historical texts are used in order to shed light on the personality of two Sultans, Mehmed II and Bayezıd II. The bindings are examined with respect to their techniques of production and decoration. Types of bindings and a list of binders are given in the appendices. Colour photographs illustrate the variety of these bindings, which were made of leather or by using silk textiles. This volume is the first study of its kind.

1116   **The oriental obsession: Islamic inspiration in British and American art and architecture, 1500-1920.**
John Sweetman.   Cambridge, England: University of Cambridge Press, 1988. 327p. bibliog. (Cambridge Studies in the History of Art Series).

The book deals with the role of visual arts in the relationship between the Orient and the West (in particular the English-speaking West). It contains many illustrations of works of art which show the influence of the East and which relate directly to the East. The appendix lists buildings with Islamic associations in Great Britain and America. The work also has a useful bibliography.

Osmanlı Padişah fermanları. Imperial Ottoman *fermans*.
See item no. 1231.

Plants and gardens in Persian, Mughal, and Turkish art.
See item no. 1242.

Miniatures from Turkish manuscripts. Catalogue and subject index of paintings in the British Library and British Museum.
See item no. 1243.

Osmanlı fermanları. Ottoman *fermans*.
See item no. 1256.

Anadolu Selçuklu dönemi sanatı bibliografyası. (A bibliography for the arts of the Seljuk period.)
See item no. 1411.

Painting

1117 **Abidin Dino. Torture.**
Ali Artun, translated from the Turkish by Fred Stark.   Ankara:
Human Rights Foundation of Turkey & Galeri Nev, 1994. 110p.
Published to commemorate Abidin Dino, a Turkish painter who lived in Paris, on the first anniversary of his death, this book comprises twenty-eight drawings by the artist. The text focuses on Dino's work in relation to contemporary European art.

1118 **Ondokuzuncu yüzyıldan günümüze Türk ressamları.**
Contemporary Turkish painters.
Seyfi Başkan.   Ankara: Turkish Ministry of Culture, 1991. 221p.
bibliog.
This reference book on contemporary Turkish painters includes a glossary and illustrations. The text is in both English and Turkish.

1119 **Orientalism and Turkey.**
Semra Germaner, Zeynep İnankur, translated from the Turkish by
Nigar Alemdar, Jeremy Salt.   İstanbul: Turkish Cultural Foundation,
1989. 191p.
The book illustrates orientalist paintings depicting images from Turkey, and discusses them in relation to orientalism in general.

1120   **Post peripheral flux: a decade of contemporary art in İstanbul.**
Beral Madra.   İstanbul: Literatur Publications, 1996. 202p.
The contemporary art world in Turkey has been very active and innovative since the 1980s. Madra, an art critic, curator and gallery owner, narrates her experiences in this busy art market. Through her memoirs, the reader gains an insight into the art world of contemporary İstanbul.

1121   **A history of Turkish painting.**
Edited by Selman Pınar, Günseli Renda.   Geneva; Seattle, Washington: Palasar, in association with University of Washington Press, 1988. 2nd ed. 444p. bibliog.
The book begins with a detailed discussion of 18th-century Turkish painting, and continues up to the present day. Its five chapters are: 'Traditional Turkish painting and the beginning of Western trends', Günseli Renda; 'Painting in Turkey in the nineteenth and early twentieth century', Turan Erol; 'Post-Second World War trends in Turkish painting', Adnan Turani; 'The search for new identity in Turkish painting', Kaya Özsezgin; and a discussion of development of the art of print-making, by Mustafa Aslıer. The book contains 495 lavish illustrations.

1122   **The oriental tale in England in the eighteenth century.**
Martha Pike Conant.   New York: The Columbia University Press, 1908. 312p. bibliog. (Columbia Studies in Comparative Literature).
Oriental fiction was introduced to British literature through French imitations or translations of oriental tales. The beginning of this trend can be traced back to 1704-12 when the first English translation of the *Arabian nights* appeared. This book provides a clear description of 18th-century English oriental fiction in relation to its French sources and to the general current of English thought. The oriental and pseudo-oriental literature that appeared in English in the works of writers such as Samuel Johnson and Oliver Goldsmith are discussed. There is also an appendix of dates of publications for the works and a good bibliography. This work will be useful for all readers interested in orientalism (see also item nos. 1116 and 1119).

1950-2000.
See item no. 1220.

Cornucopia. Turkey for Connoisseurs.
See item no. 1323.

Muqarnas. An Annual on Islamic Art and Architecture.
See item no. 1350.

Music and dance

1123   Dances of Anatolian Turkey.
Metin And.   New York: Johnson Reprint, 1971. 76p. map. bibliog.
The booklet contains a survey of dance in Anatolia, covering religious dancing, dancing boys and dancing girls, theatrical dancing, mimetic dances, regional dances, formations, movements and style, music and costume for dancing.

1124   A pictorial history of Turkish dancing; from folk dancing to whirling dervishes, belly dancing to ballet.
Metin And.   Ankara: Dost Yayınları, 1976. 182p. bibliog.
A general, comprehensive survey of dance in Turkey, from its Central Asian beginnings to contemporary ballet, which uses iconographical evidence and historical testimony, and which covers both secular and sacred traditions. Dancing is also examined as a spectacle, and the choreography of the major Turkish folk dances from various regions is discussed.

1125   Some notes on aspects and functions of Turkish folk games.
Metin And.   *Journal of American Folklore*, vol. 92, no. 363 (1979), p. 44-64.
The author examines verbal and non-verbal games, games associated with the seasons and sports in rural Turkey. Some interesting photographs illustrate the article, which has implications for dance as well as theatre in Turkey.

1126   Turkish folk music from Asia Minor.
Béla Bartók, edited by Benjamin Suchoff.   Princeton, New Jersey: Princeton University Press, 1976. 288p. (New York Bartók Archive Studies in Musicology, no. 7).
The book is the fruit of Bartok's single short fieldtrip in 1935, and to that extent is only representative of one small area. This work conforms to Bartók's normal methods of analysis in its detailed attention to the structure of text and melody.

1127   Zaman, mekân, müzik. Klâsik Türk musikisinde eğitim (meşk), icra ve aktarım. (Time, place, music. Training, performance and transmission in classical Turkish music.)
Cem Behar.   İstanbul: AFA Yayınları, 1992. 176p. bibliog. (AFA – Türkiye üzerine Araştırmalar, no. 14).
An important collection of four articles illustrating various facets of the ideology of the classical tradition. The first and longest article is a well-documented study of oral transmission and the crucial role of the master-pupil relationship, while the second deals with the related issue of instrumental tuition and the concept of virtuosity.

1128 **Demetrius Cantemir. The collection of notations, part 1: text.**
Demetrius Cantemir, transcribed and annotated by Owen Wright.
London: School of Oriental and African Studies, 1992. 762p.
A study of one of the earliest noted records of Ottoman music, collected in the second
half of the 17th century, which has been transcribed into Western notation. It presents
the instrumental repertoire of the end of the century.

1129 **Cultural authority and authenticity in the Turkish repertoire.**
Walter Feldman. *Asian Music*, vol. 22, no. 1 (1990-91), p. 73-111.
The article contends that the concept of 'cultural authority which had prevailed in
Ottoman Turkey is exemplified by the conception of the "art" or "classical" repertoire
in Turkish music' (p. 73). The article illustrates why and how Turkish music is unique
in Western Asia and also serves as one of the best sources for general information on
Ottoman/Turkish music for the non-specialist reader.

1130 **Music of the Ottoman court: makam, composition and the early
Ottoman instrumental repertoire.**
Walter Feldman. Berlin: Verlag für Wissenschaft und Bildung,
1996. 560p. bibliog. (Intercultural Music Studies, no. 10).
This is by far the most detailed historical survey of Ottoman music yet to appear in
English. It is a comprehensive study of the evolution of the art-music tradition from
the 16th to the 18th centuries, and an indispensable work of scholarship. It provides
not only an extended account of the development of the repertoire, examining in turn
intonation, modal (*makam*) structure, the improvised *taksim* and the major composed
forms, *peşrev* and *semai*, but also the broader historical context, dealing with the
social position of music and its performers, and the evolution of the various instruments used.

1131 **Ottoman sources on the development of the taksîm.**
Walter Feldman. *Yearbook for Traditional Music*, vol. 25 (1993),
p. 1-28.
Contains two articles by a leading western authority on the history of Turkish music.
The first deals with the evolution of forms and repertoire, and modern attitudes to the
tradition, while the second covers the evolution of an important form of instrumental
improvisation.

1132 **The ideology of musical practice and the professional Turkish
folk musician: tempering the creative impulse.**
Irene Markoff. *Asian Music*, vol. 22, no. 1 (1990-91), p. 129-45.
After a brief overview of developments in modern Turkish history, the author discusses the current trends of thought within the Turkish folk music community
concerning contemporary performance practice and the ways in which these trends
affect the image and identity of folk musical culture in Turkey.

1133 **Introduction to Sufi music and ritual in Turkey.**
Irene Markoff. *Middle East Association Bulletin*, vol. 29, no. 2
(1995), p. 157-60.
The author provides a brief outline of the music and ritual (dance) of Anatolian
Sufism. She also provides a list of recordings available at the time of writing.

1134 **Türk mûsikîsi nazariyatı ve ûsulleri. Kudüm velveleri.** (The theory
and rhythmic cycles of Turkish music.)
İsmail Hakkı Özkan. İstanbul: Ötüken Neşriyatı, 1984. 690p.
bibliog.
The book provides an authoritative statement of orthodox, late 20th-century theory
regarding the structure of the various melodic modes (*makam*), and rhythmic cycles
(*usul*), abundantly illustrated by representative compositions.

1135 **Türk musikisi ansiklopedisi.** (An encyclopaedia of Turkish music.)
Yılmaz Öztuna. İstanbul: Millî Eğitim Basımevi, 1969-76. 2 vols.
As the only general encyclopaedia on Turkish music, this is an indispensable if occasionally subjective work of reference. Despite its scrupulous citation of historical
sources, it needs to be approached with a degree of caution.

1136 **Folk musical instruments of Turkey.**
Laurence Picken. London: Oxford University Press, 1975. 685p.
maps. bibliog.
This is a monumental work of scholarship which distils the results of extensive fieldwork. It remains unequalled not only for its detailed accounts of materials and
manufacturing processes and for the comprehensiveness of its coverage, including, for
example, various children's instruments, but also for its contextualization and breadth
of vision, culminating in an erudite and challenging essay on diffusion.

1137 **Makam: modal practice in Turkish art music.**
Karl L. Signell. Seattle, Washington: Asian Music Publications,
1977; New York: Da Capo Press, 1986. 200p.
Benefitting from consultations with the distinguished *tanbur* player Necdet Yaşar, this
is the most comprehensive study in English of modal practice in the classical tradition.
After introductory sections on the historical and contemporary repertoire, it explores,
with numerous examples, intonation, modal (*makam*) structure and melodic contour,
formulaic motifs, and the important and frequently neglected topic of modulation
between *makams*.

1138 **The Arabesque debate: music and musicians in modern Turkey.**
Martin Stokes. Oxford: Clarendon Press, 1992. 265p.
An important recent addition to the available literature on Turkish music, this work
avoids the fields of folk and art-music to concentrate on a particular form of urban
popular music and its relationship with other traditions. Especially enlightening are
the extensive analyses of the social context within which performers of *arabesk*
operate, the concepts underpinning it, and the ideological debate surrounding it.

1139 **The rise of a spontaneous synthesis: the historical background to Turkish popular music.**
Orhan Tekelioğlu. *Middle Eastern Studies*, vol. 32, no. 2 (1996), p. 194-215.

This informative and interesting article discusses the present state of all forms of Turkish music in the context of history and politics.

1140 **Mecmûa-i sâz ü söz.**
'Ali Ufki. In: *Ali Ufki: hayatı, eserleri ve mecmûa-i sâz ü söz (tıpkı basım)* (Ali Ufki: his life, works and 'Mecmûa-i sâz ü söz'). Edited by Şükrü Elçin. İstanbul: Millî Eğitim Basımevi, 1976. 328p. bibliog. (Kültür Bakanlığı, Türk Musiki Eserleri, no. 1).

This collection constitutes one of the earliest noted records on a large scale of any Middle Eastern tradition. It covers much of the vocal and instrumental repertoire of 17th-century İstanbul, and provides vital evidence about the nature and development of Ottoman music over the last three centuries. Written in the middle of the 17th century in Western notation (but from right to left) by a palace musician of Polish origin, it is published here in a rather fuzzy facsimile of the original manuscript (British Library, MS Sloane 3114). It contains a mixture of instrumental and vocal compositions.

1141 **Aspects of historical change in the Turkish classical repertoire.**
Owen Wright. In: *Musica Asiatica*. Edited by Richard Widdess. Cambridge, England: Cambridge University Press, 1988, p. 1-108.

17th-century collections of Turkish instrumental art-music include pieces that remain in the repertoire today. There is a high degree of melodic elaboration in the modern versions of some of these, compared with the simpler versions recorded in 17th-century sources. The author shows that a process of gradual amplification, necessarily accompanied by a reduction in speed of performance, has occurred, and that the process of change was already underway in the 17th century, and had largely been completed by the 19th century.

1142 **Words without songs. A musicological study of an early Ottoman anthology and its precursors.**
Owen Wright. London: University of London, School of Oriental and African Studies, 1992. 321p. map. bibliog. (SOAS Musicology Series, no. 3).

The author claims that the most characteristic Ottoman form of musical literature is to be found in the song-text collections attested from at least the 17th century. Their antecedents are earlier examples (for example from the 15th century) in Arabic and Persian. The first section of the book provides a survey of the three examples of this earlier tradition; the second section is devoted to an analysis of a 17th-century collection and its three variants; and the third section places both traditions in their wider contexts.

Dans, Müzik, Kültür, Çeviri, Araştırma Dergisi. (Folklora Doğru).
(Journal of Dance, Music, Culture, Translation, Research.)
See item no. 1325.
International Journal of Music in Turkey.
See item no. 1334.

Theatre and film

Theatre

1143 A history of theatre and popular entertainment in Turkey.

Metin And.   Ankara: Forum Yayınları, 1963-64. 144p. bibliog.

Although rather outdated, this volume is still one of the few books in English on
Turkish theatre. In part one, the author discusses the traditional Turkish theatre (guild
pageants, festivals, popular Turkish theatre, Karagöz, rural plays and dances). Part two
deals with the Ottoman theatre from the 19th century to 1923 and theatre during the
Republic. The last section contains 244 photographs illustrating forms of entertainment from Ottoman times to the 1960s.

1144 Origins and development of the Turkish theatre.

Metin And.   *Review of National Literatures*, vol. 4, no. 1 (1973),
p. 53-64.

The article discusses the direct effect of Western theatre in Turkey, covering the four
major theatrical traditions: folk theatre, popular theatre, court theatre and westernized
theatre.

1145 Culture, performance and communication in Turkey.

Metin And.   Tokyo: Institute for the Study of Languages and Cultures
of Asia and Africa, 1987. 233p. (Performance in Culture, no. 4).

The book consists of three parts: the first surveys Turco-Asian, Islamic, Western and
Anatolian local cultures; the second introduces four performance traditions (folk, popular, court, western); and the last discusses the interrelation between language,
communication and symbolism. The book emphasizes the symbolic, communicative
importance of performances in Turkey in the past and today.

1146 Karagöz: Turkish shadow theatre.

Metin And.   İstanbul: Dost Yayınları, 1987. 3rd rev. ed. 116p.
bibliog.

The book discusses the origins and development of the shadow theatre in an historical
perspective, in Turkey, in the Far East and in other parts of the world, before turning

to *Karagöz*. Its technique, characters and some representative scenarios are given in this informative and entertaining book.

1147 **Drama at the crossroads: Turkish performing arts link past and present, East and West.**
Metin And. İstanbul: Isis Press, 1991. 185p. bibliog.
The author sets out to discover the 'crossroads' where Turkey's 'spiritual' and 'cultural' inheritance meet. He discusses the basic patterns of the rituals and the early theatre of the ancient cultures of the Near East, and of Turkic and Islamic countries, before attempting to clarify the relationship between the two.

1148 **Turkish theatre: autonomous entity to multicultural compound.**
Petra de Bruijn. In: *Theatre intercontinental: forms, functions, correspondences.* Edited by C. C. Barfoot, C. Bordewijk.
Amsterdam; Atlanta, Georgia: Rodopi, B. V., 1993, p. 175-92.
From Anatolian village drama to folk theatre and westernized theatre, the article provides a brief history of the development of the Turkish theatre.

1149 **Turkey.**
Nutku Özdemir, Sevda Şenel, Ayşegül Yüksel. In: *The world encyclopedia of contemporary theatre.* Edited by Don Rubin.
London: Routledge, 1994, vol. 1, p. 852-69.
The entry on the Turkish theatre summarizes the history, roots and developments of modern Turkish theatre. It provides information on the contemporary structure of the national theatre of Turkey, theatre companies and most prominent plays and directors. There are also sections on music and dance theatre, design, criticism, research and writings related to theatre in Turkey.

1150 **The drum beats nightly: the development of Turkish drama as a vehicle for social and political comment in the post-revolutionary period: 1924 to the present.**
Bruce Robson. Tokyo: The Centre for East Asian Cultural Studies, 1976. 278p. (East Asian Cultural Studies Series, no. 17).
A critical study of modern Turkish drama which briefly looks at its historical origins (shadow play and traditional popular theatre) and influences (Europe) and then traces the gradual process by which social and then political (1960s) themes took centre stage. Several plays are examined in detail.

1151 **The Turkish shadow theatre and the puppet collection of the L. A. Mayer Memorial Foundation.**
Andreas Tietze. Berlin: Gebr. Mann Verlag, 1977. 70p.
The volume presents the puppets belonging to the L. A. Mayer Memorial Foundation. A short outline of the Turkish shadow theatre is given to enable the reader to understand the puppets. The translation of a typical play is included, as well as an explanation of the characters presented in the play. The book contains 137 plates representing the characters and showpieces used in the plays.

1152   **Modern Turkish theatre.**
Bedia Turgay-Ahmad.   *Review of National Literatures*, vol. 4, no. 1 (1973), p. 65-81.
The article summarizes Turkish entertainment before the 19th century, and discusses the westernization of entertainment, the national theatre, Turkish political drama, the new Turkish theatre, the role of the People's Houses, state and private theatres, and Turkish theatre in the 1970s.

1153   **Turkish games for health and recreation.**
Barbara K. Walker, Warren S. Walker.   Lubbock, Texas: Archive of Turkish Oral Narrative, Texas University Library, 1983. 41p.

The transformation of Turkish culture.
See item no. 16.

Turkey: from empire to nation.
See item no. 988.

Modern Turkish drama: an anthology of plays in translation.
See item no. 994.

Short dramas from contemporary Turkish literature.
See item no. 997.

Agon Tiyatro.
See item no. 1309.

Mimesis. Tiyatro, Çeviri, Araştırma Dergisi.
See item no. 1348.

Tiyatro Araştırmaları Dergisi. (Journal of Drama Research.)
See item no. 1362.

Prof. Dr. Metin And bibliyografyası. (A bibliography of Prof. Metin And's works.)
See item no. 1423.

Film

1154   **Centre vs. periphery: visual representation of the party scenes in Yeşilçam melodramas.**
Savaş Arslan.   MA thesis, Bilkent University, Ankara, 1997.
(Available from Bilkent University Library).
This study analyses the party scenes in Turkish melodrama between the early 1960s and the mid-1970s with respect to their visual representation. Arslan interprets the representation of the party scenes and the party youth in Turkish melodrama, on the basis of an antagonism between the centre and the periphery within the social context of Turkey, and in relation to the project of westernization.

1155   **Gender & Media.**
Edited by Nevena Dakovic, Deniz Derman, Karen Ross.   Ankara:
Med-Campus Project no. A126 Publications, MEDIATION, 1996.
280p.

This book is concerned with the representation of women in the media contexts of
film, print, music and broadcasting. It includes three essays on the representation of
women in Turkish cinema: 'Double faced women in Turkish melodrama and the split
structure of the political, economic and social system in Turkey' by Serhat Günaydın;
'The reflections of Turkish woman's status in Berdel' by Fatma Küçükkurt; and
'Mother-daughter relationship in the family melodrama: Teyzem' by Deniz Derman.

1156   **Turkish cinema.**
Edited by Nezih Erdoğan.
<http://www.art.bilkent.edu.tr/studies/cinstd.html>.

This page dedicated to cinema studies offers several interesting research articles on
Turkish cinema: 'Representations of the nuclear family and acquirement of gender
roles in Yeşilçam melodrama' by Osman Sezgin; '"Kara gözlüm": a case of mistaken
national identity and colonial discourse' by Nezih Erdoğan; and 'Yeşilçam versus television: "Love goddess"' by Nezih Erdoğan. Moreover, there is a section devoted to
the film 'Köçek' (Boy dancer), made in 1975 by Nejat Saydam. The articles on the
film are: 'Destroyed self and sexual identity: the case of "Köçek"' by Savaş Aslan;
'Gender and gaze in "Köçek"' by Çetin Sarıkartal; 'Woman as symptom of man: a
study of "Köçek"' by Ahmet Gürata; '"Köçek": a field of games' by Jeremy Steel;
and a review of the film in 'Gender and split identity in "Köçek"' by Nezih Erdoğan.

1157   **Türk sineması. Turkish cinema.**
Nezih Erdoğan.
<http://www.geocities.com/Hollywood/Cinema/3492/>.

Nezih Erdoğan's page 'aims to share sources, questions and problems with those who
are interested in Turkish cinema'. The contents of the web page are: 'Turkish films
index (1914-96)'; 'Sources in Turkish'; 'Sources in English', and 'Related links'.

1158   **Narratives of resistance: national identity and ambivalence in the
Turkish melodrama between 1965 and 1975.**
Nezih Erdoğan.   *Screen*, vol. 39, no. 3 (1998), p. 259-72.

Examines the dynamics by which Turkish popular cinema describes a national identity
by making use of postcolonial theory. The article describes the identity crisis that took
hold of Turkish cinema between the mid-1960s and the mid-1970s by referring to the
debates about national identity in Turkish cinema. The article concentrates on the
characteristics of Turkish melodrama as a popular genre, and analyses the film
'Karagözlüm' (My dark-eyed one) with respect to the problem of national identity as a
derivative of colonial discourse.

1159   **Filmic space in Turkish melodrama.**
Ahmet Gürata.   MA thesis, Bilkent University, Ankara, 1997.
(Available from Bilkent University Library).
This study analyses filmic space in Turkish melodrama between the years 1960-75, in the light of theoretical approaches to filmic space. It evaluates Turkish melodrama in terms of the formal aspects of filmic space by focusing on mise-en-scène, editing and sound, and the cultural and ideological preferences which influence the representation of space.

1160   **Representing romance: an investigation of design and significance in the posters of Turkish melodrama 1965-1975.**
Nazlı Eda Noyan.   MA thesis, Bilkent University, Ankara, 1998.
(Available from Bilkent University Library).
This study investigates the design and signification of posters of Turkish melodrama between 1965 and 1975, by focusing on the representation of romance. After an examination of the evolution of the film posters in Turkey, the study presents a classification of the Turkish melodrama posters with respect to their graphic characteristics and conveyed images. The study can be viewed at <http://www.geocities.com/Hollywood/Cinema/3492/>.

1161   **A chronological history of the Turkish cinema, 1914-1988.**
Agah Özgüç, translated from the Turkish by Giovanni Scognamillo.
Ankara: Ministry of Culture and Tourism, 1988. 127p. bibliog.
The book analyses the evolution of Turkish cinema since its first film in 1914, and evaluates the most distinguished films individually. The analysis relies on the results of festivals, competitions and 'the best Turkish film' lists of cinema journals in Turkey. The book includes various photographs from old and new Turkish films.

1162   **80. yılında Türk sineması. Turkish cinema at the 80th anniversary. 1914-1994.**
Agah Özgüç.   Ankara: T. C. Kültür Bakanlığı, 1988. 303p. bibliog.
A history of Turkish cinema, published to commemorate its eightieth anniversary, in Turkish and English.

1163   **Türk sinema tarihi.** (A history of Turkish cinema.)
Giovanni Scognomillo. İstanbul: Metis Yayınları, 1990. 2 vols.
The book describes the evolution and the activities of the Turkish film industry between 1896 and 1986, from a historical and sociological perspective. It documents all available information about every film made during this period, without placing the films in a hierarchical order in terms of artistic value. The book also covers the formation process, the purpose and the social appreciation of the films through quotations from related writings in journals and newspapers published during this ninety-year period. The photographs and the illustrations provided by the author increase the importance of this book, which is one of the first works of its kind. The book is in Turkish but there is an English summary.

1164   **Speaking the experience of political oppression with a masculine voice: making feminist sense of Yılmaz Güney's 'Yol'.**
Asuman Suner.   *Social Identities*, vol. 4, no. 2 (1998), p. 283-301.

The article offers a critical reading of Yılmaz Güney's film 'Yol' in the light of recent debates in postcolonial and feminist film studies. It refers to the perception of 'Yol' by the Turkish public, and to the issues of ethnic identities, gender relations and state oppression in Turkey during the period following the 1980 military coup. Besides a detailed description of the film, the article includes information about Güney's life and cinematography.

1165   **Turkish cinema.**
Edited by Christine Woodhead.   London: School of Oriental and African Studies, 1989. 43p. bibliog. (Turkish Area Study Group Publications).

A collection of short essays on Turkish cinema, which were originally papers presented at a conference.

Gece Yarısı Sineması. (Midnight Cinema.)
See item no. 1331.

25. Kare. (25th Square.)
See item no. 1340.

SineMasal. (Cine-tale / Cinematic.)
See item no. 1359.

Textiles and Costumes

Textiles

1166 A foreshadowing of 21st century art: the color and geometry of very early Turkish carpets.
Christopher Alexander.   New York: Oxford University Press, 1993.
352p. (Center for Environmental Structure, no. 7).
The author owns one of the finest collections of early Turkish carpets outside the
İstanbul museums. This book discusses the provenance of each carpet, and contains
eighty colour photographs and line drawings.

1167 Return to tradition: the revitalization of Turkish village carpets.
June Anderson.   Seattle, Washington: University of Washington
Press, 1998. 96p. bibliog.
Describes the rebirth of an almost extinct tradition of hand-knotted Turkish carpets
made in remote villages of the Aegean, and the lives of the women who make them.
As a result of a unique project, natural dyes were reintroduced and village coopera-
tives were formed to organize the production and marketing of the carpets. The book
includes 168 illustrations.

1168 Yayla: Form und Farbe in türkischer Textilkunst. (Yayla: form
and colour in Turkish textile art.)
Werner Brüggemann with Ursula Brüggemann.   Frankfurt am Main,
Germany: Museum für Kunsthandwerk; Berlin: Museum für
Islamische Kunst, 1993. 424p. bibliog.
This is the catalogue of an exhibition on Turkish textiles, which was held in Berlin (26
May-1 August 1993) and in Frankfurt am Main (9 December-4 April 1994).

1169 **Oriental rugs: a comprehensive guide.**
Murrey L. Eiland. Boston, Massachusetts: New York Graphic
Society, 1976. 214p. 3 maps. bibliog.
A comprehensive guide to 19th- and 20th-century Persian, Turkish, Turcoman and
Caucasian rugs. It is designed to serve all collectors and others interested in this area.
It covers both old and new rugs, provides a history of the art of weaving, and
describes basic rug-making materials, tools, techniques, dyes and various types of
knotting techniques. It has over 200 illustrations.

1170 **A wealth of silk and velvet: Ottoman fabrics and embroideries.**
Edited by Christian Erber with contributions by Gisela Helmecke,
translated from the German by Michaela Nierhaus. Bremen,
Germany: Edition Temmen, 1993. 288p. bibliog.
This is the catalogue of an exhibition on Ottoman fabrics and embroideries held at the
Altonaer Museum in Hamburg (25 May-15 August 1993) in conjunction with the 7th
International Conference on Oriental Carpets.

1171 **Living with kilims.**
A. Hull, N. Barnard, J. Merrell. London: Thames & Hudson, 1995.
reprint. 192p.
This book gives detailed information about kilims. It also provides information for
collectors and auction houses, and has suggestions for further reading on kilims.

1172 **Turkish carpets.**
J. Iten-Maritz. New York: Kodansha International, 1977. 353p.
This translation of the German work *Der anatolische Teppich* is one of the few books
to fully cover Turkish carpets. It gives some historical background, discusses the
development of this art, and includes colour illustrations of rugs.

1173 **Turkish embroidery.**
Pauline Johnstone. London: Victoria & Albert Museum, 1985. 96p.
Contains colour plates and black-and-white photographs of the collection at Victoria
and Albert Museum in London, which contains Ottoman embroidery from the 17th to
the early 20th centuries. There is a twenty-two page introduction.

1174 **The rugs and textiles of Hereke: a documentary account of the
history of Hereke: court workshop to model factory.**
Önder Küçükerman, Maggie Quigley Pınar. Ankara: Sümerbank
Genel Müdürlüğü, 1987. 247p. bibiog.
This book, illustrated with photographs and drawings, provides a history of the rug
factory at Hereke and its methods of production.

1175 **Yörük: the nomadic weaving tradition of the Middle East.**
Edited by Anthony N. Landreau. Pittsburg, Pennsylvania: Museum of Art, Carnegie Institute, 1978. 144p. bibliog.
This is the catalogue of an exhibition held at the Museum of Art, Carnegie Institute, Pittsburg (6 April-28 May 1978), at the Field Museum of Natural History, Chicago (22 June-22 August 1978), and at the Worcester Art Museum, Worcester (12 September-5 November 1978).

1176 **Flowers of the yayla. Yörük weaving of the Toros mountains.**
Anthony N. Landreau, Ralph S. Yohe. Seattle, Washington: University of Washington Press, 1983. 112p. bibliog.
The book introduces the reader to Yörük weavings, which are unique in colour, design and technique, and yet were made for everyday use such as camel and saddle bags, grain and storage boxes, and rugs. The work contains 100 illustrations.

1177 **Rugs and textiles.**
Louise W. Mackie. In: *Turkish art.* Edited by Esin Atıl.
Washington, DC: Smithsonian Institution, 1980, p. 299-373.
This is a clearly written, well-illustrated account of Ottoman Turkish court garments, woven silks and types of carpets.

1178 **The goddess from Anatolia.**
James Mellaart, Udo Hirsch, Belkıs Balpınar. Milan, Italy: Eskenazi, 1989. 4 vols. maps.
Volume one (Udo Hirsch) contains plates and text; volume two (James Mellaart) deals with Çatal Hüyük and Anatolian kilims; volume three (Udo Hirsch) covers the environment, the economy, cult and culture; and volume four (Belkıs Balpınar) is devoted to *kilims* of the past and present.

1179 **Yastıks: cushion covers and storage bags of Anatolia.**
Brian Morehouse. Philadelphia, Pennsylvania: Philadelphia 8th ICOC, 1996. 109p. bibliog.
This volume was published to accompany an exhibition held at the Eight International Conference on Oriental Carpets (ICOC) at Philadelphia, Pennsylvania.

1180 **Turkish embroidery.**
Gülseren Ramazanoğlu. İstanbul: Ramazanoğlu Publications, 1987. 2nd ed. 104p.
Covers the history of Turkish embroidery from the 16th century to the present, including an explanation of the stitches, designs and colours used. Colour illustrations show embroidered decorations, furnishings and clothing from the time of the Sultans to the 1980s.

1181 **Islamic carpets and textiles in the Keir collection.**
Friedrich Spuhler. London: Faber & Faber, 1979. 251p.
Two chapters of this book, which contains 146 illustrations, are devoted to classical
Ottoman and Turkish carpets, and silk textiles.

1182 **Türklerde çiçek sevgisi ve *Sümbülname*. (Turkish love of flowers and *Sümbülname*).**
Sabiha Tansuğ. İstanbul: Akbank Yayınları, 1988. 72p.
In the context of the book *Sümbülname* (1736), the author illustrates the Turkish love
for flowers as depicted in miniatures, textiles, embroidery and prints. The book is both
in Turkish and English, and contains photographs.

1183 **Ottoman embroidery.**
Roderick Taylor. Wesel, Germany: V. Hulsey, 1993. 224p.
The book looks at a whole range of embroidered textiles produced within the Ottoman
Empire. It draws widely on textiles from private and museum collections in Turkey,
Europe and America, covering a wide range of examples from handkerchiefs and
robes to decorated tents. It includes 140 coloured plates, and over 50 line drawings.
The sections of the book are entitled: 'Background to an Empire'; 'The embroidered
textiles'; 'Large embroideries'; 'Influence of the Ottomans'; 'Designs and patters';
'Materials'; 'Techniques'; and 'Collectors and collection'.

1184 **Atlaslar atlası: pamuklu, yün ve ipek kumaş kolleksiyonu (Cotton, woolen and silk fabrics collection).**
Hülya Tezcan. İstanbul: Yapı Kredi Yayınları, 1993. 272p. bibliog.
(Yapı Kredi Collections, no. 3: Catalogue of the Yapı Kredi Bankası
Textile Collection).
Reviews the history of Turkish textiles, including an account of fabrics, dyes and
decoration. This is followed by a fully illustrated catalogue of the textiles collection of
the Bank, which includes samples from the 17th to the 19th centuries. The text is in
Turkish and English.

1185 **Floral messages: from Ottoman court embroideries to Anatolian trousseau chests.**
Ulla Ther, Michaella Nierhus. Bremen, Germany: Temmen, 1993.
300p. bibliog.
Turkish domestic embroideries are usually seen as being unworthy of serious study,
but here Ulla Ther successfully proves the opposite. This beautifully produced and
well prepared book is the catalogue to an exhibition on domestic embroideries held at
the Altonaer Museum in Hamburg. The volume begins with an introduction to the
types of domestic embroideries and nomenclature which covers the following subjects: their use, role and appreciation; materials and techniques; the origin,
development and symbolism of the motifs used; dating; provenance and ethnic group;
and collections and museums. The introduction is followed by a section of coloured
plates of the collection pieces. This book will be invaluable for all those interested in
embroidery.

1186   **Kilim: history and symbols.**
Dario Valcarenghi.   Milan, Italy: Electra, 1994. 214p. bibliog.
Deals with the myths and history of the Anatolian kilim, and the meanings of the
different symbols in the designs.

1187   **Turkish flat weaves: an introduction to the weaving culture of
Anatolia.**
William T. Ziemba, Abdülkadir Akatay, Sandra L. Schwartz.
Vancouver: Yörük Carpets and Kilims, 1979. 143p. map. bibliog.
The work contains a brief introduction to Anatolian geography and history, followed
by chapters on the preparation of wool, dyeing, weave types, representative technical
analyses (of the plates in the book) and designs. A bibliography is followed by a sec-
tion of colour plates and black-and-white photographs of the area and the people.

1188   **Fancy feet: traditional knitting patterns of Turkey.**
Anna Zilboorg.   London: Cassell, 1995. 128p.
This knitting pattern book contains forty-five designs for traditional Turkish knitted
socks, and provides complete instructions and charts.

Costumes

1189   **Picturesque representations of the dress and manners of the
Turks.**
William Alexander.   London: Miller, 1814. 60p. of plates.
The volume contains clear, single figure studies which illustrate the city dress of men
and women of the 19th-century Ottoman Empire, and includes sixty colour engrav-
ings.

1190   **Character and costume in Turkey and Italy.**
Thomas Allom.   London: Fisher Son & Co., 1845. 48p.
The book contains accurate descriptions and illustrations of Ottoman dress in the 19th
century.

1191   **Les anciens costumes de l'Empire Ottoman depuis l'origine de la
monarchie jusqu'a la reforme du Sultan Mahmoud.** (Ancient
costumes from the Ottoman Empire from the beginnings of the
monarchy to the reform of Sultan Mahmud.)
Arif Pacha.   Paris: Imp. de A. Laine & J. Havard, 1863. 47p.
The book contains coloured illustrations of official and military Ottoman dress before
the introduction of western fashions.

1192   **The pattern of a caftan said to have been worn by Selim I (1512-20) from the Topkapı Sarayı Museum.**
Janet Arnold.   *Costume: Journal of the Costume Society*, no. 2 (1968), p. 49-52.
This article describes the *caftan,* and is accompanied by notes on the cut and construction, and by drawings of the pattern pieces.

1193   **Three centuries: family chronicles of Turkey and Egypt.**
Emine Foat Tugay.   London: Oxford University Press, 1963. 323p.
The memoirs of an upper-class İstanbul family during the late 19th and early 20th centuries, which include descriptions of their dresses and social life.

1194   **The influence of Ottoman Turkish textiles and costume in Eastern Europe with particular reference to Hungary.**
Veronika Gervers.   Toronto: Royal Ontario Museum, 1982. 168p. bibliog.
A thorough and scholarly analysis of Ottoman textiles and costumes in eastern Europe. The book includes illustrations taken from the collections of the Royal Ontario Museum. A useful account of primary sources (such as household inventories) is also included.

1195   **Arabesque.**
Musbah Haidar.   London: Methuen, 1944. 244p.
The memoirs of an upper-class İstanbul family in the late 19th and early 20th centuries, with accounts of their dress and social life. It contains twelve black-and-white photographs, including family and group portraits.

1196   **The Turkish dresses in the Costume-book of Rubens.**
Otto Kurz.   In: *The decorative arts of Europe and the Islamic East, selected studies XV.*   Edited by Otto Kurz.   London: Pindar, 1977, p. 275-90.
This scholarly article discusses the impact of Turkish dress on European fashion and theatrical costume in the 17th and 18th centuries.

1197   **Languages of dress in the Middle East.**
Edited by Nancy Lindisfarne-Tapper, Bruce Ingham.   London: Curzon Press, 1997. 240p.
A study of the way in which the languages of dress connect with other social practices in the region, and with political, religious conformity. The book also discusses the dress reform laws of Turkey.

1198   **Les costumes populaires de la Turquie en 1873. Ouvrage publiee sous le Patronat de la Commission Imperiale Ottomane pour l'Exposition universelle de Vienne.** (Popular costumes in Turkey in 1873. Work published under the Patronage of the Imperial Ottoman Commission for the Universal Exhibition in Vienna.)
Osman Hamdy Bey, Marie de Launay.   Constantinople: Impr. du 'Levant Times & Shipping Gazette', 1873. 319p.
A photographic record of Ottoman city and provincial dress.

1199   **The harem: an account of the institution as it existed in the Palace of the Turkish Sultans, with a history of the Seraglio from its foundation to modern times.**
Norman Mosley Penzer.   London: Spring Books, 1965. 277p.
A standard account of the Topkapı Palace, which includes descriptions of court furnishings.

1200   **Clothing laws, state and society in the Ottoman Empire, 1720-1829.**
Donald Quataert.   *International Journal of Middle Eastern Studies*, vol. 29, no. 3 (1997), p. 403-25.
Provides the 'histories of transformation, elite formation, centralization, and state building in a new way, through the prism of regulations on the attire that the state required its servants and subjects to wear'. Section one of the article covers the clothing legislation of 1720-1808, while section two deals with the clothing revolution of Sultan Mahmud II. Eighty-two detailed endnotes and photographs accompany this exceptionally informative article which must be read by all those interested in Ottoman clothing.

1201   **Empire of the sultans: Ottoman art from the collection of Nasser D. Khalili.**
J. M. Rogers.   Geneva: Musée d'art et d'histoire; London: Nour Foundation in Association with Azimuth Editions, 1995. 285p. maps. bibliog.
This is the catalogue of an exhibition on Ottoman art and textiles, which was held at the Musée Rath, Geneva (7 July-24 September 1995).

1202   **Turquerie: Turkish dress and English fashion in the eighteenth century.**
Aileen Ribeiro.   *Connoisseur*, vol. 201, no. 807 (1979), p. 16-23.
This article discusses the use of Turkish dress as evening and masquerade wear in England during the 18th century.

1203 **Süleyman the Magnificent.**
J. M. Rogers, R. M. Ward. London: British Museum Publications, 1988. 225p. bibliog.

A lavishly illustrated and detailed catalogue of the exhibition 'Süleyman, the Magnificent' held at the British Museum between 18 February and 30 May 1988. Among the objects described and discussed are items of dress and accessories worn by members of Suleiman's family and court.

1204 **Turkish fashion in transition.**
Jennifer Scarce. *Costume: Journal of the Costume Society*, no. 14 (1980), p. 144-67.

The article is a detailed study of a woman's complete costume worn in upper-class İstanbul society around 1875. The costume is now on permanent display in the Royal Museum of Scotland, Edinburgh.

1205 **Women's costume of the Near and Middle East.**
Jennifer Scarce. London: Unwin Hyman, 1987. 192p. bibliog.

Traces the historical development and principal fashions of the Ottoman Empire, its provinces in Europe, and the Arab world, using examples from the Royal Museum of Scotland's collections. The book includes over 100 illustrations.

1206 **Principles of Ottoman Turkish costume.**
Jennifer Scarce. *Costume*, vol. 22 (1988), p. 12-31.

The author examines how Ottoman costumes had more functions than merely satisfying the needs of warmth, protection and modesty. Dealing with Ottoman costumes during the period 1500-1899, the author uses diaries, paintings and historical records to illustrate the relationship between Ottoman clothes, social status, and the maintenance of social order.

1207 **Domestic culture in the Middle East: an exploration of the household interior.**
Jennifer Scarce. London: Curzon Press with the National Museums of Scotland, 1996. 112p. bibliog.

This is a general study of domestic and social life in the three cities of İstanbul, Cairo and Tehran. The author uses examples from the 16th to the 19th centuries to look at the way in which Middle Eastern architects and artisans created the diverse interiors, and how writers and scholars shaped the understanding of space. The work contains a discussion of dress and household textiles, and has ninety-four illustrations.

1208 **Three years in Constantinople or domestic manners of the Turks in 1844.**
Charles White.   London: H. Colburn, 1846. 2nd ed. 3 vols. map.
This thorough account includes meticulous descriptions of Ottoman dress and accessories, such as cosmetics, fabric and clothing retail markets, and festivals where ceremonial dress is both displayed and worn.

Turkish embassy letters.
See item no. 33.

Food

1209 Classical Turkish cooking: traditional Turkish food for the American kitchen.
Ayla Esen Algar. New York: Harper Collins, 1991. 320p. bibliog.

Includes discussions of Turkish culinary etymology and history, personalized portrayals of places, holidays and rites of passage, as well as recipes. The book has received much praise from readers and cookery specialists because of its clear description of recipes and unfamiliar cooking techniques. It also contains recipes for ingredients which may not be easy to obtain, such as rose-water.

1210 The complete book of Turkish cooking.
Ayla Esen Algar. London: Kegan Paul International, 1995. 3rd ed. 344p.

This is a practical guide to the techniques and ingredients of Turkish cooking. It also gives a history of the cuisine, and the cultural and religious significance of the dishes described.

1211 Timeless tastes: Turkish culinary culture.
Project director Semahat Arsel, edited by Ersu Pekin, Ayşe Sümer. İstanbul: Vehbi Koç Vakfı, 1996. 297p. bibliog. (Vehbi Koç Vakfı Publications, no. 7).

The book contains Turkish dishes to suit every taste.

1212 Classic Turkish cookery.
Ghillie Basan, Jonathan Basan. London: I. B. Tauris, 1997. 256p.

A collection of recipes for both traditional Anatolian and Ottoman dishes from the imperial Palace. The descriptions are clear, and the book contains information about the spices and the ingredients, together with details about healthy qualities of authentic cooking. The book contains over 100 colour photographs.

1213   **Nurten Çevik's cookbook: selected menus.**
Compiled by Mine Çevik.   Ankara: Turkish Daily News, 1995.
2nd ed. 256p.
The recipes in the book are by Nurten Çevik and were originally published in the
Turkish Daily News during the period 1980-85 in her column. They have been brought
together by her daughter in Nurten Çevik's memory. The book contains 42 menus and
125 recipes. Ninety per cent of the recipes are of Turkish dishes, are easy to make, and
have been tried and tested.

1214   **The delights of Turkish cooking.**
Neşet Eren.   İstanbul: Redhouse, 1988. 248p.
This is a collection of selected recipes from Turkish cuisine by a master cook.

1215   **The art of Turkish cooking.**
Neşet Eren.   London: Hippocrene, 1993. 308p. (International
Cookbook Classics).
In this volume, the author, who is an authority on Turkish cooking, gives recipes for
dishes ranging from appetizers to desserts.

1216   **Nevin Halıcı's Turkish cookbook.**
Nevin Halıcı.   London: Dorling Kindersley, 1989. 176p. bibliog.
The author is a lecturer in nutrition. Her interest in local culture extends to cooking,
and she has included many recipes from her native Konya region.

1217   **Turkish cookery book.**
Turabi Efendi.   Rottingdean, England: Cooks Books, 1987. 82p.
(Reprinted from the 1862 original as a limited edition of 250 copies).
The facsimile edition of a book described in Turkish on its title page, and translated
into English, as 'A collection of receipts, dedicated to those royal and distinguished
personages, the guests of his Highness the late Viceroy of Egypt, on the occasion of
the banquet given at Woolwich, on board his Highness's yacht the Faiz-Jehad, the
16th July 1862. Compiled by Turabi Efendi from the best Turkish authorities'. With
253 recipes, this is a valuable source of information on Ottoman cookery.

1218   **Turkish cooking: a culinary journey through Turkey.**
Carol Robertson.   San Francisco, California: Frog Ltd, 1996. 224p.
The book travels through Turkey via its cuisine. The recipes are preceded by twelve
'Traveller's tales of Turkey'. There are recipes for popular mezes, soups, meat dishes,
seafood, vegetable dishes, pilavs, bread, desserts and beverages.

1219   **The Sultan's kitchen: a Turkish cookbook.**
Özcan Ozan.   New York: Periplus Editions, 1998. 160p.
The author is a chef trained in Turkey and in France, and owns a well-known restaurant
in Boston, which has won several prizes. He provides easy-to-follow recipes which
aim to recreate dishes from his restaurant in the home kitchen. The book contains 130
recipes and complete menu suggestions. The beautiful colour photographs are by Carl
Tremblay. The book has received much praise from reviewers.

Food

Eat smart in Turkey: how to decipher the menu, know the market foods and embark on a tasting adventure.
See item no. 62.

Cornucopia. Turkey for Connoisseurs.
See item no. 1323.

Geleneksel Türk mutfağı bibliografyası üzerine bir deneme. (A bibliography of traditional Turkish cookery.)
See item no. 1406.

Museums, Libraries and Archives

Museums

1220 1950-2000.
Edited by Ali Artun.   Ankara: The Central Bank of the Republic of
Turkey, 1994. 215p.
A catalogue of paintings and sculptures by contemporary Turkish artists, who are the
representatives of recent trends and styles in Turkish art.

1221 Flatweaves of the Vakıflar Museum, İstanbul.
Belkıs Balpınar, Udo Hirsch.   Wesel, Germany: Hulsey, 1982. 295p.
bibliog.
The book introduces the Vakıflar Museum and its collection of flatweaves. The text is
in English and German.

1222 Carpets of the Vakıflar Museum, İstanbul.
Belkıs Balpınar, Udo Hirsch.   Wesel, Germany: Hulsey, 1988. 343p.
map.
The book introduces the Vakıflar Museum and its carpet collection. The text is in
English and German.

**1223 In pursuit of excellence: works of art from the Museum of
Turkish and Islamic Art.**
Translated from the Turkish and edited by Robert Bragner.   Milan,
Italy: Ahmet Ertuğ Publications, 1993. 224p.
The book, illustrated by photographs, introduces the Museum of Turkish and Islamic
Art in İstanbul, which carries objects not only from the Seljuk and Ottoman periods
in Anatolia, but also samples of Islamic art from Syria, Egypt and Iraq. It has a rich
collection of carpets, manuscripts, metal work and ceramics.

1224   **Recent Turkish coin hoards and numismatic studies.**
British Institute of Archaeology, edited by C. S. Lightfoot.   London:
Oxbow Books, 1991. 150p. (British Institute of Archaeology at
Ankara Monograph, no. 12; Oxbow Monograph, no. 7).

The volume contains works by Turkish and British scholars in the field of ancient
numismatics.

1225   **Studies in ancient coinage from Turkey.**
British Institute of Archaeology, edited by R. Ashton.   London:
Oxbow Books, 1996. 168p. (British Institute of Archaeology at
Ankara Monograph, no. 17; Royal Numismatic Society Special
Publication, no. 29).

The volume contains works by Turkish and British scholars in the field of ancient
numismatics. It presents the material to be found in Turkish museums and private
collections.

1226   **Chinese ceramics in the Sadberk Hanım museum.**
John Carswell.   İstanbul: Vehbi Koç Foundation, the Museum, 1995.
146p.

This is a catalogue of the Chinese ceramics in the Sadberk Hanım museum in İstanbul.

1227   **Topkapı: the palace of felicity.**
Turkish text edited by Filiz Çağman, Engin Yenal; English text edited
by Robert Bragner, photographs by Ahmet Ertuğ.   Milan, Italy:
Ahmet Ertuğ Publications, 1990. 244p.

The Topkapı Palace is also a museum where the splendours of the Sultans and their
treasures are exhibited. This richly illustrated book describes different parts of the
Palace, and the objects stored in it. The contributors to this volume include Feridun
Akozan, Önder Küçükerman, Alpaslan Ataman, İlban Öz and Deniz Esemenli.

1228   **Sabancı kolleksiyonu.** (The Sabancı collection.)
M. Uğur Derman, Kıymet Giray, Fulya Bodur Eruz.   İstanbul:
Akbank, 1995. 479p. bibliog. (Akbank Kültür ve Sanat Kitapları,
no. 61).

A catalogue, with colour illustrations, of the paintings, sculptures and porcelain in the
private collection of Sakıp Sabancı.

1229   **Middle Eastern photographic collections in the United Kingdom.**
Compiled by Gillian M. Grant.   Oxford: M.E.L.C.O.M, 1989. 220p.

Provides a general description of the collections of photographs of the Middle East in
British archives, libraries and museums. They cover the period 1850-1970, and were
taken throughout the Arab world, Afghanistan, Iran, Israel and Turkey. The guide
describes over 250 collections, dealing mainly with loose prints and postcards or
photographs assembled in albums. Entries are arranged alphabetically by town, and
then by the name of the collection.

1230 **Chinese ceramics in the Topkapı Saray Museum, İstanbul: a complete catalogue.**
Regina Krahl, Nurdan Erbahar, John Ayers. London: Sotheby's (published in association with the Directorate of the Topkapı Saray Museum), 1986. 3 vols. bibliog.

The Topkapı Palace Museum is considered to have, after the Ardabil shrine in Iran, the second largest collection of Chinese ceramics in the world. The Ottoman court used them as tableware, and they were specially ordered for use in the palace. Volume one discusses the Yuan and Ming dynasty Celadon ware, volume two Yuan and Ming dynasty porcelain, and volume three Qing dynasty porcelain.

1231 **Osmanlı Padişah fermanları. Imperial Ottoman *fermans*.**
Edited by Ayşegül Nadir. London: Ayşegül Nadir, 1986. 173p. bibliog.

This is the catalogue of an exhibition held in İstanbul in 1987, sponsored by A. Nadir. *Fermāns* are the imperial decrees, which bore the *tuğra*, the imperial seal. The Museum of Turkish and Islamic Arts in İstanbul holds a rich collection of Islamic calligraphy and the documents bearing the *tuğra*. The exhibition not only contains the holdings of the museum, but also some exhibits from the Topkapı Palace Museum, the İstanbul Municipal Library, the Millet Library, the Museum of Divan Literature, and works loaned by the private collectors. Following the foreword by Nazan Ölçer, the introduction by Ş. Aksoy Kutlukan gives some historical background and technical information about *tuğras*. The catalogue follows a historical time-line, and provides detailed information about each item in question. This section was prepared by Tim Stanley, A. Nadir, Ş. Aksoy Kutlukan and Zarif Orgun. Following a bibliographical section, V. L. Ménage gives tips for further reading on the subject, and there is a glossary prepared by Tim Stanley. The catalogue contains lavish photographs, and is beautifully presented.

1232 **Kilimler.** (The *kilims*.)
Nazan Ölçer. İstanbul: Eren, 1988. 208p. (The Museum of Turkish and Islamic Art in İstanbul).

Discusses the collection of kilims in the Museum of Turkish and Islamic Art.

1233 **Nine thousand years of the Anatolian woman.**
Edited by Günseli Renda. İstanbul: Ministry of Culture, General Directorate of Monuments and Museums, 1994. 303p. bibliog.

The catalogue was published for the 'Woman in Anatolia' exhibitions, held in İstanbul in 1993 on the occasion of the seventieth anniversary of the Turkish Republic. The exhibitions showed women in Anatolia from the Neolithic, Classical, Byzantine, Seljuk, Ottoman and Turkish Republican periods, through works of sculpture, painting, textile, costume, photographs, engravings, miniatures and personal objects brought together from different museums and personal collections. This beautiful, illustrated catalogue can be viewed at: <http://www.turknet.com/ninethousand/index.html>.

1234   **Catalogue of the Turkish manuscripts in the British Museum.**
        C. Rieu.   Osnabruck, Germany: O. Zellner, 1978. 345p. (British
        Museum of Oriental Printed Books & Manuscripts).
This is a reprint of the earlier edition by the British Museum in 1888. The catalogue
gives the details of the Turkish manuscripts in the British Museum.

1235   **The Topkapı Saray Museum: costumes, embroideries and other
        textiles.**
        Translated from the Turkish, expanded and edited by J. M. Rogers,
        Hülya Özcan, Selma Delibaş.   London: Thames & Hudson, 1986.
        216p.
Introduces the costumes and textiles in the Topkapı Saray Museum collection.

1236   **The Topkapı Saray Museum: the albums and illustrated
        manuscripts.**
        Translated from the Turkish, expanded and edited by J. M. Rogers,
        Filiz Çağman, Zeren Tanındı.   Boston, Massachusetts: Little,
        Brown, 1986. 280p. maps.
A guide to the albums and illustrated manuscripts in the Topkapı Saray Museum
collection.

1237   **The Topkapı Saray Museum: carpets.**
        Translated from the Turkish, expanded and edited by J. M. Rogers,
        Hülya Özcan.   Boston, Massachusetts: Little, Brown, 1987. 248p.
        bibliog.
A guide to the carpets in the Topkapı Saray Museum collection.

1238   **The Topkapı Saray Museum: the treasury.**
        Translated from the Turkish, expanded and edited by J. M. Rogers,
        Cengiz Köseoğlu.   London: Thames & Hudson, 1987. 215p. bibliog.
A guide to the Treasury section of the Topkapı Saray Museum and its holdings.

1239   **The Topkapı Saray Museum architecture: the Harem and other
        buildings.**
        Translated from the Turkish and edited by J. M. Rogers, Kemal Çığ,
        Sabahattin Batur, Cengiz Köseoğlu.   Boston, Massachusetts: Little,
        Brown, 1988. 216p. map.
This book provides details on the architecture of the buildings which make up the
Topkapı Saray Museum.

1240   **Askeri müze yazma eserler katoloğu.** (The catalogue of handwritten
        manuscripts in the Military Museum.)
        Sadık Tekeli.   İstanbul: Askeri Müze ve Kültür Sitesi Komutanlığı,
        1998. 103p.
This catalogue gives details on the handwritten manuscripts held in the Military
Museum in İstanbul.

1241   **Grek ve Roma sikkeleri: Yapı Kredi koleksiyonu. Greek and
        Roman coins: the Yapı Kredi collection.**
        Oğuz Tekin.   İstanbul: Yapı Kredi Koleksiyonları, 1994. 261p.
        (Yapı Kredi Para Koleksiyonları, no. 2).
The catalogue of the Vedat Nedim Tör Museum of coin collections, which contains
seventy-seven pages of plates. The text is in both English and Turkish.

1242   **Plants and gardens in Persian, Mughal, and Turkish art.**
        Nora M. Titley.   London: British Library, 1979. 37p. bibliog.
The volume gives details of the objects from the collections of the British Library
Department of Oriental Manuscripts and Printed Books.

1243   **Miniatures from Turkish manuscripts. Catalogue and subject
        index of paintings in the British Library and British Museum.**
        Nora M. Titley.   London: British Library, 1981. 144p. bibliog.
Gives details of the miniatures from Turkish manuscripts in the collections of the
British Library Department of Oriental Manuscripts and Printed Books, and the
British Museum.

1244   **Ayasofya müzesindeki ikonalar katoloğu. (The catalogue of icons
        in the Museum of Ayasofya).**
        Nilay Yılmaz.   Ankara: Turkish Ministry of Culture Publications,
        1993. 2 vols.
This is a catalogue, in Turkish and English, of all the Byzantine icons preserved in the
Ayasofya Museum.

Urartu: a metalworking centre in the first millennium B.C.
See item no. 145.

**The Anatolian civilizations: the Council of Europe XVIIIth European
art exhibition.**
See item no. 1095.

The age of Sultan Süleyman the Magnificent.
See item no. 1110.

Konuşan maden: tombak ve gümüş madeni eserler kolleksiyonu. (Gilding
copper [*tombak*] and silver metalwork collection).
See item no. 1111.

Yörük: the nomadic weaving tradition of the Middle East.
See item no. 1175.

Atlaslar atlası: pamuklu, yün ve ipek kumaş kolleksiyonu (Cotton, woolen and silk fabrics collection).
See item no. 1184.

Floral messages: from Ottoman court embroideries to Anatolian trousseau chests.
See item no. 1185.

Libraries

1245 **American Research Institute in Turkey (ARIT) library, İstanbul.**
<http://arit.dartmouth.edu/arit>.
Founded in 1964, the American Research Institute in Turkey is a consortium of forty North American Universities, museums and institutes with an interest in the scholarly study of Turkey in the fields of humanities and social sciences. ARIT Ankara Library focuses on Anatolian archaeology, while the holdings of the İstanbul Library are concerned with Turkey from the Byzantine to the present day. The holdings of the library can be accessed at this website.

1246 **Elyazması eserler katoloğu. (Catalogue of handwritten manuscripts).**
Abdullah Ceyhan.   Ankara: Diyanet İşleri Başkanlığı Yayınları, 1988. 2 vols.
This is a catalogue, in Turkish and English, of Islamic manuscripts held in the library of the Diyanet İşleri Başkanlığı (Directorate of Religious Affairs) in Ankara.

1247 **The Women's Library and Information Centre Foundation: the first and only library on women's history in Turkey.**
Aslı Davaz-Mardin.   *TASG News: Newsletter of the Turkish Area Study Group*, no. 47 (1998), p. 26-30.
This library was opened in 1990 through the efforts of a group of women, who also volunteer to work in the library. It publishes a newsletter, an illustrated diary and books. This article, written by one of the founding members of the library, provides the history of the library and comprehensive information about its collections, as well as a contact address and telephone numbers.

1248　**İstanbul kütüphaneleri Arap harfli süreli yayınlar toplu katoloğu: 1828-1928.** (Union catalogue of the periodicals in Arabic script in the libraries of İstanbul.)
Compiled by Hasan Duman.　İstanbul: Research Centre for Islamic History, Art and Culture (IRCICA), 1986. 602p. (Bibliographical Series, no. 3).

This volume covers periodicals in Ottoman Turkish, Arabic, Persian and Urdu, some combined with twenty-two other languages, which are found in the ten leading İstanbul libraries. It contains entries for 1,809 titles, printed in different parts of the world, with Turkish-language periodicals making up the majority of the titles. The entries, in Turkish, give the name of the periodical, a list of the subject matter, the name of the owner of the concession, the directors in charge, the editors-in-chief in order of appointment, artists and writers associated with the publication, frequency, date of first and last issue, the size, and the name of the İstanbul library where the periodical is held. The catalogue has subject indexes in Turkish, English and Arabic, together with an Arabic script index of titles.

1249　**Archaeological Museum library.**
Havva Koç.　*TASG News: Newsletter of the Turkish Area Study Group*, no. 47 (1998), p. 24-25.

Written by the librarian of the museum, the essay provides the history of the library and an idea of its contents.

1250　**The Süleymaniye library.**
Günay Kut.　*TASG News: Newsletter of the Turkish Area Study Group*, no. 47 (1998), p. 17-20.

Describes the building which houses the Süleymaniye library and its collection, and gives a contact address and telephone numbers.

1251　**The library of the Topkapı Palace museum.**
Banu Mahir.　*TASG News: Newsletter of the Turkish Area Study Group*, no. 47 (1998), p. 22-23.

The author briefly summarizes the contents of the library and its history.

1252　**Süleymaniye library, İstanbul.**
Research Centre for Islamic History, Art and Culture (IRCICA).
IRCICA Newsletter, no. 46 (1998), p. 12-14.

Provides information about the library, and presents a list of its collections. There are five libraries of İstanbul which have rich collections of manuscripts attached to the Süleymaniye Library. These libraries are listed separately in the article.

1253　**İstanbul libraries.**
Turkish Area Study Group.　*TASG News: Newsletter of the Turkish Area Study Group*, no. 47 (1998), p. 14-16.

This issue of the Newsletter carries a very handy list of İstanbul libraries, their addresses and telephone numbers.

1254 **Catalogue of Islamic manuscripts (Arabic, Turkish, and Persian) in the libraries of Turkey.**
Edited by Ekmeleddin İhsanoğlu, and prepared by R. Şeşen, C. Akpınar, C. İzgi. İstanbul: Research Centre for Islamic History, Art And Culture (IRCICA), 1984. 524p.
The catalogue contains a preface in English and in Arabic, and author and title indexes. Numerous medical manuscripts, by 450 authors and scattered in 129 libraries in Turkey, have been brought together. This is useful source material for researchers of the history of medicine.

1255 **Catalogue of Turkish manuscripts in the Bodleian library.**
Günay Kut, Michael Daly. Oxford: Oxford University Press, 1996. 400p. bibliog.
Part two of the 1930 catalogue of the manuscripts in the Bodleian Library at the University of Oxford, which were acquired before 1900, was devoted to Turkish manuscripts. This catalogue is a supplement and cites all the Turkish manuscripts acquired since 1900 by the Bodleian Library (356 entries). A reprint of the original catalogue (approximately 280 entries) is also given. The entries are classified by subject, such as the Koran, Sufism, Islamic history and legend, jurisprudence, history and legend, biography, medicine, botany, geography, encyclopaedias, dictionaries and grammars.

Archives

1256 **Osmanlı fermanları. Ottoman *fermans*.**
İsmet Binark, Necati Aktaş. İstanbul: Devlet Arşivleri Genel Müdürlüğü, Osmanlı Arşivi Daire Başkanlığı, 1994. 2nd ed. 177p. bibliog. (Devlet Arşivleri Genel Müdürlüğü, Osmanlı Arşivi Daire Başkanlığı, no. 19).
One way in which the Ottoman Sultans communicated their decisions to the administrators of the Empire was by *fermans*. The calligraphy of these written texts, as well as the *tugras* (royal cipher) of the Sultans, which legalized the text, had an aesthetic quality. The book is a guide to collections which carry these *fermans*, and is in English and Turkish.

1257 **Osmanlı arşivi, Yıldız tasnifi, Ermeni meselesi. Ottoman archives, Yıldız collection, the Armenian question.**
Ertuğrul Zekâi Ökte. İstanbul: Tarihi Araştırmalar ve Dökümantasyon Merkezleri Kurma ve Geliştirme Vakfı, 1989. 3 vols. maps.
These volumes contain the facsimiles of documents from the Ottoman archives, Yıldız Palace collection, relating to the Armenian population of the Ottoman Empire during

the late 19th and early 20th centuries. The text is in Turkish and English, and the documents are in Ottoman Turkish, modern Turkish and English.

1258 **British documents on Ottoman Armenians.**
Edited by Bilal Şimşir. Ankara: Türk Tarih Kurumu Basımevi, 1982-90. 4 vols. (The Turkish Historical Society, serial no. 7).
The work, in English and French, carries documents dealing with correspondence related to the Armenians in Anatolia during the second half of the 19th century. Volume one covers the period 1856-80; volume two 1880-90; volume three 1891-95; and volume four 1895.

1259 **Başbakanlık Osmanlı arşivi rehberi.** (Guide to the Prime Ministry Ottoman archives.)
Türkiye Cumhuriyeti Başbakanlık Devlet Arşivleri Genel Müdürlüğü.
Ankara: Devlet Arşivleri Genel Müdürlüğü, 1992. 634p. (T. C. Başbakanlık Devlet Arşivleri Genel Müdürlüğü Osmanlı Arşivi Daire Başkanlığı, no. 5).
This is the most complete guide to the documents in the Ottoman archives, and in the introductory section also provides clear, general information about the collection and its classification.

1260 **Başbakanlık Osmanlı arşivi katologları rehberi.** (Guide to the catalogues of Prime Ministry Ottoman archives.)
Türkiye Cumhuriyeti Başbakanlık Devlet Arşivleri Genel Müdürlüğü.
Ankara: Devlet Arşivleri Genel Müdürlüğü, 1995. 320p. (T. C. Başbakanlık Devlet Arşivleri Genel Müdürlüğü Osmanlı Arşivi Daire Başkanlığı, no. 26).
This volume, which was out of print soon after it was published, is a guide to the catalogues of the Ottoman archives. It has an index, and the appendices contain a listing of the codes and abbreviations used for the Ottoman archives, together with the dates of reigns for Sultans and their Grand Viziers.

1261 **Başbakanlık Devlet Arşivleri Genel Müdürlüğü Dökümantasyon Daire Başkanlığı rehberi.** (Information guide of the Prime Ministry General Directorate of State Archives Department of Documentation.)
Türkiye Cumhuriyeti Başbakanlık Devlet Arşivleri Genel Müdürlüğü.
Ankara: Devlet Arşivleri Genel Müdürlüğü, 1996. 2nd rev. ed. 23p. (T. C. Başbakanlık Devlet Arşivleri Genel Müdürlüğü Dökümantasyon Dairesi Başkanlığı Yayınları, no. 11).
This small booklet is a very valuable publication because it lists all the publications of the different departments (the publications of the Directorate itself, Ottoman archives and Republican archives, as well as the Department of Documentation) of the Prime Ministry General Directorate of State Archives. Some of these publications have English subtitles which usually show that they contain bibliographical information on works written in other languages than Turkish.

1262 **Enformasyon bülteni.** (Information bulletin.)
Türkiye Cumhuriyeti Başbakanlık Devlet Arşivleri Genel Müdürlüğü.
Ankara: Devlet Arşivleri Genel Müdürlüğü, 1997. 99p. (T. C.
Başbakanlık Devlet Arşivleri Genel Müdürlüğü, Dökümantasyon
Daire Başkanlığı, no. 50).

A publication by the General Directorate of State Archives, Directorate of
Documentation, which has been issued once every two months since May 1989 (the
first four issues were published under the name *Duyuru bülteni*). It contains bibliographical records of books, articles, conference papers and seminar papers published
in Turkey during the time specified. There are also author and subject indexes.

1263 **Arşiv belgelerine göre Kafkaslar'da ve Anadolu'da Ermeni
mezâlimi. Armenian violence and massacre in the Caucasus and
Anatolia based on archives.**
Türkiye Cumhuriyeti Başbakanlık Devlet Arşivleri Genel Müdürlüğü.
Ankara: Devlet Arşivleri Genel Müdürlüğü, 1995-98. 4 vols.
(Osmanlı Arşivi Daire Başkanlığı, no. 23-2, 34-35).

The first volume of the work, which covers the period 1906-18, contains archival
documents (256 records) on the movements and the actions of the Armenian guerrillas
(helped by the Russians), and the atrocities committed by them in the area. The second
volume contains 209 records of atrocities under 38 headings between January-August
1919, and the third and fourth volumes cover the period 1919-22. General information
on the content of the original records is given in the first volume. The volumes contain
transcriptions and summaries of the documents in Turkish and in English, an index
and a bibliography, and photocopies of the documents.

1264 **Topkapı Sarayı müzesi Osmanlı arşivi katoloğu: fermanlar.
I fasikül no. E. 1-12476.** (Catalogue of Ottoman archives in Topkapı
Palace Museum: the fermans.)
Compiled by İ. H. Uzunçarşılı, İ. K. Baybura, Ü. Altındağ. Ankara:
Türk Tarih Kurumu Basımevi, 1985. 105p. (Türk Tarih Kurumu
Series VII, no. 81).

The *ferman* fascicule presented in this catalogue contains 1,021 entries listed in
chronological order from 1453 to 1920, and is preceded by two isolated survivors
from the 14th century. Each entry gives: the date; a content summary, identifying the
sultan and the addressee, and the principal details of the occasion and subject of the
ferman; a physical description of the item; and the call number.

1265 **Archive of Turkish oral narrative: preliminary catalogue II.**
Compiled by Warren S. Walker, Michael D. Felker, Elizabet K.
Brandt. Lubbock, Texas: Archive of Turkish Oral Narrative, 1988.
211p.

The Archive of Turkish Oral Narrative (ATON), which was set up by Warren and
Barbara Walker and which is housed in Lubbock, Texas, at the library of Texas
Technical University, is an indexed, accessible collection of Turkish folk-tales and
related forms. This guide catalogues around one-third of the narratives held by the
archive.

1266   **The Republic of Turkey: an American perspective. A guide to**
        U.S. official documents and government sponsored publications.
        Julian W. Witherell.   Washington, DC: Library of Congress, African
        and Middle Eastern Division Research Services, 1988. 211p.
        This guide lists publications from the period 1919-86. The titles are taken from four
        principal sources: the US Agency for International Development abstracts and
        microfiches; the American Statistics Index (Congressional Information Service);
        Government Reports, Announcements & Index (Department of Commerce); and
        Resources in Education (Educational Resources Information Center). The book
        includes a brief description of most of the 1,702 titles, and a comprehensive list of
        topics and authors. The titles reflect the development of diplomatic and economic ties
        between the United States and Turkey; for example, the largest category deals with
        US assistance to Turkey. The work is also available in microfiche.

Bibliography on manuscript libraries in Turkey and the publications on
the manuscripts located in these libraries.
See item no. 1414.

Arşivcilik bibliyografyası: Türkçe ve yabancı dillerde yayınlanmış
kaynaklar, 1979-1994. A bibliography on archival studies: includes
Turkish and foreign sources, 1979-1994.
See item no. 1431.

Mass Media

General studies

1267 **Dogs, women, cholera, and other menaces in the streets: cartoon satire in the Ottoman revolutionary press, 1908-11.**
Palmira Brummett. *International Journal of Middle Eastern Studies*, vol. 27 (1995), p. 433-60.
The author analyses the cartoons published during the Young Turk period (1908-11), placing them in their cultural and political context.

1268 **The press and the consolidation of democracy in Turkey.**
Metin Heper, Tanel Demirel. *Middle East Studies*, vol. 32, no. 2 (1996), p. 109-23. (Special Issue. *Turkey: identity, democracy, politics).*
The authors give a concise summary of the development of the press in Turkey, and evaluate the role of journalists and daily newspapers.

1269 **Representation of women and men in Turkish newspapers.**
Olcay E. İmamoğlu, Yeşim Gültekin, Bahar Köseoğlu, Afife Cebi. *Journal of Human Sciences*, vol. 9, no. 2 (1990), p. 57-67.
The authors report on the results of two studies of the direct and indirect representations of stereotyped gender roles in selected newspapers in 1988. The results show that traditional gender roles were perpetuated in all the newspapers to varying degrees, and that the politics of the newspapers was not a factor in their portrayal of gender roles.

1270   **A fait accompli: transformation of media structures in Turkey.**
A. Raşit Kaya. *Middle East Technical University Studies in Development*, vol. 21, no. 3 (1994), p. 383-404.
One of the results of Turkey's transition to a market-based strategy for economic modernization in the 1980s, was the introduction of a more information-based economy and a transformation of its media structures. The author argues that the political parties and the government in Turkey react in ways that demonstrate the lack of any coherent media policy, a situation which, in effect, facilitates the corporate interests of big businesses.

1271   **Media imperialism and VCR: the case of Turkey.**
Christine Ogan. *Journal of Communication,* vol. 38, no. 2 (1988), p. 93-106.
The author claims that 'media imperialism thesis' is invalidated because of the invention of the VCR (video cassette recorder), and illustrates her claim with Turkish examples.

1272   **Media, migrants and marginalization. The situation in the Federal Republic of Germany.**
Manfred Oepen. *International Migration Review*, vol. 18, no. 1 (Spring 1984), p. 111-21.
The author examines the situation of Germany's *gastarbeiter* (guest workers), focusing on the media consumption of Turkish workers. He claims that Turkish-origin newspapers and videos tend to go beyond fostering a sense of cultural identity, reflecting the tendency toward 'ethnic revival' in order to counter feelings of inferiority. On the other hand, the lack of media support for integration is due to German officials' unwillingness to grant migrants full societal participation, and to a lack of recognition of migrant cultural identity and special communications needs.

1273   **Packaging Islam: cultural politics on the landscape of the Turkish commercial television.**
Ayşe Öncü. *Public Culture*, vol. 8, no. 1 (1995), p. 51-71.
During the 1991 election, the pro-Islamic Welfare Party launched a television media campaign that avoided using typical Islamic religious symbols. This campaign brought Islam on Turkish television into focus. There were two alternative packages: Islam-as-a-viewpoint and Islam-as-global-machination. These competing images engaged the audience, and forced them to clarify their stand on Islam. The author describes a particular knowledge of Islam which is constructed by commercial television in Turkey, and its influence on Turkish politics.

1274   **Global media and cultural identity in Turkey.**
Haluk Şahin, Asu Aksoy. *Journal of Communication*, vol. 43, no. 2 (1993), p. 31-41.
The authors study the influx of telecommunications technology in the early 1990s, which profoundly affected Turkey's culture and national identity, and the constitutionally established monopolistic state-run system, which lost almost forty per cent of its audience to private television and radio stations.

1275 **Turkish media after the 1980s.**
L. Doğan Tiliç. In: *Contrasts and solutions in the Middle East.*
Edited by Ole Hoiris, Sefa Martin Yürükel. Aarhus, Denmark:
Aarhus University Press, 1997, p. 401-16.

The author provides a comprehensive summary of the components of the contemporary media in Turkey. He gives a summary of the political structure of Turkey during the 1980s and continues with a section on the private holdings and persons controlling the Turkish media. There is also a section on Turkish journalists and their audience.

Gender & Media.
See item no. 1155.

Newspapers and general periodicals

Newspapers

1276 **Akit.** (Agreement.)
İstanbul, 1993- . daily.

A pro-Islamic daily which often takes a strongly anti-secular line. It can be viewed at: <http://www.akit.com.tr.>.

1277 **Bizim Gazete.** (Our Paper.)
İstanbul, 1995- . daily.

The publication of the Turkish Journalists' Association.

1278 **Cumhuriyet.** (The Republic.)
İstanbul, 1924- . daily.

This left-of-centre daily has a circulation of around 70,000. It also has a well-established book club, and a radio station. It is published weekly in Europe under the name *Cumhuriyet Hafta.* It can be viewed at: <http://www.Cumhuriyet.com.>.

1279 **Dünya.** (The World.)
İstanbul, 1981- . daily.

One of the ten biggest economy newspapers of Europe, where it is published weekly. It has fifty outlets in Turkey, and it carries economic news from the Anatolian provinces as well as from the big centres. It is owned by the Globus Group which also owns 'Dardanel TV' and 'Dardanel Radio'. It also publishes a series of monthly journals and provides the teletext news for NTV (the news channel in Turkey). It has a circulation of around 45,000 in Turkey, but seventy-five per cent of its readers are subscribers. The address for 'Dünya Online', which is in Turkish and English, is: <http://www.dunya-gazete.com.tr/>.

1280   **Fanatik.** (The Fanatic.)
       İstanbul, 1995- . daily.
A daily sports newspaper with a circulation of around 220,000. It focuses on soccer, paying particular attention to Turkey's four major football teams. It is owned by Doğan Medya Group and can be viewed at: <http://www.fanatik.com.tr.>.

1281   **Finansal Forum.** (Financial Forum.)
       İstanbul, 1996- . daily.
Targeted at business, industry, government, and academia, this paper claims to fill a gap in the Turkish market for a high quality business daily. It has a low circulation, but is aiming for a high profile target audience of 26,000 subscribers.

1282   **Gözcü.** (Observer.)
       İstanbul, 1996- . daily.
A mass market, populist broadsheet daily, whose circulation is around 160,000.

1283   **Hürriyet.** (Liberty.)
       İstanbul, 1948- . daily.
Owned by the Doğan Medya Group, *Hürriyet* has a circulation of around 600,000, which makes it one of the three dailies with the highest circulation in Turkey. It follows a secular and Republican editorial policy, which can be classified as central and liberal. It is an influential newspaper, often with inflammatory, sentimental headlines. It employs 1,400 people, and is printed in five different locations. It attracts forty-four per cent of all newspaper advertising. It is also published in America and Europe, and can be viewed at: <http://www.hurriyet.com.tr.>.

1284   **Milli Gazete.** (National Newspaper.)
       İstanbul, 1973- . daily.
A pro-Islamic daily owned by Yeni Neşriyat A.Ş.

1285   **Milliyet.** (Nationality.)
       İstanbul, 1949- . daily.
This is a liberal daily with an average daily circulation of over 600,000. It became the best selling paper in 1996. It belongs to the Doğan Medya Group, which also owns the television channel 'Kanal D'. The paper is well known for its investigative journalism and series on socio-political and economic issues. It is also published in Europe and can be viewed (in Turkish with summaries in English) at: <http://www.milliyet.com.tr>.

1286   **Posta.** (The Mail.)
       İstanbul, 1997- . daily.
A low-price, mass market daily which is the result of a merger in 1997 of two separate dailies. It is owned by the Doğan Medya Group. Its circulation is around 215,000.

1287 **Radikal.** (Radical.)
İstanbul, 1996- . daily.
This is the third largest newspaper in the Doğan Medya Group, with a circulation of around 190,000. It is targeted at young, westernized, urban readers, and it carries articles by some of the most outspoken and provocative writers. Its coverage of international news is also above average. It can be viewed at: <http://www.radikal.com.tr>.

1288 **Resmi Gazete.** (Official Gazette.)
Ankara, 1930- . daily.
The *Resmi Gazete* publishes all laws, regulations, official decisions and appointments related to government and state matters. It has recently been made available online at: <http://www.rega.com.tr>.

1289 **Sabah.** (Morning.)
İstanbul, 1985- . daily.
This daily has a circulation of over 540,000. Alongside *Hürriyet* and *Milliyet*, the central-liberal daily *Sabah* is one of the most influential newspapers in Turkey. It has several prominent columnists, who often express contradicting views or strong criticism of one another. It is also widely distributed in Europe. It can be viewed at: <http://www.sabah.com.tr>.

1290 **Turkish Daily News.**
Ankara, 1961- . daily.
This is the first and only English-language daily in Turkey. It was co-founded by the Çelik family, and İlnur Çevik is the current editor. It is an independent, liberal newspaper, and has an electronic news and information service on the Internet which is updated daily. It also publishes the *Turkish Globe*, a full-colour magazine. It can be viewed at: <http://www.turkishdailynews.com.>.

1291 **Türkiye.** (Turkey.)
İstanbul, 1970- . daily.
A right-wing, pro-Islamic daily owned by İhlas Holding, which also owns the television station TGRT. It has a circulation of over 425,000 and is also published in Europe.

1292 **Yeni Asır.** (New Age.)
İzmir, Turkey, 1895- . daily.
This is one of the oldest publications in Turkey, and until recently it was an influential regional paper. It is now part of the Sabah Group.

1293 **Zaman.** (Time.)
İstanbul, 1986- . daily.
A conservative daily with a circulation of around 300,000. Its sister television channel is 'Samanyolu TV'. It targets a moderate Islamic community, and has a reputation of allowing other opinions to be expressed. It is printed in twelve countries, including the former Soviet Union, and can be viewed at: <http://www.zaman.com.tr>.

General periodicals

1294 **Adam Sanat.** (Adam Art.)
İstanbul, 1987- . monthly.
This journal deals with art and literature in general. It carries literary reviews, translations, poetry and short stories by Turkish authors, book reviews, interviews with Turkish artists, and reviews of their work.

1295 **Aksiyon.** (Action.)
İstanbul, 1994- . weekly.
This right-of-centre weekly paper carries national and international news.

1296 **Aktüel.** (Contemporary.)
İstanbul, 1991- . weekly.
This magazine has a circulation of around 20,000. It carries special features on Turkey and the world, as well as news of social and cultural events in Turkey, and information on tourism.

1297 **Ankara Kültür ve Sanat Haritası. Ankara Culture and Arts Map.**
Ankara, 1995- . monthly.
This useful monthly is prepared by Toplumsal Araştırmalar Kültür ve Sanat için Vakıf (Foundation for Social Research, Culture and Arts). It contains details of all cultural and artistic activities in Ankara, including radio, theatre, films, books, exhibitions and lectures. The text is generally in Turkish. The inclusion of addresses of museums and art galleries, and telephone numbers for hospitals and emergency services make this publication very useful.

1298 **Atlas.**
İstanbul, 1993- . monthly.
A journal devoted to nature and travel, with many colour photographs.

1299 **Babıali Magazin.** (Babıali Magazine.)
İstanbul, 1988- . monthly.
This monthly carries news about the Turkish press.

1300 **Bilim ve Teknik.** (Science and Technology.)
Ankara, 1968- . monthly.
This is the popular science journal of Türkiye Bilimsel ve Teknik Araştırma Kurumu (The Scientific and Technical Research Council of Turkey [TÜBİTAK]).

1301 **Ekonomist.** (Economist.)
İstanbul, 1991- . weekly.
A distinguished journal on money, banking and economics, which also carries a special supplement on the stock market.

1302   **İstanbul Life.**
İstanbul, 1995- . monthly.
This popular city guide for İstanbul is full of useful information.

1303   **Kitap Günlüğü.** (Book Diary.)
İstanbul, 1997- . monthly.
Provides information about new books and contains articles about authors, the problems of publishers and publishing in Turkey. Each issue carries two supplements: a list of books published the previous month; and a dictionary of books which introduces publishers and their publications. It is in Turkish.

1304   **Milliyet Sanat.** (Milliyet Art.)
İstanbul, 1972- . fortnightly.
This journal covers the arts and literature, also carrying news about past and coming cultural activities.

1305   **Nokta.** (The Dot.)
İstanbul, 1982- . weekly.
Carries articles and news on national political and socio-economic issues, and features on world news. It can be viewed at: <http://www.medyatext.com>.

1306   **P-Sanat kültür antika dergisi.** (P-magazine of art, culture,
        antiques.)
        İstanbul: Portakal Sanat ve Kültür Evi, 1996- . four issues annually.
This beautifully produced, lavish magazine, with colour photographs, carries articles on antiques and art, as well as news about the art world. It is in Turkish.

1307   **Sinema.** (Cinema.)
İstanbul, 1994- . monthly.
Focuses on popular cinema, and introduces domestic and foreign films on release or coming soon at Turkish cinemas. It provides information about their topics, directors and actors, in the form of short descriptions, critical essays and interviews accompanied by numerous photographs. Although the journal has occasional special 'files' which provide more in-depth information on specific topics, like film genres, the writing in general is in the form of popular, easily readable pieces rather than extensive, critical research papers.

1308   **Turkey Briefing.**
London: Turkey Briefing Group, 1987- . bimonthly.
This newsletter carries political news about Turkey and recently published book reviews.

Cornucopia. Turkey for Connoisseurs.
See item no. 1323.

25. Kare. (25th Square.)
See item no. 1340.

Professional
Periodicals

1309 Agon Tiyatro.
Ankara, 1993- . four issues annually.
Carries articles on Turkish theatre, translations and reviews of plays, as well as research articles on drama. It is in Turkish.

1310 American Association of Teachers of Turkic Languages (AATT) Bulletin.
Princeton, New Jersey, 1987- . biannual.
The *Bulletin* carries articles on topics of interest to teachers of language and literature, as well as workshops and reports, book reviews, advertisements and announcements.

1311 Anatolian Archaeology: Reports on Research Conducted in Turkey.
British Institute of Archaeology in Ankara.   London, 1995- . annual.
The first three issues on this annual publication were edited by Gina Coulthard and Stephen Hill. There are about thirty pages in each issue, illustrated with photographs and line drawings. Most of the brief entries are reports on excavations and surveys, museum-based research, post-excavation and publication initiatives, conferences and grants. This is the companion publication to *Anatolian Studies* (see item no. 1312).

1312 Anatolian Studies: Journal of the British Institute of Archaeology at Ankara.
British Institute of Archaeology in Ankara.   London, 1951- . annual.
Includes reports on excavations, and analytical articles on the archaeology of Turkey. For example, the 1997 issue of this major journal of record and research contains 31 pages of photographs, and 224 pages of text illustrated by maps, plans and line drawings. Indexes to the journal are published separately.

1313   **Anatolica: Annuaire International pour les Civilisations de l'Asie
Antérieure.** (Anatolica: International Yearbook of the Civilizations
of Anatolia.)
Nederlands Historisch-Archaeologisch Instituut te Istanbul.   Leiden,
the Netherlands, 1967- . annual.

This is the journal of the Netherlands Institute for History and Archaeology in
İstanbul. Published in German, French or English, it produces preliminary reports on
the excavations of many nationalities in Turkey.

1314   **Ankara Üniversitesi Hukuk Fakültesi Dergisi.** (Journal of Ankara
University Faculty of Law.)
Ankara Üniversitesi Hukuk Fakültesi.   Ankara, 1943- . quarterly.

Although mainly in Turkish, there are articles in English as well as in French and
Italian.

1315   **Banka ve Ticaret Hukuku Dergisi.** (Journal of Banking and
Commercial Law.)
Banka ve Ticaret Hukuku Araştırma Enstitüsü (Research Institute of
Banking and Commercial Law).   Ankara, 1961- . quarterly.

Although the journal is mostly in Turkish, every issue has a translation of the contents
page into English, and some articles appear in English.

1316   **Belleten. Türk Tarih Kurumu.** (Bulletin. Turkish Historical
Society.)
Türk Tarih Kurumu.   Ankara, 1937- . quarterly.

The official publication of the Turkish Historical Society. It includes scholarly articles
on Turkish and Anatolian history, principally in Turkish.

1317   **Birikim.** (Accumulation.)
Ankara, 1989- . monthly.

The journal describes itself as a 'monthly socialist journal of culture', and it carries
research articles by social scientists and journalists on issues concerning all fields of
Turkish culture, politics, economy, law and international relations.

1318   **Bitig: Journal of the Turkic World.**
Research Centre for Turkestan and Azerbaijan (SOTA).   Haarlem,
the Netherlands, 1991- . quarterly.

This bilingual journal in Turkish and English aims to provide a forum for discussions
on topics related to the Turkic peoples of the world. It contains articles (both academic
and journalistic) on different aspects of the Turkic world, as well as news, announcements of meetings and conferences, and book reviews. More information on SOTA
and the journal can be obtained at: <http://www.turkiye.net/sota/sota.html>.

1319   Boğaziçi Journal. Review of Social, Economic and Administrative
        Studies.
        Boğaziçi University.   İstanbul, 1987- . biannual.
This journal is published in English, and includes research papers in the fields of
politics, public administration, economics, and sociology, mainly related to Turkey.
The journal has been published under different names: *Boğaziçi University Journal of
Social Sciences* in 1973; and *Journal of Economics and Administrative Sciences* until
1986.

1320   **British Journal of Middle Eastern Studies.**
        British Society for Middle Eastern Studies.   Abingdon, England:
        Carfax, 1991- . biannual.
This is the journal of the British Society for Middle Eastern Studies (BRISMES),
published under the title *BRISMES Bulletin* between 1974 and 1991. It carries
academic articles on all subject areas concerning the Middle East, as well as book
reviews.

1321   **CEMOTI: Cahiers d'Études sur la Méditerranée Orientale et le
        Monde Turco-Iranien.** (CEMOTI: Study Papers on the Western
        Mediterranean and the Turko-Iranian World.)
        Association Française pour l'Étude et les Recherches Internationales,
        Fondation Nationale des Sciences Politiques.   Paris, 1985- .
        biannual.
Carries scholarly articles (normally in French but occasionally in English) on the
history, culture and contemporary political, social and economic developments of the
Balkans, the Mediterranean, Turkey, Iran, Central Asia and the Caucaus, including
Xinjiang.

1322   **Central Asian Survey.**
        Abingdon, England: Carfax Publishers, 1982- . quarterly.
Concerned primarily with the history, politics, cultures, religions and economies of the
Central Asian and Caucasian regions. Many issues contain articles referring to Turkey,
to the Turkic states of the former Soviet Union, or to the Turkic peoples of the
Russian Federation.

1323   **Cornucopia. Turkey for Connoisseurs.**
        İstanbul, 1992- . quarterly.
An illustrated review about Turkey, past and present. It features articles on history,
art, architecture, design, fashion, interior decoration, gardens, country life, eating out
(outside Turkey as well as in Turkey), cookery, recipes, exhibitions and auctions,
travel, maps, guides, hotels, shopping, business, finance and real estate, as well as
book reviews. With its attractive illustrations and well-written expert articles, this is a
very informative and beautifully published journal on Turkey. It not only gives news
from Turkey, but also of cultural activities in Europe and in the United States concerning Turkey. It can be viewed at: <http://www.cornucopia.net/>.

Professional Periodicals

1324   **Çağdaş Türk Dili.** (Contemporary Turkish Language.)
Dil Derneği.   Ankara, 1987- . monthly.
The monthly publication of the Dil Derneği (Language Association), and is the
alternative and opposing journal to the monthly publication of the Turkish Language
Association. It carries articles on language and literature in Turkish.

1325   **Dans, Müzik, Kültür, Çeviri, Araştırma Dergisi. (Folklora
Doğru).** (Journal of Dance, Music, Culture, Translation, Research.)
Boğaziçi Folklor Klübü.   İstanbul, 1969- . biannual.
This is the publication of the Folklore Club of Boğaziçi University. Its articles are
principally concerned with different areas of Turkish folklore and oral tradition.

1326   **DEİK Bulletin.**
Foreign Economic Relations Board.   İstanbul, 1986- . monthly.
The Foreign Economic Relations Board (Dış Ekonomik İlişkiler Kurulu [DEİK]) was
established in 1986 by the following bodies: the Turkish Union of Chambers of
Commerce, Industry, Commodity Exchanges and Maritime Chambers of Commerce
(TOBB); the Union of Turkish Chambers of Agriculture (TZOB); the Turkish
Confederation of Employer Associations (TISK); the Turkish Industrialists' and
Businessmen's Association (TÜSIAD); the Turkish Foreign Trade Association
(TURKTRADE); the Economic Development Foundation (IKV); the Turkish
Contractors' Association (TMB); the Association for Foreign Capital Coordination
(YASED); and the Turkish Exporters Assembly (TIM). It is a non-profit private sector
organization, whose objective is to improve Turkey's external economic relations and
to contribute to the integration of the Turkish economy with the world economy
through bilateral Business Councils established with various countries. The head-
quarters, in İstanbul, provides information on every aspect of Turkish economy and
foreign trade, and its library is open to all researchers. As well as a monthly *Bulletin*
on recent economic news, DEİK also publishes reports, handbooks and booklets on
Turkish foreign trade. The organization can be reached at <deik@servis.net.tr.>.

1327   **Dil Dergisi. Language Journal.**
Türkçe Öğretim Merkezi (TÖMER).   Ankara, 1992- . monthly.
One of the publications of the language centre at Ankara University. It carries research
articles on the Turkish language, mostly in Turkish, but occasionally in English,
French and German. It also carries news of cultural and academic activities in Turkey
concerning language and language teaching, and book reviews.

1328   **Dilbilim Araştırmaları Dergisi.** (Journal of Linguistic Research.)
Ankara, 1986- . annual.
Aims to encourage research on modern Turkish in the light of contemporary
linguistics. The language of the publication is primarily Turkish but it does carry some
articles in English.

1329   **Edebiyāt. New series. A Journal of Middle Eastern and Comparative Literature.**
Yverdon, Switzerland: Harwood Academic Publishers, 1993- . biannual.
One of the few English-language journals devoted to the critical study of Middle Eastern literatures. This publication frequently includes articles about Turkish literature and almost always contains something of interest for Turkish studies. Between 1987 and 1988, it was published in Philadelphia by the Middle East Center, University of Pennsylvania.

1330   **Eurasian Studies.**
Turkish International Cooperation Agency (TICA).   Ankara, 1994- . quarterly.
Published in separate editions in English, Turkish, Kırgız, Uzbek, Turkmen and Kazakh, this journal carries articles on current political, social and cultural developments in the 'Eurasian region' (Turkey, the Black Sea countries, Central Asia and the Caucasus).

1331   **Gece Yarısı Sineması.** (Midnight Cinema.)
İzmir, Turkey, 1998- . four issues annually.
Includes both informative and critical essays on erotic, science-fiction, action, adventure, trash and underground films while focusing in particular on horror films. Although the essays mostly consist of examinations of films of foreign directors in these genres, the journal also includes essays on Turkish commercial films. It is the first Turkish cinema journal of its kind.

1332   **Hacettepe Journal of Education.**
Ankara, 1983- . annual.
A publication of Hacettepe University in Ankara. It carries refereed research papers on all fields of education, summaries of theses and dissertations of the research students of the Faculty of Education of Hacettepe University, book reviews and announcements. The languages of the journal are Turkish, English, French or German with abstracts in English and Turkish.

1333   **International Journal of Middle Eastern Studies.**
The Middle East Studies Association of North America (MESA).
New York; Cambridge, England: Cambridge University Press, 1968- . quarterly.
This journal publishes articles and reviews concerning the area encompassing Iran, Turkey, Afghanistan, Israel and Pakistan, from the 7th century to modern times. Spain, Southeastern Europe and the former Soviet Union arc also covered for those periods when their territories were under the influence of Middle Eastern civilizations. The periodical is interdisciplinary, and deals with history, political science, economics, anthropology, sociology, philology, literature, folklore, comparative religion, law and philosophy.

1334 **International Journal of Music in Turkey.**
İstanbul, 1997- . quarterly.
This is the journal of the Turkish Society for Musicology, and the only one of its kind in English. It covers all aspects of music and all styles and genres, including traditional Turkish art music, folk music, popular music and contemporary music in Turkey, as well as reviews. Its editorial board is composed of Turkish and international scholars.

1335 **İstanbul Üniversitesi Hukuk Fakültesi Dergisi.** (Journal of İstanbul University Faculty of Law.)
İstanbul, 1924- . quarterly.
Carries research articles on law, in Turkish with summaries in English.

1336 **Journal of Faculty of Architecture of Middle East Technical University. Orta Doğu Teknik Üniversitesi Mimarlık Fakültesi Dergisi.**
Ankara, 1986- . biannual.
This journal carries research articles on all areas of architecture.

1337 **Journal of South Asian and Middle Eastern Studies.**
Pakistan-American Foundation. Villanova, Pennsylvania, 1977- . quarterly.
Published in English, this journal frequently carries important papers and book reviews on Turkey's domestic politics and international relations, besides covering the Middle East in general and (occasionally) South Asia.

1338 **Journal of Turkish Literature.**
Ankara, September 1999- . quarterly.
Edited by Talat S. Halman, this is the first international journal in English devoted solely to Turkish literature, from its origins to the present day. It carries scholarly articles on Turkish literature from Turks in Asia, the Middle East, the Balkans and elsewhere. However, its main focus is on modern Turkish, Ottoman, Seljuk and Central Asian literatures.

1339 **Journal of Turkish Studies. Türklük Bilgisi Araştırmaları.**
Cambridge, Massachusetts, 1977- . irregular.
Contains scholarly articles about the Turkish world and the cultural regions with which Turks have had relations in the course of their history. Even though the journal is not exclusively dedicated to literature, it regularly contains articles on the philology and literatures of the Turkic languages. Articles are in English, French, Turkish or German.

1340 **25. Kare.** (25th Square.)
Ankara, 1990- . four issues annually.
Includes informative, critical and theoretical essays on world cinema (Turkish cinema, third world cinema, Hollywood cinema, European cinema, etc.), covering a wide

range of topics from classical narrative cinema to underground and avant-garde cinema, and written from a wide range of perspectives (Marxist, psychoanalytical, feminist, etc.). It also provides much useful information on a variety of topics, from film theories to film festivals, as well as translations from foreign authors. The journal brings together essays by both academics and non-academics.

1341   **Kitap-lık.** (The Bookcase.)
Yapı Kredi Bankası.   İstanbul, 1988- . quarterly.
This is the journal of the Yapı Kredi Bank publications. It carries book reviews, articles on art, literary criticism (on Turkish and world literatures), philosophy, and translations into Turkish. It also introduces booksellers and antique books. It is in Turkish.

1342   **Menas Associates' Turkey Focus.**
Berkhamsted, England, 1997- . monthly.
An independent monthly journal which carries news and analysis of economic, political and financial developments in Turkey.

1343   **METU Studies in Development.**
Faculty of Economics and Administrative Sciences of the Middle East Technical University (METU).   Ankara: METU Press, 1972- . quarterly.
The publication carries articles written either in English or in Turkish, with an abstract in the other language. The articles are by Turkish and foreign academics, covering various areas of the social sciences, including economics, sociology, public administration, management and political science.

1344   **The Middle East Journal.**
The Middle East Institute.   Bloomington, Indiana, 1947- . quarterly.
Covers a vast geographical area from the Western Sahara to Pakistan, Central Asia and Caucasus. It carries articles on politics, economy, culture, ethnicity and religion. As well as research articles, each issue contains a chronology organized by subject and country, book reviews, annotations of recent publications, and a bibliography of periodical literature. The activities of the Institute can be viewed at <http://www.mideasti.org/mei>.

1345   **Middle East Review of International Affairs (MERIA).**
Edited by Barry Rubin.   BESA Center for Strategic Studies, 1996- .
This is the first journal on the Middle East to be distributed electronically. MERIA is a project edited and directed by Barry Rubin, which aims to advance research on the Middle East and foster scholarly communication and cooperation. MERIA includes: 'MERIA News', a monthly newsletter including short analyses, reviews and conference announcements, websites and publications, as well as readers' research queries; 'MERIA Journal', a quarterly academic journal on Middle East issues and topics; 'MERIA Seminars', closed discussion lists for experts wishing to hold intensive exchanges on specific topics; and 'MERIA Books', which covers a variety of topics on the Middle East. MERIA can be reached at: <http://www.biu.ac.il/SOC/besa/meria.html>.

1346 **Middle East Studies Association Bulletin.**
The Middle East Association of North America. New York;
Cambridge, England: Cambridge University Press, 1966- . biannual.
The bulletin carries research articles on the languages, literature, religion, music, history, art and culture of Middle Eastern countries. The website for the bulletin is: <http://w3fp.arizona.edu/mesassoc/>.

1347 **Middle Eastern Studies.**
London: Frank Cass, 1964- . four issues annually.
This periodical carries research articles on the history and politics of the Middle East, especially in the 19th and 20th centuries.

1348 **Mimesis. Tiyatro, Çeviri, Araştırma Dergisi.** (Journal of Theatre, Translation, Research.)
Boğaziçi University. İstanbul, 1989- . annual.
This journal, published in Turkish, carries translations of plays and research articles on world drama.

1349 **Monthly Bulletin.**
Capital Markets Board (Sermaye Piyasası Kurulu). Ankara, 1994- . monthly.
The publication is in Turkish, but there is a summary in English. It provides information about the prime markets, securities outstanding, secondary market, İstanbul Stock Exchange, mutual funds, investment companies and real estate investment companies.

1350 **Muqarnas. An Annual on Islamic Art and Architecture.**
Leiden, the Netherlands: E. J. Brill, 1983- . annual.
Carries scholarly articles on Islamic art and architecture.

1351 **Newsletter.**
Organization of the Islamic Conference, Research Centre for Islamic History, Art and Culture (IRCICA). İstanbul: IRCICA, 1983- . quarterly.
This publication carries news from Islamic countries, cultural events, information about academic and cultural institutions in Islamic countries, book reviews, and announcements of the Centre's own publications. It is published in Turkish, Arabic, English and French.

1352 **New Perspectives on Turkey.**
The Economic and Social History Foundation of Turkey. İstanbul, 1986- . biannual.
Published first by Vassar College, the journal deals with studies in social and historical sciences on subjects directly or indirectly related to Turkey. It is a very important source for everyone interested in Turkish studies.

1353 **Newspot.**
Directorate General of Press and Information. Ankara, 1984- .
monthly.
The journal is in English and it is distributed free upon request. It contains articles on Turkish geography and history, Turkish culture and arts by experts, accompanied by colour photographs. It is full of useful information and makes good reading. The journal is also available on the Internet at <http://www.byegm.gov.tr.>.

1354 **Nüfusbilim dergisi. The Turkish Journal of Population Studies.**
Hacettepe Institute of Population Studies. Ankara, 1979- .
irregular.
Although erratic in publication times, this journal carries research articles in English and Turkish with summaries in either language. It occasionally contains abstracts of theses and lists of recent publications on demography.

1355 **Osmanlı Araştırmaları. The Journal of Ottoman Studies.**
İstanbul: Enderun Kitabevi, 1980- . annual.
This journal is devoted to Ottoman studies and carries research articles in Turkish, English, French and German.

1356 **Perceptions.**
Centre for Strategic Research. Ankara, 1996- . quarterly.
This publication has links with the Turkish Ministry of Foreign Affairs, and carries research articles covering various aspects of Turkish foreign policy, and regional and global issues of interest to Turkey. Contributors include academics, diplomats, journalists, and politicians from inside and outside Turkey.

1357 **Quarterly Bulletin.**
The Central Bank of the Republic of Turkey. Ankara, 1982- .
quarterly.
The *Quarterly Bulletin* is in Turkish and in English. It provides tables of production and price statistics, interest and exchange rates, figures of foreign trade, balance of payments, external debt statistics, money and banking statistics, as well as other financial statistics.

1358 **Sağlık ve Sosyal Yardım Vakfı Dergisi.** (Journal of Health and
Social Welfare.)
Sağlık ve Sosyal Yardım Vakfı (Health and Social Welfare
Foundation). Ankara, 1947- . quarterly.
This publication, in Turkish, carries articles on various aspects of health and social welfare in Turkey.

1359   **SineMasal.** (Cine - tale / Cinematic.)
Dokuz Eylül University, Faculty of Arts.   İzmir, Turkey, 1998- .
four issues annually.

A scholarly journal of film and communications, which includes articles on particular communication media such as film, television and advertising. The majority of the articles published analyse the products of the media from a social perspective, in other words, the characteristics and aspects of Turkish society as revealed in Turkish films and television.

1360   **Tarih ve Toplum.** (History and Society.)
İstanbul, 1983- . monthly.

The editorial board of this journal is composed of Turkish and international historians and social scientists. It carries research articles, in Turkish, on history and social life and will be of interest to both academics and general readers.

1361   **TASG News. Newsletter of the Turkish Area Study Group.**
Turkish Area Study Group (TASG).   Cambridge, England, 1975- .
biannual.

Provides news and information about Turkey and Turkish peoples on matters of educational, social and cultural interest, both historical and contemporary. The newsletter carries scholarly articles and book reviews as well as news of meetings and conferences about Turkey. It is distributed to over 300 individuals and teaching/research institutions internationally.

1362   **Tiyatro Araştırmaları Dergisi.** (Journal of Drama Research.)
Ankara Üniversitesi Dil ve Tarih Coğrafya Fakültesi.   Ankara,
1970- . annual.

The journal carries research articles on drama and Turkish theatre written by academics, as well as translations from other languages into Turkish. It also provides a bibliography of theses completed by the drama students at Ankara University.

1363   **Toplum ve Bilim.** (Society and Science.)
İstanbul, 1978- . quarterly.

The editorial board of this journal includes well known social scientists, and the articles in the journal are indexed in *Sociological Abstracts*. Each issue carries weighty research articles in Turkish.

1364   **Toplumbilim.** (Sociology.)
İstanbul, 1995- . biannual.

This journal covers the social sciences and arts. Each issue is dedicated to a special topic, such as Turkish sociology or visual arts. It is in Turkish.

1365   **Turkic Linguistics Post (TULIP).**
Mainz, Germany, 1991- . irregular.
An informal circular which offers information about on-going research in the field of Turkic linguistics, as well as book reviews, news about conferences, etc. It carries items in English, French, German, Russian and Turkish. Its web home page can be viewed at <http://www.uni-mainz.de/FB/Philologie-III/Orientkunde>.

1366   **Turkic Languages.**
Wiesbaden, Germany: Otto Harrassowitz, 1997- . biannual.
The journal is devoted to studies on all aspects of Turkic languages. It contains research articles, review articles, discussions, reports and surveys of publications. The preferred languages of publication are English and German.

1367   **Turkish Journal of Agriculture & Forestry.**
Türkiye Bilimsel ve Teknik Araştırma Kurumu (TÜBİTAK).
Ankara, 1976- . six issues a year.
Published by the Scientific and Technical Research Council of Turkey (TÜBİTAK), the journal carries scientific articles on agriculture and forestry in Turkish and English.

1368   **Turkish Journal of Biology.**
Türkiye Bilimsel ve Teknik Araştırma Kurumu (TÜBİTAK).
Ankara, 1976- . four issues a year.
Published by the Scientific and Technical Research Council of Turkey (TÜBİTAK), the journal carries research articles on genetics, molecular biology, microbiology and cytology in Turkish and English.

1369   **Turkish Journal of Botany.**
Türkiye Bilimsel ve Teknik Araştırma Kurumu (TÜBİTAK).
Ankara, 1976- . six issues a year.
Published by the Scientific and Technical Research Council of Turkey (TÜBİTAK), the journal carries research articles in English on different areas of botany.

1370   **Turkish Journal of Chemistry.**
Türkiye Bilimsel ve Teknik Araştırma Kurumu (TÜBİTAK).
Ankara, 1976- . four issues a year.
Published by the Scientific and Technical Research Council of Turkey (TÜBİTAK), the journal carries research articles on chemistry and chemical engineering in English.

1371   **Turkish Journal of Earth Sciences.**
Türkiye Bilimsel ve Teknik Araştırma Kurumu (TÜBİTAK).
Ankara, 1976- . quarterly.
Published by the Scientific and Technical Research Council of Turkey (TÜBİTAK), the journal carries research articles in English on different fields of earth sciences.

1372 **Turkish Journal of Electrical Engineering and Computer Sciences.**
Türkiye Bilimsel ve Teknik Araştırma Kurumu (TÜBİTAK).
Ankara, 1992- . quarterly.
Published by the Scientific and Technical Research Council of Turkey (TÜBİTAK), the journal carries research articles in English on electrical engineering and computer sciences.

1373 **Turkish Journal of Engineering and Environmental Sciences.**
Türkiye Bilimsel ve Teknik Araştırma Kurumu (TÜBİTAK).
Ankara, 1976- . quarterly.
Published by the Scientific and Technical Research Council of Turkey (TÜBİTAK), the journal carries research articles in English and Turkish on engineering, earth sciences, electronics and electrical engineering.

1374 **Turkish Journal of Mathematics.**
Türkiye Bilimsel ve Teknik Araştırma Kurumu (TÜBİTAK).
Ankara, 1976- . quarterly.
Published by the Scientific and Technical Research Council of Turkey (TÜBİTAK), the journal carries research articles in English on mathematics.

1375 **Turkish Journal of Medical Sciences.**
Türkiye Bilimsel ve Teknik Araştırma Kurumu (TÜBİTAK).
Ankara, 1976- . six issues a year.
Published by the Scientific and Technical Research Council of Turkey (TÜBİTAK), the journal carries research articles in English on medicine and health sciences.

1376 **Turkish Journal of Physics.**
Türkiye Bilimsel ve Teknik Araştırma Kurumu (TÜBİTAK).
Ankara, 1976- . monthly.
Published by the Scientific and Technical Research Council of Turkey (TÜBİTAK), the journal carries research articles on physics and astrophysics in English.

1377 **Turkish Journal of Zoology.**
Türkiye Bilimsel ve Teknik Araştırma Kurumu (TÜBİTAK).
Ankara, 1976- . four issues a year.
Published by the Scientific and Technical Research Council of Turkcy (TÜBİTAK), the journal carries scientific articles on zoology in Turkish and English.

1378 **The Turkish P.E.N.**
Turkish P.E.N. Centre. İstanbul, 1991- . annual.
Edited by Suat Karantay, the publication contains translations of selected texts from Turkish literature, as well as biographies of the authors of the texts, news of cultural events, literary prizes and new developments in the Turkish literary scene. It also acts as the newsletter of the Turkish P.E.N. The publication is annual although it was published biannually in 1994 and 1995.

1379   Turkish Public Administration Annual.
Institute of Public Administration and the Middle East.   Ankara, 1974- . annual.
This annual publication carries research articles on central and local administration, law, education, urbanization and environment, where the issues are treated on theoretical and practical perspectives. Some of the volumes contain articles written in English, German and French as well as in Turkish.

1380   Turkish Review of Balkan Studies.
Foundation for Middle East and Balkan Studies.   İstanbul, 1993- . annual.
Contains articles covering historical issues and recent and current problems relating to the Balkans and Turkish foreign policy in that region. The contributors are scholars working inside and outside of Turkey.

1381   Turkish Review of Middle East Studies.
Foundation for Middle East and Balkan Studies.   İstanbul, 1986- . annual.
Originally published as *Studies on Turkish-Arab Relations*. It covers Iran and Israel as well as Arab states, with articles on historical, economic and socio-cultural issues and current problems related to the Middle East and Turkish foreign policy. The contributors are Turkish and international academics.

1382   Turkish Studies Association Bulletin.
Turkish Studies Association.   Grand Rapids, Michigan, 1976- . semi-annual.
The bulletin of the Turkish Studies Association of America. It publishes short research articles on all areas of Turkish studies, reports of meetings and conferences, and book reviews, and has a section on the activities of departments of Turkish studies world-wide, and news about its members. It is a valuable source for everyone interested in Turkish studies. The website for the Association is at: <http://bsuvc.bsu.edu/~tsa/>.

1383   Turkish Yearbook of Human Rights.
Institute of Public Administration for Turkey and the Middle East. Ankara, 1976- . irregular.
Carries articles on issues relating to human rights, especially law.

1384   The Turkish Yearbook of International Relations.
Ankara University Faculty of Political Sciences.   Ankara, 1960- . annual.
This publication carries research articles by prominent academics, in particular on the international relations of Turkey.

1385   **Türk Dili.** (Turkish Language.)
Türk Dil Kurumu.   Ankara, 1951- . monthly.
The official journal of the Turkish Language Society. It is in Turkish and includes articles, short stories, poems, literary criticism and book reviews.

1386   **Türk Dilleri Araştırmaları. Researches on Turkic Languages.**
Ankara, 1991- . annual.
This annual publication carries research articles on Turkish and Turkic languages. The principal language of the publication is Turkish, but articles in other languages are published with a summary translation in Turkish.

1387   **Türk Dünyası Araştırmaları.** (Researches on the Turkic World.)
İstanbul, 1979- . six issues annually.
Carries both journalistic and research articles on a variety of topics concerning Turkic peoples and culture.

1388   **Türkiye Günlüğü.** (Diary: Turkey.)
Ankara, 1989- . six issues annually.
The journal carries research articles by Turkish social scientists on all areas of culture, politics, economy and international relations of Turkey.

1389   **Türklük Bilgisi. Review of Turkish Studies.**
İstanbul: Bulak, 1998- . monthly.
Contains reviews of books (published inside and outside Turkey) on any field of Turkish studies in Turkish, English and Russian parallel texts, lists of recent books and articles, titles of theses from Turkish universities, sections on necrology, news of conferences (national and international), and a bulletin board.

1390   **Varlık.** (Existence.)
İstanbul: Varlık Yayınları, 1933- . monthly.
One of the first and longest-running journals in Turkey in the field of general literature, poetry, literary criticism and the arts. Some of the best-known authors of Turkey have published their first works in this journal. It is in Turkish.

1391   **Yapı Kredi Economic Review.**
Yapı Kredi Bank.   İstanbul, 1986- . biannual.
This economics journal, in English, is distributed widely, both nationally and internationally.

Turkish Economy Statistics and Analysis.
See item no. 766.

Monthly Bulletin of Statistics.
See item no. 861.

Encyclopaedias and Reference Works

1392   **The encyclopedia of Islam. New edition.**
Edited by Th. Bianquis, C. E. Bosworth, E. van Donzel, W. P.
Heinrichs.   Leiden, the Netherlands: E. J. Brill, 1991- .
This is a well-known, comprehensive source for all subjects connected with Islam and
the lands in which Muslims live. For Turkey, there are entries on authors, literature,
history, geography and many other fields. It is published in three or four double issues
per year. The project is continuing and, when completed, will comprise eleven volumes of text, one 'Supplement', and one volume of 'Index'. It is also available on
CD-ROM.

1393   **Press guide.**
Directorate General of Press & Information.   Ankara: BYGM, 1997.
168p.
Although this useful guide is prepared for the foreign missions and journalists in
Turkey, it should be owned by everyone interested in Turkey. It contains brief
information about the country, names and addresses of press organizations, information about residence permits and visas for foreign press members, local area codes
in Turkey, airline services, addresses of foreign embassies and consulates, and
information about Turkish and foreign media in the major cities of Turkey. It is full of
other useful names, addresses and telephone numbers as well as tips on travel and
sightseeing. The Directorate General of Press and Information can be reached at:
<http://www.byegm.gov.tr>. This site carries information about the Directorate, as
well as about Turkish media, including a full list of newspapers and journals published
in Turkey.

1394 **Middle East contemporary survey.**
Edited by Bruce Maddy-Weitzmann. Boulder, Colorado: Westview Press, 1996. 760p. maps. (Moshe Dayan Center for Middle Eastern & African Studies, Tel Aviv University).

A reference work on contemporary Middle Eastern affairs. It covers the year 1995, and is the nineteenth volume in a series of annuals that provide a continuing, up-to-date record and analysis of the area's politics and economy. The section on Turkey is by Hugh Poulton.

1395 **Directory of Sport Research Institutes.**
H. Mechling, J. Schiffer, G. Simonis. Cologne, Germany: Council of Europe, 1990. 173p. (Bundesinstitut für Sportswissenschaft).

This volume lists institutions and researchers involved in sports research in Austria, Belgium, Denmark, Finland, Greece, Germany, Luxembourg, Netherlands, Portugal and Turkey.

1396 **Perspectives on the evolution of Turkish studies in North America since 1946.**
Howard A. Reed. *Middle East Journal*, vol. 50, no. 1 (1997), p. 15-31.

Examines the emergence of Turkish studies as an academic field after the Second World War, and Princeton University's pioneering leadership. In the 1990s, there were over twenty Turkish studies programmes and hundreds of courses in many colleges and universities across the United States and Canada. This article provides encyclopaedic information on the subject.

1397 **Sicill-i Osmanî yahut Tekzire-i meşahiri Osmaniyye.** (Ottoman registers. Encyclopaedia of Ottoman biographies.)
Mehmed Süreyya. İstanbul: Sebil Yayınevi, 1995-98. 4 vols.

Sicill-i Osmanî provides the biographies of the personalities who occupied various state offices from the foundation of the Ottoman state to 1899. In the original, it consists of two parts. The first part covers the biographies of sultans and the royal personages of the Ottoman dynasty. The second part contains the biographies of famous individuals and families who excelled in the Ottoman Empire and in the Seljuk state, including the Khans of Crimea, some Muslim scholars, and governors of Mecca. These two parts have been transliterated into Latin script and published in four volumes, together with indexes of names.

1398 **Seventh Five-year Development Plan (1996-2000).**
Turkish Republic State Planning Organization (SPO). Ankara: SPO, 1996. 308p.

The English text of the Five-year Development Plan, which carries important and useful summary data and statistics about Turkey, as well as future projections.

1399 **Dünden bugüne İstanbul ansiklopedisi.** (An encyclopaedia of İstanbul.)
Türkiye Ekonomik ve Toplumsal Tarih Vakfı. Ankara, İstanbul: Kültür Bakanlığı & Türkiye Ekonomik ve Toplumsal Tarih Vakfı, 1992-95. 8 vols. bibliog.

This encyclopaedia, in Turkish, contains 10,000 items and thousands of photographs, engravings and maps, covering the whole of İstanbul's 2,000 years of history.

1400 **Günümüz Türkiyesinde kim kimdir. Who's who in Turkey.**
Kim Kimdir. İstanbul, 1985- . annual.

The Turkish version of the well-known 'Who's who' series.

Historical dictionary of Turkey.
See item no. 10.

A cultural atlas of the Turkish world.
See item no. 18.

Non-governmental Organizations guide (main establishments).
See item no. 600.

Bibliographies

1401 **Türk dış göçü, 1960-1984: yorumlu bibliyografya.** (Turkish out-
migration, 1960-84: annotated bibliography.)
Nermin Abadan-Unat, Neşe Kemikiş. Ankara: Ankara Üniversitesi
Siyasal Bilgiler Fakültesi, 1986. 642p. (Ankara University Political
Science Faculty Publication, no. 555).

The publication covers 1,255 titles by 660 individual and institutional authors. Not all
of the entries are annotated, but there is a subject index. Abadan-Unat gives a
summary account of migration from and back to Turkey between 1960 and 1984,
together with a review of the relevant literature on the period.

1402 **Türkiye-Avrupa Topluluğu bibliyografyası, I: 1957-1990.**
(Turkey-European Community bibliography, I: 1957-90.)
İsmet Binark, Erdoğan Öztürk, İbrahim Karaer. Ankara: Devlet
Arşivleri Genel Müdürlüğü, 1990. 837p. (T. C. Başbakanlık Devlet
Arşivleri Genel Müdürlüğü Dökümantasyon Dairesi Başkanlığı,
no. 2).

Contains over 8,000 bibliographical entries on books, articles, seminar and conference
papers, and reports, published in Turkish and in foreign languages.

1403 **Türkiye-Avrupa Topluluğu bibliyografyası, II: 1990-1992.**
(Turkey-European Community bibliography, II: 1990-92.)
İsmet Binark, Erdoğan Öztürk, İbrahim Karaer. Ankara: Devlet
Arşivleri Genel Müdürlüğü, 1992. 150p. (T. C. Başbakanlık Devlet
Arşivleri Genel Müdürlügü Dökümantasyon Dairesi Başkanlığı,
no. 7).

Contains 810 entries, organized by author's surname. The works deal with different
aspects of Turkish-European Community relations.

1404 **Türkiye dışındaki Türkler bibliyografyası. A bibliography of Turks out of Turkey.**
İsmet Binark, Erdoğan Öztürk, İbrahim Karaer. Ankara: Devlet Arşivleri Genel Müdürlüğü, 1992. 2 vols. (T. C. Başbakanlık Devlet Arşivleri Genel Müdürlüğü Dökümantasyon Dairesi Başkanlığı, no. 5).
The two volumes contain 10,818 bibliographic entries on published works dealing with the Turkic peoples of the world. The works included are written in foreign languages as well as Turkish.

1405 **Türkiye dışındaki Türk vatandaşları bibliyografyası. A bibliography of Turkish citizens out of Turkey.**
İsmet Binark with Zeki Dilek, Musa Okur, İbrahim Karaer. Ankara: Devlet Arşivleri Genel Müdürlüğü, 1993. 187p. (T. C. Başbakanlık Devlet Arşivleri Genel Müdürlüğü Dökümantasyon Dairesi Başkanlığı, no. 10).
The volume includes 943 bibliographic entries for books, articles, reports, conference and seminar papers, published in Turkish and other languages, on Turkish citizens living outside Turkey.

1406 **Geleneksel Türk mutfağı bibliyografyası üzerine bir deneme.**
(A bibliography of traditional Turkish cookery.)
Selma Birer, Zümrüt Nahya. Ankara: Ankara Üniversitesi Basımevi, 1990. 165p. (Milli Folklor Araştırma Dairesi Yayınları).
This work includes 1,135 entries.

1407 **DPT bibliyografyası. 1990-1995.** (State Planning Organization bibliography. 1990-95.)
Devlet Planlama Teşkilatı. Ankara: MGS Yayın ve Temsil Dairesi Başkanlığı, 1997. 256p.
This is a useful publication for those who are able to go to the library of the State Planning Organization in Ankara. It contains a listing of publications by the different sections of the SPO, reports of its various commissions, and results of the projects carried out by its personnel. It is not for sale but is distributed free of charge upon request.

1408 **DPT yayın kataloğu, 1996.** (State Planning Organization catalogue of publications, 1996.)
Devlet Planlama Teşkilatı. Ankara: Devlet Planlama Teşkilatı, annual.
A useful catalogue for the specialist, who knows Turkish and who is able to go to the library of the State Planning Organization. It contains all publications issued by different sections of the SPO, reports of its commissions, and the results of research projects carried by its personnel. It is not for sale but is distributed free of charge upon request.

1409 **Kadın süreli yayınları bibliyografyası: 1928-1996. Hanımlar Âlemi'nden Roza'ya.** (A bibliography of women's periodicals: 1928-96. From 'The World of Women' to 'Roza'.)
Aslı Davaz-Mardin. İstanbul: Kadın Eserleri Kütüphanesi ve Bilgi Merkezi Vakfı & Tükiye Ekonomik ve Toplumsal Tarih Vakfı, 1998. 549p.

A bibliography of women's periodicals, published between 1928 (the date of the Language Reform) and 1996, therefore periodicals printed in the Latin alphabet. The volume contains 195 periodicals and provides full bibliographical information about each one, reproductions of their cover pages and their first editorials. An interesting feature of the volume is the section where, through quotations taken from their first editorials, the aims of the periodicals and their attitudes towards women are given. There is a chronological listing of the titles of the periodicals, as well as lists of the holdings of the Turkish National Library and the Women's Library and Information Centre. This bibliography is somewhat unusual as it makes interesting reading for everyone. (Aslı Davaz-Mardin is one of the founders of the Women's Library and Information Centre, located in İstanbul.)

1410 **Türkiye, Türkler ve Türk dili bibliyografyası.** (Bibliography of Turkey, Turks and the Turkish language.)
Directorate General of Press and Information. Ankara: Directorate General of Press and Information, 1986. 593p.

The volume lists 4,437 publications on all aspects of Turkey's history, culture and economy and 773 titles of higher degree dissertations. There are indexes by topic and author. Most of the works presented in the volume are in English, but Turkish, German and French are also represented. Coverage is patchy, there are misspellings and some entries do not relate to Turkey.

1411 **Anadolu Selçuklu dönemi sanatı bibliyografyası.** (A bibliography for the arts of the Seljuk period.)
Aynur Durukan, Mehlika Ünal. Ankara: Atatürk Kültür, Dil ve Tarih Yüksek Kurumu, 1995. 187p. (Atatürk Kültür Merkezi Yayını, no. 86).

Covers books and articles published since the end of the 19th century in Turkish and in other languages on Seljuk art and architecture in Anatolia.

1412 **Turkey.**
Meral Güçlü. Oxford: Clio Press, 1981. 331p. map. (World Bibliographical Series, no. 27).

This is the first edition of the present work. It is strongly suggested that Güçlü's volume is consulted, especially for publications on Turkey which predate the 1980s, the majority of which have not been included in the present volume.

Bibliographies

1413   **1928'e kadar İzmir'de çıkmış Türkçe kitap ve süreli yayınlar katoloğu.** (A catalogue of books and periodicals in Turkish published in İzmir until 1928.)
Ömer Faruk Huyugüzel.   İzmir, Turkey, 1996. 101p.
This catalogue introduces books, newspapers and journals/periodicals separately, and includes an index of persons, places and publishers.

1414   **Bibliography on manuscript libraries in Turkey and the publications on the manuscripts located in these libraries.**
Edited by Ekmeleddin İhsanoğlu, compiled by Nimet Bayraktar, Mihin Lugal.   İstanbul: Research Centre for Islamic History, Art and Culture (IRCICA), 1995. 337p. (Bibliographical Series, no. 4).
The main body of this guide is in Turkish and consists of three parts: a list of all libraries in Turkey which contain Islamic manuscripts in Turkish, Arabic or Persian; a bibliography of bibliographies and guides pertaining to these libraries; and a bibliography of publications pertaining to these manuscripts. There are colour photographs which show examples of different types of manuscripts, including miniatures and bindings. The introduction, in English, gives a history of libraries and librarianship in the Ottoman Empire and the Turkish Republic.

1415   **Türk-Ermeni ilişkileri bibliyografyası.** (Bibliography of Turco-Armenian relations.)
Erdal İlter.   Ankara: Ankara Üniversitesi, 1997. 300p. (A. Ü. Osmanlı Tarihi Araştırma ve Uygulama Merkezi Yayınları).
The bibliography consists of two parts. The first gives the titles of the works screened for the preparation of the bibliography, and the archives related to the subject. The second section comprises the bibliography under the following subsections: periodicals; written reports/records of conferences, symposiums and seminars; archives (in Turkish, American, Armenian, English, French and German); books, brochures, theses, reports, almanacs and albums; and articles and conference papers. It contains 1,545 entries in eight languages (Turkish, English, French, German, Italian, Russian, Armenian and Arabic).

1416   **Turkologischer Anzeiger/Turkology annual.**
Institut für Orientalistik.   Vienna: Orientalisches Institut der Universität Wien, 1975- . annual.
Volumes one and two were published as part of *Wiener Zeitschrift für die Kunde des Morgenlandes* (The Vienna Journal for Oriental Studies), but since 1977 the work has appeared as an independent publication of the Institut für Orientalistik in Vienna. It is a classified listing of books, articles and reviews (with indexes of authors and of books reviewed), published in any language, on Turkish studies, including the Arab provinces of the Ottoman Empire. Since 1977, it has included American doctoral dissertations, and since 1980, non-Ottoman Turkic languages and literature (excluding works on history and those published in the USSR).

345

Bibliographies

1417 **İstanbul kütüphanelerindeki eski harfli Türkçe kadın dergileri bibliyografyası (1869-1927).** (A bibliography of women's periodicals in İstanbul libraries, written in Ottoman script [1869-1927].)
Kadın Eserleri Kütüphanesi Bibliyografya Oluşturma Komisyonu. İstanbul: Metis Yayınları, 1993. 390p. (Kadın Eserleri Kütüphanesi ve Bilgi Merkezi Vakfı).

Prepared by the Bibliography Preparation Committee of the Women's Library and Information Centre in İstanbul (Zehra Toska, Serpil Çakır, Tülay Geçtürk, Sevim Yılmaz, Selmin Kurç, Gökçen Art and Aynur Demirdirek). This bilingual (Turkish and English) bibliography contains a bibliographical description of the periodicals selected by the Committee, a detailed listing of the contents of each issue, and the photograph of a cover page from each periodical. The periodicals are listed alphabetically.

1418 **Cyprus.**
Compiled by Paschalis M. Kitromilides, Marios L. Evriviades.
Oxford: ABC-CLIO Ltd, 1995. 2nd rev. ed. 264p. map. (World Bibliographical Series, vol. 28).

This bibliography has been prepared along the general editorial guidelines of the World Bibliographical Series and includes easily accessible major works on all aspects of Cyprus. Readers may find it useful to read this work in conjunction with the present volume.

1419 **Türkiye'nin arkeoloji, epigrafi ve tarihi coğrafyası için bibliyografya.** (Bibliography for the archaeology, epigraphy, and historical geography of Turkey.)
Arif Müfid Mansel.   Ankara: Türk Tarih Kurumu Basımevi, 1993. 616p.

The volume contains works published in different languages up to 1944.

1420 **Türk folklor ve etnografya bibliyografyası.** (Bibliography of Turkish folklore and ethnography.)
Mili Folklor Enstitüsü.   Ankara: Ankara Üniversitesi, 1971-75. 3 vols. (Milli Folklor Enstitüsü Yayınları).

A comprehensive compilation of works about Turkish folklore. Each of the three volumes is designed as an independent entity. Entries are organized under the following categories: general works about folklore and ethnography, folk literature, folk music, folk traditions, folk beliefs, folk entertainment, material culture, folk architecture, folk costumes and folk cookery. The first volume has 5,219 entries, the second volume 1,104 and the third volume 4,743. The work is seriously outdated; however, this is still considered to be the best bibliography on Turkish folklore.

1421 **Anadolu ve Rumeli'de gerçekleştirilen ulusal ve yerel kongreler ve kongre kentleri bibliyografyası.** (Bibliography of national and regional congresses held in Anatolia and in Rumelia, and of the provinces where they were held.)
Orta Doğu Toplumsal Araştırmalar Kuruluşu. Ankara: Dönmez Offset, 1993. 5 vols. (TBMM Kültür, Sanat ve Yayın Kurulu Yayınları [Board of Culture, Art and Publications of the Turkish Grand National Assembly], no. 59).
This bibliography deals with the period between 1918 and 1920, the years of national struggle after the Mondros Armistice which led to the foundation of the Republic. It covers national resistance movements, local congresses, meetings and their records or minutes. Each volume also provides the background to local meetings, followed by a bibliography of works. Volume one covers the national congresses between 1918 and 1920; volume two local congresses held in Kars, Ardahan, Oltu and Trabzon; volume three local congresses held in İzmir and Balıkesir; volume four local congresses held in Alaşehir, Nazili, Muğla and Afyon; and volume five local congresses held in Edirne, Lüleburgaz and Pozantı. This is a very important work for specialists.

1422 **Index Islamicus 1981-1985: a bibliography of books and articles on the Muslim world.**
Compiled and edited by G. J. Roper. London: Cassell, 1991. 2 vols.
The volumes contains the entries from issues of *The Quarterly Index Islamicus*, volumes 6-10 inclusive. There are 30,000 entries arranged in broad categories. Entries for monographs have longer annotations, and the name index includes editors, compilers, translators and biographers. There is also a subject index.

1423 **Prof. Dr. Metin And bibliyografyası.** (A bibliography of Prof. Metin And's works.)
Mahmut Şakiroğlu. Ankara: Turhan Kitabevi Yayınları, 1993. 65p.
Metin And is a very well known name of Turkish performing arts and culture. This bibliography lists all of his works, demonstrating And's personality and interests (theatre, ballet, opera, performance theories, aesthetics, history and miniatures).

1424 **Bibliography of ancient numismatics for Anatolia. (Antik Anadolu nümismatiği bibliyografyası).**
Oğuz Tekin. İstanbul: Arkeoloji ve Sanat Yayınları, 1993. 231p. (Sikke, Madalya, ve Mühür Katologları Dizisi, no. 2).
This bibliography, in English and Turkish, is one of the few works on ancient Anatolian numismatics.

1425 **Turkish national bibliography, 1993/1.**
Turkish National Library. Ankara: Milli Kütüphane Basımevi, 1996. 154p.
Consists of bibliographical records of publications sent to the National Library, including books, periodicals and audio-visual material. The National Library call number is given for each item, and there are separate indexes for authors and

corporate bodies, book titles, periodicals titles, and ISBN and ISSN numbers. The items are given under the subject numbers of the Library. The Internet address for the National Library is: <http://www.mkutup.gov.tr/index.html>.

1426   **Türkiye makaleler bibliyografyası. (The bibliography of articles in Turkish periodicals).**
       Turkish National Library.   Ankara: Türk Tarih Kurumu, 1952- .
       annual.

This bibliography covers all articles and reviews in periodicals sent to the National Library in Ankara, and all papers submitted to conferences, congresses, seminars and other similar meetings in Turkey. It also covers all agreements, laws, regulations, decrees, circulars, decisions, standards and statues published in the *Official Gazette* since January 1992. The entries are arranged according to the Dewey Classification system, and there is also an author index. It was published in Turkish and French until 1974, and in Turkish and English since 1975.

1427   **Armenians in Ottoman documents (1915-1920).**
       The Turkish Republic Prime Ministry General Directorate of the
       State Archives.   Ankara: Başbakanlık Basımevi, 1995. 641p. (The
       Turkish Republic Prime Ministry General Directorate of the State
       Archives, no. 25).

The work contains 272 records related to the Armenians in the Ottoman Empire between the years 1915 and 1920. The introduction provides a summary of Turco-Armenian relations throughout history, and the events leading to and during the deportation of the Armenian population from Anatolia, as supported by the documents. The second part of the book gives the transcriptions and the summaries of the records, and the bibliography of the sources used. The third part contains photocopies of the records. The identities and location of the records are also provided.

1428   **Bibliography on national sovereignty, democracy and human rights (1840-1990).**
       Türkiye Büyük Millet Meclisi Kültür, Sanat ve Yayın Kurulu.
       Ankara: THK Matbaası, 1992. 3 vols. (TBMM Kültür, Sanat ve
       Yayın Kurulu Yayınları, no. 51).

The bibliography, commissioned by the Board of Culture, Art and Publications of the Turkish Grand National Assembly, and prepared by a private company (ODAK) with contributions from E. Özbudun and A. Mumcu, contains major works in English, French and German on the late Ottoman and Republican periods. Volume one, 'National sovereignty', contains works on various aspects of the formation of the nation state, including foreign relations ('in so far as national sovereignty corresponds to the sovereignty of the state over a given territory'). Volume two, 'Democracy', contains works on Turkish domestic politics in general, and encompasses political, social, cultural and economic levels of analysis. Volume three, 'Human rights', includes major works on society, trade and industry, and employment, including trade agreements with foreign countries. The entries are organized by author's surname.

1429 **Irak Türkleri bibliyografyası. A bibliography of Iraqi Turks.**
Türkiye Cumhuriyeti Başbakanlık Devlet Arşivleri Genel Müdürlüğü.
Ankara: Devlet Arşivleri Genel Müdürlüğü, 1994. 426p. (T. C.
Başbakanlık Devlet Arşivleri Genel Müdürlüğü Dökümantasyon
Dairesi Başkanlığı, no. 12).
Contains 4,101 bibliographical entries of written documents (including newspaper
articles) on the history, culture, social and economic circumstances of the Turks of
Iraq.

1430 **Arşiv belgelerine göre Kafkaslar'da ve Anadolu'da Ermeni
mezâlimi, I: 1906-1918; II: 1919; III: 1919-1920; IV: 1920-1922.
Armenian violence and massacre in the Caucasus and Anatolia
based on archives.**
Türkiye Cumhuriyeti Başbakanlık Devlet Arşivleri Genel Müdürlüğü.
Ankara: Başbakanlık Basımevi, 1995-98. 4 vols. (T. C. Başbakanlık
Devlet Arşivleri Genel Müdürlüğü Osmanlı Arşivi Daire Başkanlığı,
no. 23, 24, 34, 35).
The first volume contains 256 records collected under 26 summary headings related to
the events which occurred between 1906 and 1918. The second volume contains 209
records collected under 38 summary headings pertaining to the period between
January and August 1919. The third and fourth volumes contain the records of
incidents between late 1919 to 1922. The volumes contain summaries, transcriptions
and photocopies of the records which detail the atrocities perpetrated by the
Armenians against the Turkish population.

1431 **Arşivcilik bibliyografyası: Türkçe ve yabancı dillerde
yayınlanmış kaynaklar, 1979-1994. A bibliography on archival
studies: includes Turkish and foreign sources, 1979-1994.**
Türkiye Cumhuriyeti Başbakanlık Devlet Arşivleri Genel Müdürlüğü.
Ankara: Başbakanlık Devlet Arşivleri Genel Müdürlüğü, 1995.
3 vols. (T. C. Başbakanlık Devlet Arşivleri Genel Müdürlüğü
Dökümantasyon Dairesi Başkanlığı, no. 14).
This publication is aimed at students of archival studies and contains 11,241 bibliographical entries of works published in Turkish and other languages.

1432 **Batı Trakya Türkleri bibliyografyası. A bibliography of Western
Thrace Turks.**
Türkiye Cumhuriyeti Başbakanlık Devlet Arşivleri Genel Müdürlüğü.
Ankara: Başbakanlık Devlet Arşivleri Genel Müdürlüğü, 1996. 329p.
(T. C. Başbakanlık Devlet Arşivleri Genel Müdürlüğü
Dökümantasyon Dairesi Başkanlığı, no. 17).
A bibliography of works on the Turkish population of Western Thrace. It contains
4,584 entries of books, official reports, theses, periodical articles, newspaper articles
and new items written in different languages on the subject. The works cited in the
bibliography are dated between 1924 and 1995.

Bibliographies

1433 **Ege sorunu bibliyografyası. A bibliography of the Aegean question.**
Türkiye Cumhuriyeti Başbakanlık Devlet Arşivleri Genel Müdürlüğü.
Ankara: Başbakanlık Devlet Arşivleri Genel Müdürlüğü, 1997. 190p.
(T. C. Başbakanlık Devlet Arşivleri Genel Müdürlüğü
Dökümantasyon Dairesi Başkanlığı, no. 20).

This bibliography aims to be of help to researchers working on Turkish-Greek relations. It is divided into five parts: part one covers bibliographies, catalogues and reference works on the issue; part two books, reports and theses; part three articles and research papers; part four newspaper and periodical articles; and part five news as reported in newspapers. The first four parts are arranged alphabetically, while the last part is chronological, covering the period 1992-96.

1434 **Periodicals in Turkish and Turkic languages: a union list of holdings in U.K. libraries.**
Edited by Muhammad Isa Waley.   Oxford: Middle East Libraries Committee (U.K.), 1993. 95p.

This work covers eleven libraries, including collections in London, Oxford, Cambridge, Durham and Manchester. The 1,200 entries are listed according to international bibliographical standards, and Ottoman and non-Turkish titles are systematically romanized. The criteria for inclusion is linguistic, so that periodicals and academic works on Turkish topics in non-Turkic languages are excluded. Each entry includes title, subtitle, location, using source, dates, publication location, issues held in a library, and additional information in many cases. Library shelf marks are given to identify the collections where listed titles can be found.

Historical dictionary of Turkey.
See item no. 10.

Indexes

There follow three separate indexes: authors (personal or corporate); titles; and subjects. Title entries are italicized and refer to the main titles. The numbers refer to bibliographical entry rather than page number. Individual index entries are arranged in alphabetical sequence: for non-Turkish languages, accented characters are treated in the same way as the same characters without accents, while for Turkish words accented characters are treated according to Turkish ordering, namely: CcÇç . . . GgĞğ . . . IıIi . . . OoÖö . . . SsŞş . . . UuÜü.

Index of Authors

A

Aarssen, J. 423
Abadan-Unat, N. 8, 452, 476, 833, 890, 1017, 1401
Abbott, G. F. 21
Abou-El-Haj, R. A. 915
Abu-Haidar, F. 435
Abu-Husayn, Abdul-Rahim 617
Acar, F. 479, 504, 551, 668
Adam, J. H. 394
Adıvar, H. E. 996
Agenor, P. R. 733
Ağaoğlu, A. 997, 999
Ağaoğulları, M. A. 580
Ahmad, F. 1, 162, 192, 259, 528, 551, 560, 850
Ahmet Mithat Efendi 274
Ajdari, Z. 697
Akan, P. 484, 781
Akar, A. 1103
Akarlı, E. D. 529
Akatay, A. 1187
Akatlı, F. 1017
Akay, İ. 804
Akbal, O. 989, 996
Akçay, A. A. 330
Akçay, C. 530
Akçelik, R. 343-44
Akdavar, Y. 512

Akder, H. 463, 804, 809
Akdikmen, R. 384-85
Akın, A. 508
Akman, A. 540
Akpınar, C. 1254
Aksal, S. K. 989
Aksan, V. H. 262
Aksoy, A. 1274
Aksu-Koç, A. 415
Akşit, B. 330, 476, 509-11
Akşit, B. T. 476, 509-12
Aktan, O. H. 790
Akural, S. M. 442, 565
Akurgal, E. 125
Al-Asad, M. 944
Al-Rabghuzi 431
Al-Shahi, Ahmed 447
Alderson, A. D. 392
Alemdar, N. 1119
Alexander, C. 1166
Alexander, W. 1189
Alexandris, A. 314
Alford, J. 676
Algan, R. 1091
Algar, A. 444
Algar, A. E. 1209-10
Algaze, G. 126
'Ali Ufki 1140
Aliş, Ş. 274
Alkım, V. B. 386
Allom, T. 1190
Alpay, Ş. 553
Altındağ, Ü. 1264

Altstadt, A. 430
Altun, A. 913, 1104
Altunışık, M. 703
AMATEM Team 512
Ambraseys, N. N. 102
Ambros, E. 1002
Amsden, A. H. 801
And, M. 8, 565, 988, 1105, 1123-25, 1143-47
Anday, M. C. 989, 997
Anderson, B. 40
Anderson, E. 40
Anderson, J. 1167
Anderson, S. P. 263
Andrews, P. A. 315
Andrews, W. G. 992, 1003-04
Angın, Z. 522
Ansal, H. K. 801
Ansay, T. 590, 669
Anscombe, F. F. 202
Antel, N. 386
Apaydın, T. 996
Aral, İ. 999
Aral, J. 512
Aras, B. 690, 713
Arat, Y. 453, 480-81, 484, 504, 552, 890
Arat, Z. F. 482, 484
Aresvik, O. 805
Arıcanlı, T. 734, 814
Arık, R. 8
Arık, U. 660

Arif Pacha 1191
Arnold, J. 1192
Arsel, S. 1211
Arslan, S. 1154
Artemel, S. 988
Artun, A. 1106, 1117, 1220
Asad, T. 464
Asatekin, G. 903
Ash, J. 67
Asher, R. E. 381-83
Ashton, R. 1225
Aslan, S. 1156
Aslanapa, A. 1106
Aslıer, M. 1121
Ataç, K. 544
Atalık, G. 331
Ataöv, T. 653, 668
Atasoy, N. 1107-08
Atasü, E. 999
Athanassopoulou, E. 561
Atıl, E. 1109-10, 1177
Attias, J.-C. 325
Avery, R. 386-89
Ayata, S. 438, 890
Aybet, G. 667
Aydın, Z. 880
Aydın-Wheater, N. 881
Ayers, J. 1230
Aykan, M. B. 714
Ayliffe, R. 41
Aytaç, K. 977
Aytaçlar, S. 512
Azemoun, Y. 393
Azmaz, A. 332

B

Backus, A. 416, 423
Baedeker 42
Bağış, A. İ. 670, 715
Bahçeli, T. 724
Bain, R. N. 1078
Bainbridge, M. 2
Balamir, A. 903, 953
Balan, J. 878
Balım, Ç. 435, 530
Balkır, C. 668, 703
Ballantine, J. 959
Balpınar, B. 1221-22
Banks Association of Turkey 735

Banuazizi, A. 691
Barakat, H. N. 914
Baran, S. 999
Barchard, D. 544
Bardak, M. 527
Barfoot, C. C. 1148
Barkey, H. J. 316, 716, 782
Barkey, K. 179, 618
Barlas, D. 649
Barnai, J. 325
Barnard, N. 1171
Barrows, L. 960
Bartal, I. 325
Bartlett, W. 902
Bartlett, W. 902
Bartók, Béla 1126
Basan, G. 1212
Basan, J. 1212
Baser, K. H. C. 121
Başaran, M. 989
Başarın, H. H. 345
Başarın, V. 345
Başbakanlık Devlet Arşivleri Genel Müdürlüğü 1256, 1259-63
Başgelen, N. 904
Başgöz, İ. 8, 558, 961, 988, 1067-73, 1076
Başkan, S. 1118
Batur, S. 946, 1239
Baybars, T. 1042
Baybura, K. 1264
Bayerle, G. 396
Baykay, Ö. 544
Baykurt, F. 989, 996
Bayraktar, N. 1414
Bayraktaroğlu, A. 43, 410
Bayraktaroğlu, S. 410
Baytop, T. 124
Bean, G. E. 44-45, 127-28
Beaumont, P. 104
Beck, B. H. 22
Beckman, G. M. 129
Beeley, B. 331, 333
Behar, C. 291, 455, 530, 1127
Behçet Mahir 1090
Bekman, S. 962-63
Belge, M. 3
Beller-Hann, I. 471
Benatar, R. 580

Benbassa. E. 325
Benedict, P. 105
Bener, Vüs'at O. 996
Benninghaus, R. 315
Bent, J. T. 264
Berik, G. 483, 504, 834
Berk, İ. 989, 1000
Berkes, N. 439, 541
Berktay, F. 504
Berktay, H. 218, 625
Berman, P. 511
Bernhard, J. 978
Berrett, A. M. 698
Berta, Á. 417
Bezmez, S. 387-90
Bianchi, R. 531
Bierman, I. A. 915
Bilgin, C. 120
Bilgin, P. 718
Bilginsoy, C. 834
Binark, İ. 1402-05
Birand, M. A. 532-33
Birer, S. 1406
Birsel, S. 989
Bıçak, V. 591
Black, C. E. 204
Black, N. 992
Blake, G. H. 104
Blake, L. G. 274
Blakney, R. 390
Blank, S. J. 651, 697
Blasing, R. 1039-41, 1043
Blaustein, A. 592
Board of Culture, Art and Publications of the Turkish Grand National Assembly 1421, 1428
Böcker, A. 334, 339
Bodger, A. 192
Boerma, J. T. 513
Boeschoten, H. E. 77, 418-20, 431
Bolak, H. C. 504
Bombaci, A. 1036
Bon, O. 265
Boratav, K. 560, 736
Bordewijk, C. 1148
Bornstein-Makovetsky, L. 325
Borowiec, A. 677
Bosworth, C. E. 1392
Bosworth, R. J. B. 192
Bourgignon, R. 669

Bournoutian, G. A. 180
Bouzek, J. 130
Boyacıgiller, N. 484
Bozdoğan, S. 453, 952
Bölükbaşı, S. 653, 726
Braam, H. 431
Bragner, R. 922, 1106, 1111, 1223
Bramley, G. 902
Brandt, E. K. 1265
Braude, B. 205
Brendemoen, B. 417
Bridge, F. R. 192
Bridge, J. 544
Bright, W. 379
Brinkmann, R. 103
Brosnahan, T. 34, 46-47
Brown, C. H. 387, 390
Brown, F. E. 881, 883, 887, 901
Brown, J. F. 655
Brown, L. C. 203-04
Brown, P. M. 593
Browne, E. G. 1012
Brubaker, R. 179
Brüggemann, U. 1168
Brüggemann, W. 1168
Brummett, P. 219, 540, 1267
Buckwell, A. 804
Buğday, K. M. 77
Buğra, A. 552, 783-84
Bulut, A. 513
Bulutay, T. 835-36, 855
Burak, S. 996, 999
Burelli, A. R. 923
Burnaby, F. G. 75
Burrill, K. 988, 1005
Burrows, B. 669
Buxton, C. R. 266

C

Cafer Efendi 916
Calabrese, J. 717
Cameron, I. 594
Canby, J. V. 131
Candemir, Y. 822
Cansever, E. 989
Carley, P. M. 705, 716
Carswell, J. 1226
Cebi, A. 1269

Cemal Süreya 989, 1000, 1017
Cendrovitz, M. 653
Centre for Turkish Studies (Bonn) 335
Cerrah, İ. 454
Ceyhan, A. 1246
Ceylan, M. 993
Cezzar, M. 917
Chambers, R. L. 196
Chandler, R. 76
Chatterjee, L. 884-85, 893, 895
Childs, T. W. 181
Childs, W. J. 79
Chipman, J. 659
Christie, R. 993, 1035, 1052, 1057
Cimok, F. 909
Cizre-Sakallıoğlu, Ü. 561, 837
Clark, R. 988
Clauson, G. L. M. 391
Clawson, P. 697
Clot, A. 267
Coggins, P. 346
Cohdem, A. 207
Cohen, A. 206
Comrie, B. 372-73, 378
Conant, M. P. 1122
Coode, M. J. E. 114
Couloumbis, T. A. 678
Cox, S. S. 24
Crane, H. 916
Criss, N. B. 182, 718
Csato, E. A. 376, 426
Cuinet, V. 106
Cullen, J. 114
Cumalı, N. 989, 994, 996, 1032
Cunningham, A. 190, 196
Çağatay, N. 504
Çağman, F. 1107, 1227, 1236
Çakmak, D. 512
Çapan, C. 1028
Çeçen, A. A. 737
Çelen, A. 411
Çelik, Z. 905, 918
Çevik, M. 1213
Çığ, K. 946, 1239
Çınarlı, M. 989

Çilingiroğlu, A. 132-33
Çoban, N. Y. 822

D

Dabir-Alai, P. 738
Dağı, İ. 561
Dağlarca, F. H. 989, 1033
Dağlı, Y. 78
Dakovic, N. 1155
Dallaway, J. 90
Daly, M. 1255
Damar, A. 989
Danielson, M. N. 635, 882
Danilov, V. I. 560
Dankoff, R. 77, 268, 430, 1066
Darke, D. 48
Darling, L. T. 220
Davaz-Mardin, A. 1247, 1409
Davies, E. 1036
Davis, F. 485
Davis, P. H. 114
Davison, R. H. 5, 162, 183-84, 196
Dawn, C. E. 162
Dayıoğlu, G. 999
de Bruijn, P. 1148
de Busbecq, A. G. 23
de Launay, M. 1198
Dede Korkut 1079, 1085
Dedoğlu, N. 514
Delaney, C. 441, 476
Delforge, M. 472
Delibaş, S. 1235
Demetrius Cantemir 1128
Demirağ, İ. 530
Demirel, T. 561, 1268
Demirsar, M. 54
Dener, A. 883
Denktash, Rauf 731
Denniston, R. 185
Denton, G. 669
Deny, J. 374
Dereli, T. 838
Deringil, S. 186, 652-53
Derman, D. 1155
Derman, M. U. 1228
Desai, A. 33
Devereux, R. 542, 595
Devrim, Ş. 269

Sayın, S. 703
Scacciavillani, F. 762
Scarce, J. 1204-07
Schamiloglu, K. 430
Schaufeli, A. 423
Scheel, H. 374
Schick, I. C. 580
Schiffauer, W. 476
Schiffer, J. 1395
Schiffer, R. 90
Schmitt, M. N. 610
Schofield, R. 711
Schönig, C. 417
Schwartz, S. L. 1187
Scognomillo, G. 1161, 1163
Seal, J. 71
Seccombe, R. L. 341
Selby, B. 73
Selçuk, F. 703
Selous, F. C. 288
Serageldin, İ. 953
Seton, L. 152
Settle, M. L. 74
Sezer, D. B. 650, 654, 662, 681, 706
Sezgin, A. H. 907
Sezgin, O. 1156
Sezgin, S. 764
Shaffer, B. 697
Shaker, S. 763
Shami, S. 894
Shankland, D. 444, 450, 471, 476
Shapland, G. 723
Sharman, A.-M. 501
Shaw, S. J. 8, 166, 196-97, 326-27
Shmuelevitz, A. 561
Shorter, F. C. 301-03, 513, 522
Sılay, K. 1001, 1016
Siegl, H. 1087
Signell, K. L. 1137
Simon, R. 565
Simonis, G. 1395
Simons, J. 511
Sinclair, T. A. 154
Singer, A. 627
Sipahigil, T. 1045
Sirman, N. 456, 463, 473, 502, 504
Slobin, I. 434

Smith, G. M. 1094
Smith, K. 65
Smolansky, O. M. 705
Social Insurance
   Institution 523
Somel, K. 814
Sonyel, S. R. 727
Soucek, S. 251
Southeast Anatolia Project
   (GAP/SEAP), Regional
   Development
   Administration 815
Soviet Government 92
Soysal, S. 999
Soysal, Y. 553
Sönmezoğlu, F. 660
Sözen, M. 908
Spandounes, T. 176
Spuhler, F. 1181
Stagos, P. N. 608
Stanley, T. 1231
Stark, F. 1117
Starr, J. 474
State Institute of Statistics
   113, 252-55, 291-92,
   304-12, 503, 519,
   581-85, 611, 765-74,
   792-99, 816-20, 827-30,
   851-55, 858-62, 871-74,
   973-75, 986
State Planning
   Organization 1398,
   1407-08
Stearns, M. 686
Stech, T. 131
Steel, J. 1156
Steele, J. 66, 953
Steinbach, U. 565
Stirling, P. 450, 471, 476, 544
Stokes, M. 476-77, 1138
Stoneman, R. 31
Suchoff, B. 1126
Sugur, N. 561, 791, 843
Suleiman, Y. 435-36
Summers, G. D. 153
Sunar, İ. 662
Suner, A. 1164
Sunier, T. 366
Suzuki, P. 478
Sümer, A. 1211
Sümer, F. 1085
Sümer, G. 997

Süreyya, M. 1397
Svanberg, I. 367
Svolopoulos, C. 318
Sweetman, J. 1116
Swietochowski, T. 691
Symes, M. S. 881, 883, 887, 901
Szajkowski, B. 355
Szyliowicz, J. S. 586, 800
Şahin, H. 1274
Şakiroğlu, M. 1423
Şen, F. 342, 368, 662
Şen, M. 330
Şenel, S. 1149
Şenesen, G. 484
Şeni, N. 504
Şenses, F. 801, 856
Şenyapılı, T. 890
Şeşen, R. 1254
Şimşir, B. N. 369, 1258

T

Tabak, F. 239
Tachau, F. 550-51, 558, 565, 587
Taji-Farouki, S. 347, 364
Talasubramanyam, V. N. 775
Talbot Rice, D. 1097
Talbot Rice, T. 177
Tamer, Ü. 989
Tan, T. 648
Taner, H. 994, 996, 1054-55
Tanındı, Z. 1115, 1236
Tanışık, M. N. 610
Tanju, S. 289
Tanker, M. 524
Tanpınar, A. H. 996
Tansel, A. 525, 976
Tansuğ, S. 1182
Tapper, R. 451
Taraklı, D. 877
Tarr, G. D. 742
Tartter, J. R. 4
Taşhan, S. 669, 707, 719
Taylor, J. L. 897
Taylor, R. 1183
Taymaz, E. 802, 855
Tecer, A. K. 1056

360

Index of Titles

Genel nüfus sayımı. İdari bölünüş. 21.10.1990 304
General agricultural census. Results of the agricultural holding (households) survey, 1991 819
General agricultural census. Results of village information survey, 1991 820
General election of representatives: results by districts, 24.12.1995 583
General election of representatives: results by provinces, 24.12.1995 582
Generals' coup in Turkey: an inside story of 12 September 1980 532
Genocide Files 725
Geology of Turkey 103
Global media and cultural identity in Turkey 1274
Globetrotter travel map of Turkey 37
Goddess from Anatolia 1178
Gözcü 1282
Grammar of Orkhon Turkic 408
Great powers and the end of the Ottoman Empire 192
Greece and Turkey, adversity in alliance 676
Greek minority of İstanbul and Greek-Turkish relations: 1918-1974 314
Greek-Turkish relations since 1955 724
Grek ve Roma sikkeleri: Yapı Kredi koleksiyonu. Greek and Roman coins: the Yapı Kredi collection 1241
Gross domestic product by cost components, 1987-1995 770

Gross domestic product by provinces, 1987-1994 769
Guide to Eastern Turkey and the Black Sea coast 48
Günümüz Türkiyesinde kim kimdir. Who's who in Turkey 1400

H

Hacettepe Journal of Education 1332
Hagia Sophia: architecture, structure and liturgy of Justinian's great church 910
Haifa in the late Ottoman period, 1864-1914. A Muslim town in transition 216
Handbook of Turkish law 614
Handbook of world education. A comparative guide to higher education and educational systems of the world 979
Handbuch der türkischen Sprachwissenschaft. Teil I 375
Harem: an account of the institution as it existed in the Palace of the Turkish Sultans, with a history of the Seraglio from its foundation to modern times 1199
Health and social inequalities in Turkey 514
Health statistics year book of Turkey. 1987-1994 527
Herb drugs and herbalists in Turkey 121
High level manpower in economic development: the Turkish case 849

Higher education in Turkey. Monographs on higher education 960
Higher education reform in Turkey – the university in the service of the community: results after three years of application 965
Historical dictionary of Turkey 10
Historical geography of Asia Minor 88
Historical geography of the Ottoman Empire from earliest times to the end of the sixteenth century, with detailed maps to illustrate the expansion of the Sultanate 112
History of astronomy literature in the Ottoman period 230
History of Mehmed the Conqueror 178
History of Middle East economies in the 20th century 242
History of Ottoman architecture 925
History of Ottoman poetry 1012
History of the Ottoman Empire and modern Turkey 166
History of theatre and popular entertainment in Turkey 1143
History of Turkish painting 1121
Hittite myths 129
Hittites 137
Hittites and their contemporaries in Asia Minor 143
Household consumption expenditures survey results, 1994 774
Household consumption expenditures survey: summary results of 19 selected province centers, 1994 773

380

387

Index of Subjects

A

Abdülhamid II 199, 280, 930
Accountancy 530
Achaemenid period 148
Adana 79
Administration 617-48, 1319, 1343, 1379
  Ottoman 163, 166, 170, 225, 268, 617-34, 898, 900
  finance 220
  Haifa 216
  military 209
  Turkish Republic 534, 635-48
    metropolitan 646
    municipal 895-96
    university 484
Aegean coast 37-38, 40, 57, 60, 66, 127
Aegean question 676, 678
  bibliography 1433
Afghanistan 12, 702
Agriculture 27, 32, 111, 463, 468, 530, 804-20, 876, 1367
  change 464, 544, 844, 878
  conditions 809-11
  development 805
  economics 807-08, 812-14, 842
  employment 302
  European Community 804
  GAP/SEAP 750
  Ottoman 253, 627
  policies 463, 812-13
  production 805
  technology 809
  trends, 1950-85 808
Ağaoğlu, Adalet 1020
Ağca, M. A. 548

Ahmet Resmi Efendi 262
Akdamar monastery 912
Al-Rabghuzi 431
Albania 26
Albanians 29
Aleppo 79
Alevism 445, 448, 450
Algiers 210
American Research Institute in Turkey 1245
Anatolia 76, 91
  4,000-3,000 BC 151
  4,000-2,000 BC 158
  2nd millennium BC 141
  1st millennium BC 142, 145, 161
  3rd century BC 146
  Achaemenid 148
  architecture
    houses 903, 936
  Byzantine 146
  Celts in 146
  Central 3, 79
  Chalcolithic 160
  dance 1123
  Eastern 79
  Hellenistic 148
  housing and settlement 886
  inner 80
  Iron Age 148
  Late Bronze Age 148
  Neolithic 144, 154, 160
  Ottoman 154
  prehistoric 159-60
  Roman 146
  South West 135
  urbanization 887
Ancient Near East 134
And, Metin
  bibliography 1423
Ani-Taurus 154

Ankara 111, 1297
  dining 64
  heating systems 866
  history 897
  light rail transit system 824
  planning 881
Antiquities 44-45, 80, 85, 125, 135
  Ephesus 127
  Lydia 128
  Miletus 127
  Pergamon 127
  Smyrna 127
Aphrodisias 3, 45
Arab rebellion 270
Ararat 154
Archaeological Museum library 1249
Archaeology 45, 52, 66, 125-61, 131-33, 135-36, 138, 140, 144-45, 147-49, 151, 154-61, 1311-13
  bibliography 1419
  Greece, South East Europe and Western Turkey 130
Archaeology and prehistory 125-61
Architects 51
Architecture 16, 18, 51, 58, 60, 66, 903-58, 1336
  Byzantine 909-12, 915
  conservation law 958
  contemporary 952-58
  education 955
  Greek 140
  Hayat House 936
  Mamluk 914
  Middle Ages 913
  mosques 906, 953
  Muslim religious 906

393

Government 27
  local 643, 647
    decentralization 640
    İstanbul 641
  municipal
    decentralization 638
Gökalp, Ziya 541-42, 555,
  574
Grammars
  Chagatay 404
  Orkhon Turkic 408
  Ottoman Turkish 405
  Turkish 406-07, 409
Grand Bazaar 926
Graves, Robert Windham
  290
'Great Game' 188
Greece 14, 28-29, 76, 660,
  706, 725, 732
  Aegean dispute 676,
    678
  Classical 132-33
  Ottoman architecture
    957
Greek invasion (1919) 193
Greek revolt (1821) 193
Gross Domestic Product
  769-70
Guides 40-66
Güney, Yılmaz 1164

H

Hagia Sophia 53, 910
Haifa 216
Hajj 223
Halicarnassus 45
Halide Edib Adıvar
  272-73
Hall, A. S. 135
Handicrafts 8
Harborn, William 264
Hatay 154
Health and welfare
  508-27, 519, 1358
  abortion 508, 515
  breastfeeding 520
  children 521
  contraception 508, 519,
    522
  maternal 521
  maternity 508

primary care 510
public 27
smoking 525
social inequalities 514
statistics 527
tourism 518
women 492-93
Hecatomnid Caria 140
Hecatomnid Labraunda
  140
Hellenism 88
Hellenistic period 148
Herbal medicine 121
Herbert, Aubrey 81
Hijaz 223
Hiking 49
Historic buildings 51
Historical surveys 21-33
Historical topography 135
History 4, 7-8, 10, 17-19,
  28-29, 31-32, 41, 52,
  60, 69, 110, 134, 139,
  162-290, 1316, 1323,
  1352, 1355, 1360-61
  1st millennium 132
  7th-10th centuries 109
  11th-14th centuries 109,
    168-78
  15th century 5, 109
  16th century 5, 82, 109
  17th century 5, 21, 77,
    89, 109
  18th century 5, 76, 109,
    179-201
  19th century 5, 20, 85,
    87-88, 90, 106, 109
  20th century 1, 5, 20,
    109, 270, 658
  biographies and
    memoirs 262-90
  business 783
  national congresses
    bibliography 1421
  Ottoman
    domains 202-17
    social, cultural and
      economic 218-61
  pre-Islamic 18
  republican
    bibliography 1428
  Seljuk 18
  social 105, 233-34
  sources 22-23

Hittite Empire 153
Hittite mythology 129
Hittites 137, 143
Holy Land 89
Homeric epics 130
Hopa 72
Horseback travel 68, 75
Hotels 61
Housing 889-91, 902
Human development
  863
Human rights 602, 609,
  612, 1383
  European Convention
    on 594
Hunting 288
Hyde, Henry 271

I

ICARDA (International
  Center for
  Agricultural Research
  in the Dry Areas)
  809
Iconography 141
Icons 1244
Identity
  Alevi 448
  in architecture 953
  in art 1121
  Crimean Tatar 212
  female 1019, 1022,
    1047
  in film 1156, 1158
  immigrant Turks 371,
    1022, 1031, 1047,
    1272
  Islamic 589
  Kurdish 322, 561
    and language 435-36
    in music 1132
  Muslim Balkan 364
  Turkic 708
  Turkish 453, 460, 561,
    587, 589, 1274
Immigration 339
  from Balkans 337, 682
  policy 338
Import Substitution
  Industrialization 782
Industrialization 801

Manufacturing 249-50,
787
Manuscript libraries
bibliography 1414
Manuscripts 1234, 1236,
1240, 1242-43, 1255
Directorate of Religious
Affairs 1246
Islamic 1254
Mapping 80
Maps 34-39, 92-101
Cyprus 100
East Black Sea 38
Eastern Anatolia 38
Eastern Turkey 35
energy resources 97,
101
geological and thematic
95-101
İzmir 37
Marmara 37
Marmara region 38
mineral resources 96
Mount Ararat 39
South Coast 38
Southern Anatolia 38
topographic 92-94
Turquoise coast 37
West and Southwest
coast 38
West Black Sea 38
Western Turkey 36
Maraş 79
Maritime history 245
Marmara 37-38
Marmaris 70
Marxism 568
Mausoleion 140
Me'ālī 1002
Mecca 210, 223
Media 1267-1308, 1341
contemporary 1275
history 1270
Islam 1273
newspapers 1276-93
periodicals 1294-1308
press, development of
1268
press guide 1393
Medicine
herbal 121
modernization 516
Medina 210

Mediterranean coast
56-57, 60, 66
Mehmed Aga 916
Mehmed II (Mehmed the
Conqueror) 168, 178
Melek Ahmed Pasha 268
Mellink, Machteld J. 131
Memoirs see Biographies
and memoirs
Menemencioğlu, Numan
652
Mesopotamia 141
Metalwork 9
Mevlevihane 940
Middle East 14, 162, 233,
242, 713-23, 1320-21,
1333, 1337, 1344-47,
1394
gender studies 496
water 715, 723
Midhat Pasha 280
Migrant workers 341, 833,
846, 848
Migration 180, 295,
330-42, 452, 471, 478
America 356
Australia 343-45,
351-52, 354
Austria 365
Belgium 362
bibliography 1401
Bulgaria 369-70
Denmark 363
Europe 334
European Community
335, 342
external 833, 846, 848
France 371
Germany 340, 347, 355,
371
Alevi Turks 361
Sunni Turks 361
internal 893
Islamic movements 355
labour market 349
Lausanne Convention
(1923) 318
Netherlands 347
Islamic organizations
366
Nordic countries 353
Ottoman policy 356
rural change 333

rural-urban 330, 462
Sweden 367
United Kingdom 346
women 332, 360
Miletus 3, 66, 127
Military 18
Military coup (1980) 532,
536, 554
Military engineering 91
Military Museum
manuscripts 1240
Mimar Sinan (architect)
923-24, 938, 950
Mineral resources 96
Miners
safety and working
conditions 847
Miniatures 9, 1243
collections 1107
history 1105, 1107
Minorities
assimilation 359
Balkan Muslims 364
Bulgaria 688
Bulgarian Muslim
Turks 348, 357,
369-70
Europe 833, 846, 848
Franco-Jewish Alliance
324
Greek 314
Kurds 316-17, 321-23
racism 368
Sephardic Jews
319-20
Turks in America 358
Turks in Germany 368
Mongol Empire 7
Montagu, Lady Mary
Wortley 33
Morier brothers 278
Mortality
child and infant 509,
511, 513, 519, 526
trends 301
Motherland Party 551,
673
Motoring 57
Mount Ararat 3, 68, 73
Mountaineering 65
Mountains 65, 68
Muğla 45

Map of Turkey

This map shows the more important features.

ALSO FROM CLIO PRESS

INTERNATIONAL ORGANIZATIONS SERIES

Each volume in the International Organizations Series is either devoted to one specific organization, or to a number of different organizations operating in a particular region, or engaged in a specific field of activity. The scope of the series is wide-ranging and includes intergovernmental organizations, international non-governmental organizations, and national bodies dealing with international issues. The series is aimed mainly at the English-speaker and each volume provides a selective, annotated, critical bibliography of the organization, or organizations, concerned. The bibliographies cover books, articles, pamphlets, directories, databases and theses and, wherever possible, attention is focused on material about the organizations rather than on the organizations' own publications. Notwithstanding this, the most important official publications, and guides to those publications, will be included. The views expressed in individual volumes, however, are not necessarily those of the publishers.

VOLUMES IN THE SERIES